THE SINTRA COLLAR

PREHISTORIC
AND
ROMAN STUDIES

COMMEMORATING THE OPENING
OF THE DEPARTMENT OF
PREHISTORIC AND ROMANO-BRITISH
ANTIQUITIES

EDITED BY
G. DE G. SIEVEKING

PUBLISHED BY
THE TRUSTEES OF THE BRITISH MUSEUM
1971

PRINTED IN GREAT BRITAIN
AT THE UNIVERSITY PRESS, OXFORD
BY VIVIAN RIDLER
PRINTER TO THE UNIVERSITY

The archaeological papers in this volume concern certain important individual pieces or classes of antiquity in the collections of the Department of Prehistoric and Romano-British Antiquities of the British Museum. They are offered as a contribution towards the proper publication of the collections and to commemorate the creation of the Department in 1969.

The contributors include members of staff and friends; scholars whose researches led them to the Departmental collections at this time, and members of the former Department of British and Medieval Antiquities who were responsible for these collections at different times in the last fifty years, including Professor C. F. C. Hawkes and Sir Thomas Kendrick who inspired and undertook the first moves which led eventually to the creation of the Department.

CONTENTS

vii

PLATES

ix

xi

FOREWORD

THE British Museum now has a Department of Prehistoric and Romano-British Antiquities. The decision of the Trustees at their Board meeting on 12 April 1969 was historic, in more senses than one. It set the seal on intentions which had long been cherished; and it opened the way to new developments in two Departments, the new one and the old one from which the new one had been 'hived off'.

It had been clear for many years that there was not much in common between Hinton St. Mary and post-Renaissance clocks or between Roman grave-stones and eighteenth-century porcelain. The spread of the former Department was intolerably wide; so it seemed no more than practical good sense to split it.

This has happened in the Museum more than once before; for instance, the separation of Western Asiatics from Egypt, and of Orientals from the Ethnographers. And nobody can doubt that the separate establishments are healthier than one Department could be if its frontiers, in time and space, were unduly far-flung. To be fissiparous is not laudable in itself. But if a Department is to prosper it must have a *principium individuationis*, in time or in space or in both, and this was what the former Department lacked. A wide embrace may be a good thing; but there are practical limits to successful embracing—and there was an understandable feeling that Dr. Bruce-Mitford's Department lacked the homogeneity which sound and fruitful growth demands. Hence the Trustees' decision to draw a chronological line and substitute two commands for the former one.

There was, of course, nothing sudden or unexpected about this. Plans had been maturing for years, and preparations made, with his customary thoroughness, by Mr. Brailsford. So the Trustees' decision was, from one point of view, an endorsement of the *status quo* or, at least, of a *status* which could come into existence at the drop of a laurel wreath. We therefore hail the new Department and its first full-blown (if he will forgive the word) Keeper of Prehistoric and Romano-British Antiquities as the inevitable outcome of inexorable development.

So much for the past, immediate, and more remote. But the present point is the future. There can be no doubt that both Mr. Brailsford, in his new independent role, and Dr. Bruce-Mitford, with the prehistorics off his back, will be able to pursue and develop their own lines with more satisfaction to themselves and (what is more important) to British and international scholarship. There is an immense amount to be done, in both the Departments; and nobody knows this better than the two Keepers. The world awaits the publication of Sutton Hoo, and that is why the Trustees have made the rather unusual arrangement of

I   B relieving Dr. Bruce-Mitford of departmental duties so that he can devote his considerable energies to this special task. Similarly, there are almost endless opportunities, inside Britain and elsewhere, for Mr. Brailsford and his colleagues to enrich, in breadth and in depth, the Museum's collections of Prehistoric and Romano-British material.

For that is what we come back to—the collections. I am aware thát earlier in this brief article I have often used the word 'Department'; and I am equally aware of the *frisson* of distaste which this word produces in 'a good Museum man'. But the word is simply a neutral administrative description (very outward and not very visible) of the really living and growing entity, a collection. We have made this division in what was formerly Dr. Bruce-Mitford's bailiwick simply with the intention of fostering the growth and vitality of two distinguishable collections. And everybody will wish the two Keepers well in their newly defined responsibilities.   JOHN WOLFENDEN

IN THE 1920s

IN a university vacation of 1920 Louis Clarke[1] took Tom Joyce and myself out to lunch in London. Louis and I were both reading Anthropology at Oxford, and Joyce, who was to become a great friend of mine, was in charge of the ethnological collections of the British Museum. After lunch we went to the Museum and toured the Ethnographical Gallery; then we went to the long study in the offices of the Department of British and Medieval Antiquities where Joyce had his desk in the south-east corner. On entering the big room, our path was crossed by a shortish man, bald, little moustache, pince-nez, stove-pipe collar, dark-coated, who was carrying a tray on which were some stone axes. 'Reginald!', Louis called, 'Now *what* have you got there? Come and show us, and let me introduce to you a young man who ...' The great Reginald Smith (for at once I identified him) muttered ungraciously and continued a rapid bolt to his desk in the north-east corner of the study. So my first contact with the prehistoric collections of the British Museum, lasting about two seconds, was sadly unpropitious, the reason for the snub being that in Smith's opinion Louis and I were in bad company.

In the Pitt-Rivers Museum, Oxford, Henry Balfour, the Curator, taught us prehistory and ethnography as one subject; but when I joined the British Museum staff in 1922, just after the empire of Sir Hercules Read[2] had been partitioned, I found that Ethnography, at least for administrative purposes, had been married to Ceramics (Oriental Antiquities plus Western Ceramics), and that Joyce had a new office well away from our premises. I discovered almost at once that O. M. Dalton, who was Keeper of the residual British and Medieval

Department, was still interested in the lost ethnographical collections of which he had once been in charge before the arrival of Joyce, that he had helped Read in the study of our Benin bronzes and had also given Joyce assistance in the preparation of the *Handbook to the Ethnographical Collections*. But with Smith it was different, and I found that where I was concerned an affection for ethnography was something suspect, rather like an unwise friendship at school with a boy in another house. However, my job was to work under Smith 'in the field of Prehistoric, Romano-British, and Anglo-Saxon antiquities'. The Anglo-Saxon end of the field was fenced off against my intrusion as the *Guide* was being written; but, even so, in other parts of this very large field there seemed to be no reason why I should not soon prove myself to be a promising young man.

Alas for human hopes! At that time Smith did not want a participating colleague. The galleries were already arranged, and their contents frozen into position by the *Guides*, published or about to be published, excellent and admirably illustrated hand-books that toured each room case by case. I was allowed to do some tidying and straightening of labels, and occasionally it was my privilege to force a new acquisition into the crowded ranks of its own kind. I do not complain on that score and I do not complain of drudgery, for I had expected drudgery. What depressed me was the discovery that Smith thought that I should never be fit for anything else. My previous knowledge (work on megaliths and in museums at home and in France, following the Pitt-Rivers course) was unacceptable, like press-cuttings of triumphs in amateur theatricals when one wants a job on the legitimate stage. I understood that. The trouble was that Smith did not like me. He was an austere vegetarian and had that and many other reasons for disapproving of his gluttonous assistant. He tried to get me transferred to the St. Albans Museum.

The drudgery was varied by being of three kinds. The first was the sorting (not indexing) of mounds of off-prints that had accumulated since the days of Sir Wollaston Franks.[3] Though the taskmaster himself seldom made any use of these pamphlets when they had been classified and put into box-containers, preferring to send for the bound copy in the Library of the periodical containing the article he wanted, Smith considered pamphlet-sorting as fascinating and honourable employment for his assistants, and he was devoted to the imposition of this exercise as to a fetish. When E. C. R. Armstrong left the National Museum of Ireland in the time of the Troubles and joined us in an understandably nervy state, Smith at once prescribed occupational therapy for him in our haystacks of pamphlets. Armstrong had been Keeper of Irish Antiquities and was an antiquary of high repute; he had expected to be asked to work on our own Irish collections, so he was thankful when he found a better place of refuge, as Bluemantle, in the College of Arms.

The second task was the identification and indexing of the subjects of glass negatives, mostly old and obsolete. The third drudgery was the task of moving the recently acquired Sturge collection of flint implements from one to another of its first three basement homes. It contained much fine and valuable material; but it weighed in all, so I was told, twenty-two tons, and to the removal man and his assistant it seemed to be mainly a collection of very large, very heavy flint cores. 'And where are we going to lay our road-metal today?' W. W. Winkworth (Ceramics) inquired as I pushed my loaded trolley past him.

As I have said, the Prehistoric Room was arranged before I joined the staff, and very well arranged by our standards at that time. It was also very well labelled, at any rate for a visitor with a good knowledge of prehistoric archaeology. We did not cater for those without that equipment. The collections, as far as was reasonably possible, were all on parade, and some archaeologists liked the Prehistoric Room that way. But it was not a part of the Museum Beautiful nor of the Museum Comfortable. To house our collections from prehistoric sites abroad there was a fascinating little iron gallery in the North Wing reached by two narrow spiral staircases, and itself so narrow that only a child or a contortionist could get a close look at anything on the lower shelves of the wall-cases, wall-cases that could not be opened fully and, when partly opened, both blocked the passage-way and imprisoned the curator.

For my part nothing in the Prehistoric Room exceeded in interest the two table-cases in the South Wing in which we showed flints from the Grime's Graves and Cissbury flint-mines. The cases were crowded with a jostle of white, creamy, grey, blue, and black flints, some with orange iron-stains, and each had a buff label bordered in scarlet (red ink and gum, our speciality), labels that proclaimed Smith's persistent belief that the flint-mine industry might belong to the Aurignacian period of the Upper Palaeolithic; most of these labels bore references to illustrations of Aurignacian flint implements in foreign books and periodicals and commanded our visitors to compare the cited picture with the flint at which they were looking. There was, however, a black sheep in the fold, a polished axe of darkish basalt; but it was not permitted to disturb the harmony of the flock of flints; nor were potsherds from Cissbury or the bones of hitherto supposedly Neolithic animals. When he first (1912) advanced his controversial views on this subject, Reginald Smith operated courageously on a wide front.

In due course Smith recognized my existence by allowing me to take over his cherished duties as the Department's registrar. This was a compliment. Ask to see the beautiful registers kept by Smith with their accurate thumbnail drawings, and then turn on a bit. You will see what I mean. But he kept me out of the circle of his approved friends. I never even spoke to his most frequent visitor, the pleasant and friendly Reid Moir, until after Smith had retired and I was Keeper of the Department. I think Smith felt that I was indiscreet in making

4

so many friends who were not in the circle I have just mentioned, troublesome people, for instance, with contrary views to ours. I think immediately of Hazzledine Warren and my visits to his anti-eolith collection at Loughton. And there were friends I made who had displeased Smith in other ways; I found them amusing, informative, and sometimes very generous to us. I think I helped also by welcoming prehistorians of other countries and of my own generation. Once I was handed a visiting-card and told that Smith, presumably otherwise engaged, wished me to 'deal with this gentleman'; the card bore the name of a distinguished young Catalan archaeologist who had come to pay a courtesy call on Smith. Obediently I went into our Waiting Room and there met for the first time Professor Bosch Gimpera. We got on very well. We went to lunch at Scott's. Writing to acknowledge my greetings on his seventieth birthday, Bosch recalled the menu of that happy meal.

My first chance to justify myself publicly as a British Museum man came when Dalton suggested that I should write a short, popular handbook to be called *Flints*, adding that he would have a word with Smith about the project. I was delighted and made plans for the text and the illustrations. Eagerly I waited for the word 'go'; but the only 'go' was the departure of Smith's text of *Flints* to the printer.

Yet it was not all that long before I began to know Reginald Smith as a kindly man and a just one. He defended me bravely on at least two occasions when I was accused of an offence that was the result of Smith's own forgetfulness. As I mellowed a little, became less bumptious, and learnt to moderate my voice (in his presence anyway) Smith and I became friends. He really did at last approve of some of my enterprises, such as my visit in 1926 to the painter George Bonsor in his castle at Carmona, near Seville, and my return with the finds from the stone graves in the Isles of Scilly that Bonsor had excavated long ago and gave to me for the British Museum. I discovered that Smith was always ready to talk about flowers and robins and suchlike, and that he liked to be told of outstanding displays in florists' windows. There was much to admire in him. He was tough in his archaeological views, and his intensive typological study of his British Museum collections and amazing knowledge of 'the parallels' (book-illustrations of relevant material elsewhere) gave him certainties that served the Museum well. An example was his refusal to be shaken by the attacks on the authenticity of the Mesolithic harpoons from Holderness; they were to stay on exhibition, he said, and eventually he had the satisfaction of hearing that similar harpoons had been dredged up from the bed of the North Sea.

Though I had little success in the field of prehistory, in the field of Romano-British antiquities I won glory. However, before the trumpets sound, I must admit to being rebuked. 'The identity of the owner is immaterial, Kendrick. Hats, coats, and scarves are not to be left on sarcophagi.' That was the Director speaking, Sir Frederic Kenyon, for I had erred in granting this cloak-room facility to Professor R. G. Collingwood who was studying an inscription not far away from us in what was then the Roman Gallery on the ground floor. How right Kenyon always was! Of course the apparel of visitors, however distinguished, should not be left on sarcophagi. But I have only reported this incident for the purpose of adding my deep and still warm gratitude to Kenyon for his kindness to me in these early days. I was still very lame, and he did not like to see me standing when he found me at work in the galleries. 'Get Mr. Kendrick a chair', he would command. Nice for me, but bad luck on the warder addressed, as the only available chair was usually that from which the warder had risen in order to salute the dignified, top-hatted Sir Frederic.

The glory I won resulted from the excavation and removal to London in 1927 of the Roman pavement at Horkstow in north Lincolnshire that Mr. John Hele had asked us to accept and exhibit on permanent loan. I was put in charge of the operations, and many were the difficulties that I had to overcome. I will tell here of only one of these, a serious disruption of the dig and a great sorrow to us all caused by the death *in mediis rebus* of our foreman, Albert Pinker, son of the Museum's Master Mason. Albert was skilled, hard-working, and devoted to the service of the Trustees. He collapsed on the site, and, when I took him that evening in an ambulance to Grimsby Hospital, his few coherent remarks were apologies for the trouble he was giving us. He died in the night. We all combined to bury Albert with the honour he deserved, his coffin covered by a Union Jack.

A big event was Dalton's visit to the excavation, and, knowing his distaste for such a journey and a night in a small-town hotel, I was very grateful for the encouragement of his coming. The visit, however, began badly. Dalton arrived on the site in one of the distressing states of shyness that sometimes overwhelmed him. This similarly embarrassed his waiting hosts, the farmer and myself, for even when he had reached us our visitor took no notice of our presence and just stood there, staring up at the surrounding trees. The astonished farmer at last succeeded in opening the conversation by announcing loudly that it was very hot, and was further flummoxed when Dalton, now forced to recognize us, replied, 'Oh, but surely this mead is most pleasantly umbrageous?' He did, very occasionally, talk like that. This time we recovered quickly. Dalton was interested in the excavation and he was a charming guest of honour at the Vicarage luncheon. Back in the Museum he commended me to the Trustees, and later I received a holograph letter from Kenyon telling me what a splendid person I was in the opinion of the Trustees and in his own opinion. I ought to have framed that letter and worn it during the rest of my Museum service flapping on my chest like a phylactery.

Dalton described the affliction of his shyness in his sad and lovely book *Apologia Diffidentis*.[4] As might be expected, this *diffidentia* was the cause of one or two painful scenes between us that I recall with dismay, sadly aware that stupidities on my part in a nervousness induced by his, assuredly aggravated our common distress. But my admiration of, and respect for, Dalton were great indeed, almost amounting to a juvenile hero-worship. As a chief, he was friendly, courteous, and encouraging. I enjoyed the grace of his conversation; for me his books and catalogues set unattainable standards; I liked being bewildered by his deep and wide learning, though it was only with the help of the Loeb Library that I was able to cope with his oral and written communications.

I think Dalton had some confidence in me. He asked me several times to attempt tasks that we in the Department all knew to be formidable. My peace mission to Sir Wallis Budge,[5] intended to heal a Read–Budge feud, was one of them. Clutching a dirty Coptic textile with a strange device, I set forth. Try not the pass, indeed! In the Babylonian Room that was the cry of H. R. Hall,[6] all smiles and jangling his keys merrily, and in the last Egyptian Room, in the cheerless company of the mummies, Budge's Cerberus, a well-known warder whose nature was I suspect merciful, tried in my own interests to prevent my knocking on the door of Budge's study. It might be wiser, I gathered, to approach the great man on another day. As all this is outside the 'field of prehistoric etc., etc.', I relate only that after much knocking that finally evoked from inside a sound like the yelp of a wounded dog, I opened the door, entered, and, after a few moments of explanation, received a wonderfully kind and generous welcome. I stayed about twenty minutes, delighted both at Budge's geniality and at his large stock of discreditable tales about other great men of the British Museum.

The senior Assistant Keeper, Alec Tonnochy, had, like myself, beginning difficulties, but they were not the result, as in my case, of a badly managed *fervor novitium*. His misfortune was that he had been posted to the Museum from a Civil Service pool without inquiry into his aptitude for or interest in museum work, and at first, as he told me, he had little of either. He made a short, unhappy start in Read's time and then Tonnochy went off to the First World War. I joined the Department soon after his return, and it was obvious that he was not yet at ease there. Smith ignored him, and I was not much help to Tonnochy, for though he enjoyed some of the drudgery that we shared, he was unresponsive, I suppose reasonably enough, to my inquisitive interest in the collections (medieval and later) that were his appointed business. But Dalton understood him and was kind to him, making him take a share in the preparation of the *Guide to Mediaeval Antiquities* (1924) and encouraging him to write a short paper for the *Antiquaries Journal*. This sympathy had the desired effect, and Tonnochy became reconciled to his museum destiny. He was a truly learned man and also a dependable observer of rules and regulations, a combination of qualities that later made him a good Keeper of the Department. I soon found it very easy to appreciate him as a helpful and often very amusing colleague.

7

I may have given the impression that my joining the Department completed a quartet of rather odd people. Yet, be that as it may, I declare that in spite of short-lived surface acrimonies, the four of us maintained successfully a pleasant harmony in our life together. There were no long sulks or sustained quarrels. Dalton would have never permitted anything of that kind. Our duties to the Museum, according to our then understanding of the museum-craft, were performed smoothly and as an agreeable common interest. For my part, I now know that in a departmental set-up like ours, a zeal for study and a constantly pricking curiosity provoked by study, combine to make a museum man invincible when assailed by the small discords that inevitably occur. *Labor omnia vincit.* It has been said before. Let us say it again.

T. D. KENDRICK

[1] L. C. G. Clarke, Curator of the University Museum of Archaeology and Ethnology, Cambridge (1922–37); Director of the Fitzwilliam Museum, Cambridge (1937–46).

[2] Keeper of the Department of British and Medieval Antiquities and Ethnography (1896–1921).

[3] Keeper of the Department of British and Medieval Antiquities and Ethnography (1866–96).

[4] For the trilogy of books written under the pen-name W. Compton Leith, see Sir George Hill's obituary notice of Dalton, his close friend, *Proc. British Acad.* 31 (1945), pp. 365–7. The *Apologia* was published in 1908, *Sirenica* in 1913, and *Domus Doloris* in 1919, this third book being an account of Dalton's experience in hospital. All three came from the Bodley Head, and all three are disturbing works of uncommon beauty and sensitivity.

[5] Keeper of the Department of Egyptian and Assyrian Antiquities (1893–1924).

[6] Keeper of the Department of Egyptian and Assyrian Antiquities (1924–30).

ENVOI

ON 12 April 1969 the Trustees took the decision to declare what had been the Sub-department of Prehistory and Roman Britain within the Department of British and Medieval Antiquities from that date a Department in its own right, to be known as the Department of Prehistoric and Romano-British Antiquities. At the same time they appointed J. W. Brailsford, formerly Deputy Keeper in charge of the Sub-department, to be the first Keeper of the new Department.

By this date, after a long but successful haul, the Sub-department had far more than restored the fortunes that these fields, so wide-ranging and active, had enjoyed in the Museum before the war. The new Department was a lusty baby; indeed, somewhat overdue in its formal appearance. It began life with a staff of seventeen, having already occupied for nearly two years a new and independent set of offices. Here it has its own conservation workshop, small, but the best-equipped of its kind in the country, with three Conservation Officers. It has an academic staff of Keeper, three Assistant Keepers, and two Research Assistants. It has new specially designed accommodation for its first-line later reserve collections, a well-lit, attractive Students' Room for the post-Mesolithic

8

collections, a Quaternary Room offering virtually ideal conditions for the study of the great Palaeolithic collections, and a well-found library. The war damage (Pls. II *b* and IV *a*) which, incredibly, remained unrepaired for a quarter of a century, has been replaced by new construction within (Pls. III *a* and IV *b*) and outside (Pl. I *a, b*) the walls that stood and which, with one exception, set limits to the possibilities of expansion. Great credit goes to Mr. Brailsford for the sensible, clear-sighted, and persistent way in which these major moves and developments have been planned and carried through; and to the staff of the Sub-department for conspicuously hard, able, and devoted work. We must also thank the Director during these important years, Sir Frank Francis, for his part in pushing the programme through, getting us the extra staff we asked for, and conceiving the idea of building the offices for the new Department on top of Library buildings which lay concealed just beyond the outside wall (Pl. I *a*). Our efforts to create more space in the rebuilding had led to proposals for cantilevering out for offices at first-floor level to east and west of the big North Wing of the old Central Saloon. The solution proposed by Sir Frank Francis was much better. The new office block coheres, instead of being split into two as it would have been with the cantilevering proposals. It has good daylight lighting, the morning sun, and a roof-scape from its east-facing windows.

In rebuilding the bombed exhibition galleries it was not found possible, for a variety of reasons, to do much with the Central Saloon, as it has always been called, at the head of the great stairs from the Front Hall; or with its small South Wing; or the Roman-Britain Room, straight ahead from the main stairs and beyond the Central Saloon, apart from giving this latter a new roof, a measure of dust-filtration, and a broad balcony down the north side (Pl. IV *b*). The main dividends in the rebuilding of the bombed galleries were squeezed out of the large North Wing. Here, the exhibition floor was raised 8 feet above the general level, so that a slab of the first-line reserve collections could be accommodated underneath (Pl. III *a* and Fig. I *c*). Headroom for the exhibition area was cut to $15\frac{1}{2}$ feet; and over the whole wing, above roof level, with excellent daylight top and side lighting, a large Students' Room, Illustrator's office with photographic annexe, rooms for an Assistant Keeper and for clerical and executive staff, and for the reception of the visitors, were constructed (Pl. V *b*, and Fig. I *a*). Visitors now reach the Department and Students' Room quickly and simply by lift direct from the Front Hall of the Museum. The simplified plans in Figs. I and 2 give the layout of the new Department. The achievement which the new Department represents can best be appreciated by recalling the state of affairs in 1945. The condition of the public galleries at the time may be seen from Pls. II *b* and IV *a*. In 1939 these galleries had been heavily packed with exhibits. The large North Wing carried a long balcony around its walls, reached by two spiral staircases (Pl. II *a*). Sir Thomas Kendrick recalls this balcony on page 4.

9   C

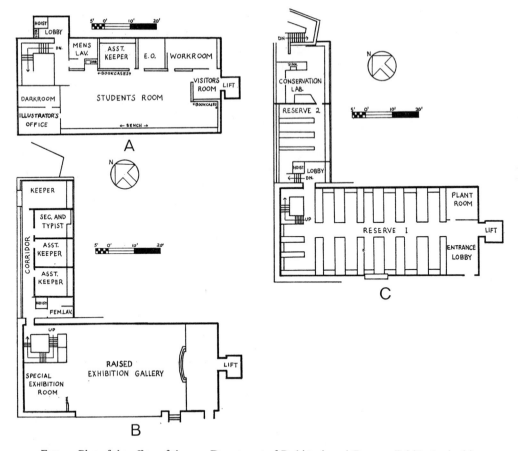

FIG. 1. Plan of the offices of the new Department of Prehistoric and Romano-British Antiquities:

(a) Top floor (Students' Room)
(b) Mezzanine floor (Early Man Gallery)
(c) Principal floor level

Here the stone implements of the Palaeolithic world were massed (Pl. v a). The area below contained chiefly the great Bronze Age collections, including the entire Greenwell collection, with such things as the Loose Howe Bronze Age canoes and the fascinating material from the Swiss lake-dwellings. The Central Saloon was full of Bronze Age weapons. The Early Iron Age was equally densely displayed in half of an outlying gallery, the Iron Age Gallery, now devoted to Renaissance and later ceramics and metalwork. A whole generation taught themselves prehistoric archaeology in these crowded rooms, where everything important was on view. Apart from what was visible, drawers and cupboards under table-cases were full of the reserve material. All this material, brought back from wartime evacuation, had to be stored in the White Wing basement

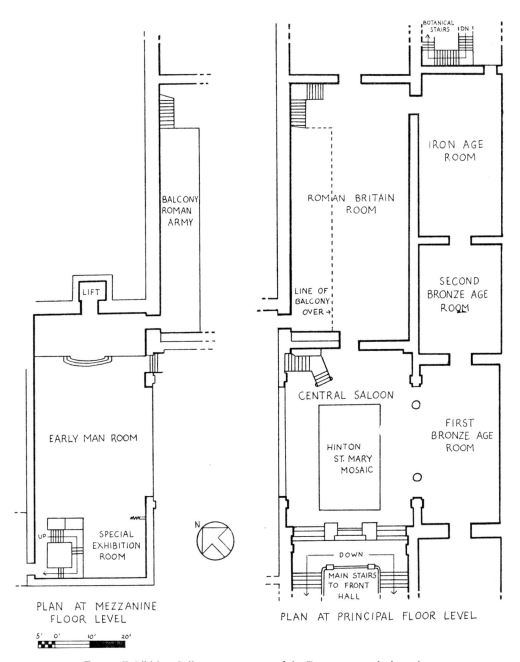

BOTANICAL STAIRS | DN

IRON AGE ROOM

BALCONY ROMAN ARMY

ROMAN BRITAIN ROOM

SECOND BRONZE AGE ROOM

LIFT

LINE OF BALCONY OVER →

CENTRAL SALOON

FIRST BRONZE AGE ROOM

EARLY MAN ROOM

HINTON ST. MARY MOSAIC

N

UP

SPECIAL EXHIBITION ROOM

DOWN

MAIN STAIRS TO FRONT HALL

PLAN AT MEZZANINE FLOOR LEVEL

PLAN AT PRINCIPAL FLOOR LEVEL

5' 0'   10'   20'

FIG. 2. Exhibition Gallery arrangements of the Department at its inception.

11

which, even before the war, had been already full; and here they were augmented by the steady intake of the thirty years since 1939. From May 1949, after the transfer to Oriental Antiquities of William Watson, who had just finished for us a new version of Reginald Smith's *Flint Implements*, until December 1956, when Gale Sieveking arrived, these enormous and growing collections of European and world scope remained in the care of a single Assistant Keeper, John Brailsford, helped out by our old friend and Assistant, E. M. M. Alexander, O.B.E., F.S.A., who was not a member of the staff. Alexander left us in September 1955, at the age of sixty-eight. There were at the time no departmental conservation workshops. Under the same Assistant Keeper also came the geographically limited but active field of Romano-British studies, with its mosaics and monuments.

The situation was an absurdity for a great National Museum. Our ability to compete internationally may be gauged by the fact that at this time in Sweden, in the Statens Historika Museum, an academic staff of nine, plus a Schools Officer, covered the Prehistoric periods up to the end of the Scandinavian Iron Age, for collections consisting only of Swedish material. There was no Roman occupation of Sweden, otherwise there would have been at least thirteen scholars covering, for native Swedish antiquities which had stayed put, what one Assistant Keeper had to cover in the British Museum with collections of European and world scope that had been evacuated for six years and returned to a building where their galleries no longer existed. One has to remember also that Swedish museums are only open to the public for relatively short periods in the week, and that the pressure of routine business in a Scandinavian capital does not compare with what has to be handled in London.

The division of the old Department of British and Medieval Antiquities into two Departments is the last in a long series of such divisions. In 1861 there was one Antiquities Department in the British Museum. Now there are eight. The story of this increased specialization in the National Museum, with provision in staff and funds for the development of specific fields, epitomizes a great century in the history of Archaeology. In 1861 the single Department of Antiquities was divided into three Departments—Coins and Medals, Greek and Roman, and Oriental (by which was primarily meant Egyptian and Assyrian). Five years later, in 1866, the Department of British and Medieval Antiquities and Ethnography was formed, these collections being stemmed off from 'Oriental'. In 1886 the Department of Egyptian and Assyrian Antiquities was formed. In 1921, after the retirement of its keeper Sir Hercules Read, the unwieldy mass, British and Medieval Antiquities and Ethnography, was divided, a new Department of Oriental Antiquities, Ceramics, and Ethnography being set up. In 1921 a Central Laboratory was set up for research into the problems of conservation and for conservation itself; it was under the then Department of Scientific and

Industrial Research, who financed it, while the Trustees provided accommodation. In 1931 it was incorporated fully into the Museum and given departmental status. In 1938 Oriental Antiquities and Ethnography became two separate Departments, and European Ceramics came back to British and Medieval. In 1955 the Department of Egyptian and Assyrian Antiquities was split into the two new Departments of Egyptian and of Western Asiatic Antiquities. Finally, in 1969, after 102 years, the Department of British and Medieval Antiquities has ceased to exist, being replaced by the two Departments, Medieval and Later Antiquities, the parent body, and Prehistoric and Romano-British Antiquities.

It is seldom possible in a great institution or Ministry for any one Department to secure the money and staff needed to develop freely, as internal logic may require, the many different sides of its field. The creating of a new Department gives the field of a study, and the part of the collections thus singled out, new status in its own right. Each such creation in the Museum has resulted in new activity, more intensive specialization, new aspirations and objectives. As with previous divisions, the setting up of the new Department of Prehistoric and Romano-British Antiquities must not be thought of as mere formal recognition of an existing state of affairs, but as a new beginning, auspicious for British prehistory and Romano-British studies.

The blueprint establishment envisaged for the Department of Prehistoric and Romano-British Antiquities, accepted in principle by the Trustees, is twenty-six, in all grades.[1] The present staff with which the Department opens is seventeen. There is still a build-up to take place, before Students' Rooms can be fully manned and all the services we want (such as the efficient upkeep of the national index of Bronze Implements) be carried out. The idea behind this establishment is that the curatorial staff (Keeper and Assistant Keepers) should be adequately supported at all lower levels; and substantially relieved of academic routine by the introduction of the new professional graduate grade, Research Assistants, who take on many important functions and assist in very various ways. Such routine now presses with unprecedented weight because of great increase in public interest and in the important requirements of mass media of communication and of education at all levels. We hope that the curators, thus relieved, will be better able to augment the collections through excavation; to play a full part in the national and international field; to find time for research, a fundamental part of their duties; and to publish the collections. Sounding this cheerful note, and recognizing a great step forward, it should be said at this time that the new Department still has large and clearly seen problems ahead of it.

To display the collections and illustrate the fields of Prehistory and Roman Britain as they would wish, the staff consider that they need three times the exhibition space now available, for the space for prehistoric and Romano-British exhibitions is in fact, after the rebuilding, a little less than it was in 1939.[2]

13

The galleries are now concentrated and in the vicinity of the offices; in this space, however, to suit modern display requirements, very much less can now be put on show (cf. Pls. II *a* and III). The proportion which cannot be exhibited is consequently very much greater, and all the time the collections have been growing, as they still are growing, and will continue to grow. The space for the reserves is already quite full, and there is no place for expansion. There is also a lack of the kind of working space (for spreading out, classifying, drawing, and so on) that cataloguing, conservation, and field-work (a relatively new official activity of the Department) demand. On all these points the new Department can now speak for itself; and they are problems of which the Trustees are aware. The Department can at least plan ahead on generous lines for the promised move-out of the Library Departments, an event that will be comparable in the history of the Museum to the departure from Great Russell Street of the Natural History collections, giraffes and all, in 1880–3.

When the Trustees set up the new Department they decided at the same time that the reduced parent Department (now also able to expand) should be known by a more rational title, that of Medieval and Later Antiquities. The old British and Medieval name never gave any real indication of the scope of this pantechnicon Department. It misled and confused people. It will be seen that both Departments have lost from their title the general cover of the adjective, 'British'. *Romano-British* does indeed survive, making the point that the Department has some special responsibility for our national antiquities, but making it only incidentally. But the express declaration in their names that these Departments contain the native antiquities of the British Isles, and bear responsibility for our national antiquities, in all periods, has gone. In 1866 the word *British* in the title of the newly formed Department under Franks was all-important, for it had been in response to powerful outside criticism of neglect by the National Museum of our national antiquities that the Department had come into being. Criticism had begun to be vocal about 1845, when Lord Prudhoe made it a condition of the Trustees' acceptance of the Stanwick bronzes that two rooms should be set aside in the Museum for the British collections. In 1854 a government Commission was set up to inquire into the matter of the British collections, to which many of the Trustees agreed that they had given no thought. It should be remembered that when all this was going on, and for almost twenty years after the British and Medieval and Ethnography Department was set up, the Natural History collections were still housed in the building. The Trustees had a great deal on their minds. The story of 'The British Museum and British Antiquities' has been told with characteristic wit and brilliance by Sir Thomas Kendrick[3] and need not be repeated here; but, in 1866, 'British' in *British and Medieval* was included not so as to give a true idea of the scope of the extraordinary *omnium gatherum* to which the name was applied, the subsequent breakdown of which into separate Departments has been described above, but to satisfy an outraged public that the National Museum did value and cater for our national antiquities. It made a nationalistic point. The dropping of 'British' now allows titles to be devised which reflect the scopes of the Departments more accurately and rationally. It also recognizes that the need to stress the nationalistic point no longer applies. A hundred years of steady growth has made the British collections well known and prized; and Reginald Smith's and Mr. Brailsford's Guides and other departmental publications have contributed. The publicity attached to such finds as the Mildenhall Treasure, the Sutton Hoo ship-burial, the Snettisham and Ipswich torcs, the Hinton St. Mary early Christian pavement, and so on, have helped to make the Museum's role as a home for national antiquities well known. Today, moreover, there are many fine provincial collections of British antiquities and the subject is not so exclusively dependent on the National Museum.[4]

It is sometimes still said, by people who do not seem to have thought sufficiently about it, that, as was being urged in the 1850s, we should have in this country a Museum of National Antiquities, like other countries, and as is the case today in Wales and Scotland. Sir Thomas Kendrick, with the profundity often concealed by his wittiest passages, dealt with this very well. Modern national frontiers may create barriers, but otherwise have little or no significance in archaeology.

To those who have worked in the unique milieu of the British Museum, to fragment it would be to throw away something irreplaceable, which exists nowhere else. The British Museum is the supreme affirmation of the fact that archaeology is one and indivisible. The only gain from a Museum of National Antiquities might be that such an institution, though spiritually impoverished, could have a fine new building and plenty of room to expand and could be tailor made for its modern functions. It would have got, not a bigger slice of the cake, but a cake all to itself. This is a real point. But such a new independent Museum should at least be a Museum of Prehistoric Archaeology, or of Medieval Art and Archaeology; not one which isolates things found in this country from those found on the continental mainland or in the Middle East, or the rest of the world. Provision on an ideal scale, it is true, can never be realized while Prehistory and Romano-British studies remain the care of one Department out of fourteen in a great institution. But to balance this are unique gains which in days of increasing specialization it is not possible to over-estimate and which should be our national pride.

I wish the new Department and its keen and able staff a glorious future.

RUPERT BRUCE-MITFORD
(*Keeper of British and Medieval Antiquities 1954–69*)

15

PLATE I *a*

The main offices of the Department of Prehistoric and Romano-British Antiquities, built on top of offices used by the Department of Printed Books. The Reading Room is seen on the right. The block containing the Front Hall, with Prehistoric Saloon above, is on the left. Across the bottom of the picture runs the roof of the passage leading from the Front Hall into the Reading Room. At the top, left, above the old roof level, the new Students' Room can be seen, with part of the staircase-block connecting it with the new offices.

PLATE II *a*

The old Central Prehistoric Saloon, looking through into its North Wing, showing the balcony housing the palaeolithic displays, with access by spiral staircases. The date of the photograph is not recorded but the Witham shield, the Somme-Bionne burial, the bronze head of Hadrian and the Ribchester helmet are recognizable. This indicates that the Roman Britain Room and Iron Age Gallery were not yet in use for these collections.

[1] This does not include the gallery warding staff, which is centralized.

[2] We have lost, on the ground floor, the south half of the old Roman Portrait Sculpture Gallery, where the Museum bookstall now is. This used to contain Romano-British mosaics and monuments. We have lost upstairs the long balcony round the North Wing of the Prehistoric Saloon (Pl. 11*a*), and half of the old Iron Age Gallery. The old Coin Cast and Plaquette Rooms, now the Third and Fourth Prehistory Rooms, were gained in lieu.

[3] T. D. Kendrick, 'The British Museum and British Antiquities', *Museums Journal*, li (1951), pp. 139–49.

[4] R. L. S. Bruce-Mitford, 'National Museums and Local Material', *Museums Journal*, lv (1956), pp. 251–8.

THE SEDGEFORD TORC

THE Sedgeford torc was brought to light on 6 May 1965 when a field called Polar Brek at West Hall Farm, Sedgeford, in Norfolk[1] was being worked over with light tractor-drawn harrows. The field had been ploughed within the preceding few years, but at the time of finding the torc must have been practically on the surface of the ground, since the teeth of the harrows would only have penetrated about an inch. The findspot of the Sedgeford torc lies some two miles west of the site of the Snettisham finds.[2] The Sedgeford torc is made of gold, and at an inquest held at Sedgeford on 29 December 1966 it was declared treasure trove. It was subsequently acquired by the British Museum through the Duchy of Lancaster, with the consent of Her Majesty the Queen. The finder, Mr. A. E. Middleton, was paid the full market value of £3,300. The acquisition was made with the aid of a contribution from the Christy Trust. The Trustees of the British Museum are having a replica made, to be presented to the Castle Museum, Norwich.

The Sedgeford torc (Pl. vi *a*) is of the multi-strand ring terminal type, the same form as the great torc from Snettisham.[3] The hoop is made up of eight twists of gold wire, each twist having six strands. The massive terminals are decorated with embossed ornament of Snettisham type. Such torcs may be dated on the evidence of the finest example, that from Snettisham, one of the terminals of which contained a Gallo-Belgic Dc (Atrebatic) quarter-stater.[4] A worn specimen of this type of coin was found in the Le Catillon hoard, so that this type of coin, and presumably the great Snettisham torc, must date from somewhat before 56 B.C. This is consistent with Piggott's dating[5] of 60–50 B.C. for the Cairnmuir terminal,[6] which was associated with Gaulish gold 'bullet' coins.

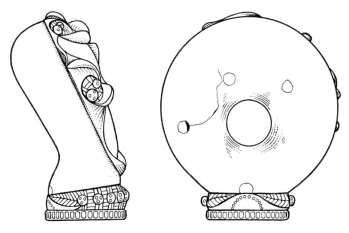

FIG. 1. The Sedgeford Torc Terminal. Side view and inner face. (Scale ¼).

The embossed ornament on the one surviving terminal of the Sedgeford torc (Pl. VII, Figs. 1 and 2) comprises the following elements:

1. A flowing pattern of curved ridges, which unlike its counterpart on the great Snettisham torc, extends over the whole outer surface of the terminal.

2. Filling the smaller spaces enclosed by 1, a 'matting' pattern executed in shallow grooves. This also occurs on the outer part of the neck of the terminal.

3. Associated with 2, a series of small almost spherical bosses. An interesting detail of these is the group of three punch marks impressed on each boss; an identical treatment is found on the great Snettisham torc and on the Cairnmuir terminal.

(The roundels of concentric ridges found on the great Snettisham torc and on the Cairnmuir terminal do not occur on the Sedgeford torc.)

Unlike the four decorated torcs in the hoard found on the outskirts of Ipswich in 1968 (Pls. VIII–IX) the Sedgeford torc is clearly a finished product. The plain surfaces within the pattern are smooth, the ridges and bosses well modelled, and the 'matting' filling inserted where appropriate. But the most interesting technological feature of the Sedgeford torc is the ancient repair of a serious crack on the back of the terminal (Pl. VI *b* and Fig. 1) by means of three rivets passing through it from face to face. Whether the damage occurred during or after manufacture,

17   D

the torc was in either case considered an object of sufficient value to deserve an elaborate repair. On the other hand, the smith would not have carried out the repair unless the owner, actual or prospective, were prepared to accept the torc in its repaired condition. As originally executed, the repair was no doubt practically invisible, at least on the outer face.

FIG. 2. The decoration on the Sedgeford Torc Terminal. (Scale ¼).

Snettisham-type ornament

The incidence of the elements of Snettisham-type ornament among a group of objects bearing this type of decoration is shown in the table.

TABLE

The Incidence of Elements in Snettisham Ornament

Present = × Absent = —	Curved ridges	Matting	Small spherical bosses (with three punch marks ××)	Roundels of concentric ridges	Zig-zag ridges	Lines of dots	Notched ridges
Snettisham torc	×	×	× ×	×	×	×	—
Cairnmuir terminal	×	×	× ×	×	—	×	×
Sedgeford torc	×	×	× ×	—	—	—	×
Clevedon terminal	×	×	×	—	—	—	×
Ipswich torc no. 2	×	—	—	—	—	—	—
,, ,, 3	×	—	×	—	—	—	—
,, ,, 4	×	—	×	—	—	—	×
,, ,, 5	×	—	×	—	—	—	×
Snettisham bracelet	×	×	×	—	—	—	—
Thames helmet	×	×	×	—	—	—	—
Needwood Forest torc	—	—	×	—	×	×	—

The three most distinctive elements, curved ridges, 'matting', and small spherical bosses are present on all examples quoted in the table except the Ipswich torcs, which were not finished, and the Needwood Forest torc, which is only marginally in the 'Snettisham' class, and may be earlier than many other examples. On the Snettisham torc, the Cairnmuir terminal, and the Sedgeford torc, the small spherical bosses are further distinguished by the presence of three fine punch-marks. This correspondence in the finest detail surely indicates that these three pieces at least are from the same workshop. This conclusion is not unexpected for the Snettisham and Sedgeford torcs, which were found only two miles apart. It is, however, more surprising for the Cairnmuir terminal, which comes from the other end of the country.

The Ipswich torcs, found in October 1968, and now in the British Museum, are of outstanding interest because of their unfinished condition, which reveals unique evidence of the processes used by the Iron Age goldsmith. The torc shown in Plate VIII is apparently almost straight from the mould. The ornament has been only roughly blocked out, and the surface reproduces without change that of the wax model from which it had been cast, except perhaps for some hammering.

On the other three decorated torcs from Ipswich (e.g. Pl. IX), a start had been made with the finishing of the ornament by tooling with a punch or chisel. However, the work had not been completed, and the terminals have been left in a rough and scarred condition, very different from the beautifully finished terminals of the great Snettisham torc. Moreover, on the Ipswich torcs the 'matting' ornament had not yet been applied.

J. W. BRAILSFORD

[1] The National Grid Reference of the farm is 53/709 365.

[2] R. R. Clarke, 'The Early Iron Age Treasure from Snettisham, Norfolk', *Proc. Prehist. Soc.* XX (1954), pp. 27–86.

[3] Clarke, op. cit. 1954, pl. xvi; *Later Prehistoric Antiquities of the British Isles*, 1953, Frontispiece.

[4] D. F. Allen, in (ed.) S. S. Frere, *Problems of the Iron Age in Southern Britain*, p. 111.

[5] S. Piggott, 'The Carnyx in Early Iron Age Britain', *Ant. Journ.* XXXIX (1959), p. 31.

[6] Clarke, op. cit. 1954, pl. xvii, nos. 1 and 2.

THE HEATHERY BURN CAVE REVISITED

AN ESSAY TOWARDS THE RECONSTRUCTION
OF A WELL-KNOWN ARCHAEOLOGICAL DISCOVERY

IT is a day, not to be more closely specified, in the early sixties of the last century. William Greenwell is journeying to the small market-town of Stanhope, 'capital of upper Weardale', in the county of Durham. He is a clergyman, but this visit is not occasioned by his calling. For the Revd. Mr. Greenwell is also an enthusiastic antiquary, and he has recently learnt of remarkable discoveries at a site just north of the town. His interest is by no means purely one of academic detachment: a particular passion with him is the collection of antiquities, and he has heard that much has already been found, and is no doubt in grave danger of imminent dispersal. He is in luck:

> I was fortunate enough to make the acquaintance of the late Mr. George Tinkler, and his son, Mr. Thomas Tinkler. . . . Through them I have been enabled to become possessed of the greater part of the articles found, and of specimens of almost every variety of weapon and implement. I also learnt many valuable details connected with the different finds and their attendant circumstances.

The quotation comes from Greenwell's paper, 'Antiquities of the Bronze Age found in the Heathery Burn Cave, county Durham'. He read this to the Society of Antiquaries of London on the 5th of May 1892, and it was published two years later in *Archaeologia* (Greenwell, 1894). It is a careful record of all that he had been able to find out concerning the discoveries in the cave.

We can no longer visit the Heathery Burn Cave, except in imagination. The same process of quarrying by which the antiquities were gradually brought to light has in the end destroyed it entirely. Greenwell's own collection from the site has come to the British Museum. So has much of the other material, and the Museum now has nearly all that survives.

The site and the finds from it deserve our consideration. The Bronze Age antiquities, as Greenwell rightly appreciated, are one of the outstanding assemblages of that period from anywhere in Britain, while the circumstances of their deposit present an intriguing problem. We have two sources of information: the surviving finds, and the old accounts of their discovery. A first requirement must be a fuller presentation of the archaeological material than Greenwell's own brief descriptions. Here the Trustees of the Museum have recently given valuable support, by publishing a set of *Inventaria Archaeologica* devoted to the site and the antiquities from it that are still extant (Britton, 1968).

The purpose of the present paper is to touch on certain topics that were implicit in the *Inventaria* publication, but which could not be dealt with systematically within its form of presentation. These topics are: the sequence of discoveries in the cave and their original publication, the correlation of the material mentioned by Greenwell with what now exists, the extent of our knowledge of what has been lost, and the problem of assigning the surviving finds to their original locations in the cave.

As an appendix, I have welcomed the opportunity of publishing again the analyses by optical spectroscopy that were made on bronze implements from the site.

THE SEQUENCE OF DISCOVERIES IN THE CAVE AND THEIR ORIGINAL PUBLICATION

Greenwell records the finding of antiquities in the cave on two occasions, in 1843, and during the years 1859–72. There may have been a third, considerably earlier. The evidence is in a letter written by the Revd. W. Wilson to the Revd. J. Hodgson, which is dated 29 February 1816, and was published in the first volume of *Archaeologia Aeliana* (Wilson, 1822*b*). At that time Mr. Wilson was the rector of Wolsingham, a town five miles down Weardale from the Heathery Burn Cave. The Revd. John Hodgson was the distinguished Secretary of the Society of Antiquaries of Newcastle-upon-Tyne, which had been founded just three years before, in 1813. Mr. Wilson's letter included the following passage.

> The sleeve of mail armour I have sent you, was found fifty or sixty years ago, I believe in Hatherburn Cave, near Stanhope; a cave that extends, it is said, a mile in length. I believe it to be Roman.

It seems reasonable to suppose that this is in fact a reference to the Heathery Burn Cave. In the absence of more details, it is not easy to assess the discovery. Mail armour is armour made of rings, or chains, or of overlapping plates. Mr. Wilson thought the find was Roman, but possibly he was mistaken. For in a slightly earlier letter, dated 6 February 1816, and also to the Revd. John Hodgson, he had confidently interpreted a hoard of characteristic Late Bronze Age metalwork found at Haggate (two or three miles west of Stanhope) as 'the arms, etc., of a single Roman foot soldier . . . together with all the tools or accoutrements for repairing, sharping, or burnishing' them (Wilson, 1822*a*, 13).

If Wilson's report is correct, the discovery in the cave was made some time in the 1750s or 1760s. Nothing more seems to be known about the circumstances of the find or its character.

The earliest discovery of antiquities that is mentioned by Greenwell is that of 1843, when the construction of a tramway destroyed the entrance to the cave (Greenwell, 1894, 91). Eight bronze rings were found, which were said to have been on a piece of bronze wire. The find was in itself quite unspectacular, and it appears to have aroused no special interest nor been a stimulus to further exploration.

We come now to the series of discoveries made from 1859 to 1872, and their first publication. In his paper in 1894 Greenwell observed:

The finding of various relics began in 1859, and continued to be made at intervals, as the work of quarrying the limestone was carried on, until 1872, after which time I have no knowledge that anything has been found, the work since then having been discontinued [Greenwell, 1894, 92].

Heathery Burn Cave
Locations and Dates of discoveries (Greenwell (1894): source for all details)

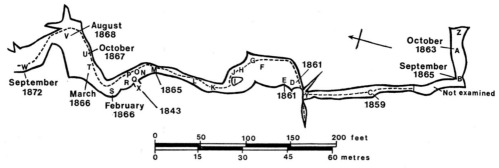

FIG. 1. Plan of the cave. Letters indicate find-spots.

The early discoveries of these years were promptly reported and discussed by several writers. The first were J. Elliott and S. J. Mackie. Elliott wrote two papers for *The Geologist* (1862*a*, *b*), and Mackie gave a short account in the *Archaeological Journal* (1862). Soon afterwards Mackie supplemented his first paper with some remarks published in the *Proceedings of the Society of Antiquaries* and occasioned by his exhibition to the Society of material from the cave on 5 June 1862 (Mackie, 1861–4). Meanwhile, as Mackie informs us, the human remains found during 1861 had been examined by Professor Huxley (this is T. H. Huxley), Mr. Carter Blake, Mr. Busk, 'and other anatomists' (Mackie, 1862). Two of these scientists contributed papers which mentioned these remains to *The Geologist* in the same year that Elliott had published his (Huxley, 1862; Blake, 1862).

Clearly by the early 1860s the cave, and the discoveries that continued to be made there, had become well known in antiquarian circles. This situation gives the context for Greenwell's own first visit and his fruitful relationship with George and Thomas Tinkler (Greenwell, 1894, 92). In 1865 the British Museum comes into the story for it was in that year, as A. W. Franks reported to the Society of Antiquaries, that the Museum acquired, through Greenwell, its first specimens from the site (Franks, 1864–7, 236). These were a cast disc of bronze with four loops, and two 'armlets' of bronze (in fact, nave-bands).

During the following years the discoveries at the Heathery Burn Cave passed into the general currency of archaeological knowledge. They are naturally referred to in specialist papers, but also appear as examples in such famous and widely read books as the *Cave Hunting* of Boyd Dawkins (1874, 141–4) and John Evans's *The Ancient Bronze Implements, Weapons, and Ornaments of Great Britain and Ireland* (1881, *passim*: see index on p. 500).

Finally, in 1894, Greenwell published his classic paper, about thirty years after his first visit and more than twenty years after discoveries had ceased (Greenwell, 1894). He not only took into consideration the earlier accounts, but added very much to them from his own observations and those of George and Thomas Tinkler. It is to these three, after the initial reports of Elliott and Mackie, that we are so largely indebted for our contemporary knowledge of this remarkable site.

There is one other person to whom we should be especially grateful. This is not on account of what he wrote about the discoveries, but because he acquired and preserved a considerable part of the antiquities that survive. Nearly all these are now in the British Museum and derive from two sources. One, of course, was Greenwell himself. The other was the Revd. Henry Slater, of Larentia, Stawell, Bridgwater, in Somerset, from whom the Museum acquired fifty-four items (1911, 10–21, 1–54). To see how Mr. Slater was able to possess this important collection, we should turn not to Stawell and Larentia (Larentia is best known as the (second) foster mother of Romulus and Remus), but to his career in the north of England. This may be conveniently followed with the aid of *Crockford's Clerical Directory*, in the editions of 1882 and 1890.

Henry Slater had been a scholar of St. Catherine's College, Cambridge, where in 1847 he graduated B.A. Entering the Church, he became a deacon in the following year, and in 1849 he was ordained priest. The first appointment he held was in the north of England, as curate of St. Andrew's, Liverpool, from 1848 to 1850. His second brought him to Weardale, when in 1850 he was made senior curate of Stanhope and curate of Eastgate. This was nine years before the main series of discoveries had begun, but he remained in these curacies until 1866. It was in this position, as we may reasonably imagine, that he became familiar with the Heathery Burn Cave, and that he had the opportunity to acquire antiquities found there (cf. Slater, 1865, 169, for some hints of this). And even when he finally received preferment and became vicar of Bywell St. Andrew with St. James, at Riding-Mill, he was not impossibly remote. There he continued as vicar for many years, at least until 1890, and long after finds at the cave had ceased. In 1889 he was made an Honorary Canon of Newcastle-upon-Tyne.

Greenwell stressed the richness of the Late Bronze Age finds from the cave, both in quantity and variety. In describing these antiquities he first grouped them broadly by the materials of which they were made, and then classified them within this framework in the usual way according to types (Greenwell, 1894, 96–110). His account today appears rather brief and sketchy. Recently the *Inventaria* publication has attempted to provide a short catalogue of what has survived and so is still available for direct study (Britton, 1968).

It seems reasonable now to correlate these two accounts. This would not only make comparison easier, but bring out any differences between the material mentioned by Greenwell and that which exists at the present time. Such a correlation is attempted in the list on the opposite page.

Note on the presentation

The *first* column gives (in brackets) the serial numbers used in the *Inventaria* publication.

The *second* column is a brief description of each category of artifact. It combines the terms used by Greenwell with those of the *Inventaria*. Where they differ significantly, the *Inventaria* term is given second (in brackets).

The *third* column gives the quantity of artifacts in each category, fragments counting as whole items, according to Greenwell. A plus sign ($+$) means that at least this number was found. A question mark (?) indicates some uncertainty in the correlation.

The *fourth* column gives (in brackets) the quantity of artifacts in each category, fragments counting as whole items, as given in *Inventaria*.

THE EXTENT OF OUR KNOWLEDGE OF WHAT HAS BEEN LOST

The list given above makes it clear that some of the antiquities mentioned by Greenwell are now lost. Brief references to some of these were made in the *Inventaria* publication, but it was not possible there to attempt a more detailed appraisal. Below will be found set out such information as there is on the archaeological material that is no longer extant. (For references to surviving antiquities, the serial numbers of the *Inventaria* publication are used.)

Bronze penannular bracelets

Greenwell mentions the following: 'three armlets, and the half of a fourth, of the ordinary form, penannular with dilated ends' (1894, 101). He continues: 'They are all small, one remarkably so. Of the two I have had an opportunity

(1)	Gold penannular ornament, triangular in section	1	(1)
(2)	Gold penannular bracelet	1	(1)
(3–5)	Bronze penannular bracelet	4	(3)
(6)	Bronze bracelet of slender rod	1	(1)
(7–10)	Jet or lignite bracelet (ring)	4	(4)
(11)	Part of jet ring (?)	0	(1)
(12)	Bronze finger-ring	1	(1)
(13)	Amber bead	1	(1)
(14–15)	Stalagmite (stone) bead, cylindrical	3	(2)
(16–17)	Stone with perforation (pendant)	2	(2)
(18–20)	Perforated shell	3	(3)
(21–3)	Perforated dog tooth (canine)	2	(3)
(24–6)	Perforated incisor tooth of horse	3	(3)
(27–8)	Antler (or bone) with three perforations (cheek-piece)	5	(2)
(29–39)	Bronze ring	22+	(11)
(40)	Probably part of bronze ring	0	(1)
(41)	Bronze button	1	(1)
(42)	Bronze disc with attached flat ring (strap-distributor)	1	(1)
(43)	Bronze disc with five loops on back and concentric ridges on face	1	(1)
(44–9)	Bronze disc with four loops on back	6	(6)
(50–7)	Bronze 'hoop of thin metal' (nave-band)	8	(8)
(58)	Bronze 'caldron' (bucket)	1	(1)
(59–60)	Bronze sword	3	(2)
(61–9)	Bronze spearhead	8+	(9)
(70)	Bronze tongs	1	(1)
(71)	Bronze mould for socketed axes	1	(1)
(72)	Waste runner of bronze (casting 'jet')	1	(1)
(73)	Piece of copper (piece of copper or bronze ingot)	1	(1)
(74–84)	Bronze socketed axe	19+	(11)
(85–7)	Bronze gouge	3	(3)
(88)	Bronze socketed chisel	1	(1)
(89)	Bronze chisel or awl	1	(1)
(90)	Bronze awl	0	(1)
(91)	Bronze 'razor'	1	(1)
(92–3)	Bronze two-edged knife, socketed	2	(2)
(94)	Bronze two-edged knife, tanged	1	(1)
(95–108)	Bronze pin	15+	(14)
(109–10)	Flat slivers of bone, with one end pointed	?	(2)
(111–19)	Bone 'pin' (pointed implement)	?22+	(9)
(120)	Lignite 'pin' (pointed implement of jet)	1	(1)
(121–40)	Pointed implements of bone	?22+	(20)
(141)	Bone 'chisel'	0	(1)
(142–5)	Bone 'gouge'	3	(4)
(146–61)	Bone implement: 'cf. paper knife' (bone spatula)	11+	(16)
(162–9)	Antler with one perforation (probably toggles or handles)	8+	(8)
(170–1)	Small toggle of bone	0	(2)
(172–4)	Antler object with slot, probably handle	0	(3)
(175)	Antler tine with cutting at base	2 or 3	(1)
(176)	Lead spindle-whorl	1	(1)
(177–8)	Bone spindle-whorl or button	3	(2)
(179–81)	Circular piece of stone with central perforation (probably spindle-whorl)	2	(3)
(182)	Whetstone (polishing stone)	1	(1)
(183)	Whetstone (hone)	1	(1)
(184)	Flint, 'thick flake 3½ in. long', fabricator	1	(1)
(185)	Flint barbed and tanged arrowhead	1	(1)
(186–8)	Flint flake	2	(3)
(189–96)	'Fragmentary pieces' of pottery (sherd)	Large quantity	(8)
	'Indeterminate small pieces of bronze'	Some	(0)
	'Piece of bronze wire'	?1	(0)
	Bone bead	1	(0)
	Knife of split boar's tusk	1	(0)
	Fragment of worked bone or horn	Many	(?)
	Shaped piece of wood	Several	(0)

of examining, the largest is 2⅝ inches on the outside diameter, the other being only 1⅜ inch.' The two which Greenwell saw for himself may be identified with (3) and (4), both of which come from the Greenwell Collection. The third surviving bracelet is complete (5). So the missing item appears to be 'the half of a fourth' bracelet, which was found at A on Fig. 1 (Greenwell, 1894, 92–3).

It is interesting that one of the surviving antiquities was at one stage part of a penannular bracelet. This piece is (12), probably a finger ring, which has been made out of just such an object. Greenwell describes it, but does not refer to this feature (1894, 103–4). Nor does he give any information on where it was found. There seems at least the possibility that (12) and the 'half of a fourth' penannular bracelet might be the same object.

Stalagmite (stone) beads

Greenwell states that 'three beads made of stalagmite' were found at O (1894, 95). Elsewhere he comments: 'Two beads made from stalagmite were found; they are both cylindrical and measure 1¼ inch in length' (1894, 106). Two stone beads survive and both are cylindrical. One (14) is 1·35 in. long, and the other (15) is 0·85 in. Perhaps the most likely interpretation would be that one stone bead is lost, and that this is the other of the two described as cylindrical and 1¼ in. in length.

Cheek-pieces

In his discussion of implements 'made from tines and the beams of red deer's antlers', Greenwell mentioned five that seem to be cheek-pieces, although they were not accepted as such by him (1894, 108–9). These five appear to be of the same general pattern as (27) and (28). He describes three, of which one, shown in his fig. 30, may be identified with (28). The second, not illustrated by him, is of the straight form, and might very well be (27). Both (27) and (28) are from the Greenwell Collection. Of the third, now lost, there is the following account: 'A third, also straight, which is imperfect and in fragments, has had at least three series of short very finely-cut straight lines upon it, one being of five, another of seven lines.' Nothing more seems known of the further two, which are also lost.

It may be appropriate to comment here on the familiar illustration in V. G. Childe's *Prehistoric Communities of the British Isles* (1949, fig. 61 on 181), which purports to show two cheek-pieces from the Heathery Burn Cave. Neither of these is in fact any of the objects just mentioned. The lower item is a cheek-piece from a Swiss 'lake-dwelling' that was cited by Greenwell for comparison (1894, 109; fig. 31). The upper, reproduced from Greenwell's fig. 32 (1894, 109), is not a cheek-piece, but probably a toggle or handle.

Bronze rings

Eight bronze rings were discovered in 1843 and given to Mr. C. Rippon of Stanhope Castle. If they exist, their whereabouts seems unknown. Greenwell, who saw them, wrote: 'They are plain rings of different sizes, precisely like others found in the cave' (1894, 91). From 1859 to 1872 another fourteen rings at least were found. Eleven complete rings (29–39), and what may be part of a twelfth (40), survive. For the other two, or three, that are lost, we have only Greenwell's general comment on the whole category: 'They are all quite plain, and, though differing in thickness, are rather thin' (1894, 101).

Bronze swords

Two swords and part of a third were found. There exist now one sword that is nearly complete, although broken into three pieces (59), and a fragment from the blade of another (60). The sword now lost, which was discovered at A, had already gone when Greenwell wrote. 'One, which was whole, has disappeared without my having had an opportunity of examining it, though I have seen a tracing' (1894, 93, 97). Commenting on this and (59) together, he remarked: 'They are of the ordinary leaf-shaped form, well cast and finished, with a handle-plate and holes for rivets to attach the bone or wood, which, in addition to the plate, constituted the handle' (1894, 97).

Bronze socketed axes

At least nineteen socketed axes were discovered. Eleven are listed in the *Inventaria* publication (74–84), of which two had been illustrated by Greenwell, (84) in his fig. 8, and (83) in fig. 9 (1894, 99–100). Writing generally of the axes found, Greenwell commented: 'They are all of the socketed type, with a single loop at the side . . . and the greater number are ornamented with three vertical short ribs upon each face . . .' (1894, 99). These remarks are quite appropriate to the surviving axes, and nothing more seems known of the eight or more that are lost. (Some of the 'lost' axes may in fact survive. Mr. C. B. Burgess has kindly informed me that a socketed axe attributed to the Heathery Burn Cave is now in the Musée Dobrée at Nantes!)

Bronze pins

Greenwell refers to 'at least fifteen' bronze pins (1894, 101). The *Inventaria* publication includes fourteen (95–108). Probably there is no real disparity, since one of Greenwell's pins is described by him as follows: 'A thinner and more needle-shaped one, but without an eye, has no head; it is $2\frac{1}{8}$ inches long.' Though he has no figure, this seems clearly the same object as (90), which in the *Inventaria* publication is classified as an awl.

Antler tines with cutting at base

Greenwell noted that 'Two or three tines of red deer's antler, cut off at the base but not perforated, were met with. They do not look like unfinished implements, and they appear to have been used at the pointed end' (1894, 110). He gives no details of where they were found and does not figure any. One may probably be identified with (175), a tine detached in this way. The other one or two may be represented by two other antler tines from the cave, which also derive from the Greenwell Collection (British Museum: WG 1401 and WG 1404). As with (175), their function, if indeed they are completed and not in process of manufacture, is not clear. One (WG 1401) has been polished smooth and is about 5 in. long. The other (WG 1404) is only a fragment, now 2·4 in. long, with possible traces of cutting. Both these have been identified as of red deer antler by Miss J. E. King (British Museum, Natural History).

Bone spindle-whorls or buttons

Two survive. Greenwell records the finding of three at M, all of them about 1½ in. in diameter (1894, 94, 108). He figures one of these (fig. 29 on 108), and it is clearly not (177). It may perhaps represent (178), being similar in form and size. But the likeness does not seem quite conclusive, and (178) is not from the Greenwell Collection but from that of the Revd. H. Slater. So it is perhaps possible that Greenwell's illustration shows the example that is lost.

Pottery

There is no doubt that the losses in this category are the most significant. What survives seems to be no more than a small fraction of the original quantities. Greenwell gives the following account:

So far as I know no perfect vessel, or indeed anything like one, was found. A large quantity of fragmentary pieces, principally small, was discovered in all parts of the cave, but the greater portion has unfortunately not been preserved. All the vessels, the remains of which I have seen, have been rather rudely hand-made, without the application of the wheel, but fairly baked, though at an open fire and not in a kiln. The colour varies, but is principally of a pale yellowish tinge with a tendency to red. None of the pieces show any signs of ornamentation but a fragment of a rim is of a well-made vessel which has had a shoulder, and another has had two perforations immediately beneath the lip, made after it was fired [Greenwell, 1894, 110].

In the *Inventaria* publication eight sherds were published (189–96). There are also several body sherds in the Yorkshire Museum at York. In general terms Greenwell's remarks might accord with these surviving pieces. More specifically the rim fragment 'which has had a shoulder' could be (189), and that with 'two perforations beneath the lip' could be (190). Mackie, writing more than thirty years before Greenwell (1862, 359), had referred to 'fragments of urns rudely ornamented'. This comment need not be incompatible with Greenwell's version, which seems to be based on that part of the material that he was able to see for himself. None of the surviving sherds is ornamented at all, not even 'rudely'.

Greenwell observed that pottery was found 'in all parts of the cave', and mentioned its discovery specifically at A, D, H, J, K, M, T, and V. At least in some of these places the amounts seem to have been considerable: 'much broken pottery' at H and J and a 'great quantity' at A (1894, 92–6). The original locations of the sherds now extant are not known.

'Indeterminate small pieces of bronze'

None survive, and our knowledge is limited to two comments by Greenwell. In describing the finds at D, he referred to 'a small piece of bronze since lost' (1894, 93); and writing generally of the metalwork, he remarked 'Some small indeterminate pieces of bronze were met with' (1894, 105).

'Piece of bronze wire'

The only information is that given by Greenwell in his account of the finding of bronze rings at X in 1843. These were 'said to have been placed upon a piece of bronze wire' (1894, 91). But he appears somewhat sceptical, since he adds: 'I have seen the rings, but not the piece of wire, which, if it ever existed, has been lost.'

Bone bead

In describing the beads found Greenwell mentions 'a long one of bone' (1894, 106). It does not seem to have survived and nothing further is known about it.

Knife of split boar's tusk

Boar's tusks were found at a number of places in the cave (Greenwell, 1894, 92–6, 110), and nine are in the British Museum (WG 1382, WG 1390–5, and two unregistered). Although these appear to be in more or less their natural state, one that is lost seems to have been deliberately modified:

> A single specimen of another kind of knife was met with. It has been made from the tusk of a boar, split in half down the middle and brought to a sharp edge by rubbing. It is $5\frac{1}{2}$ inches long.

This is compared by Greenwell with 'similar knives in barrows accompanying an interment', for which he refers to his own work, *British Barrows* (1877, 215, 274). He also cites for comparison others from 'some of the Swiss lake-dwelling sites', and here refers to the book by Keller (Keller, edited by Lee, 1878, i, 30; ii, pl. xx, no. 16).

Fragments of worked bone and horn

'Many fragments of worked bone and horn were discovered, which cannot be classed with any of the implements above described' (Greenwell, 1894, 110). Of the material in the *Inventaria* publication, it is perhaps possible that Greenwell would have put under this head (109) and (110), which are flat slivers of bone, pointed at one end. The rest appear to be lost, except perhaps for two fragments of bone in the Museum collection, one at least of which may be worked (WG 1398 and WG 1399).

Shaped pieces of wood

'Some pieces of wood, evidently shaped, were found, but not in a condition to admit of their being identified as parts of any certain instrument' (Greenwell, 1894, 110). No information is given on where they were found. The only possible survivor seems to be one piece of wood, 7·5 in. long and embodying part of a knot-hole, now in the British Museum (WG 1403).

Boyd Dawkins's account and the gold ornaments: an additional note

In his general review of the discoveries at the cave Boyd Dawkins refers to *two* 'ornaments of the horse-shoe, or split-ring type, made of thin plates of gold' (1874, 141–4). The only one of this sort which exists, and the only one known to Greenwell, is that published in the *Inventaria* (1). Perhaps Boyd Dawkins accidentally included under this type the other gold ornament (2), a penannular bracelet.

THE PROBLEM OF ASSIGNING THE SURVIVING FINDS TO THEIR ORIGINAL LOCATIONS IN THE CAVE

The archaeological material had been preserved because it was sealed under a layer of stalagmite 2–8 in. thick. As quarrying advanced and this layer was broken up, some notice (but not, it seems, a full record) was taken of the finds and where they were made. Details of this kind were given by Elliott in his second paper in *The Geologist*, for the parts cleared up to that time (1862*b*; plan on p. 168). Greenwell later added many more, and included also the subsequent discoveries (1894, 92–6; plan: Pl. xii. See Fig. 1 on p. 22). Both Elliott and Greenwell indicated by letters the places where finds had been made, and described the discoveries at each in turn. Antiquities were recorded at twenty-two locations, and described by Greenwell in terms of about forty categories.

An attempt is made to summarize this information in Table 1 and to provide a key to the table that relates, so far as appears reasonable, the categories of description used by Greenwell to the *Inventaria* publication. (In that publication Greenwell's plan, as shown in Fig. 1 on page 22, was reproduced in a slightly modified form on Card 10.)

TABLE I

Location of Different Categories of Archaeological Material in Heathery Burn Cave

CATEGORIES	A	B	D	E	F	G	H	J	K	L	M	N	O	P	Q	R	S	T	U	V	W	X	TOTALS
1																	1						1
2																1							1
3	1								1			2											4
4									1														1
5				1															1				2
6								1															1
7													3										3
8										3													3
9																				1			1
10																				3			3
11										1		4			3						1	8	17
12															1								1
13												1											1
14												1											1
15	6																						6
16	8																						8
17																					1		1
18	2																	1					3
19	7							1															8
20														1									1
21					1																		1
22	7						2		8				1							2			20
23							1													2			3
24														1									1
25										1													1
26																					1		1
27								1															1
28						1						6			1			1	1				10
29	4	1			1	1	1	1											1	4			14
30								1															1
31		1					1					2			1					4			9
32											3												3
33															1								1
34		1																					1
35															x								x
36	x	x					x	x	x	x								x		x			x
37		1																					1
38							1			1													2
39												2		1									3
40																						1	1
	35	3	1	1	1	4	5	5	9	5	8	15	4	1	8	1	1	2	3	13	7	9	

31

The Categories of Archaeological Material in Table 1

The *first* column gives (in brackets) the serial numbers used in the *Inventaria* publication. The *second* column gives the number of the category in the table.

(1)	1	Gold penannular ornament, triangular in section	(74–84)	22	Bronze socketed axe
			(85–7)	23	Bronze gouge
(2)	2	Gold penannular bracelet	(88)	24	Bronze socketed chisel
(3–5)	3	Bronze penannular bracelet	(91)	25	Bronze 'razor'
(6)	4	Bronze bracelet of slender rod	(92–3)	26	Bronze two-edged knife, socketed
(7–11)	5	Jet or lignite bracelet (ring)			
(13)	6	Amber bead	(94)	27	Bronze two-edged knife, tanged
(14–15)	7	Stalagmite (stone) bead, cylindrical	(95–108)	28	Bronze pin
			(109–19) (121–40)	29	Bone 'pin' (pointed implement)
(18–20)	8	Perforated shell			
(21–3)	9	Perforated dog tooth	(142–5)	30	Bone 'gouge'
(24–6)	10	Perforated incisor tooth of horse	(146–61)	31	Bone 'knife' (spatula)
(29–40)	11	Bronze ring	(177–8)	32	Bone spindle-whorl or button
(41)	12	Bronze button	(179–81)	33	Stone with central perforation (probably spindle-whorl)
(42)	13	Bronze disc, larger than 14			
(43)	14	Bronze disc, smaller than 13	(184)	34	Flint: 'long and thick flake' (fabricator)
(44–9)	15	Bronze disc (group of six)			
(50–7)	16	'Broad armlet' of bronze (naveband)	(186–8)	35	Flint flake
			(189–96)	36	'Broken pottery' (sherd)
(58)	17	Bronze 'caldron' (bucket)		37	'Small piece of bronze'
(59–60)	18	Bronze sword		38	'Implement of deer's horn'
(61–9)	19	Bronze spearhead		39	'Instrument of deer's horn'
(70)	20	Bronze tongs		40	'Piece of bronze wire'
(71)	21	Bronze mould for socketed axes			

It has already been mentioned how, in one part of his paper, Greenwell reported on each in turn of the twenty-two locations where antiquities were found (1894, 92–6). In the next section he described these antiquities by type (1894, 96–110). But nowhere did he correlate the two accounts. Nor did he use any method, such as numbering, by which his descriptions may be identified individually and directly with the material as we have it today. Some of these correlations have been attempted in the present paper, in the list on page 25 above, and in Table 1 with the explanation of its categories. With due caution, they may be used as a basis for carrying the discussion a stage further, by taking them in conjunction with Greenwell's original account.

The problem is how far the surviving finds may be assigned to their original locations in the cave. The *Inventaria* publication gave some brief indications on these lines. But since its form does not admit discussion, the question could not be explored fully nor the arguments involved made explicit. In fact for some items the location seems certain, while for others there is no evidence at all. The degree of certainty or ignorance may perhaps be examined by classifying the kind of information we have. Below seven classes are proposed and in terms of these are grouped all the antiquities known to be extant.

Class 1

In twelve instances Greenwell gave the location of an antiquity that he figured. For all these a surviving artifact can be identified unambiguously with his illustration. It follows that if Greenwell's account is correct, the original locations of these items are known with certainty. They are listed here.

The *first* column gives the *Inventaria* numbers (in brackets), the *second* column the number of Greenwell's figure, and the *third* the location.

(1)	2	T	Gold penannular ornament, triangular in section	(85)	15	W	Bronze gouge
				(87)	16	H	Bronze gouge
(2)	1	S	Gold penannular bracelet	(88)	13	R	Bronze socketed chisel
(6)	20	K	Bronze bracelet of slender rod	(91)	7	N	Bronze 'razor'
(41)	23	Q	Bronze button	(93)	5	W	Bronze two-edged knife, socketed
(70)	11	Q	Bronze tongs				
(71)	10	G	Bronze mould for socketed axes	(94)	6	H	Bronze two-edged knife, tanged

Class 2

Often Greenwell gave details which go beyond the bare designation of type. By this means we may sometimes make correlations between the sections of his paper which deal with location and with typology, and between these and a surviving antiquity. These conditions seem to be met, either with certainty or nearly so, for twenty items, which are listed below. (Greenwell's text should be referred to for the details in each case.)

The *first* column gives the *Inventaria* numbers (in brackets), the *second* column the location.

(18–20)	L	Perforated shells: three, forming a necklace	(59)	A	Bronze sword, broken into three pieces
(44–49)	A	Bronze discs with four loops on back: six, found together	(60)	U	Fragment of bronze sword: 'piece from the middle of the blade'
(50–57)	A	Bronze 'hoops of thin metal' or 'broad armlets' (nave-bands): eight similar, found together	(184)	B	Flint: long and thick flake (fabricator)

Class 3

Sometimes Greenwell mentions, both in his section on locations and in that on typology, a category of artifact that is represented by only one example. Besides the instances that have been already included, there are two more where the references of this sort may be identified with the single examples of surviving objects that come within these categories. (There is the assumption of course that only one example of the category ever existed.) These cases are set out on the next page.

33   F

The *first* column gives the *Inventaria* numbers (in brackets), the *second* column gives Greenwell's descriptive category (cf. Table 1), and the *third* the location.

(13)	6	J	Amber bead
(58)	17	W	Bronze 'caldron' (bucket)

This argument may be extended to a further instance. Greenwell mentions the finding of three bronze gouges, of which two have already been located by information of Class 1. By applying the argument to the third, we get the following:

(86)	23	W	Bronze gouge

Class 4

A similar argument to that just mentioned may be used for categories with several examples found at one location, if the numbers given by Greenwell and those of the surviving objects are the same. (Again there is the assumption that no more examples of the category ever existed.) Thus:

(24–6)	10	V	Perforated incisor teeth of horse (three examples)

In one further case the argument may also be applied by combining two of Greenwell's descriptive categories, each of which is represented by a single example, and each of which is defined in terms of the other (cf. Table 1). These are:

Category 13	Bronze disc, larger than 14
Category 14	Bronze disc, smaller than 13

For the present purpose these may be treated as one category with two examples found at one location, N. Probably they are to be identified as follows:

(42)	13	N	Bronze disc with attached flat ring (strap-distributor)
(43)	14	N	Bronze disc: five loops on back; concentric ridges on face

It may be noted that the only other bronze discs mentioned by Greenwell are the six of Category 15 in Table 1, which appear to be items (44–9) of the *Inventaria* publication. According to information of Class 2, these were found at A.

Class 5

There are two more of Greenwell's categories for which the information is somewhat like that of Class 4. Again, there are several examples of the category, all found at one location. But in these instances the number of surviving artifacts differs from that in Greenwell's account. Perhaps this disparity should suggest caution. The cases are these:

(14–15)	7	O	Stalagmite (stone) beads, cylindrical (three found; two survive)
(177–8)	32	M	Bone spindle-whorls or buttons (three found; two survive)

34

Classes 1–5 tell us all we know about the locations of individual antiquities that are still extant. These details may be summarized by location, as follows:

The *first* column gives the location, the *second* column the *Inventaria* numbers (in brackets), the *third* the class of information.

A	(44–9)	2	Bronze discs with four loops on back
	(50–7)	2	Bronze 'hoops of thin metal' (nave-bands)
	(59)	2	Bronze sword
B	(184)	2	Flint: long and thick flake (fabricator)
G	(71)	1	Bronze mould for socketed axes
H	(87)	1	Bronze gouge
	(94)	1	Bronze two-edged knife, tanged
J	(13)	3	Amber bead
K	(6)	1	Bronze bracelet of slender rod
L	(18–20)	2	Perforated shells
M	(177–8)	5	Bone spindle-whorls or buttons
N	(42)	4	Bronze disc with attached flat ring (strap-distributor)
N	(43)	4	Bronze disc: five loops on back; concentric ridges on face
	(91)	1	Bronze 'razor'
O	(14–15)	5	Stalagmite (stone) beads, cylindrical
Q	(41)	1	Bronze button
	(70)	1	Bronze tongs
R	(88)	1	Bronze socketed chisel
S	(2)	1	Gold penannular bracelet
T	(1)	1	Gold penannular ornament, triangular in section
U	(60)	2	Fragment of bronze sword
V	(24–6)	4	Perforated incisor teeth of horse
W	(58)	3	Bronze 'caldron' (bucket)
	(85)	1	Bronze gouge
	(86)	3	Bronze gouge
	(93)	1	Bronze two-edged knife, socketed

Class 6

Greenwell mentions where examples of thirteen further categories were found. But the information he gives is not so specific that individual objects among the surviving material may be assigned to their original locations. The details available are summarized below.

The *first* column gives the *Inventaria* numbers (in brackets), the *second* column Greenwell's descriptive category (cf. Table 1), and the *third* the location.

(3–5)	3 AJN		Bronze penannular bracelet
(7–11)	5 EU		Jet or lignite bracelet (ring)
(21–3)	9 V		Perforated dog tooth
(29–40)	11 LNQWX		Bronze ring
(61–9)	19 AJ		Bronze spearhead
(74–84)	22 AHKOW		Bronze socketed axe
(95–108)	28 GNQUV		Bronze pin
(109–19) (121–40)	29 ABFGHMTV		Bone 'pin' (pointed implement)
(142–5)	30 J		Bone 'gouge'
(146–61)	31 BGMQV		Bone 'knife' (spatula)
(179–81)	33 Q		Stone with central perforation (probably spindle-whorl)
(186–8)	35 Q		Flint flake
(189–96)	36 ADHJKMTV		'Broken pottery' (sherd)

TABLE 2

Heathery Burn Cave. Analyses of Bronze Implements

Inv. Arch. GB. 55	No. of analysis	Type of artifact	Cu	Sn	Pb	As	Sb	Ni	Bi	Fe	Ag	B.M. Reg. no.
(6)	107	Bracelet of slender rod	83·0	10·4	5·5	0·34	0·42	0·18	0·010	0·0072	0·075	1911, 10–21, 4
(47)	108	Disc with four loops on back	85·9	7·3	6·0	0·14	0·23	0·13	0·0055	< 0·006	0·13	1911, 10–21, 2
(51)	111	Cylindrical casting (nave-band)	80·7	11·0	6·4	0·46	0·80	0·34	0·023	0·010	0·17	65, 2–7, 1
(58a)*	451*	Ring-handle of bucket	[100]	[8·5]	[> 15]	[n.d.]	[0·20]	[0·075]	[0·070]	[< 0·006]	[0·13]	WG 1271
(58a)	96	Ring-handle of bucket	81·1	8·4	10·1	< 0·1	0·098	0·058	0·019	0·019	0·070	WG 1271
(58a)	97	Staple for handle of bucket	79·7	12·4	7·6	0·12	0·16	0·092	0·018	0·01	0·10	WG 1271
(58a)	99	Sheet metal of bucket	86·0	12·2	1·6	n.d.	< 0·05	0·027	0·0064	0·0074	0·038	WG 1271
(58b)	98	Base-plate of bucket	94·1	5·2	0·66	n.d.	< 0·05	0·023	0·011	0·0075	0·0090	WG 1271
(59)	109	Sword	83·7	8·4	6·5	0·38	0·48	0·18	0·067	< 0·006	0·21	1911, 10–21, 6
(64)	101	Spearhead	79·5	13·3	6·7	0·12	0·18	0·097	< 0·005	0·0077	0·11	WG 1276
(69)	100	Spearhead	79·8	12·0	6·9	0·34	0·51	0·23	0·013	0·0070	0·14	WG 1275
(71)	110	Mould for socketed axes	79·7	12·5	7·0	0·27	0·34	0·15	0·013	< 0·006	0·12	1911, 10–21, 9
(76)	102	Socketed axe	88·1	5·0	6·4	0·13	0·20	0·10	< 0·005	< 0·006	0·12	WG 1283
(83)	103	Socketed axe	81·3	11·7	6·5	0·18	0·15	0·081	0·010	0·0080	0·068	WG 1286
(88)	106	Socketed chisel	80·4	11·9	6·9	0·18	0·28	0·16	0·011	0·0072	0·13	WG 1318
(93)	105	Socketed knife	80·3	9·6	4·9	0·12	0·16	0·086	< 0·005	< 0·006	0·050	WG 1314
(94)	104	Tanged knife	78·1	15·6	5·5	0·24	0·32	0·14	0·0078	0·017	0·14	WG 1313

* in reference to Analysis no. 451 means that because of the high proportion of lead the results are approximate only, and are expressed in relation to 100 parts of copper.

n.d. in Analyses nos. 98, 99, 451, means 'not detected'.

The following abbreviations are used:

Ag silver   Cu copper   Pb lead
As arsenic   Fe iron   Sb antimony
Bi bismuth   Ni nickel   Sn tin

Class 7

For the rest of the antiquities now extant, Greenwell gives no information on where they were found. This situation is our Class 7, and the items concerned are listed below.

(12)	Bronze finger-ring
(16–17)	Stones with perforation (pendants)
(27–8)	Antler (or bone) with three perforations (cheek-pieces)
(72)	Waste runner of bronze (casting 'jet')
(73)	Piece of copper (piece of copper or bronze ingot)
(89)	Bronze chisel or awl
(90)	Bronze awl
(92)	Bronze two-edged knife, socketed
(120)	Lignite 'pin' (pointed implement of jet)
(141)	Bone 'chisel'
(162–9)	Antler with one perforation (probably toggles or handles)
(170–1)	Small toggles of bone
(172–4)	Antler objects with slot, probably handles
(175)	Antler tine with cutting at base
(176)	Lead spindle-whorl
(182)	Whetstone (polishing stone)
(183)	Whetstone (hone)
(185)	Flint barbed and tanged arrowhead

DENNIS BRITTON

APPENDIX

Analyses by Optical Spectroscopy of Bronze Implements from the Heathery Burn Cave

Greenwell published one analysis, presumably chemical, of a socketed axe—which one is not known (1894, 97). The result was:

Copper	65·20	Iron	0·10
Tin	8·06	Arsenic	traces
Lead	24·30	Sulphur	0·18

Total: 97·86

More recently Mrs. Blin-Stoyle has published seventeen analyses by optical spectroscopy on bronze implements from the site. Thirteen antiquities were analysed, and a series of five analyses made on different parts of the bronze bucket. All these objects are in the British Museum. The original publication is not widely accessible (Blin-Stoyle, 1959), and the paper by Mrs. Brown and Mrs. Blin-Stoyle which comments on these results does not include the figures obtained (1959, especially 197). Furthermore their interest has been enhanced by subsequent metallurgical studies of Bronze Age material from the north of England (Dr. R. F. Tylecote, in Burgess, 1968, 48–56). It therefore seems a good idea to give the analyses again here, correlating them with the serial numbers used in the *Inventaria* publication. This has been done in Table 2.

REFERENCES

BLAKE, C. C., 1862. Further Notes on Human Skulls from Heathery Burn Cave, Weardale, Durham; with a notice of the river-bed skeleton from Leicester. *The Geologist*, 5, 313–16.

BLIN-STOYLE, A., 1959. Spectrographic Analysis of British Middle and Late Bronze Age Finds. *Archaeometry*, 2; Supplement.

BOYD DAWKINS, W., 1874. *Cave Hunting*. London.

BRITTON, D., 1968. *Late Bronze Age Finds in the Heathery Burn Cave, Co. Durham (Inventaria Archaeologica. Great Britain, 9th Set : GB. 55)*. London.

BROWN, M. A., and BLIN-STOYLE, A. E., 1959. A Sample Analysis of British Middle and Late Bronze Age Material, using Optical Spectrometry. *Proceedings of the Prehistoric Society*, 25, 188–208.

BURGESS, C., 1968. *Bronze Age Metalwork in Northern England c. 1000 to 700 B.C.* Newcastle-upon-Tyne.

CHILDE, V. G., 1949. *Prehistoric Communities of the British Isles*. 3rd ed. London.

DAWKINS, *see* BOYD DAWKINS, W.

ELLIOTT, J., 1862a. On the Discovery of Human and Animal Bones in the Heathery Burn Cave, near Stanhope. *The Geologist*, 5, 34–7.

—— 1862b. Further Discoveries in Heathery Burn Cave. Ibid. 167–71.

EVANS, J., 1881. *The Ancient Bronze Implements, Weapons, and Ornaments of Great Britain and Ireland*. London.

FRANKS, A. W., 1864–7. [An account of additions to the collections of the British Museum in 1865]. *Proceedings of the Society of Antiquaries (2nd ser.)*, 3, 233–42.

GREENWELL, W., 1877. *British Barrows*. Oxford.

—— 1894. Antiquities of the Bronze Age found in the Heathery Burn Cave, County Durham. *Archaeologia*, 54, 87–114.

HUXLEY, [T. H.], 1862. Notes upon Human Remains from the Valley of the Trent, and from the Heathery Burn Cave, Durham. *The Geologist*, 5, 201–4.

KELLER, F. (translated and arranged by LEE, J. E.), 1878. *The Lake Dwellings of Switzerland and other parts of Europe*. London.

MACKIE, S. J., 1862. [Account of the Heathery Burn Cave, and the discoveries there.] *Archaeological Journal*, 19, 358–9.

—— 1861–64. [Remarks on finds in the Heathery Burn cave, which he exhibited to the Society of Antiquaries on 5 June 1862.] *Proceedings of the Society of Antiquaries (2nd ser.)*, 2, 127–32.

SLATER, H., 1865. Early British remains from Allendale and Weardale. *Archaeologia Aeliana (new ser.)*, 6, 168–9.

WILSON, W., 1822a. [Letter to the Revd. J. Hodgson, dated 6 February 1816.] *Archaeologia Aeliana*, 1, 13.

—— 1822b. [Letter to the Revd. J. Hodgson, dated 29 February 1816.] Ibid. 16.

THE SINTRA GOLD COLLAR

OF the works in fine metal possessed by our Museum from the ancient Iberian Peninsula, the noblest is from Portugal: the massive gold collar discovered reputedly at Sintra (Fig. 1, frontispiece, and Pls. x–xii).[1] A location there or near, among the famous steep hills between Lisbon and the ocean, suits the find well enough, and may doubtless be accepted. The Lower Tagus country and the regions all round, from the Beira heights to the Sado and the middle Guadiana, form a region where prehistory, distinctive earlier, met the dawn of history distinctively again: in a cultural blend to which the goldsmith's craft, amongst much else, is an outstanding witness.

The collar, all gold, weighs 1·262 kilograms (short by only some 2½ ounces of 3 pounds avoirdupois). Its form is composite, with penannular body, swollen to its biggest in the middle—thus the front—and tapered in symmetry to

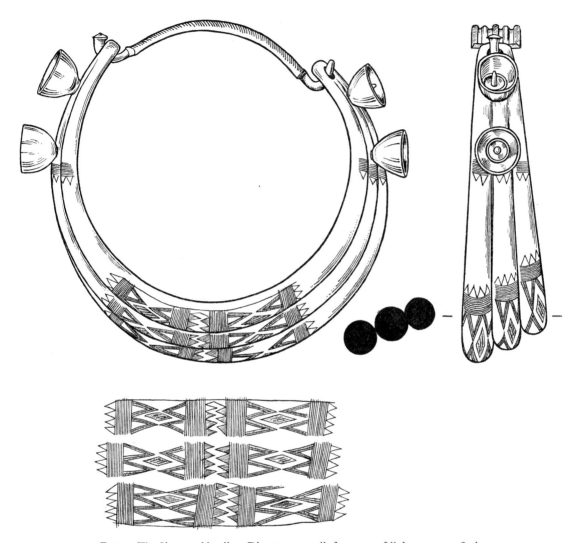

FIG. 1. The Sintra gold collar. Diameter over all, from top of link: 13·1 cm. Scale *c.* 2:3

extremities behind, some 7·7 cm. apart and almost rigid. A human neck inserted, for a comely fit—the inner diameters, of 10–11 cm., give English collar-size 12 to 13—will have been an adolescent or a slender grown woman's. The weight and splendour must suggest ceremonial; such a lady might have worn it when performing as a priestess. The notion is in keeping with the context and date that we shall find suggested by its features.

Two of these attract us to its upper part first. One is functional, the link that fastens it behind; the other is wholly ornamental. Where the collar curves forward, to cross the wearer's shoulders, it has cup-like projections, in line and two a side, moulded each alike, pegging into it beneath (Figs. 1 and 2). From their hollow cup's bottom (6 mm. deep), ringed in relief, there rises a spike (5 mm. tall) like the stamen in a lily. The cups are thus simplified renderings of flowers: strange to prehistoric European decoration, but here to be seen as something else—Orientalizing. From the eighth to the seventh/sixth centuries B.C., long before the seizing of the Straits by Carthage, the Peninsular south was frequented by Phoenicians, from the east Mediterranean littoral and Cyprus. This maritime enterprise, ahead of any Greek, was above all aimed at the country's wealth of metals.[2] Tartessos (as the Greeks would spell it), strong in their supply, was the chief native power to be enriched by the trade (map, Fig. 3); behind it was the way by land to the Tagus. Natives could thus acquire Oriental products; and the gold hoard of El Carambólo (close to Seville), on its diadem-panels and its breast-plaques and armlets, has many rows alternately of bosses and of cups, the cups with an inner petalled flower in relief—with a centre that also could be heightened by a gem, as on the diadem in the comparable hoard of La Aliseda, inland towards the Tagus (prov. Cáceres).[3] The spike, used as centre in our Sintra flower-cups, was used in rows, non-florally, on native gold armlets (Estremoz and Portalegre, Portugal; Villena, SE. Spain); so here we see floral convention passed out of Oriental into plain native terms.[4] The Berzocana pair of collars (prov. Cáceres again),[5] of a swollen-stemmed form like the Sintra one but simpler (Fig. 3, where cf. inset *a*), lacks the cups, but can still attest Oriental contact, being found with a foreign-looking sheet-bronze bowl: hammered bronze-work, previously strange to the West, seems another Phoenician introduction.[6] So does the technique of casting bronze joints free, for handle-rings or swivels—which our collar shows, in gold, employed for attachment of the link that fastens it: the feature that we noticed at the outset (Fig. 2).

The interest of this, and of the floral cups too, does not end with their Eastern derivation. Both can be seen amongst diffusions further north, carried by voyaging up the outer coasts of Europe. And such voyaging, in return, brought further features back, which are embodied in our same Sintra collar. When Eastern enterprise first passed the Straits, towards the early eighth century B.C., its merchant ships could soon be found fit to risk coasting, in summer, on the outer ocean. With natives, doubtless used to it in skin-clad boats, exchanges of knowledge could extend such voyages, perhaps in Tartessos-built Eastern-type ships, very soon to Britain and to Ireland. Thus adaptations from the East, of its hammered bronze cauldrons (with the free-cast handles)[7] and its V-notched shields[8]—even, too, a model boat suggesting such ships[9]—may be explained here within the eighth century already. We have also bronze examples of the

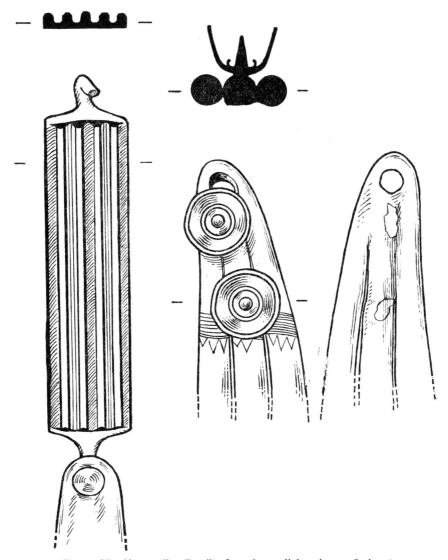

FIG. 2. The Sintra collar. Details of attachment link and cups. Scale 9:8.

floral cup: spikeless for the head of an Irish kind of dress-pin—though one has a pimple (Point of Sleat hoard, Skye)[10]—and spiked for the cup-like ends of one bracelet, mounted on the sword-hilt from Whittingham (Northumberland).[11] Further, our collar has connections more distant. They are north-European, and reflect a shift of sea-route, away from western Britain to the Channel and North Sea. In Armorica—Brittany, with the harbours round the Loire—was a people whose resources and prominent position, at the corner of the Continent, suited

41 G

it for trade in both its own and other peoples' products. The Tartessians, by sailing here as customers for both, could let Armoricans, in skin-boats, ply the traffic on farther; what they told of this to Greeks, a while after 600, was what had started thus more than a hundred years before.[12] For the Armoricans, from the later eighth century onwards, went along with the Tartessians in new-model armament, using swords with blade straight and most often tipped for stabbing; such weapons, very like the Tartessian in form, they distributed and diffused up the Loire and up the Channel, even to the boundaries of northern Europe[13]— a land whose people and traditions were its own. One of those traditions was its mode of metal collars. Of the types of our period, single-stemmed or composite, most have rather widespread regions of occurrence, in the lands around the western Baltic. But one, on the Mecklenburg coast, is an exception: its single stem is swollen, and its three known specimens come all from the islands of Usedom and Rügen (Fig. 3). On Usedom, the first (Fig. 4b) was in the Ziemitz hoard, whence the type was called the 'Ziemitz type' by Sprockhoff; the contents let us date it in the seventh century.[14] This specimen and the next, from Rügen (Fig. 4a), have a link, eyed for a hook and at its other end a swivel, with hammer-closed substitute for free-cast joint; and on the link of the first, and the shoulders of them both, stand solid but indubitable cup-shaped projections. Even the other Rügen collar, from Tetzitz (Fig. 4c), though linkless, has button ends recalling Berzocana; and while the stems of all are ridged, hollow-backed, and fringed with openwork (as Fig. 4a)—Northern features all—yet the likenesses to Sintra, in the links and projections, seem hard to reject.

A relation for Peninsular collars with the Baltic was claimed nearly forty years ago by Bosch Gimpera.[15] Among the Northern types in bronze, he saw that one (triple or multiple) seemed copied by multiple cast-bronze collars in the Bronze Age culture of Mallorca; the Peninsula, having trade in that direction with Sardinia, could give the required intermediacy by sea.[16] The North had, moreover, some collars with a link, such as the Ziemitz type hook, and which could anyhow be broadened (in the Late Bronze Age) to an ornamented 'link-plate'.[17] And this is just what the Sintra collar has (Figs. 1 and 2; cf. 4a), with swivel and terminal hook. The eyes for these indeed are in the collar's own ends, as on another Portuguese one in gold, from Machorros near Serrazes (Fig. 3).[18] But the gold hoard of Herdade do Alamo, near Moura,[19] shows the link-plate with eyes and the collar-ends with hooks, as again on one in gold (with further fragment) from Almoster, north of Sintra (though with no link found);[20] and this hooked form is one originally Northern.[21] Conversely, the linkless type remarked from Berzocana, with button-like ends (which the Tetzitz piece recalls), appears in Portugal more often: in gold though at bracelet size, there are examples from near Guimarães,[22] from the Serra da Estrêla (closer to the Tagus),[23] and from Veiga da Pousadinha near Telões (stem eight-faceted).[24]

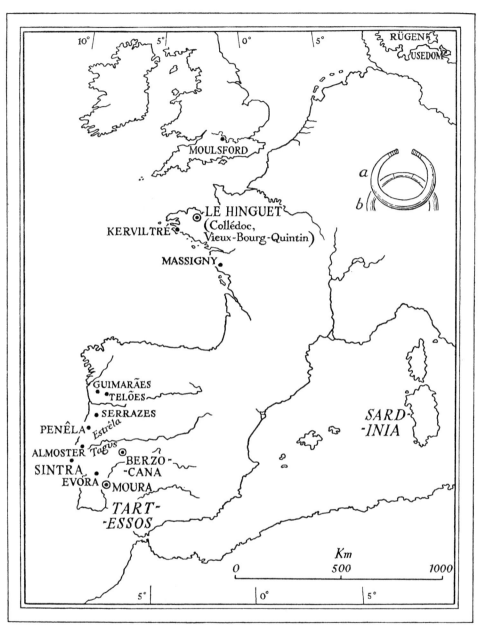

Fig. 3. Map to show localities named in the text. Discs mark those of gold collars (or bracelets), ringed where of two or more in hoard. For RÜGEN and USEDOM see Fig. 4.

Insets: (a) the button-ended form, Brittany (three sites) and Berzocana;
      (b) closed fastening of the Évora form (cf. fig. 5d, Penêla).

(Drawn by Marion Cox.)

43

The Sintra collar's dominating feature, however, is its body, which is triple: formed of three swollen stems—graded in their size, to fit one within the other for display on the wearer's neck and chest (Pl. xii). This is just as in the Northern composite collars, and otherwise is found nowhere else. Its presence here, as

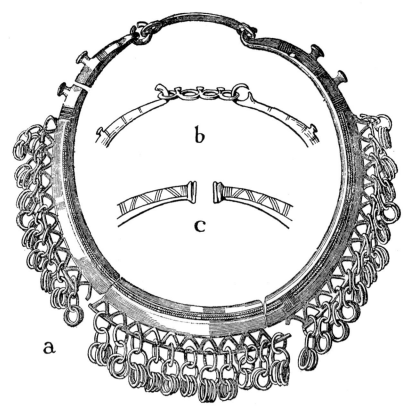

FIG. 4. Bronze collars, Ziemitz type, from Baltic coastal islands ($\frac{2}{5}$).

    (a) Rügen (no loc.).
    (b) Usedom (from the Ziemitz hoard). Sketch of shoulders and link.
    (c) Rügen (from Tetzitz), sketch of terminals.
(All after Sprockhoff.)

Bosch Gimpera from the first has seen, is his claim's best point by far. The Northern bronze analogues may have flat or hollow backs, or be wholly flat and sickle-shaped;[25] the likeness still remains. The Moura type, single, does repeat the flat shape. But the Sintra collar shows us a unique adaptation, of the Northern triple body to a massive gold form.

    As a product of the maritime relations of the age, which let its Northern features dominate, its Eastern be ancillary, the seventh century (earlier half) appears its best date. But their combining on a collar so splendid, yet feminine,

44

leaves questions to ask on those relations themselves. Was their covering such distances a new thing now, due, through Tartessos, to the Eastern impulse? And were they simply for commerce, in goods and techniques, or has the collar yet more to suggest? Two more features remain to be observed: its swollen-stemmed shape and its surface decoration. Both these bear upon the first question anyhow; the way to the second lies through it.

The decorative patterns on the body, first of all, must be distinguished from the knurling on the link-plate. That, along its middle and its outermost ribs (Fig. 2), is simply meant to imitate Oriental filigree. But these, on all three of the body's members equally, are entirely European, and are done in fine tracer-work.[26] Bands of close lines, right across the three members, are drawn once on either side just below the flower-cups, and four times to span the main decorative panel on the middle portion of the body in front. To the outer bands here, and to the two below the cups, are added chevrons forming plain dog-tooth borders, which define, on each side, an undecorated space. To connect the two inner bands are further chevrons, hatched, against a zigzag ribbon left plain in between them; to connect them with the outer bands, the panel uses larger ones, hatched and edged in contrast—double-edged on each member—and placed point to point. The intervals they leave, thus diamond-shaped, are plain, but enclose lesser diamonds which are, in turn, hatched. These tracer-worked patterns as a whole (Figs. 1 and 5) are descended from the Early Bronze Age, when Wessex gold plaques, and Irish lunulas,[27] had each their versions of the style. While in the British Isles it faded *c.* 1200 B.C., at the transition from sheet-gold orna-ments to twisted,[28] it was brought to fresh development, on massive ones, in Brittany. And those, as has been shown by J. Briard, of Rennes, declare this jointly in their tracer-worked style and in the form of their penannular stem, which is swollen. For in Britain the style makes its latest known appearance on the sheet-gold terminals of the Moulsford torc (Berkshire),[29] where the stem, already twisted, is of four strands together (Fig. 5*a*), bound by ties (as one remains to show) but bulging. And from that, of *c.* 1200, the Breton gold collars took the bulge or swelling of their massive form of stem (Fig. 3, with inset *a*); their ornament may even copy versions of the twist, while the ties could be rendered in its tracer-work as bands. Briard,[30] with the Kerviltré and Massigny collars (Finistère and Vendée), cites the great gold treasure of Le Hinguet (Collédoc near Vieux-Bourg-Quintin, Côtes-du-Nord): 8·018 kilograms of ornaments,[31] melted after finding in 1832, but in France published later, from the buyer's notes and drawings,[32] and in England by the Revd. J. B. Deane, from his own, in *Archaeologia* for 1838 (whence here Fig. 5*b–c*, two of the collars).[33] Briard's date for their climax, *c.* 1000–900, must have seen the type passed down the coast towards Portugal: so were bronzes, also then, from both sides of the Channel.[34] The movement, thus, was well before Phoenicians

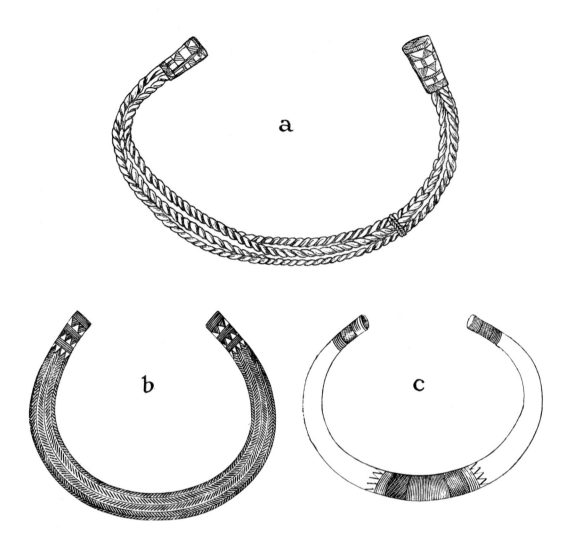

reached the Straits; and as sequels, in the same resplendent tradition, we may place the famous collars from Penêla[35] and Évora[36] (Fig. 5d; and Fig. 3, inset b). Their massive gold stems show the tracer-work continuing, the swollen form too, and have a portion made detachable (with hidden peg-and-socket joints) to close them behind: a novelty likeliest towards the eighth century, followed then, towards the seventh, by a further one, the link—at Moura seen plain, on the Sintra piece embellished.

So our first question anyhow is answered. Gold works can truly reflect sea-connections before, as well as after, the Eastern impulse came. When it did come, indeed, it extended them still further, adding the stretch between Channel and Baltic to that between Channel and Peninsula. The opening of this ocean-

46

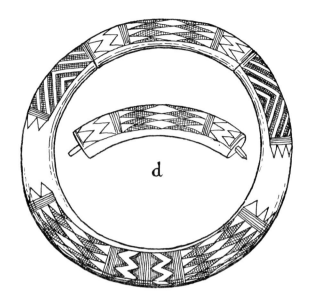

FIG. 5. Gold collars: England, Brittany, and Portugal. (Scales *a–c* $\frac{2}{5}$, *d* $\frac{1}{2}$).
    (*a*)   Moulsford (Berkshire: Mus. and Art Gallery, Reading).
    (*b–c*) From treasure of Le Hinguet (Collédoc nr. Vieux-Bourg-Quintin, Côtes-du-Nord).
    (*d*)   Penêla (district Coimbra: Mus. Etnolog. National, Lisbon-Belem).
               (After (*a*) Briard, (*b–c*) Deane, (*d*) Cartailhac.)

coast stretch, moreover, can be due to migration southward along it: towards 900 there were newcomers in Brittany, and then very soon in the Peninsula too, as though taking direction from migrants in retreat. Few in numbers, such venturers can yet have been important. Goldsmiths and their gold, at least, were somehow involved—while treasure like the hoard of Le Hinguet was buried. Why was Bronze Age society so concerned for all this finery? For collars of such weight as those from Évora and Penêla? and then for that from Sintra, most elaborate of its kind, with its Eastern and Northern seventh-century affinities? This is our second question. The nature of the work, and its transmission in such detail, point to more than commerce; more too, surely, than the pride of native chieftains. Our collar was a woman's. Were not many more besides? Religion—so with priestesses to wear them in its service, and with sanctuaries for treasure-hoarding—must have meant more, to such societies, than many of us usually admit. What reality is hidden by the mythical Hesperides? Ocean, for the ancients, washed the Baltic islands too—though the finery there was only bronze. I see the voyages and the treasures, which Phoenicians sought for trade, as like those of megalithic times: somehow involved with a feminine religion. Distantly perceived, it reminds the prehistorian that man will not live by bakery alone.

C. F. C. Hawkes

[1] Purchased 1902 (B.M. Reg. no. 1900, 7–27, 1), as from Cintra, formerly so spelt, some 22 km. north-west of Lisbon; discovered 1895, and stated to have been found, 'among rocks', at the Casal de S. Amaro there: Mário Cardozo in *Revista de Guimarães*, lxvii (1957), 29 with fig. 25, resuming J. Leite de Vasconcellos, *O Archeólogo Português*, i (1895), 160; ii (1896), 17–23; vii (1901), 155; cf. E. Cartailhac, *L'Anthropologie*, vii (1896), 373–4; S. Reinach in *Antiq. Journ.* v (1925), 123–5 with fig. 3 (and see n. 35 here below); P. Bosch Gimpera, *Etnologia de la Península Ibérica* (1932), 225, fig. 185; H. N. Savory, *Spain and Portugal* (1968), 219, 251, 313, photo pl. 56. To replace the figure in our *Bronze Age Guide* (1903 and 1920), reproduced so often, the Department has honoured this article with the new ones, done with fine skill by Mr. Philip Compton (figs. 1–2), and with the Studio's new photographs including one in colour (Frontispiece); I thank the executants and all concerned, Mr. G. de G. Sieveking especially.

[2] With D. Harden, *The Phoenicians* (1962), 64, 148, 160 ff., refs. 245–9, and A. Arribas, *The Iberians* (1964), 47 ff., 179 ff., refs. 197, 202, see J. M. Gomez-Tabanera (ed.), *Las Raíces de España* (Inst. Esp. de Antrop. Aplicada, Madrid, 1967), 120 ff., 167 ff., and the symposium-volume *Tartessos y sus Problemas*, ed. J. Maluquer (V. Symp. Prehist. Penin., Univ. Barcelona, 1969).

[3] Arribas cit. n. 2, with pls. 1–7: boss-and-cup design, pl. 7, El Carambólo (182 ff., 254); cup with central gem (remains of) among those on pl. 5, La Aliseda 'diadem' (179 ff., 253).

[4] Estremoz (district Évora) bracelet, in Mus. Arq. Madrid, technique and comparisons: A. Blanco in *Cuadernos de Estudios Gallegos*, xii (1957), 6–10; hence W. Schüle in *Jahrb. d. R.-G. Zentralmuseums Mainz*, vii (1960), 79 ff., Abb. 28–9, comparing El Carambólo armlet; Mário Cardozo in *Conimbriga*, i (1959), 17–25, with refs. from 1912 (*Rev. Arch.* xx. 375–80, S. Reinach, for whom the technique was rediscovered by his famous B. Champion). Portalegre (east of Lisbon, south of Tagus) bracelet: Cardozo ibid. 17, 22–7, whence Savory (cit. nn. 1, 19), 313, pl. 59, 219–21, adding, to the Estremoz comparisons, others from the new Villena hoard (Alicante) where C14 shows the non-floral spikes were prior: J. M. Soler, *El Tesoro de Villena* (1965).

[5] A. Blanco in *Zephyrus*, xi (1960), 250–5.

[6] Blanco cit. n. 5 claims the Berzocana bowl as Cypriote; prior to it, and to the better-known handled pans and flagons, should be the earlier of the shields of n. 8 below, and of the cauldrons of n. 7, with their free-cast handle-joints as here next remarked on.

[7] C. F. C. Hawkes and M. A. Smith in *Antiq. Journ.* xxxvii (1957), 131–98, modified for the Peninsula by Hawkes in *Tartessos . . .* (1969, cit. n. 2), 191–2.

[8] J. M. Coles in P.P.S. xxviii (1962), 156–90, with A. M. Snodgrass, *Early Greek Armour* (1964), 55–6.

[9] I have ventured for *Tartessos . . .* (cit. nn. 2 and 7) to compare the Caergwrle (Flintshire) model boat in the National Museum of Wales, fig. 27 in Grimes, *Prehistory of Wales*, with the merchant ships (or 'round' ships, Harden cit. n. 2, 169) shown in the Phoenician fleet on the relief that Dr. R. D. Barnett published in *Antiquity*, xxxii (1958), 226, pl. 22b; Harden 169, 233 (n. 174) and pl. 50, with 308.

[10] Irish cup-headed pins, Eogan cit. n. 28, 305–7, fig. 16, 4, with Coles in *Proc. Soc. Antiq. Scot.* xciii (1962), 111–12, on that in Point of Sleat hoard, ibid. iii (1857–60), 102, where fig. shows its pimple, overlooked by Coles despite J. D. Cowen (cit. n. 11), 285, after Evans.

[11] In the Whittingham hoard: Cowen and Maryon, *Arch. Aeliana*, ser. vi, xii (1935), 280–309; hilt's 'antennae' formed by bracelet, with the cup ends spiked, Cowen 281–8, comparing Sleat pin (n. 10), but doubting relevance of Sintra: the flower-cup evidence from Spain was still unknown.

[12] I here allude to the lost western 'Periplus', seen by Adolf Schulten as sixth-century, of Greek Marseilles, and as used by later writers, whence finally Avienus in his *Ora Maritima*. The resourceful and busy folk of lines 90–114, with their boats, have a geography that only fits Armorica (cf. 146–51: beyond the Bay of Biscay); so this was the 'Oestrymnis' which, as Greeks then would learn, was frequented by traders from Tartessos (113–14). In Schulten's *Fontes Hispaniae Antiquae*, i (1922: requiring some prudence), see pp. 31 ff. 55–7, 79–84.

[13] J. Briard, *Les Dépôts Bretons et l'Âge du Bronze Atlantique* (Rennes, 1965), 228–9 on these 'carp's tongue swords' (complete map, fig. 86); distribution up to North, 236–7.

[14] E. Sprockhoff, *Jungbronzezeitliche Hortfunde der Südzone des Nordischen Kreises, Periode V* (Mainz, R.-G. Zentralmus. Katalog 16, 1956), vol. i, 132 ff. on composite 'Halskragen' collars, 146–61 on single-stemmed collars (some in sets);

this 'Ziemitz type', 143–4, with Abb. 38 and in vol. ii Taf. 25, 1–2, whence my fig. 3*a*, *b*, *c*.

¹⁵ P. Bosch Gimpera, *Etnología de la Península Ibérica* (Barcelona, 1932), 225, 237–9.

¹⁶ This Northern composite collar-type with 'close-hatched basket-pattern' (Sprockhoff cit. n. 14, 137–9, Abb. 36, nos. 3–4) runs throughout period IV to start of V, *c*. 800 (when no. 5 breaks the pattern, and leads off to 6–9); modern dating, lower than when Bosch was writing, thus can just allow its rendering, from around 800, in the still hatched composite collars of Mallorca (cast all in one: his fig. 197). For the Peninsula-Mallorca-Sardinia relationship, see his 231–9 and Mrs. Margaret Guido, *Sardinia* (1963), 151–72.

¹⁷ Of period V and first before the end of IV, as in the Skindbjerg hoard, Jutland, M76 in Broholm's *Danmarks Bronzealder*, iii (1946), 200, on a three-stemmed 'close-hatched basket-pattern' collar: see preceding n. 16.

¹⁸ R. Severo in *Portugalia*, ii. 1 (1905), 109, fig. 1.

¹⁹ H. N. Savory, *Spain and Portugal: the Prehistory of the Iberian Peninsula* (1968), 219, 251, 313, pl. 55, following Cardozo (cit. n. 1), 29, 40 with prior refs., fig. 23 (pl. xiii).

²⁰ Severo (cit. n. 18), 72–4, fig. 1.

²¹ Sprockhoff (cit. n. 14), 132: ends when not plain have primarily hooks; alternatively, loops.

²² From Cantonha near Guimarães, and evidently late: Cardozo (cit. n. 1), 29, 40 with prior refs., fig. 24 (pl. xiii); multiple, the two inner bands with spikes as Estremoz and Portalegre (n. 4), the two outer stems knob-ended in the Iron Age manner (hence Cardozo's dating), but with tracer-work in Sintra style still, though simplified.

²³ Cardozo in *Revista de Guimarães*, lx (1950), 409 ff., fig. 2.

²⁴ Severo in *Portugalia*, ii. 2 (1906), 283, fig. 2; from the faceting, could be late like the multiple Estrêla one (n. 22).

²⁵ Sprockhoff (cit. nn. 14, 16), 136–41, Abb. 36, nos. 6–9.

²⁶ Herbert Maryon on the tracer, from his own experiments, *Antiq. Journ.* xviii (1938), 243–7, figs. 1–13, and *Oxford History of Technology*, i (1954), 642 with fig. 433: it is applied like the punch, whereas the graver 'ploughs' (so is of steel, 648–9, and unknown to Bronze Age art). I thus say 'tracer-work' in tribute to Maryon, and his years in the Museum's Research Laboratory.

²⁷ *P.P.S*, Joan Taylor, xxxiv (1968), 259–65; eadem, *P.P.S.* xxxvi (1970), 38–82.

²⁸ In the line of Fox and Piggott, Margaret Smith and others, now Eogan, ibid. xxx (1964), 273 ff., and in *J.R.S.A. Ireland*, xcvii (1967).

²⁹ Hawkes in *Antiquity*, xxxv (1961), 240–2.

³⁰ *Les Dépôts Bretons* (cit. n. 13), 146–8, with fig. 47 (1 Moulsford, whence my fig. 4*a*, 3 Kerviltré); Massigny, Breuil in *L'Anthrop.* xiv (1903), 173–8, fig. 1.

³¹ Briard, *Les Dépôts* (cit. n. 13), 144–6, where Le Hinguet = Collédoc in P. R. Giot, *Brittany* (1960), 163.

³² P. du Chatellier, *Matériaux*, xviii (1884), 102–4, whence Briard's fig. 46; his fig. 47, 2 shows one of the two collars electrotyped for Rennes (with two bracelets), and figured 1886 in the *Trésors de l'Armorique*.

³³ This Revd. John Bathurst Deane, F.S.A., when the treasure was discovered, was on holiday near by; he quickly drew it all, took the weights in troy, and proceeded to a study which he read before the Antiquaries 18 Feb. 1836: *Archaeologia*, xxvii (1838), 1–14, with engravings (from copies of his drawings) pls. i–ii, whence his nos. 4 and 10 are my fig. 5 *b* and *c* (photos. R. L. Wilkins, Oxford Inst. of Archaeology).

³⁴ Savory (cit. n. 19), 221–7, from prior studies of his own, and of MacWhite's as 269, which could allow of more firm interpretation later on.

³⁵ Penêla (or Penella) collar: E. Cartailhac, *Les Âges Préhistoriques de l'Espagne et du Portugal* (1886), 297, fig. 421, whence my fig. 4 *d*, redrawn by Mrs. Cox; previously, Bosch Gimpera (cit. n. 15), 222, fig. 182, and S. Reinach (cit. below), 124 with pl. xiii, fig. 2. Site (in district Coimbra), is near Condeixa-a-Velha; weight was not 1·8 but 1·95 kg., Mário Cardozo (cit. n. 1), 28–9 with prior refs.: stolen in the revolution of Oct. 1910 from the Palácio das Necessidades at Lisbon; formerly in the collection of Maria II's consort, Dom Fernando II, the 'Rei Artista'. Cardozo in *Conimbriga*, i (1959), 16, cites from *Actas y Memorias Soc. Esp. de . . . Prehistoria*, vi (1927), 263, the belief of J. Cabré that it existed then abroad, in a museum unaware of its identity.

³⁶ Found 1882; acquired then first by the same Cavaleiro da Silva who appears, rather later, to have secured the Sintra collar and disposed of it for London (n. 1); from a younger J. da Silva, in 1920, France gained the Portel (Évora) collar, by purchase for Saint-Germain (Mus. des Ant. Nationales), facilitated, at Lisbon, by a director lacking funds (Cardozo cit. n. 1, 28–9, from Vergilio Correia in 1925: *Terra Portuguesa*, 41, 89,

n. 1). The Évora collar was published then by Salomon Reinach, *Antiq. Journ.* v (1925), 123–34: descr. 123–6, with pls. xiii–xiv, figs. 1 and 6–7; its weight is 2·3 kilograms. The Hallstatt comparisons adduced in his discussion are recognized today as sixth century, not seventh (Schüle cit. n. 4, 79–87), so priority remains with our Atlantic diffusion.

THREE IRON AGE BROOCHES
FROM HAMMERSMITH

THE three fibulae A–C on Pl. xiii came into the British Museum at the end of the last century with the provenance 'Hammersmith'. Little is known about the circumstances of their discovery, and there can be no question of a strict archaeological context, but fibulae B and C are probably those mentioned in passing by Smith (1905, 346) after noting 'the occurrence on the site of the Hammersmith pile-dwelling of four bronze pins in the British Museum. On the same site and at the same time, though not in indisputable association, were found three thin bronze discs with openwork centres and two bronze brooches of the type known as La Tène I'. With its similar inventory number and provenance in the *British Museum Catalogue*, fibula A doubtless came from the same 'site'. The pins were illustrated and discussed by Smith in the above paper (1905) and one of the bronze discs was figured by him in the *British Museum Iron Age Guide* (Smith, 1925, fig. 170), but these three fibulae do not appear to have been illustrated before.

Fibula A (B.M. 98. 6–18. 27; length 38 mm.). The bow is hollow. At the rear, the casting is pierced through, twice horizontally and once vertically. The horizontal holes are almost completely blocked, apparently by corroded iron; the vertical piercing retains a bronze rod or stud that is fitted flush underneath but is broken off at the top. The separate pin is of rectangular cross section; the loop at the end is blocked with corroded iron.

The profile of this brooch immediately suggests a close relationship with the 'decorated foot' (*mit Fusszier*) range of fibulae that are characteristic mainly of the Hallstatt D2 stage of development in areas around the northern periphery of the Alps (Zürn, 1942). If this fibula could be shown in fact to belong to a specific continental Ha D2 type, it would be of a certain interest, since although some slight contact between the main Ha D areas and Britain is implied by rare imports (Hawkes and Smith, 1957, 197), by influences in the design of British daggers (Jope, 1961) and, more doubtfully, by influences in pottery (Hodson, 1962, 142), not a single Ha D2 fibula has yet been published from Britain. Since fibulae are the commonest metal item in the late Hallstatt sites of eastern France, Switzerland, and southern Germany, their complete absence from Britain makes it difficult to accept the idea of any very close contact between the two zones at this time (roughly the later sixth century and early fifth century B.C.), whether in the form of invasions or even of a very lively direct trade (for example, the supposed tin trade from Britain to Massalia via Vix). With this dearth of evidence for contact at this period, even one fibula would be something.

However, a closer comparison of Hammersmith A with continental examples makes it difficult to accept this brooch as a continental 'Fusszier' fibula. The squatness of the raised ball-foot is unusual but not completely out of sympathy with continental examples (e.g. Joffroy, 1960, pl. 20, 14–16; pl. 21, 1–9; pl. 22, 7–9). Again, although the pin mechanism is lost, it could have resembled the regular late Hallstatt cross-bow construction where a pin with its functional, symmetrical spring is located on the fibula body by a rod passing through the coils and through a hole at the base of the bow. However, a pin has survived with Hammersmith A: it has a simple, expanded, pierced end and could never have formed part of a functional spring-and-pin, but would have pivoted freely on the hypothetical iron rod. Even if this pin were rejected as not absolutely certainly belonging, yet a further feature, the rearward projection or finial with its additional horizontal and vertical piercings would separate this brooch from regular continental types. In the absence of close parallels, it is difficult to guess at embellishments that these mountings originally supported. However, the vertical stud very probably secured some added decoration. This could have been a raised globe similar to and balancing the front 'Fusszier': there is space on the extension for a second casting of this shape and size. Symmetry rather like this was a characteristic of La Tène A double-headed bird fibulae, a general type with three centres of distribution in Provence/Liguria, the Middle Rhine, and north-west central Spain (Dehn, 1966). In Spain, further symmetrical fibulae develop, presumably from the fifth century B.C. onwards, for example, double-tower fibulae (Schüle, 1960, fig. 27). But these analogies would be of a most general kind.

More likely, perhaps, the embellishment on top of the rear finial of Hammersmith A may have been much smaller than the front 'Fusszier'—no more than a simple globe. Small globes, generally of coral, and roughly in this position were, in fact, a feature of some further Early La Tène fibulae on the Continent (cf. Joffroy, 1960, pl. 24, 2, 4). If either of these reconstructions is correct, the continental feature would be of Early La Tène rather than Late Hallstatt date. The rear horizontal piercing of Hammersmith A is less easy to restore even hypothetically. It could conceivably have held a second iron rod and skeuo-morphic spring in the spirit of some very Late Hallstatt and provincial La Tène fibulae (cf. Joffroy, 1960, pl. 23, 1; pl. 25, 4), but no continental examples seem really close to this feature of Hammersmith A.

This rather brief survey of possible continental parallels has implied that Hammersmith A is unlikely to be a continental product but that many of its features are derived from continental fibulae of Late Hallstatt and early La Tène types. An attempt may now be made to supplement the above hypothetical

51

reconstruction and interpretation by discussing some other fibulae from the British Isles. The feature most difficult to parallel was the rear, pierced finial, and this provides a good starting-point for discussion. An extension behind the spring was, of course, regular on some Romano-British fibulae in the first centuries A.D., but a cursory search has produced several other, earlier, fibulae with this feature. At least three are of direct relevance.

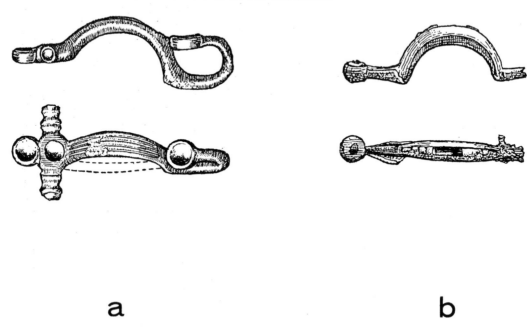

a   **b**

FIG. 1. Fibulae from Hunsbury (*a*) and Woodeaton (*b*). (From Smith, 1912, and Taylor, 1917.) Scale ¼.

The first, from Great Chesterford, Essex (Pl. xiv*b*), is the most instructive. Although far more ornate than Hammersmith A, it shows the same combination of 'Fusszier' and rear extension that was not paralleled on the Continent. Here, although fragmentary, the rear extension preserves traces of a setting with white incrustation in a position that corresponds with the vertical stud at the rear of Hammersmith A. Unfortunately, the pin and its fastening are lost, but the short horizontal bronze stud at the rear of the bow suggests a pivot of some kind.

Second, a frequently illustrated brooch from Hunsbury (e.g. Fox, 1958, fig. 7*c*) has an 'Early La Tène' foot, but also a rear finial with depressions to hold added decoration (Fig. 1 *a*). An interesting further detail is the surviving skeuomorphic crossbow spring cast in with the bow. This is a feature at home in Atlantic rather than central areas of Europe, and is seen in Britain on the fibulae from Harlyn Bay and Plymouth that have reasonably been claimed to demonstrate such Atlantic contacts (Read, 1907; Fox, 1958, pl. 31, 24–5).

The third brooch, from Woodeaton (Fig. 1 *b*), although very fragmentary, displays a similar mixture of features that are late Hallstatt (the stud at the front of the catch-plate, presumably to support a 'Fusszier'), La Tène (the coral (?) strip sunk into the top of the bow), and insular (the rear finial) (Taylor, 1917, fig. 3).

Hammersmith A and these three brooches thus form a motley but instructive group, emphasizing once again the complexity of the evidence for continental influences on British Iron Age metalwork. They offer a remarkably close analogy to the more impressive daggers from the Thames studied by Jope (1961), and they show that insular experiments in brooch design, often thought to start relatively late in the Iron Age, were much more deeply rooted.

One further well-known brooch from the Thames must be mentioned in connection with this 'rear-finial' group. The fibula from Datchet, Bucks. (Evans, 1895; Fox, 1958, pl. 41) presents a much more disturbing mixture of features than anything mentioned so far. Fox (1958, 55) reasonably classified it as La Tène III on account of the cast frame construction of its foot, and yet it has rear-finial embellishments in just the spirit of the brooches described and which have been traced to continental inspiration of the fifth century B.C. The form of the frame-shaped finial and the position of the rear glass bead on this 'La Tène III' fibula are in fact closer to Early La Tène prototypes than are those of the Hammersmith A group. It seems impossible to escape one of three conclusions:

1. The exact replication of La Tène III construction at Datchet is a complete coincidence.
2. The close replication of rather specific features of some continental Early La Tène fibulae at Datchet is a complete coincidence.
3. Ultimately fifth-century continental features did survive in Britain, presumably via brooches of the type discussed and others (e.g. Arras, Queen's Barrow: Fox, 1958, pl. 9) into the first century B.C.; they could then have helped to influence later fibula developments up to and after the Roman conquest.

Fibulae B and C (Pl. XIII). These are clearly 'La Tène I' in one sense or another, as Smith apparently described them (1905, 346). It has long been recognized that fibulae are one of the best indicators of chronological horizons for the continental Iron Age, and since 1908 a reliable key to the stylistic development of many specific La Tène fibula types has been available through the work of Wiedmer-Stern at Münsingen. Here it was possible to retrieve the sequence of fibula fashions through rich associations in graves and through the linear arrangement of the cemetery. This arrangement is dictated to a certain extent by factors other than time, but is able to provide a check on the evidence of association (Schaaf, 1966; Hodson, 1968). The sequence of some principal types at this cemetery is shown on Pl. XV. This sequence is unlikely to have been retrieved by a theoretical typology alone, as experiments have confirmed (Hodson, Sneath, and Doran, 1966), and it is unfortunate that theoretical typologies have played such a prominent part in British Iron Age chronology. The classification of British Early La Tène fibulae by Fox (1927) was a theoretical typology of this kind, put forward tentatively but often accepted as a basis for dating other finds and events.

Fibula B (B.M. 98. 6–18. 24; length 53 mm.) shows in an extreme form the straightening of the bow that has been noticed on many British fibulae (Jope, 1962, 26). Fig. 2 *a* shows a fibula from Münsingen with similar, though not such extreme, proportions and profile. In that cemetery brooches like this with very short catch-plates and low bows (although not otherwise as straight) are concentrated in a relatively short period of time, the Ib (early) stage. However, Hammersmith B is distinguished from continental La Tène fibulae of that stage by two features: first, the foot, although clearly distorted from its original position, would never have been tilted at the acute angle that was regular on the Continent (see Fig. 2 *a* and Pl. xv). Second, the pin is not sprung but pivoted. This would be a most unusual feature on continental La Tène fibulae, and is not, for example, attested once at Münsingen. Evidence suggesting that this is not due to a repair at Hammersmith, but is an original feature, will be presented in discussing the next brooch.

Fibula C (B.M. 98. 6–18. 25; length 46 mm.). It seems reasonable to discuss this fibula as one of three from the Thames that together form a closely knit type or 'species'. The second, from Woodeaton, is without a foot, but conserves more of the spring (Fox, 1927, fig. 18B). The third brooch, from 'London', is well known from previous publications (e.g. Smith, 1925). Because of its completeness, it will form the basis of this discussion (Pl. xiii *d*. B.M. 62. 2–12. 5; length 40 mm). Although quite distinct in general shape from the straight-bow fibula just described, many specific features are shared with it. The decorative motif on the bow of each is basically the same, as is the construction and shape of the foot. But perhaps the most remarkable relationship is indicated in the construction of the skeuomorphic spring (Pl. xiv *a*). In each case the pin, together with the same coil of the non-functional spring, is separated from the outer coil, the division being carefully disguised on the underside. The exact uniformity itself suggests that this is an original feature and not due to later repair. However, there are further considerations as well. A pivoted pin implies a different conception in fastening than a sprung pin. If a sprung pin were the fashion, a repair could be effected by replacing a complete, new spring. This type of repair seems to have been standardized on the Continent (cf. Fig. 2 *b* with Jope, 1962, fig. 1, 3). The sprung pin, which was virtually exclusive with central La Tène fibulae, never regularly replaced the pivoted version in Atlantic coastal areas. Indeed, the most developed insular La Tène fibulae in Britain have extremely

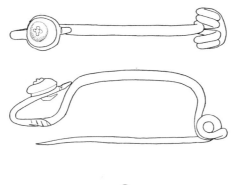

a

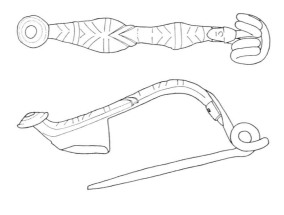

b

FIG. 2. Fibulae from Münsingen graves **91**(*a*) and 46(*b*). Scale ¼.

elaborate versions of pivots but not true springs (e.g. Fox, 1958, figs. 4, 5, 8, 9, 11; pls. 8, 9). For Britain, a respectable ancestry for this feature may now be seen in the Hammersmith A fibula group.

A typologically intermediate stage between these two main series is provided, once more at Hammersmith, by the large, disc-footed fibula in the London Museum (Fox, 1958, fig. 13*f*). This, like several other British fibulae, has close analogies with the continental La Tène Ia series (Hodson, 1964*a*, 137) and is quite distinct from Hammersmith B and C. However, it has a disguised pivoting mechanism like that illustrated on Pl. xiv and emphasizes the consistency of this Hammersmith workshop practice.

Hammersmith C, then, belongs to a restricted 'species' of fibula in the Thames valley, and is morphologically distinct from Hammersmith B, but it shares with it and with many other British fibulae sufficient major features to suggest a class or type of insular La Tène fibula that is distinct from all continental types. The basic definition of this general type would be through the foot profile, which preserves the near-horizontal element of Münsingen Ia alongside the short catch-plate and low bow of Münsingen Ib (Early). It remains to be seen from inspection how consistently the second main insular feature, the non-functional skeuomorphic spring, also recurs. Many La Tène I fibulae from southern Britain and especially from Wessex share at least the first characteristic, and the presence of rods through the springs of many, suggests some skeuomorphism at least rather than, necessarily, 'an expedient by which the fibula after being broken was made serviceable again' (Goddard, 1908). It is perhaps not surprising to find that this insular type of brooch is the one favoured on typically insular sites in Wessex like All Cannings Cross and Rotherley. It could perhaps be regarded, with the insular ring-headed pin, as an integral feature of the Woodbury complex, a pattern of recurring types (a 'culture' in Childe's archaeological sense of the word (Childe, 1956, 16)), which may represent the indigenous Bronze Age substratum retaining its identity into the Iron Age (Hodson, 1964b). Sites on the Thames, like Hammersmith, could represent this native substratum in a more commercial, indeed in a truly metropolitan setting.

SUMMARY AND CONCLUSIONS

Three fibulae from Hammersmith (Pl. XIII, *a*, *b*, and *c*) have led to the discussion of two classes of insular fibulae. The first, a 'rear-finial' group, demonstrates a combination of continental and insular features rather like the Thames daggers studied by Jope. This fibula series should start in the fifth century B.C., but may survive into the first, if the shape of the Datchet brooch is accepted as more than a coincidence. The second class is an insular La Tène I type of brooch, distinguished by its foot and bow profile and its tendency to have a pivoted pin located by a rod to a skeuomorphic spring, a feature perhaps derived from the rear-finial group. This second class includes a number of distinct 'species' whose definition and interpretation require further study. However, it is possible that the class as a whole represents the absorption and transformation of different continental types by the native population.

F. R. HODSON

ACKNOWLEDGEMENTS

My knowledge of Hammersmith A is due to a drawing by G. C. Dunning, one of many kindly presented by him to the London University Institute of Archaeology. I would also like to thank Professor Martyn Jope for helpful discussions on these and other Iron Age topics.

REFERENCES

CHILDE, V. G., 1956. *Piecing Together the Past*. London.

DEHN, W., 1966. Die Doppelvogelkopffibel aus dem Val-de-Travers. In *Helvetia Antiqua: Festschrift Emil Vogt*, ed. R. Wyss, 137.

EVANS, S., 1895. *Proc. Soc. Ant. Lond*. xv. 191.

FOX, C., 1927. A La Tène Brooch from Wales. *Arch. Camb*. lxxxii. 67.

—— 1958. *Pattern and Purpose*. Cardiff.

GODDARD, E.H. 1908. Notes on Objects of 'Late Celtic' Character Found in Wiltshire. *W.A.M.* xxxv.389.

HAWKES, C. F. C., and SMITH, M. A., 1957. On some Buckets and Cauldrons. *Ant. J.* xxxvii. 131.

HODSON, F. R., 1962. Some Pottery from Eastbourne. *Proc. Prehist. Soc*. xxviii. 140.

—— 1964a. La Tène Chronology. *Bull. Inst. Arch. Lond*. iv. 123.

—— 1964b. Cultural Grouping within the British Pre-Roman Iron Age. *Proc. Prehist. Soc*. xxx. 99.

—— 1968. The La Tène Cemetery at Münsingen-Rain. *Acta Bernensia*, v.

—— SNEATH, P. H. A., and DORAN, J. E., 1966. Some Experiments in the Numerical Analysis of Archaeological Data. *Biometrika*, liii. 311.

JOFFROY, R., 1960. *L'Oppidum de Vix et la Civilisation Hallstattienne finale Pub. Univ. Dijon*, xx.

JOPE, M., 1961. Daggers of the Early Iron Age in Britain. *Proc. Prehist. Soc*. xxvii. 307.

—— 1962. Iron Age Brooches in Ireland. *Ulster J. Arch*. xxiv–xxv. 25.

READ, C. H., 1907. *Proc. Soc. Ant. Lond*. xii. 372.

SCHAAF, U., 1966. Zur Belegung Latènezeitlicher Friedhöfe der Schweiz. *Jb. R-G. Z. Mainz*, xiii. 49.

SCHÜLE, W., 1960. Probleme der Eisenzeit auf der Iberischen Halbinsel. *Jb. R-G. Z. Mainz*, vii. 59.

SMITH, R. A., 1905. *Proc. Soc. Ant. Lond*. xx. 344.

—— 1912. The Hunsbury Hill Finds. *Arch. J.* xviii. 430.

—— 1925. *British Museum Guide to Early Iron Age Antiquities*. London.

TAYLOR, M. V., 1917. Woodeaton. *J.R.S.* vii. 98.

WIEDMER-STERN, J., 1908. *Das gallische Gräberfeld bei Münsingen*. Bern.

ZÜRN, H., 1942. Zur Chronologie der späten Hallstattzeit. *Germania*, xxvi. 116.

SPUR-SHAPED BRONZES OF THE IRISH EARLY IRON AGE

IN the British Museum collections, among bronze bridle-bits of the Early Iron Age from Ireland, are six large bronze spur- or wishbone-shaped objects, and a fragment of a seventh. These belong to a type characteristic of Ireland, and not found in Britain at all. All those in the British Museum are either from Irish findspots or unprovenanced (see catalogue below, pp. 59–61). Two of them, unfortunately in poor condition, form a pair, while the most elaborate example has a feature suggesting it was one of a pair, namely the concentration of the decoration on one side. This latter[1] was the subject of a paper by Sir Charles Hercules Read in 1915[2] and he mentions that, at the time, there were thirty-three of these objects in the museum at Dublin. There are now at least fifty-six in Dublin, in addition to examples in other museums, mainly in Ireland.[3]

These bronzes, because of their association with bridle-bits, have always been regarded as an item of horse-harness, though their exact function has not as yet been defined with any certainty. In his publication Read quotes a theory, current in his time, that the objects, hung beneath the horse's neck, were an arrangement to prevent the reins from tangling. He pointed out that this was unlikely, since the purpose was served by the terret, but he did not mention that terrets, while common in the British Iron Age, are very rare indeed in Ireland.[4] In actual fact, there is no definite evidence even for chariots in Ireland at this period. One may, however, cite the yoke from Northern Ireland, which is now in the National Museum of Antiquities in Edinburgh.[5] Read's own suggestion for the use of the objects was that they were mounted behind the horse's ears as a decorative crest. He says that he was told they fitted a big model racehorse in the Dublin Museum in this position; the Celtic chariot pony would, however, have been much smaller than such a horse.

Another theory holds that the objects were used for leading the ponies, attached in some way beneath the animal's head. This seems unnecessarily complicated; the most that would have been needed would have been a short leading-rein attached to the bridle. The existing reins would, in fact, have been perfectly adequate. Chariot ponies must have been well trained and disciplined, and a complex apparatus for leading them would not have been necessary. In any case, a fairly large object fixed to the bridle in this way would have been a nuisance. The decorative value of articles suspended beneath the pony's head or neck, as Read recognized, would have been small.

A recent article on the yoke-saddle in ancient harnessing, by Mrs. Mary Littauer,[6] suggests a more plausible explanation of the Irish material than any yet put forward. While Mrs. Littauer's discussion of the yoke-saddle is based on material chronologically and geographically far removed from Early Iron Age Ireland, the similarities between her examples and the enigmatic Irish objects are very striking. Briefly, she argues that the yoke-saddle was part of an attempt to adapt the yoke-and-pole method of harnessing, straightforward when applied to bovine animals, to the different physical characteristics of the horse family. A complete solution was not arrived at until the invention of the horse-collar in the tenth century A.D.[7] Methods based on a girth and breast- or throat-strap tend to weaken the equine animal's power of traction by bringing pressure to bear on the windpipe. The yoke saddle as described by Mrs. Littauer and shown in her illustrations, while far from perfect, did do something to alleviate this, and was probably reasonably adequate where the horse or pony was in any case only taking a half-share in drawing a light chariot. This harnessing still would not have enabled horses to pull heavy loads.

The yoke-saddle itself was a spur-shaped object of wood or metal; the finial was attached to the yoke beam, and the saddle was placed on a leather pad on the horse's neck, just above the withers. The throat-strap and a loose girth, encircling the horse behind the elbows, formed the rest of the harness. Whether the throat-strap and girth were both attached to the ends of the yoke saddle, or whether the former could have been attached to the saddle pad, does not seem quite clear. Perhaps either would be possible. The Egyptian relief illustrated by Mrs. Littauer[8] also shows that the reins were guided through or under the yoke-saddle, thus dispensing with the need for terrets. This harness would sit securely without chafing the horse, and some of the pull would be taken off the throat by the shoulders moving against the legs of the yoke-saddle.

It is not suggested that the Irish objects necessarily worked in exactly the same way as the Egyptian ones discussed by Mrs. Littauer, even if the functioning of the latter were completely clear, but it is proposed that this was broadly the way in which they were used. The size of the bronzes would seem about right for a small chariot pony, as the neck is narrow at the crest, only thickening towards the throat.

One objection that may be raised is that the bronzes show little trace of wear. The finial in particular could be expected to be worn, if it had been lashed to the yoke beam. Raftery says, however, 'the only signs of wear on them are found on the tops of the rings or loops, and occasionally on the slender shafts'.[9] The strap junctions vary in type on our examples; the fine piece published by Read, which appears to be exceptional, has two well-made sets of strap terminals, one piece[10] has plain rings, and two have only small holes on the inside of their concave terminals,[11] more suitable for sewing the object on to the saddle pad than attaching reins. Metal ring junctions could have been passed through these small holes, but should in that case have survived, at least in some instances. Examination of far more than the six pieces studied here is needed to decide these questions.

There are a number of problems in trying to decide the precise method by which these items were used, but in spite of this the explanation of these enigmatic bronzes as yoke-saddles seems more satisfactory than any yet proposed.

CATHERINE JOHNS

CATALOGUE

1. Pl. xvi *b*

No registration number; acquired by the British Museum in 1915 from the Tower Armouries. The piece has no known provenance or other history.

Total length: 27·5 cm.
Length of finial: 7·5 cm.

Width between terminals: 15·4 cm.

Width between upper strap junctions: 13·3 cm.

The object is in good condition, dark green, with some areas of smooth brown surface remaining.

This is by far the most elaborate of the pieces discussed here, both in the decoration and in the provision of two sets of strap terminals. It may be suggested that the hinged pair served for the girth, the fixed for the throat strap.

2. Pls. XVI *a* and XVIII *a*

B.M. Reg. no. 54. 7–14. 294.
Found in County Mayo, possibly at Ballynacostello.

Total length: 32·5 cm.
Length of finial: 12·5 cm.
Width at terminals: 16·3 cm.
Width between rings: 14·6 cm.

The condition is very good, with a gold-brown patina. The detail photograph (Pl. XVIII *a*) shows the small cast rings within the terminals. These would not have been suitable for the attachment of straps, though they could have served for attaching the yoke saddle to the saddle pad. Straps could have been attached directly to the yoke saddle only by looping them around the legs of the object and sewing them in place. This piece is different in type from (1) above and (4) and (5) below. It may be referred to as Type 2.

3. Pl. XVII *a*

No registration number; no provenance.
Total length: 29·5 cm.
Length of finial: 10·8 cm.
Width at terminals: approximately 10·5 cm.
Width between rings: approximately 9·5 cm.

In good condition apart from the missing terminal; brown patina.

The piece is of Type 2, and as in (2) above, the finial-knob and the terminals match; in this case they are decorated with a zigzag line in relief. The space between the legs is very narrow, and this is the original width, not the result of any distortion.

4. Pls. XVII *b* and XVIII *b*.

B.M. Reg. no. 1913. 7–15. 1.
Found at Mullingar, County Westmeath.

Total length: 24 cm.
Length of finial: 11·8 cm. (6·5 cm. to the curve).
Width: 15·5 cm.

Yellow-brown patina. The surface has a grooved, wrinkled appearance, which seems to have been in the casting. The finial has probably been bent into its present right-angled form, and though the end is very smooth, there could perhaps have been a knob terminal which has been lost.

The simple ring terminals would have served satisfactorily for at least one set of strap-ends; they are much worn (Pl. XVIII *b*). This piece constitutes a third type. It was found with two others, one of which is now in Cambridge and is of Type 2.

5 and 6. Pl. XIX *a, b*.

B.M. Reg. no. 53. 5–28. 4 and 5.
Found near Galway.
Total length cannot be estimated.
Length of finials: (5) 15·5 cm.
             (6) 14·5 cm.

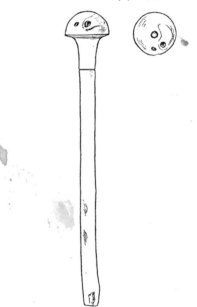

FIG. I. Bronze Finial. Catalogue no. 7. Scale ½.

Width would have been approximately 15 cm.

The patina is grey-green, and the metal is deeply pitted and corroded. The finial-knobs are separate hollow castings, rivetted to the shafts of the finials. The two pieces seem to form a pair, and although the type cannot be ascertained with complete certainty, since the terminals are missing, they seem most likely to be Type 3, like (4) above.

7. Fig. 1
B.M. Reg. no. 1921. 12–6. 36.

Found in County Antrim.
This is a finial only, and measures 15·5 cm.

The patina is golden, and the type is exactly the same as (5) and (6) above, the knob being separately cast, and attached to the finial by means of a rivet, the head of which is finished flush with the surface of the knob.

[1] Pl. xvi *b*.
[2] Sir Charles Hercules Read, 'On a Bronze Object of the Late-Celtic Period recently added to the British Museum', *Archaeologia*, lxvi (1915), 349.
[3] I am indebted to R. G. Haworth for this information, and also for a number of other very helpful comments.
[4] J. Raftery, *Prehistoric Ireland* (1951), p. 195.
[5] Stuart Piggott, 'An Iron Age Yoke from Northern Ireland', *Proceedings of the Prehistoric Society*, xvi (1949), 192.
[6] Mary Aiken Littauer, 'The Function of the Yoke Saddle in Ancient Harnessing', *Antiquity*, xlii, no. 165 (1968), 27.
[7] *History of Technology*, ii (Oxford, 1956), 554.
[8] Mary Littauer, op. cit., pl. v *b*.
[9] J. Raftery, loc. cit.
[10] Pl. xviii *b*.
[11] Pl. xviii *a*.

THE WITHAM SHIELD

THE Witham shield[1], excellently preserved and virtually complete (Pl. xx), is one of the finest and largest of all works of early Celtic art and craftsmanship. It was taken from the bed of the River Witham a few miles east of Lincoln about 1826, and came to the Museum in 1872.[2]

What survives is the thin bronze (0·3–0·2 mm.) facing of a wooden shield about 8 mm. thick,[3] oblong with rounded corners, and very slightly waisted down the long sides. It is made up of two sheets (1m. 1·8cm. long) not closely fitting down the middle, but with the ragged join covered by a spine down the whole length, hammered out of one piece of bronze 0·8 mm. thick, to give a swelling, almost hemispherical spindle-umbo near the middle, and at each end an elaborate patera-like disc. The bronze facing had an outer edge-binding. All this is a *tour de force* in beaten bronze-work.

This shape of shield with spindle-boss was well known in the Italic world from the seventh century B.C. onwards,[4] but taken by Celtic tribes from people on their southern fringe, later became known as the 'Gaulish' shield. From Celtic Europe there are no shields known with complete bronze facing; this idea came from Etruscan and Greek armour.[5] In Celtic Europe the shields were wholly of wood, with the spindle-shaped bosses carved out of wood,[6] sometimes (from the second century B.C.) held by an iron strap;[7] only in the later first century B.C. were there metal covers more closely shaped to cling to the full spindle form,[8] except in Italy where some are known earlier.[9]

The spine, with all its detail, is worked by beating and chasing from one sheet of bronze 0·8 mm. thick (thinned to 0·3 in the highest relief), cut to shape to leave a flange with a zigzag border made by punch-work on alternate sides of a reserve line left between two grooves.[10]

The umbo (Pl. xxi) has a subtly slewed surface-pattern worked in low relief (not modelled very fully in the round), giving a taut whip to the vertical axis down the shield. The composition is made from two groups of interlocking loop-and-pelta figures[11] which unwind on either side of the mid-line into a twinned comma-leaf figure[12] sprouting a dart in its tip which jabs down the spine, its slew creating the whip. Within the interlocked peltas smooth slightly domed egg-shapes rise gently from the umbo surface to create a play of light (Pl. xxii). The two loop-and-pelta compositions are held, as if on a mat, by papyrus-like palmettes in the pseudo-axillar spaces, set diagonally over the umbo. The central ring contains three pinned-on almonds of rich cherry grained coral.[13] Buns in the adjacent loops are also of this coral; the lower loops each contain a five-petalled flower embossed and tooled in the metal.

The terminal paterae of the spine are carried on animal heads[14] (equine or bovine to taste), doing duty perhaps like the gorgoneion as ghost-layers. In the angles between head and patera, set like horns and ears combined, are five-leaved palmettes, and on the nasal a seven-leaved palmette clings under the round pop-eyes (giving, by the setting of their internal segments, a sly sideways glance). These palmettes are of classical quality; throughout Celtic Europe palmettes are rarely given more than three leaves.[15]

From the animal mouth hangs a patterned tongue (or a bib, Pl. xxiii); an S-figure with swelling body[16] and in its top end-scroll an involution like those developed on Swiss scabbards of the second century;[17] from a coalescing hair-spring on the bottom end-scroll a dart is poised, aimed directly down the spine at the opposing dart from the umbo.

The terminal paterae are bordered with a fluttering wavy ribbon rising in relief[18] from a broad rounded rim, and growing from the border-tips of paired relief whorl-leaves (recalling the wavy ivy-borders of so many Italic mirrors of the third century and earlier).[19] Inside this lies a planar annulus given a texture with broadly worked flowing line-pattern composed asymmetrically from S-scroll sequences, recalling the ornament developed on Middle La Tène sword-scabbards and other weapons produced by Swiss[20] or north Italian[21] armourers, with some reminders of the low-relief intertwining as seen on the Waldalgesheim pieces,[22] but always with the underlying flavour of Hellenistic foliate ornament. The centrepiece is a cupped boss with a central dome worked as a seven-petalled

62

flower; silver bowls with comparably reticent petalled omphaloi were being produced by western Greek workshops in the third century.[23]

Two main themes pervade and unify the whole decor and ornament-composition on the shield: the whorl-leaf with a strand growing somewhat unbiologically from its tip, and the dot-ended vein-line. Neither is common on continental Celtic work; the latter recurs in many ages and is an effective trick of fine-metal- (particularly silver-) workers.[24] The former probably arose out of ornament such as that on the back of a Swiss brooch,[25] and in Britain is the germ-theme of another Witham antiquity, the sword with foliate ornament rather more freely drawn.[26]

Lurking on the surface of the bronze facing is the profile outline[27] of a boar-emblem, with immensely long but muscular legs,[28] placed as though draped about the shield umbo (fig. 1). The figure had been applied, nailed through the bronze to the wood, and thus easily wafted away in the river when the wood rotted. It was probably of a contrasting metal (it may even have had some embossed modelling, which would have given the whole shield design more substance); it was in two parts divided at the midriff of its very slender body, the ends tucked under the shield-spine.[29] The strange profile of his face can be understood in terms of ears, tusks, and muzzle, and hence perhaps (by transference) equally strange facial profiles of other Celtic animals such as the Uffington White Horse.[30] The Witham shield boar has no prominent

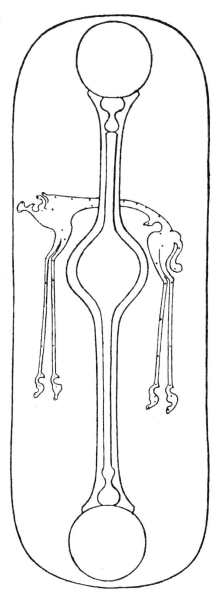

Fig. 1. The Witham Shield, to show Boar in relation to modelled ornament.

spine-crest as on Celtic boars, though such was evidently in mind by the way the neck rises to the top of the ears. On Celtic boars these spine-crests often have patterns of bristles or openwork; even this convention, though it looks barbaric, had its roots firmly in ancient Italy.[31]

The miscellany of themes, in varying degrees archaic, brought into harmony

63

on this shield makes the dating of the work difficult. Many of the exotic themes make us look towards the southern world for their sources. With their variously archaic nature in mind, where more probable that its highly skilled craftsman-designer acquired his experience and thematic stock than among those ateliers of southern Gaul or beyond in Italy itself, where copies of Greek fifth-century or of Hellenistic silverware and bronzes were being turned out for the wealthy in the third century or later?[32]

So these ancient themes need not mislead us. We must seek out the details with the latest initial usage, to show the earliest possible time of making for this shield. The most cogent of these seem to come from the Celtic world just north and south of the Alps as its crafts and arts glided from terminal Early into Middle La Tène manners, in the later third and perhaps into the second century B.C.: the involution hanging from the mouths of the spine-heads[33] (Pl. XXIV a), and the slantwise implication of the line-pattern layout in the patera annuli.[34] Nothing positively demands a later date: the reserve-zigzag border has good examples of this age both in Europe[35] and in Britain.[36]

Part of another shield of this design, from the Thames at Wandsworth[37] (Pl. XXIV b), also in the Museum, enforces this later third- or second-century dating. Though it has the southerly tectonics of the Witham shield, with boss, spine, and end-discs (here separate pieces and not preserved), its detail is taken not from the south but from the Transalpine world, a translation into insular emboss-ing of a style devised in tooled solid metal among the East Celts of the third century B.C.[38] (and filtering a little westwards in Europe). Thus among this family of shields, the Witham shield with its features both structural and decorative so largely southerly or Alpine, should be regarded as the primary example, introducing this structural design into Britain, rather than Wands-worth with its duality of sources, East-Celtic-derived ornament worked over the surfaces of southerly tectonics. Though an undoubted masterpiece of repoussé, the whole aspect of the Wandsworth spine and umbo (especially the ghost-laying mask) is not so urbane as the Witham shield; in this Wandsworth piece we have fully entered the shaded mysteries of the Barbarian Celtic world.

The imposing scale of the Witham shield might prompt us to ask whether it could be later; but (apart from its place in the sequence of British shields)[39] the style of its detail is not really in accord with the trends in taste into the first century B.C. or beyond, especially remembering the Snettisham gold atelier not far away. All seems in place in the second century which appears thus the most reasonable dating.

It remains to look at its possible milieu in the Lincoln area during the second century B.C. It was probably made in a workshop in this district, for several of its tricks either were already (e.g. the dot-ended vein-lines on the third-century Wisbech dagger sheath)[40] or soon to become (e.g. the three almond slugs set in a ring) characteristics of ornament in this part of eastern Britain. It seems unnecessary to suggest that the finished shield was brought northwards from, say, Thames valley workshops.

Such a costly and delicate work could hardly have been for use in battle; it must have been ceremonial, and if its age be any earlier than the second century we should see it in the hands of a noble spearman,[41] for the earliest La Tène swords in Britain are not before that.[42]

In Britain these fine shields and many of the weapons of the Iron Age have come from rivers, and as we have so few cemeteries or wealthy burials we must again ask the question whether insular aristocratic funerary rites involved freeing the spirit from the flesh in a sinking boat.

E. M. JOPE

APPENDIX

Production of the Witham Shield Replica

OUTLINE PROCEDURE

The process used to reproduce a faithful copy of the Witham shield was based on the one known as electrotyping.

Electrotyping requires a mould to be taken from the object to be copied, in this case the Witham shield. The mould is then coated with a suitable conductive powder and placed in a tank of electrolyte solution. The mould is connected to the negative terminal of an electrical supply and a copper anode is connected to the positive terminal. The resultant flow of current redeposits the copper from the anode on to the mould. When the copper deposit has built up to the required thickness the mould, with its attached deposit, is removed from the tank and washed.

The mould is separated from the copper deposit. The edges of the copper deposit are cleaned with a piercing saw and file until all excess copper is removed and the edges coincide with those of the original.

The several pieces needed to form a shape are then fitted and soldered together.

The electrotype is copper—the shield is bronze. A chemically deposited surface-covering of brass is applied in a similar way by electrotyping until the appearance is as required.

The entire electrotype is carefully cleaned and dried and then a coat of lacquer brushed on to prevent discoloration of the surface due to handling or atmospheric contamination.

ACTUAL PROCEDURE

The moulding process for the Witham shield was difficult because not only is it fragile but it is also large (3 ft. 9 in. × 1 ft. 6 in.). It can be taken apart and reduced to three pieces, being two halves and a central spine. The two panels measure roughly 3 ft. 9 in. × 8 in. and the spine 3 ft. 6 in. × 6 in.

A tank was constructed to contain an economical amount of electrolyte, which amounted to nine gallons (41 litres). The electrolyte was made up with distilled water, copper sulphate, and sulphuric acid in their correct proportions.

The moulding material was required to have ease of application, flexibility to ensure ease of removal, structural weakness so that it would tear before damaging the original antique, resistance to the electrolytic solution, setting or curing to its usable state at room temperature, and able to form a faithful mould.

Silicone Rubber, or Silastomer, has all these properties and so makes acceptable its one disadvantage, which is shrinkage. This, however, is so slight that it is of little consequence being less than $\frac{3}{16}$ in. in the 3 ft. 9 in. length of the shield. This is when used immediately. After a period of three months the shrinkage had increased to nearly $\frac{3}{4}$ in.

The central spine was moulded as for gelatine moulding. The spine was placed upon a bed of plasticine and a plaster of Paris casing formed over it allowing $\frac{1}{2}$ in. space in which the Silastomer could flow and so completely cover the spine, the decorative end discs, and the central boss. The spine was lacquered, with the joins between the coral decoration and metal sealed with Durofix to avoid damage, and placed in position, the plaster case placed over it and the Silastomer poured into each of six pour holes. When the Silastomer had cured, the case was removed and a fibreglass form made to replace it. This was to keep the flexible Silastomer in the correct shape while in the tank of electrolyte.

The fibreglass case was taken off and then the Silastomer mould was removed from the spine and found to be satisfactory in its reproduction of detail.

The mould was replaced into the fibreglass case and the reproductive surface coated with conductive powder. This was then wired to the negative terminal and placed into the tank of electrolyte.

The copper anode was then wired to the positive terminal and introduced into the tank. The current was adjusted, by means of a rectifier which gave $\frac{1}{4}$ volt initially and then 1 volt, to 4 amperes.

Three weeks later the redeposited copper was of a sufficient thickness so the mould was removed from the tank and it, with the copper, was washed and dried. Before removing the Silastomer mould it was considered to be a safety precaution to coat the inside of the redeposited copper with soft solder to strengthen any weakness or thin areas in the deposit. This was done and then the Silastomer mould removed to reveal a perfect reproduction.

The edges were cleaned and the various holes drilled, pierced and filed to conform to the original.

The two side panels were dealt with in a slightly different manner in the formation of the mould. The Silastomer was poured on to each panel in turn and strengthened with nylon net. This method was used so that the Silastomer should remain sufficiently flexible to make possible its removal from the fragile, brittle metal of the original shield.

The Silastomer was backed with fibreglass to maintain the contours of the side panels and then coated and connected as for the spine.

In addition to applying soft solder to the copper deposit a 14-gauge brass wire was soldered continuously following a line an inch in from the outside edge on the underside of the panel which was less than $\frac{1}{16}$ in. thick and required stiffening. Two cross-bars were added, to hold the side panels in the correct position, to which the spine was attached by screws.

After all soldering and cleaning-up had been finished the chemical colouring was applied. A suitable tank was made and various appearances achieved, ranging between copper and brass, before the final effect was considered acceptable.

After thorough washing and drying the panels and spine were coated with Ercalene, a cellulose-based lacquer, to reduce change of appearance caused by atmosphere and handling.

OBSERVATIONS

On the Silastomer mould and the copper replicas the detail of design, both embossed and chased, was more clearly defined than on the original, due to the lack of confusing patination with its resultant changes of colour.

Also reproduced and brought into greater clarity are the assembly marks of the original assembly. These are for the location of the central spine upon the two side panels. Such are the marks and rivet holes that they suggest a domed oblong of uncertain depth. The side panels are domed but being of thin brittle metal are so distorted that the true shape would be very difficult to obtain. There is evidence of repairs carried out in antiquity to the central spine at the lower end and to one side of the central boss. The crack at the junction of the lower disc and the spine has been patched by riveting. A crack 3 in. above this, where the pattern separates causing a structural weakness, has been drilled at its extremities and a rivet fitted to strengthen it and to hide the fault. A similar crack at the top of the spine has not been so riveted, presumably being caused at a later date, not being subject to the abuse of being rested on the ground and having greater rigidity on account of the shorter distance between the upper disc and the central boss.

The repair in the side of the boss is probably due to a fault in the casting made worse by working-up the design.

In each disc, adjacent to the spine, is a trefoil piercing with three associated rivets. On the boss, above and below the central motif, is a triangular and a circular piercing with attendant rivets. These would indicate a backing, possibly of leather, of a coloured decorative nature. A dissimilar metal is considered unlikely due to lack of corrosive evidence.

The stylized boar outline on the side panels is as legible on the replica as on the original. The difference in its body width, as it passes beneath the central spine, is noticeable.

The side panels were apparently beaten to the requisite thickness, as there are several small areas indicating faulty smelting where the metal sheet has laminated during beating. The sheets do not have the appearance of having been annealed. They are stiff to the touch, very brittle, and crack or tear very easily.

P. H. T. SHORER

[1] This account summarizes the detailed discussion in P. Jacobsthal and E. M. Jope, *Early Celtic Art in the British Isles* (in press = *ECABI*).

[2] B.M. Reg. no. 72.12–13.1; length 1 m.11·8 cm. *Archaeologia*, 23 (1831), 97. The circumstances of finding are obscure; it came to the armoury collection of Col. Meyrick at Goodrich Court in Herefordshire, through the good offices of Earl Brownlow who got it from the Rector of Washingbourne in Lincolnshire, near whose estate it had been found.

[3] It was evidently of wood as some of the holes in the bronze seem to have been for nails; the thickness is given by the rivet lengths to the internal washers.

[4] P. Coussin, *Les Armes Romaines* (1927), 65, fig. 26; O. Montelius, *Civ. Prim. Ital.* (1895), pl. 175; L. A. Milani, *Studi e Materiali*, ii (1901–2), pl. 10, fig. 51 (tomb-covers).

[5] A. M. Snodgrass, *Early Greek Weapons and Armour* (1964), 51 f., 54, 226, n. 3.

[6] G. Rosenberg, *Hjortspringfundet* (1937), 48; P. Vouga, *La Tène* (1923), pls. xvi–xviii; W. Kimmig, in *Germania*, 24 (1940), 106–11.

[7] A type widespread through Celtic second-century Europe, J. Déchelette, *Manuel d'Archéol.* iv (1927), pp. 556–90, 675, 679.

[8] *Acta Archaeologica*, 20 (1951), 46 ff.; *Mainzer Z.* 29 (1934), 55.

[9] O. Klindt-Jensen, *The Cauldron from Brå* (1953), fig. 26a; Mr. David Ridgway kindly informs me that this is a fifth-century grave. *Not d. Scavi*, 1888, pl. 2. 2.

[10] This technique for reserve zigzag line is seen in the third century on La Tène Ic brooches in the Tirol (*Germania*, 38 (1960), 21, pl. 2. 2) or on the openwork daggersheath from Hammersmith (*Proc. Prehist. Soc.* 27 (1961), pl. xxvii b).

[11] This use of interlocking pelta-units is seen in the work of the late fourth-century Waldalgesheim master and his followers in the subsequent century (P. Jacobsthal, *Early Celtic Art* (1944), pp. 94 f. The peltas arise when round settings replace foot scroll whorls, PP 450a, b). How figures may come to lose their outgrowth finial-bosses to become peltas may perhaps be seen on the Standlake scabbard-mount (*Problems of the Iron Age in Southern Britain* (ed. Frere, 1959), pl. v a).

[12] Cf. *ECA*, P 359.

[13] Identified as coral by the X-ray diffraction technique. The research was carried out by H. Barker at the British Museum Research Laboratory in 1964.

[14] Many Etruscan mirrors have a head thus placed.

[15] P. Jacobsthal, *ECA*, p. 88.

[16] For the double line within the swell, compare the La Tène Ic brooches, *Germania*, 38 (1960), pls. 1, 1a, 2a and 5.

[17] P. Vouga, *La Tène* (1923), fig. 7.

[18] Made by hammering an oblong punch in zigzag alternation along the inside of the roll-mould.

[19] W. Lamb, *Greek and Roman Bronzes* (1929), pls. xliv, lx; E. Gerhard *et al.*, *Etruskische Spiegel*, *passim*; for modelled wavy bordering, *J. Hell. Stud.*, 69 (1950), pl. ii a; J. Boardman, *Greek Art* (1964), fig. 152.

[20] For the curlew-bill on Pl. xxiii, cf. the spearhead, *ECA*, no. 129.

[21] *ECA*, no. 103.

[22] *ECA*, pls. 37–9, 44–5, 96–9.

[23] D. E. Strong, *Greek and Roman Gold and Silver Plate* (1964), 94–5, pl. 248.

[24] Cf. *ECA*, no. 381.

[25] *ECA*, no. 333, P 349; F. R. Hodson, *The La Tène Cemetery at Münsingen-Rain* (1968), tomb 50.

[26] *Burlington Mag.* 75 (1939); T. D. Kendrick, in *Antiq. J.* 19 (1939), 194.

[27] What we now see seems to be a combination of contact-corrosion and trimming marks.

[28] Long-legged boars ('greyhound pigs') are often shown in Celtic contexts, e.g. on coins.

[29] The register across the spine is not quite exact, and the boar-body is narrower on one side than the other (as is precisely shown in the Museum's *Guide to Early Iron Age Antiquities* (1925), fig. 113). There would seem therefore no reason for seeing in this boar an early stage in the shield's history; the boar *could* even have been a later addition, though I see no reason to suggest this.

[30] The convention was not confined to insular Celtic animals, for it is seen on an east Celtic coin (I. Hunyady, *Die Kelten im Karpatenbecken* (vol. of plates 1942), pl. c. 6).

[31] e.g. the boars incised on Etruscan helmets, P. Jacobsthal, *Early Celtic Art* (1944), pl. 222a, b.

[32] The Museum has, for instance, both ancient originals and copies of *phialai* from Èze in the Alpes Maritimes: G. M. A. Richter, *Ancient Italy* (1955), 58, figs. 188–9 (also in the Museum); *Amer. J. Archaeol.* 54 (1950), 359 ff.; D. E. Strong, *Greek and Roman Gold and Silver Plate* (1966), 81.

[33] P. Vouga, *La Tène* (1923), fig. 7e, pl. v. 5.

[34] Slantwise layout on sword scabbards is a Middle La Tène characteristic.

[35] e.g. on the back of the Tirolese brooch, *Germania*, 38 (1960), 21, pl. 2. 2.

[36] The openwork sheath of a dagger from Hammersmith, probably of the third century, has a rough version of this technique, *Proc. Prehist. Soc.* 27 (1961), pl. xxiii e.

[37] *Later Prehistoric Antiquities* (1953), pl. xx. 2.

[38] *ECA*, nos. 175, 176, 222, 267–74. This matter is more fully treated in *ECABI*.

[39] The Museum possesses also the two other finest British shields, Battersea and the Wandsworth roundel, the central unit from a shield of Battersea type (with its strong Augustan flavour). This Wandsworth roundel again probably has a poor copy of the relief wavy-line technique of Witham and the Wandsworth mask shield, and with its sense of perspective—the oblique view of a bird rising from the water (Pl. xxv)—seems to follow silver-ware of Augustan age.

[40] *Proc. Prehist. Soc.* 27 (1961), pl. xxiv.

[41] For Italic conventions compare the procession of spearmen bearing just this kind of shield, on the Arnoaldi situla of c. 400 B.C. (*Arte delle Situle* (1961), pl. 38).

42 The Standlake sword seems the earliest
known, first made up as a sword probably about
200 B.C. (*ECABI*, chap. 3, revising the dating of
this composite piece in *Proc. Prehist. Soc.* 27
(1961), 315, 320; in concord with J. M. de
Navarro, in *Ber. R.G. Komm.* 40 (1959), 91,
note 25).

SOME WILTSHIRE PALAEOLITHS

IN this communication the significance is discussed of certain stone implements from neighbouring localities in the periglacial region of Wiltshire.
From this part, near and around the Ridgeway on Hackpen Hill, belonging
technically to the Thames basin, a number of Lower Palaeolithic forms were
made known nearly sixty years ago by the Revd. H. O. Kendall.[1] My interest
in them was stimulated by actual field experience in the district and inspection
of comparable specimens in the museums at Avebury, Devizes, and Marlborough, particularly during the summer of 1960. Since, I have studied the
palaeoliths derived from Kendall's pioneer excavations that are in the Wellcome
Prehistoric Collection, now in the British Museum, and similarly found artifacts
already among the national series. Recent advances in Palaeolithic archaeology
and in the British Pleistocene have enabled a reconsideration of the evidence from
Kendall's Wiltshire sites and an evaluation of some hitherto unrecorded material.
It is the purpose of this paper to emphasize the importance of sites such as these
and of man's industrial products from them in the study of the Palaeolithic Age
in Britain.

I. THE RIDGEWAY SITE

(*a*) *Historical*

Using the terminology current when he wrote on Hackpen Hill, Kendall
spoke of chipped flints. Nor did he always make it clear in his contribution in
1916 to the *Proceedings of the Society of Antiquaries*,[2] if he meant true artifacts or
split, broken, and edge-injured stones brought to their condition by natural
agencies. Seven years before,[3] he had referred frequently to eoliths, but with
commendable shrewdness and reserve he put them outside the real scope of his
later paper. Even so, it is plain that several of the excellent drawings in his
second communication image accurately these products of nature's workshops
alongside illustrations of unambiguous Palaeolithic tools. One can now explain
the roughened surfaces, the long and short flake-scars affording no striking-
plane and often disposed at angles impossible to achieve in intentional flaking,
together with marginal scalloping and scaling of manifestly different periods,
staining and multiple coloration. Similar scathing and surface alteration also
appear on many of the palaeoliths which have been traced and studied in different
collections. Some of these artifacts, like the entirely natural objects, bear

innumerable short scratches. The real implements must, therefore, have been subjected to the same maltreatment as their companions which were excusably attributed to man's work.

The first of the specimens coming under Mr. Kendall's generalization were found in the ground inside hollows near the Ridgeway. Their presence therein caused the finder to conclude that they were from an implementiferous bed, the existence of which might be revealed by digging. Numerically poor as was the archaeological yield of the operations he conducted, it nevertheless proved instructive in 1916 but not conclusive. For it gave rise then to speculation on the character of the deposits explored and on the chronological place of the artifacts.[4] As understood today, the Lower Palaeolithic output and the site are, I believe, even more interesting than they first appeared.

From the excavation report and the accompanying drawings of the section[5] beside the Ridgeway one cannot recognize distinctive stratification as in fluviatile deposits. It can be said, however, that most of the man-made objects were extracted from the gravel (4, Fig. 4, p. 76, below), at little depth from the surface. Irrespective of the containing bed, they vary in condition. Only a few are virtually unblemished though slightly lustrous; others have blunted edges and crushed ridges, to the degree indeed of being almost indistinguishable from rolled pebbles and cobbles. Ferrous cement from the enclosing layer adheres to some of the artifacts and other stones, and certain artifacts show striations.

The naturally and artificially scarred pieces from the pits are mostly of a good grade of rich brown and greenish flint, often banded and mottled. In the heavily coated and stained specimens the true colour of the material is discernible where some late injury has affected the surface. Kendall, however, has mentioned black implements, excavated or turned up by the plough.[6] Their smoother and glossier surfaces would distinguish them from tools of later execution. We shall see that in some of the artifacts of post-Palaeolithic facies the flint used is light or dark grey.

While the numbers of palaeoliths from Hackpen Hill are not imposing and the actual artifacts not impressive, yet the clutch is comprehensive. Thus bifacially worked forms and flake-tools were found, besides pieces so worn along the edges as to suggest that with the simplest of added dressing their natural contours were convenient and serviceable. Of course these last are not ranked with the naturally scathed specimens regarded as artifacts by Mr. Kendall. Cores, also, though not stressed by him, deserve particular comment.

(b) Facies

On the standards accepted today the Hackpen Hill series is demonstrably Acheulian, albeit rather poorly expressed. Low quality and small numbers, however, need not surprise if one takes into account, first, a lack of suitable raw

70

material on the high ground for making large bifacial implements by fine shallow flaking, and, second, the probability that occupation here by man in Lower Palaeolithic times was only seasonal.

Although some of the artifacts would certainly appear to have been produced by exponents of early Acheulian industry, yet the abraded and grossly pebbled condition of so many composing the assemblage makes separation difficult, the more so because of the nature of the containing soil. However, in my opinion none of the palaeoliths can be attributed to workmanship more advanced than Middle Acheulian, the facies contemporary with the Middle Gravel on the 100-ft. (30 m.) terrace at Swanscombe, Kent,[7] and with fluviatile gravel resting on the equivalent benches upstream along both banks of the Thames, notably at Lent Rise, Burnham, Bucks., and Furze Platt, Maidenhead, Berks.[8] Hand-axes of similar facies are recovered from the gravels on the counterpart shelf lining the main rivers of the Solent drainage.[9]

(i) *Bifaces*. Wrought by short flaking, the bifaces range in length from 3·55 in. (9 cm.) to 4·55 in. (10·5 cm.). Pebbles, small cobbles, and thick flakes went to their manufacture into quite usual forms.

The hand-axes of the most ordinary type are first illustrated to show the short striations which score their surfaces in bewildering confusion and lend peculiar interest to the specimens. Fig. 1, nos. 1 and 2 are made on a pebble and on a flake respectively.

Ovates, core-tools, are also represented. Heavy, bulging, and scratched, no. 3 is an example with crushed edges and attrite flake-ridges. Less stout and even more abraded, a companion, no. 4, has apparently been reduced from normal oval to squarish outlines. Being now so smoothed and bruised of edge, these two implements are hardly distinguishable from water-rolled stones. Another, no. 5, pocked by thermal fracture, is a shapely cordiform tool. Heavily coated, ochreous brown, and better preserved than its associates, it exhibits the marks of well-developed Acheulian workmanship. No. 6, a dihedral and equally well-made form, can be placed with the ovates.

(ii) *Flakes and derivatives*. The chronicler of the investigations carried out over fifty years ago around Hackpen Hill showed unusual perspicacity at a time when so many searchers thought only of amassing the finest Lower Palaeolithic tools, mainly hand-axes and the like. Owing, however, to Kendall's carefulness, worn or worked flakes and pieces were collected. Many are now seen to supplement the bifaces, and these increase our knowledge of the Lower Palaeolithic industries in Wiltshire.

Among the flakes from Kendall's excavations on Hackpen Hill are several that could be described as Levalloisian. However, some of these are waste from bifaces in the making, for example, a number retaining nodular cortex such as Fig. 2, nos. 1 and 2. Some of this residue of hand-axe manufacture bears signs of

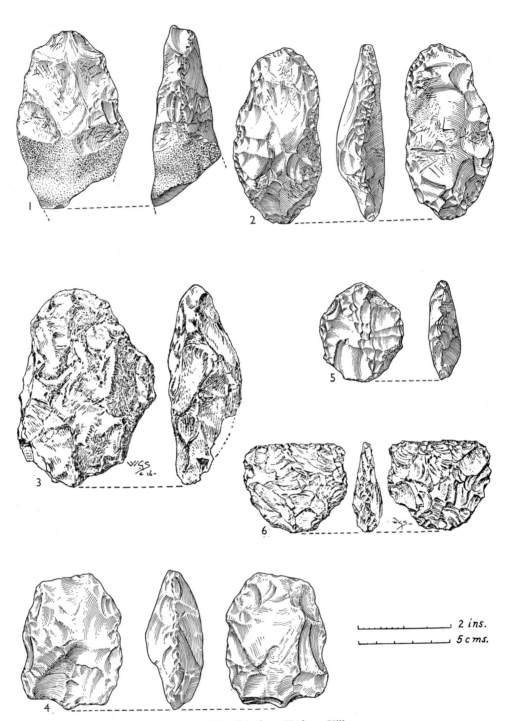

FIG. 1. Palaeoliths from Hackpen Hill.

Bifaces: 1, Wellcome Prehistoric Collection, no. 82450; 2, 4, and 5, B.M. Reg. nos. 1916, 2–10, 2; 1916, 7–6, 1; 1911, 12–2, 5. 3 and 6 after Kendall, 1916 (reproduced by permission of the Society of Antiquaries).

72

the utilization and trimming. Thus, fine steep dressing along the left edge of no. 1 converted this flake into a side-scraper. Its feeble hollow right margin is worked boldly on both faces, the upper showing much wear, not unlike that along the edges of no. 2, which may be due simply to natural bruising against other stones rather than to use. Intentional retouch, however, is plain along the short oblique edge on the right side of the squat compound scraper on a flake, no. 3, recorded 6–12 in. (15–30 cm.) below grass-level. The drawing shows how the natural roughening of the margin at the base of the high left side compares with the intentional work. Again, along the edge of the pronounced lateral hollow in no. 4, the bruising appears to be wear rather than deliberate treatment.

Discoveries over the past forty years in Pleistocene deposits have established that many flakes, exactly resembling nos. 5 and 6 in Fig. 2, occurred associated with well-developed Middle Acheulian bifaces and parent cores in the valleys of the Thames,[10] Bristol Avon,[11] and the Trent.[12]

The crenellated scraper, no. 6, shows that the basic form of the edge-retouched and worn flake was determined before the slice was struck from a prepared core. Another is also suggested by the vertical butts of the three flakes, plain in no. 5 and faceted in nos. 6 and 7. On its upper surface no. 6 also displays large truncated facets resulting from the working down of the original lump. Not being separable geologically or otherwise from their bifacially worked Acheulian companions, these flake-implements are not attributable to a pure Levalloisian industry, but provide further evidence in that the ingenious and widespread technique had its inception in the long-lasting Acheulian culture.

(iii) *Cores*. It is regrettable that from the pits beside the Ridgeway no cores were taken of the familiar 'tortoise' type prepared to give the knapper flakes and blades such as nos. 5, 6, and 7 in Fig. 2. On the other hand, there are some curious cores among the flints examined from the downland. As part of a varied equipment, they testify to the versatility of the Old Stone Age artisan. Thus a small cobble, no. 8, is so scarred bifacially at one end only as to indicate that the maker intended to use it as an edge-tool. A prominent knob, the roundness of the stone and the crust combine admirably as a holder. That the implement served as a chopper or heavy scraper appears from the battered condition of the edge. Used as either, it falls into the simplest class of Middle Acheulian tools deftly struck on corticated nodules.[13] Gloss in this specimen is a significant trait on every long facet. Of small prismatic pieces from which flakes or blades have been detached, one particularly, no. 9, is noteworthy for its worn convex edge. Really an improvised and not uncommon type of Lower Palaeolithic tool, it foreshadows an important and enduring order of core-scrapers. Also, among flake-scarred residual lumps of flint, no. 10 seems to be a sort of plane-scraper.

Finally, we notice an easily held, medium-sized, multi-faceted subglobular core, Fig. 3, no. 1. Hardly any part has escaped the alternate flaking that shaped

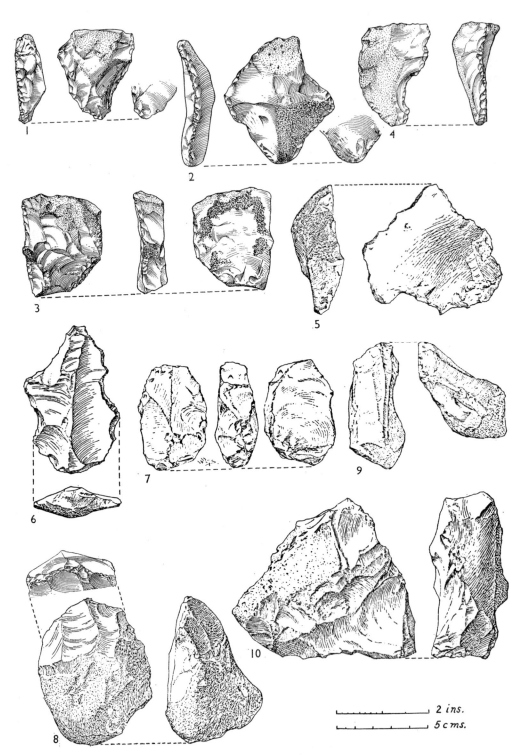

FIG. 2. Palaeoliths from Hackpen Hill. Flakes and derivatives: 1 and 3, B.M. Reg., nos. 1911, 12–2, 4; 1916, 2–10, 5. 2 and 4, Wellcome Prehistoric Collection, nos. 81986, 81986 (2463). 5–7 after Kendall, 1916. Core-tools: 8, B.M. Reg. no. 1916, 2–10, 3. 9–10 after Kendall, 1916. (5–7, 9 and 10 reproduced by permission of the Society of Antiquaries.)

and brought it to a circumferential cutting-edge. This mostly retains its pristine keenness, but the flake-ridges are dulled slightly in places and the beds show some lustre. Widespread from Lower Palaeolithic times onward, implements of this kind are enigmatic, but it has been plausibly argued that they were meant for sling-stones. Certainly their sharp sinuous edge would make them formidable weapons.

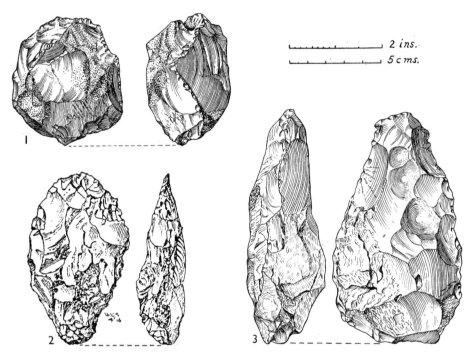

2 ins.

5 cms.

FIG. 3. Palaeoliths from Hackpen Hill and higher ground.

Subglobular core: 1, Hackpen Hill, B.M. Reg. no. 1916, 2–10, 4. Hand-axes: 2, Glory Ann Barn pit; 3, Totterdown, Avebury Museum, no. 4 B. (2 and 3 after Kendall, reproduced by permission of the Society of Antiquaries.)

2. GEOLOGICAL CONSIDERATIONS

(a) The local succession

Sediments noted by Kendall at the south end of the Hackpen range where it merges into Rough Hill,[14] and studied since his day, provide information on certain local Pleistocene conditions. The nature and origin of some of the critical deposits, exposed in shallow saucer-like pits, he hoped to determine by excavation at two sites. One, where four hollows were explored, lay immediately south of the Ridgeway near the place (SU 126725) at which the ancient track crosses the hill at right angles to the remainder of its course. The other was located about 300 yds. (275 m.) to the north-west.

75

About 200 yds. (183 m.) north-east of the depressions, at 876 ft. (267 m.) elevation, near the ruins of Glory Ann Barn, Kendall remarked a pond within the large opening that resulted here from the winning of clay.[15] Today the faces in this cavity and the talus are masked by bushes and rank grass. Gravel here was not noted by him, nor indeed is any but the most superficial to be seen now,

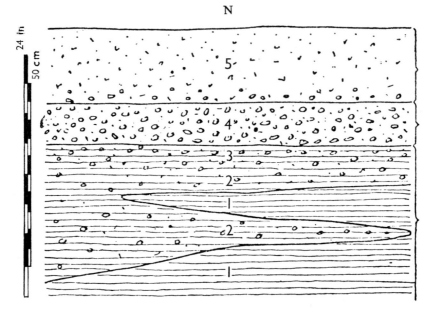

FIG. 4. Section in pit excavated beside the Ridgeway, Hackpen Hill. (Based on Kendall, 1916.) The deposits above chalk at unknown depth:

    1. Yellow clay.
    2. Irregular seams of grey and yellow clay, some stones.
    3. Thin gravel in grey clay matrix.
    4. Gravel lower part concreted and ferruginous.
    5. Top soil upper part with broken stones.

and only in the fields and tracks. Just over half a mile south, between New Totter-down and the wood Delling Penning, on the steep easterly facing cliff of the coombe, there is a long-derelict and mostly overgrown chalk-pit. As late as 1960 one of its crumbling sides showed a series of beds between the basal chalk and the grass comparable to that which can be ideally drawn from the order recorded by Kendall.

Supported by a sketch of the most comprehensive succession of layers revealed by digging in pits on the Hackpen ridge, Kendall's report is also upheld by my recent inspection of surviving exposures in the area. The sequence observed in the openings is simple. Taken with the artifact evidence, however, it is crucial in this endeavour to assess the Lower Palaeolithic facies of the district (Fig. 4).

(b) Relation to glaciated regions

Today Kendall's 'Chellean' ascription would be untenable even were the term equatable with the 'Abbevillian' which has been current in the nomenclature of prehistory for many years now.[16] Such an early placing can be as confidently ruled out as the attribution of any core or flake from the locality to the Clactonian industry.

Being referable, a few perhaps to Early, the majority certainly to Middle Acheulian manufacture, the Lower Palaeolithic relics from the openings near the Ridgeway may therefore be assigned to the period of improved climate that followed the complex of the second great glaciation in southern Britain.[17] This included the earlier episodes of the as yet imperfectly understood Old Drift.

Although never directly invaded by the Pleistocene ice nurtured in the Welsh and northern mountains, the Marlborough downland stood in a periglacial region bounded on the west, north, and east by the maximum limits of the advances. It therefore came very much under the influence of the fluctuating and not distant ice, the waxing and waning of which, with attendant variations of climate and vegetation, affected the habitability of the area by warm-blooded forms including man.

For centuries, nay thousands of years, snow lay on the heights where the ground was no doubt frozen down to the chalk. With the advent and dominance of thaws during the deglaciation, masses of the congeliturbate soil, charged with the scrapings of the land-surface, bore down heavily, ravined the slopes, and filled hollows. As they slowly progressed their contents mixed; included animal remains were broken and crushed; stones, worked or not, became scratched, abraded, scarred, and scaled by contact with others moved under pressure in the sodden conglomeration. Known as solifluxion, this destructive process was of course localized and not uniform.[18] On the Wiltshire downs and other high grounds—on the Kentish downs, to take a notable example—it accounts for most so-called eoliths, once so commonly regarded as most primitive, intentionally shaped, and edge-dressed tools. Arrested when frost returned, the operation began anew with the recurrence of thaw and continued until the climate became stabilized.

Various deposits permanently register the action of solifluxion. Among them is the clay-with-flints of variable age frequently found to contain artifacts.[19] Besides stony compositions, argillaceous, chalky or otherwise, according to region, there are the cognate contorted seams of shattered and angularly fractured pebbles termed 'trail', as well as the coombe-rock, often exposed in commercial and utilitarian openings.

The dislodging of nodules in certain rocks and thereby forming cavities, as for instance in the sarsens on the Wiltshire downs[20] and the granite outcrops of Dartmoor,[21] and the rubbly overburdening on beaches as far from the theatre of ice-movements as Cornwall[22] and even Normandy,[23] also commemorate the alternating conditions of intense cold and relaxing of climatic severity, proclaiming at once how very wide was the periglacial band.

How the palaeoliths of Hackpen Hill are involved will be inferred from the emphasis laid in the foregoing paragraphs on the down-slope movements of debris under saturated conditions. Believed to be of this nature, the beds from which the artifacts were recovered in Kendall's pits are now explained. Not only so, but considering the facies of these relics, we can with assurance refer the deposits containing them to episodes of alternating thaws that succeeded the congenial period during which the Middle Acheulian implements were fashioned. What does stand out, however, is that the majority of the artifacts brought to light by the excavations on the Hackpen heights, and assignable typologically to Middle Acheulian workmanship, had been dragged from the spots where their Old Stone Age users had left them and were assimilated in moving congeliturbate masses. It is to the credit of Mr. Kendall and his collaborators that they correctly interpreted as referable to glacial activity[24] these products of solifluxion.

So clearly does the original drawing of a section in one of the pits excavated by them illustrate the character of these deposits that it has been reproduced above with a present-day reading of the sequence (Fig. 4). Containing small stony elements and completely devoid of erratics, but with firmly binding iron oxide (4) which later concreted and locally sealed the sediment beneath, they could not have travelled far. Even if congeliturbate material had been carried down from the summit of the high ground, this is not much above, and only a short distance from, the pits explored half a century ago. Nevertheless, the processes of solifluxion lasted long enough, and the small abrasive constituents sufficed in some of the accumulations in a continued and repeated movement to wear down ridges and inflict innumerable fine striae on surfaces and injure edges of artifacts and unworked stones alike.

To Kendall and his colleagues the problem of the origins of the pits and their infilling remained unsolved. After much thought I consider that processes operated that were cognate with the agencies accountable for the formation and movements of the solifluxion materials. They seem to have been produced much as were the well-known kettle-holes on the fringes of an ice-front. If in this locality ice-blocks were not responsible, then the depressions might well result from the complete or partial foundering in soft ground of hard frozen masses which subsequently thawed.

A possibility that ought not to be overlooked is that the odd, sharp, and unscathed implements, particularly the subglobular core, Fig. 3, no. 1, from between 6 in. (15 cm.) and 12 in. (30 cm.) down in one of the excavated pits, are of more advanced Palaeolithic make than the blemished and abraded artifacts

78

constituting the bulk of the Hackpen Hill assemblage. Thus, they could have been produced during such a phase of improved or interstadial climate as is now widely held to have followed a markedly cold and long interruption of the Great Interglacial. Alternatively, such objects could just as well have been fashioned even later in a highly developed Acheulian, or early Middle Palaeolithic industry, during the true interglacial period of climatic amelioration that succeeded the extended and broken thaw to which have been attributed above the forming and moving downhill of the solifluxion masses.

(c) Hand-axes from higher ground

Another palaeolith, Fig. 3, no. 2, may be adduced in illustration of the vagarious effects of solifluxion. Found only 200 yds. (183 m.) from the principal site, at an elevation a fraction over 2 ft. (61 cm.) greater [876·3 ft. (267 m.)], a cream-patinated and almost unblemished hand-axe from Glory Ann Barn pit was picked out of the clay into which it had sunk,[25] probably when the surface was soft. It therefore differs very remarkably from the deeply ochreous-stained, worn-down pebbled bifaces which have also come from this part. A point of interest is that the only Lower Palaeolithic implements from spots in England higher above sea-level are those got by Kendall 3½ miles (5·6 km.) south-by-west of Marlborough and 6 miles (9·6 km.) south-east of Hackpen Hill.[26] These sites are Milk Hill at 964 ft. (293·8 m.) and Martinsell Hill at 947 ft. (288·7 m.). Here he observed an exposure of deposits in a series similar to that noted beside the Ridgeway.

Again, from this high ground of Hackpen there have come a few palaeoliths which, though apparently unaffected by rough transport, certainly did not escape the ravages of climatic alterations after being discarded. Among the surface-finds that exhibit these effects is a hand-axe of cherty flint, no. 3. Stained deep brown like the implements already considered, and thus resembling many Palaeolithic tools from the Savernake Forest area, this biface was picked up approximately on the 800 ft. (243·8 m.) contour near Old Totterdown, a year after Mr. Kendall addressed the Society of Antiquaries early in 1916. Preserved today in Avebury Museum, it has been sadly impaired by thermal action along lines of weakness to the damage of the rather pronounced flake-scars. Deep pitting and peeling of the surface are characteristic. Time and weather have contributed to these ancient defacements without seriously dulling the long sinuous edges. Doubtless this palaeolith had lain protected for ages under the grass-covered soil or in the capping of fine gravel until eventually dislodged by agricultural operations.

3. THE PLATEAU

(a) Terrain and artifacts

Having glimpsed a Lower Palaeolithic implement in the oldest class of surface-found prehistoric relics, we can look closer at comparable examples from the plateau immediately west of and below the Hackpen ridge. These palaeoliths owe their exposure to the cutting of drainage channels and ploughing that broached the thin overlay of gravel and subjacent yellow clay, with both of which deposits the artifacts had been associated.[27]

(b) Flint

Former observations on the resemblance of some implements of post-Palaeolithic facies to 'eoliths' and deductions therefrom need not detain us. But two tools reported in 1916 and others I have handled from the plateau are significant. One is a flint hand-axe of conventional form (Fig. 5, no. 1), turned up in gravel on Whyr Farm (SU 084744) at 590 ft. (180 m.), in Winterbourne Bassett. Unscathed, sharp, and ochreous-stained, it matches the best specimens of the regional Acheulian workmanship that appears in the bifaces from gravels in a dry valley exposed in Knowle Farm pit in Savernake Forest, 9 miles (14·5 km.) to the south-east.[28] Another undersized flint hand-axe from this part, now in Avebury Museum, is indistinguishable from the last specimen or comparable Middle Acheulian tools. It is stained ochreous and though its edges are still keen and flake-ridges dulled, the scars are faintly lustrous on one face but less so on the other. This suggests that the implement had lain flat near the surface of the soil out of which it was eventually washed.

A companion (Fig. 5, no. 2), also of flint, pale brown, still sharp but slightly pitted and glazed, from the same place in Winterbourne Bassett, is the counterpart of many small Middle Acheulian bifaces from the principal palaeolith-yielding regions.

(c) Sarsen

There also comes from Winterbourne Bassett an unchanged but slightly weathered, irregular four-sided biface (Fig. 5, no. 3), almost entirely flaked over in brown sarsen with inclusions of quartz nodules and glassy particles. Sarsen implements are reported too from the top of Hackpen Hill,[29] but none has been illustrated. However, a drawing is here reproduced of the abraded butt-end of a small sarsen hand-axe (Fig. 5, no. 4), found below Winterbourne Monkton Down at 610 ft. (186 m.), but possibly derived from the high ground. Conceivably it was swept from the surface or washed out of a deposit and, becoming mixed with moving stony soil, had been roughly carried down 250 ft. (76 m.) on to the plateau. More precise as regards its finding-place, between the 550- and 575-ft. (168–75 m.) contours (at SU 113724), is a fine linguate hand-axe (Fig. 5, no. 5), now preserved in Avebury Museum. Apparently made on a thick flake of fine-grained sarsen, this implement was picked up in 1944 by Mr. A. J. Cook on the surface of a ploughed field at the foot of the spur on the same minor down.[30] It is virtually unaltered except for some rusty streaks and specks.

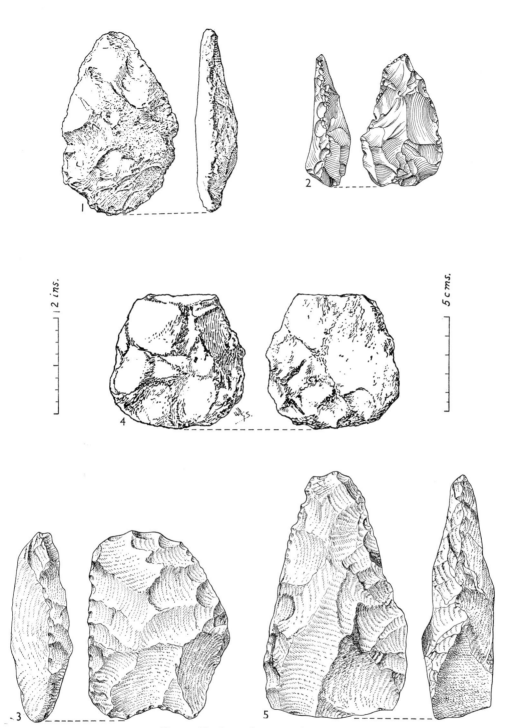

FIG. 5. Hand-axes from the Plateau.

Flint from Winterbourne Bassett:
    1. After Kendall, 1916.
    2. Avebury Museum, no. WB 110, 12–119.

Sarsen from Winterbourne Bassett:
    3. Avebury Museum, Fd. B. 6, 28-2-21 from Winterbourne Monkton.
    4. After Kendall, 1916.
    5. Avebury Museum (found June 1940).

      (1 and 4 reproduced by permission of the Society of Antiquaries.)

Weak brown staining only serves to emphasize the Acheulian character of the flake-scars and fine trimming.

In the Lower Palaeolithic province of north-eastern France and its extension in Britain a peculiar fascination attaches to the rare rools made in material other than flint and chert. It is particularly remarkable that in the Thames valley in which the supply of flint was inexhaustible, and in which innumerable palaeoliths made of it have been collected from Berkshire to Essex and Kent, there have been found several bifaces and flake-implements shaped out of difficult rocks,[31] generally Bunter cobbles. Now, in the heart of the Wiltshire downland, with its scanty muster of Lower Palaeolithic flint implements, we find a few specimens hewn by characteristic technique to true Acheulian forms in pieces of sarsen-stone. Of all kinds of rock this would be thought the most unlikely to be experimented upon by a practitioner of flaking.

4. AVEBURY AND MARLBOROUGH

We could have wished that the above enumeration had been amplified by flakes and instruments made on them. However, sufficient implements have been adduced to demonstrate that in the favourable conditions of the Great Interglacial period Acheulian bands had pushed up the highest reach of the Kennet, upper tributary of the Thames. In this regard a further increment to this list is mentioned, and because one hardly connects Lower Palaeolithic nomads with Windmill Hill. The example (Fig. 6, no. 1), from this classic site, a small sharply pointed hand-axe of whitish chert with two remnants of light-brown crust, is preserved in the museum at Devizes. Had this finely worked tool been found in stratigraphy, it would surely be put down to an Acheulian industry at least as advanced as the best represented in the Middle Gravel on the 100-ft. (30 m.) terrace of the Thames at Swanscombe. Its having been found at Windmill Hill raises problems, even the possibility that Neolithic people had brought the ancient tool to the place,[32] unless of course it be shown that solifluxion materials are present here. It has been suggested that two Lower Palaeolithic flakes known from Windmill Hill could have been obtained from just such gravels as lie at Whyr Farm and on the top of the Marlborough Downs.[33]

Single specimens may not be important diagnostically as indicators of a local industry or of full-scale upstream migration, but particular interest attaches to some. Here, therefore it is opportune to recall a small Acheulian flint, flat hand-axe (Fig. 6, no. 2), from the northern flank of Granham Hill which drops to the Kennet River opposite Marlborough College. It was picked up in 1923 by Professor J. G. D. Clark while a pupil in this famous establishment,[34] and is preserved in the school museum at Mount House. Not far from here stands the town gas-works whence there came a palaeolith (Fig. 6, no. 3), now in the University Museum of Archaeology and Ethnology, Cambridge. This implement may of course be another relic of the riverside stay of a wandering Palaeo-lithic group. Nevertheless, regarding it a word of caution must be uttered. The flint of which this biface is made, its appearance and greatly abraded condition are all such that the tool could very well have been an ingredient of a load of gravel carted from the Knowle Farm pit in the Savernake Forest.

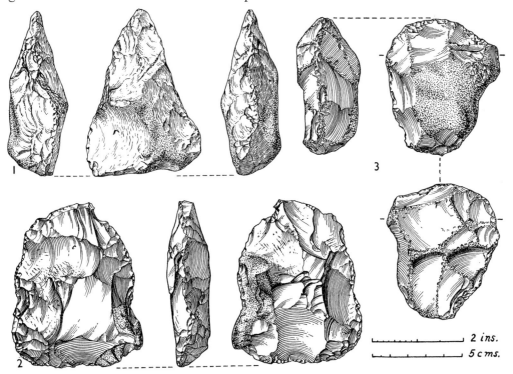

FIG. 6. Palaeoliths from Avebury and Marlborough.
Avebury: 1, Windmill Hill, Devizes Museum.
Marlborough: 2, Granham Hill, Marlborough College Museum No. 1868;
3, Gas Works, University Museum of Archaeology and Ethnology, Cambridge, No. 25–20.

It would be pleasing indeed if with the palaeoliths from this last-named pro-lific site the two specimens from Marlborough could eventually be shown to have been dropped in the direct line of a westward movement of people in early stages of Old Stone Age development.

At present it is indeterminable how over the generations the Lower Palaeo-lithic folk had reached this part of the country, either by pressing up the Thames and Kennet from the east or by following the Wiltshire Avon from the south and up the valleys of its feeders. Two of these streams, in fact, have their sources near Clyffe Peppard, where at 350 ft. (107 m.) above O.D. an ovate was found below the Lower Chalk escarpment.[35] Whether or not this implement was left behind by roamers beyond the plateau proper, say from where the hand-axe (Fig. 5, no. 1),

83

was garnered barely 2½ miles (4 km.) to the south-east at Whyr Farm, or from Hackpen Hill itself, the artifacts are memorials of far-extending human movements in Lower Palaeolithic times rather than of fixed abodes. As exponents of the Acheulian mode of life in the open, devising many forms of tools, and in their preparation developing new and improving on old methods, some of the migrants ventured far west, to both banks in the lowest reaches of the Bristol Avon,[36] up the Severn,[37] and even into what is now south Wales.[38]

4. CONCLUSIONS

1. Only a small number of Lower Palaeolithic artifacts have been found by excavation and from the scrutinizing of superficial deposits and the surface of the ground in the area considered above. Unaccompanied by datable organic remains, floral or faunal, they may be put down typologically to the Acheulian culture. They consist of such bifaces as hand-axes and ovates, flakes and cores. Some appear to be the products of early industries. Most, however, are of well-developed facies, which is upheld by flakes bearing the signs of nascent Levalloisian technique.

2. Since so few palaeoliths have rewarded years of patient searches, it seems safe to say that there was never any full occupation of the locality by Acheulian man but only rare intermittent sojourns. The implements would therefore be the relics of very small, successive bands, the sum of whose wanderings stretched over untold centuries, countless indeed because at present there are no means of dating the tools except by assigning these to the great interglacial period to which the Early and Middle Acheulian industries are referred.

3. From the circumstances of their discovery none of the palaeoliths of Hackpen Hill and the plateau beneath can be regarded as derived. For none of the first could have been carried by natural agency far from the place where they were manufactured or discarded. At the same time, virtually all the Acheulian specimens from the high ground are characteristically blemished, having been dragged from the ancient land-surface and crushed under pressure against, and scratched by, other stones in congeliturbate masses moving slowly down the western slopes. As products of solifluxion, these materials are attributed to the great thaws of the deglaciation that followed the genial period during which Acheulian people visited the locality. Although a similar phenomenon of soil-creep may well have occurred after later glacial phases, there is no evidence of man in more advanced stages of Palaeolithic development on the hill and in the region.

4. For the most part the Acheulian implements from the plateau exhibit only the signs of weathering, superficial alteration, and coloration. Found on the surface or just below it, they are in the same case as so many palaeoliths from other high-ground sites in southern England and on the European continent. Their condition and mode of occurrence proclaim that they had lain undisturbed

since they were left by their users, even escaping the brunt of the action that so affected their contemporaries on the immediately neighbouring hill.

5. To the palaeoliths from Hackpen Hill and around, in common with scores of bifaces, flakes, and cores of Early and Middle Acheulian facies from comparable sites, there pertains a peculiar significance. It has been too often ignored in the insistence by inquirers for stratigraphical data in connection with Lower Palaeolithic discoveries. As the late R. A. Smith pointed out long ago,[39] as did some before him in the field of Old Stone Age researches, relics found in just such circumstances as have been considered above furnish a clue to the date of the last serious disturbance in the upland region of their occurrence.

6. Added interest resides in the palaeoliths of Hackpen Hill, for with one exception, and this from a not distant Wiltshire downland finding-place, (Martinsell, above, p. 79) they come from the greatest altitude reached by Acheulian man in the united Lower Palaeolithic province of north-eastern France and southern England. Again, this is a reminder that he did not restrict himself to the river valleys, but ventured up the flanks on to high ground. In this respect one recalls the collections of Acheulian implements from the surface of the plateaux at over 820 ft. (250 m.) above sea-level in the famous Dordogne territory. Below, caves and fluviatile gravels have yielded identical Lower Palaeolithic relics showing with complementary evidence that our remote forerunners wandered and sojourned where they could.

A. D. Lacaille

ACKNOWLEDGEMENTS

Were it not for the facilities I have had for studying collections, these notes would have fallen short of even an attempt to deal with the Lower Palaeolithic artifacts from the area north-west of Marlborough. With pleasure therefore I acknowledge my indebtedness to the Trustees of the late Sir Henry Wellcome; to my friends in the British Museum (Bloomsbury), Dr. R. L. S. Bruce-Mitford and Mr. J. W. Brailsford, Keepers, and Mr. G. de G. Sieveking, Assistant Keeper, to whose kind help and valued suggestions this paper owes its final form. Mr. F. K. Annable, Curator of the Wiltshire Archaeological Society's Museum, Devizes, to whom I am also grateful for much information over the years, put at my disposal relevant implements. I recall useful talks with Dr. Isobel F. Smith and the late W. E. V. Young at Avebury. Both went to much trouble to display objects before me; and the second-named, then Curator of the Museum there, favoured me with the loan for illustration of selected specimens. At that time Mr. E. G. H. Kempson, President of Marlborough College Natural History Society and Hon. Curator of the College Museum at Mount House repeatedly did me the honours of this institution. To his successor in both offices, Mr. M. Hardstaff, I am beholden for permission to figure a palaeolith picked up near this place and today in the school collection. In this connection, too, I thank Professor J. G. D. Clark. He also consented to my figuring a specimen found in this Wiltshire town and now housed in the University Museum of Archaeology and Ethnology, Cambridge, the dispatch of which to me by Miss M. D. Cra'ster earns for her my appreciation. Dr. Derek Roe, Lecturer in Prehistory in the

University of Oxford, generously gave me access to references and unpublished lists. Among staff of the Nature Conservancy who did much to advance my researches in the field, I remember particularly the Regional Officers, Mrs. J. M. Kumik *née* Laptain, Messrs. J. H. Hemsley and M. J. Woodman, and the ever-helpful Warden of the Fyfield Down National Nature Reserve, Mr. Inigo Jones, besides Messrs. Frank Johnson, Manton Estate, and Ian Rands, English Farms Limited, near Rockley. To the pioneer archaeologists W. J. Andrew, Revd. H. G. O. Kendall, and G. Worthington Smith, all deceased, tribute is paid for first recognizing and attracting to notice the Lower Palaeolithic artifacts of the Hackpen ridge and its neighbourhood. For leave to reproduce certain illustrations I am obliged to the Society of Antiquaries of London, while to Miss M. O. Miller I express my gratitude for most of the drawings which embellish these pages.

[1] H. G. O. Kendall, 'Palaeolithic Implements, etc., from Hackpen Hill, Winterbourne Bassett, and Knowle Farm Pit (Wiltshire)', *Quart. Journ. Geol. Soc.* lxv (1909) [166–8], 166.

[2] Idem, 'Excavations on Hackpen Hill, Wilts.', *Proc. Soc. Ant.* xxviii (1915–16), 26–48.

[3] Op. cit. 1909.

[4] In Kendall, op. cit. 1915–16, 44–8.

[5] Ibid. 30, fig. 3.

[6] Ibid. 34.

[7] Report on the Swanscombe Skull, *Journ. Roy. Anthr. Inst.* lxviii (1938), 34–54.

[8] A. D. Lacaille, 'The Palaeoliths from the Gravels of the Lower Boyn Hill Terrace around Maidenhead', *Ant. Journ.* xx (1940) [245–71], 256–7, 262–4.

[9] R. A. Smith, *A Guide to Antiquities of the Stone Age in the Department of British and Mediaeval Antiquities*, 3rd ed. British Museum (1926), 59–60.

[10] Report on the Swanscombe Skull, cit. above, 44, 56; A. D. Lacaille, 'The Palaeolithic Contents of the Gravels at East Burnham, Bucks', *Ant. Journ.* xix (1939) [166–81], 180–1; idem, op. cit. 1940, 254, 259–62, 271; P. J. Tester, 'Early Use of the Levallois Technique in the Palaeolithic Succession of the Lower Thames', *Arch. News Letter*, iv (1952), 118–19.

[11] A. D. Lacaille, 'Palaeoliths from the Lower Reaches of the Bristol Avon', *Ant. Journ.* xxxiv (1954) [1–27], 17–19, 26–7.

[12] M. Posnansky, 'The Lower and Middle Palaeolithic Industries of the English East Midlands', *Proc. Preh. Soc.* xxix (1963) [357–94], 385.

[13] A. D. Lacaille, 'On Palaeolithic Choppers and Cleavers (Notes suggested by some Buckinghamshire examples)', *Records of Bucks*, xvi. 5 (1960), 330–44.

[14] Kendall, op. cit. 1915–16, 28–31.

[15] Ibid. 29.

[16] H. Breuil, 'Le vrai niveau de l'industrie Abbevillienne de la Porte du Bois (Abbeville)', *L'Anthropologie*, xlix (1939), 13–34.

[17] Idem, 'Le paléolithique ancien en Europe occidentale et sa chronologie', *Bull. Soc. Préh. Franç.* xxix (1932) [570–8], 575–7.

[18] Idem, 'De l'importance de la solifluxion dans l'étude des terrains quaternaires de la France et des pays voisins', *Revue de géographie physique et de géologie dynamique*, vii (1934), 269–331, 7 pls.; Kirk, Bryan, 'Cryopedology—The Study of Frozen Ground and Intensive Frost-action with Suggestions on Nomenclature', *Amer. Journ. Sci.* ccliv (1946), 622–42.

Attention should also be drawn to J. G. Evans, 'Periglacial deposits in the chalk of Wiltshire', *Wilts. Arch. Mag.* lxiii (1968), 12–26. This paper was published after the preparation of the present contribution and was not available to its author. It provides an excellent geological description of the mode of formation and topographical distribution of the periglacial phenomena in Wiltshire, and forms a useful contribution to the present discussion. Evans assigns these periglacial deposits almost entirely to the last glaciation, a conclusion at variance with the archaeological evidence cited in the present article.

[19] Smith, op. cit., 1926, 40, 65.

[20] A. D. Lacaille, 'A Cup-marked Sarsen near Marlborough, Wiltshire', *Arch. News Letter*, vii (1962) [123–9], 123–5.

[21] R. Handsford Worth, Presidential Address, 'The Weathering of Granite and other Rocks into Basins and Channels', *Trans. Devon Assoc. for the Advancement of Science, Literature and Art*, lxii (1930), 77 ff.; A. D. Lacaille, 'Stone Basins (some examples from the West of Scotland as guides to

typology)', *Trans. Glas. Arch. Soc.*, N.S. xii (1953) [41–93], 57–61.

²² W. J. Arkell, 'The Pleistocene Rocks at Trebetherick Point, North Cornwall: Their Interpretation and Correlation', *Proc. Geo. Assoc.* liv (1943), 141–70.

²³ A. Bigot, 'Les terrasses pléistocènes du littoral du Cotentin', *Livre jubilaire, Centenaire de la Société géologique de France*, i (1930), 133–49.

²⁴ Kendall, op. cit. 1916, 31.

²⁵ Ibid. 38, 44, fig. 27.

²⁶ Ibid. 38–9, fig. 19.

²⁷ Ibid. 43–5, figs. 25–6.

²⁸ Ibid. *passim*; W. Boyd Dawkins, ibid. 45.

²⁹ Ibid. 44.

³⁰ W. E. V. Young, Note in *Wilts. Arch. Mag.* lvii (1958–60), 400.

³¹ A. D. Lacaille, 'Quartzites taillés de la région londonienne', *Congrès préhistorique de France. Compte rendu de la douzième session, Toulouse-Foix, 1936* (Paris, 1937), 609–29.

³² Dr. Isobel F. Smith *in litt.*, Avebury, 19 Feb. 1968.

³³ [*Eadem*] *Windmill Hill and Avebury Ex-cavations by Alexander Keiller 1925–1939*, Oxford, 1965, 85, 168, and fig. 60.

³⁴ J. G. D. Clark, 'Notes on the Flint Implements on Granham Hill and around Panterwick', *Report of the Marlborough College Natural History Society*, no. 72 (1923) [1924, 84–9], fn. 86.

³⁵ Kendall, op. cit. 1916, 44.

³⁶ Lacaille, op. cit. 1954, above.

³⁷ *Inter alia*: Gloucestershire: M. C. Burkitt, 'A Gloucester Palaeolith', *Ant. Journ.* i (1921), 234; Mrs. E. M. Clifford, 'A Prehistoric and Roman Site at Barnwood, near Gloucester', *Trans. Bristol and Glos. Arch. Soc.* liii (1930), 208–11; eadem, 'A Palaeolith found near Gloucester', *Ant. Journ.* xvi (1936), 91. Warwickshire: F. W. Shotton, 'Palaeolithic Implements found near Coventry', *Proc. Preh. Soc. East Anglia*, vi (1930), 174–81. Worcestershire: Smith, op. cit. 1926, 10.

³⁸ H. N. S[avory], *The Bulletin of the Board of Celtic Studies*, University of Wales, Cardiff, xv (1952), note, 67; A. D. Lacaille, 'A Hand-axe from Pen-y-lan, Cardiff', *Ant. Journ.* xxxiv (1954), 64–7.

³⁹ Op. cit. 1926, 65.

WALL-PAINTINGS FROM VERULAMIUM

THE excavations carried out by Professor Sheppard Frere at Verulamium between 1955 and 1961 produced a remarkable collection of wall-paintings from a number of town-houses, including some from collapsed walls which it has been possible to reconstruct. The two sections about to be described were found in 1956 in Insula XXI. 2, and have already been briefly published by Professor Frere.¹ The property of the Gorhambury estate, they are now on loan to the British Museum. They date from the second century and comprise a stretch of the red-painted wall from the corridor, no. 3 on the plan, and part of a peopled scroll design found lying face downwards in the open courtyard outside the same corridor.²

THE RED WALL

As reconstructed the red wall measures 2 m. 59 cm. wide and 2 m. 49 cm. high (Pl. XXVI *a*). At the top, traces of yellow survive above a band of black 8·75 cm. deep. Black is also used for the vertical pilaster strips, varying in width from 26·55–29·70 cm., which appear between the red panels. The complete panel is *c.* 1 m. 80·5 cm. high and 96·5 cm. wide. Below the panels comes a black band 10·6 cm. deep, and then 7·5 cm. of yellow, part of the framework of a dado consisting of alternate black and purple rectangles divided by more yellow, which also recurs as a band below them. The black rectangles 71 by 31 cm. are placed beneath the panels, the purple ones 28·5 by 31 cm. occur below the black pilaster strips. A band of black, which probably reached to the original floor level, completes the design. Fine white lines separate the different colours.

The panels are decorated with two swags, each of which terminates in loops with hanging pendants. One end of each swag is tied to a tall candelabrum near the side of the panel and the other end is attached to a foliate line or rod, theoretically suspended from the top of the panel, in the centre (Pl. xxviii *a*). Yellow flowers with touches of white (?honeysuckle) are used for the central panel, but the panels on either side have leafier green garlands with yellow flowers near the ends. Otherwise they are made up of yellow, blue, and white buds (Pl. xxvii *b*). Below the central rod is a bluish-green motif from which dangles a yellow pendant.

The tall candelabra have yellow foliate stems ornamented with leaf sprays and also, at intervals, bluish-green motifs outlined in yellow. They rise from bluish-green bases decorated with yellow leaves and spirals, and at the top they have circular plates, painted green on the underside, carrying five lighted candles. About 33 cm. from the lower edge of the panel a yellow beaded line, 67 cm. long, joins the two candelabra (Pl. xxvii *a*). This is decorated with small yellow or bluish-green motifs. In the centre is a larger version of the green motif used for the rod at the top of the panel, with a yellow pendant suspended on either side. In the centre of the panels are birds on green perches 22 cm. long. The bird in the central panel is facing right, *c.* 17·5 cm. long and 16 cm. high, painted green with touches of white including white feathers below its wings (Pl. xxvi *b*). The birds in the panels on either side face the opposite way. The one on the left has a longer tail than its companion in the centre (Pl. xxvii *a*), and the one on the right may have had a larger beak. Possibly more than one variety of bird is represented here or the differences may be due to the panels having been the work of several painters. A graffito visible near the centre of the complete panel is probably a child's attempt to copy the bird and one of the green motifs, the scratch near the beak perhaps marking the moment when his activities were cut short (Pl. xxix *a*). Another graffito spells out the word EQVVS (Pl. xxix *b*, Fig. 1). Traces of decoration also survive dimly on the black pilaster strips between the panels. Some form of candelabrum pattern outlined in white and rising from a base with a green roundel outlined in yellow on either side seems to have been represented (Pl. xxvii *b*), and faint traces of a scroll design, probably in yellow, are just discernible on the black band below the panels.

The site occupied by the other reconstructed section of wall-painting is less certain. From the position in which it was discovered it seems to have been attached to the top of the southern courtyard wall on the outside of the red-painted corridor, no. 3. But if this was the case, it is difficult to understand how

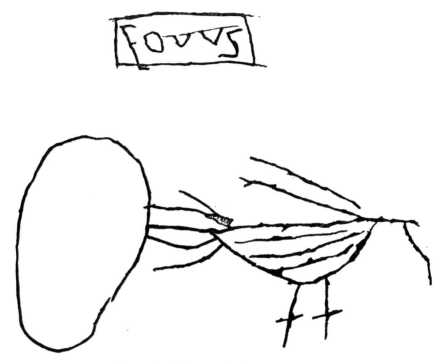

FIG. 1. Graffiti on Verulamium red wall plaster.

it escaped damage from the weather, unless some kind of veranda ran round the courtyard. At the top traces of a slight inward curve have been noted, showing that the design belongs to a frieze just below the level of the ceiling.

This section of the frieze is nearly 3 m. 66 cm. long and 99 cm. high. On a ground of golden yellow, below a dark-red band, has been painted a running scroll with black stems and tendrils and light-green leaves. Enough survives to show four complete spirals, the centre of each one being peopled alternately by pheasants or feline masks (Pl. xxx). Between the spirals is a funnel-shaped motif turned alternately up and down, with a band shaded from light to dark yellow and three large pointed red petals at the wider end. When turned upwards the rest of the motif is pale green with two grey bands outlined in black below the yellow (Pl. xxxii b). When reversed, pale yellow or deep cream is used with green bands instead of grey. The inhabitants of the spirals are painted in shades of purplish brown with touches of black. The pheasants, perhaps a cock and a hen, are in profile (Pl. xxxi *a*, *b*). The felines, probably panther masks, are portrayed full face (Pl. xxxii *a*).

These two examples of Romano-British wall-painting are among the most outstanding discoveries of such decoration so far found in this province. The frieze with its peopled scroll is unique, but parallels to the red wall can be found elsewhere. Its arrangement with a dado below a series of panels is typical of painting of this period in Britain and the neighbouring Roman provinces.[3] Often part of the dado was stippled or streaked to imitate marble wall-veneers and this decoration does occur elsewhere in the house, Insula XXI. 2, at Verulamium, but not on this wall. However, the alternation of large and smaller rectangles set in a frame of wide bands of colour is also quite familiar, and it has been found, for instance, at the Carisbrooke villa where a red and green dado outlined in white was discovered *in situ* in a room with a geometric mosaic floor.[4]

The decoration of the red wall above the dado is less typical of Britain, where in the majority of cases panels are outlined by a framework of stripes and lines of several colours. Again these appear elsewhere in Insula XXI. 2, but the design chosen for the red wall is of a more delicate nature. Apparently the pattern books used by this artist included motifs reminiscent of first-century Italy, although rather simplified. At Pompeii, for instance, the idea of swags springing from candelabra and meeting in a central feature, in this case a mask, occurs in a house near the Temple of Fortuna.[5] More swags looped along the tops of panels appear on a wall in the Macellum,[6] and also as part of the frieze in the Houses of the Vestals and Silenus.[7]

I have been unable to find any exact replicas of the Verulamium candelabra with their foliate stems and yellow or green embellishments among the numerous Pompeian examples of this motif. Possibly they are simplified forms of such candelabra as those found in the House of Castor and Pollux which seem to be entwined by two stems with tendrils, while something similar occurs in the House of Argo and Io.[8] Both Etruscan and Roman bronze candelabra, however, sometimes had shafts which attempted to imitate vegetable motifs. One in the Louvre appears to be decorated with thorns, and another from Pompeii has joints and small leaves apparently intended to depict a reed.[9] Similarly it is the actual candelabra which show best the arrangement of the prongs for the candles, sometimes placed round a circular plate at the top to which a statuette could be attached. On wall-paintings the candelabra could terminate, as at Verulamium, in a simple circle of lights, while in the House of the Bronzes at Pompeii a small vase appears above them.[10] A painting in the House of Pinarius Cerealis has a candelabrum with a stem probably imitating a palm tree, surmounted by lights.[11]

Other interesting details from the Verulamium panels include the green motifs on the candelabra. Possibly these originated in the pine-cones which occur as part of a candelabrum in the House of the Vettii.[12] Birds were obviously the form of wild life most favoured at Verulamium and they were also popular at all levels on the walls at Pompeii. Our British birds on their green perches in the middle of the panels echo some from the Houses of the Second Mosaic Fountain and the Tragic Poet, where slightly varied species looking in different directions and on the same green perches are depicted.[13]

Other sites which bridge the gap in both time and distance between Britain and Campania also enjoyed this type of fanciful decoration. Swags adorned with ribbons and various appendages were found in the Columbarium in the via Taranto, Rome,[14] where they date from the mid-first century, and also in a house of the first half of the second century in Thomasgasse, Strasbourg.[15] Candelabra used on pilaster strips dividing panels are known from the Flavian period at the Temple of Elst, near Arnhem, and from second-century houses excavated at Brotstrasse, Trier, and from under Cologne Cathedral.[16]

In Britain the closest parallel to the Verulamium panel decoration comes from excavations in 1958 on the Woolworth site at Winchester. It consists of fragments of yellow candelabra with blue and green leaves and yellow spirals, to which in one case the end of a swag is attached, on a red ground.[17] Other examples of swags from this country are less delicate. Usually they are painted in varying shades of the same colour, the darker tones presumably indicating shadow. Fragments in yellow and white, with deeper yellow or purplish brown, or blue and white shaded along one edge in dark green, on a red ground were found at Cirencester, possibly from panels with garlands using these colour schemes alternately, as at Verulamium.[18] Material preserved at the Roman villa at Brading, Isle of Wight, includes part of another swag painted in dark and light red on one fragment, and a bird below an orange swag on another.[19]

Comparative material for the scroll from our second wall-painting is less easy to find. Many examples exist in Hellenistic and Imperial times for foliate motifs of this kind, among them felines and birds from the House near the Basilica and the flowers alternating with goats or wolves from the Temple of Isis at Pompeii.[20] But none of these examples depict frontal masks such as those of our felines. The other problem is the funnel-shaped motif. The closest parallels to this seem to come from the pattern books of British mosaicists, as a form of it appears in a panel separating two sections of the fine geometric floor of mid-second-century date found at Verulamium in Insula IV. 2.[21] A smaller version of it also occurs in two small borders on either side of the dolphin and fountain mosaic from room 9 in Insula XXVIII. 3, but here it is associated with heart-shaped leaves, probably ivy rather than acanthus foliage.[22] Similarly at Bignor it is used for the fine rinceau which surrounds the bust of Venus, but the nature of the plant is here uncertain as some heart-shaped leaves are also present and small bell-shaped flowers.[23] The same flowers appear in the centre of a scroll border with the funnel motif, part of the *Bonus Eventum* pavement at Woodchester.[24]

The most striking example of this design used for a mosaic border, however, comes from Cirencester. Certainly this also seems to be again an ivy scroll, but here the motif when upright is white with a yellow band and three red petals, and when pointing downwards it has a pale-blue band and the petals are deep blue.[25] On the other pavements the bands are red and yellow, with the exception of blue bands in an ivy-leaf scroll at Dorchester.[26] Only at Cirencester does the motif alternate between two colour-schemes, as on the Verulamium wall-painting, and at Cirencester the petals are also particularly clearly indicated.

Outside Britain there is a wall-mosaic used for the dado of a second-century *frigidarium* at Buëlisacker in Switzerland where buds and tendrils grow out of a funnel-shaped sheath and ivy-leaves appear in the centre of the spirals.[27] Unpeopled acanthus foliage growing out of similar sheaths occurs on mosaics from Granéjouis near Toulouse and Tabarca, Tunisia,[28] and also from Bad Kreuznach.[29]

It is difficult to consider these two fine examples of wall-decoration from Verulamium divorced from the rest of the material to be published in the forthcoming report on the 1955–61 excavations of this exceptional Roman city.[30] The corridor with the red wall, for example, also had a purple ceiling depicting feline masks and birds set in octagons outlined by wheat-ears,[31] and more painting was found in rooms 2 and 4, and in several other houses.[32] Some of it included designs with as Pompeian an ancestry as the candelabra and swags on the red wall.[33] The fact that modern techniques of excavation and conservation make it possible to reclaim such treasures makes it increasingly feasible for scholars to recreate a true picture of house interiors in the Roman period.

JOAN LIVERSIDGE

[1] *Ant. J.* xxxvii (1957), p. 13, pls. iii *a*, iv *a*, v; xl (1960), p. 17 and plan of house XXI. 2, fig. 6.

[2] Reconstruction by Dr. N. Davey, F.S.A.

[3] For details see J. Liversidge, *Britain in the Roman Empire* (1968), pp. 86 ff.

[4] C. R. Smith, *Collectanea Antiqua*, vi (1868), p. 126, pl. vi.

[5] W. Zahn, *Die schönsten Ornamente und merkwürdigsten Gemälde aus Pompeji, Herculaneum und Stabiae*, i (1823), Pl. iii.

[6] H. G. Beyen, 'Das stilistische und chronologische Verhältnis der letzten drei pompejanischen Stile', *Antiquity and Survival*, ii, no. 4 (1958), fig. 12.

[7] Ibid., figs. 16, 19.

[8] Zahn, op. cit. ii. 2 (1844), pls. lxxxiv, lxvi.

[9] A. de Ridder, *Les Bronzes antiques du Louvre*, ii (1915), no. 3148; E. Pernice, *Die Hellenistische Kunst in Pompeji*, iv (1925); *Gefässe und Geräte aus Bronze*, fig. 73.

[10] Zahn, op. cit. ii. 2 (1842), pl. xxxiv.

[11] K. Schefold, *Vergessenes Pompeji* (1962), pl. cxl.

[12] Ibid., pl. cxxx.

[13] Zahn, op. cit. ii. 1, pl. iv; iii (1854), pl. lix.

[14] M. Borda, *La Pittura Romana* (1958), p. 65.

[15] Ibid., p. 65; R. Forrer, *Strasbourg. Argentorate*, ii (1929), pl. lvi.

[16] J. Bogaers, *De Gallo-Romeinse Tempels te Elst in de Over-Betuwe* (1954), pl. xxii; information from the Landesmuseum, Trier; O. Doppelfeld, 'Von Postumus zu Konstantin', *Wallraf-Richartz Jahrbuch*, xviii (1956), fig. 7.

[17] I am indebted to Mr. F. Cottrell, F.S.A., Curator of the City Museum, Winchester, for showing me this material. Other close parallels, found at Leicester in 1958 and unpublished, are now exhibited in Leicester Museum.

[18] J. Liversidge, 'Cirencester: Romano-British Wall-paintings from the Dyer Court Excavations, 1957', *Trans. of the Bristol and Glos. Arch. Soc.* lxxxi (1962), p. 41, pl. iv.

[19] J. Liversidge in A. L. F. Rivet, ed. *The Roman Villa in Britain* (1969), colour pl. 4.3.

[20] Zahn, op. cit. i, pl. xxix; iii, pl. xxxvii. See also J. M. C. Toynbee and J. B. Ward Perkins, 'Peopled Scrolls: a Hellenistic Motif in Imperial Art', *PBSR* xviii (1950), pls. xii. 1, xx. 1. 2.

[21] R. E. M. and T. V. Wheeler, *Verulamium: A Belgic and Two Roman Cities*, Report of the Research Committee of the Society of Antiquaries of London, xi (1936), pl. xl.

[22] *Ant. J.* xxxix (1959), pl. iv *a*.

[23] S. Lysons, *Reliquiae Britannico-Romanae*, iii (1817), pls. v, viii, ix, xix.

[24] Ibid., *An Account of the Roman Antiquities found at Woodchester* (1797), pls. xix, xx, fig. 3.

[25] Buckman and C. Newmarch, *Illustrations of the Remains of Roman Art at Cirencester* (1850), pl. vi, fig. 2.

[26] *Proc. of the Dorset Nat. Hist. Soc.* xlix (1928), pl. opp. p. 98.

[27] W. Drack, *Die Römische Wandmalerei der Schweiz* (1950), pl. xxxviii.

[28] G. Lafaye and A. Blanchet, *Inventaire des mosaïques de la Gaule et de l'Afrique*, I Fasc. i (1909), 385; II Fasc. i (1910), 940.

[29] K. Parlasca, *Die römischen Mosaiken in Deutschland* (1959), pl. lxxxviii. 2.

[30] By Professor S. S. Frere *et al.* to be published by the Society of Antiquaries of London.

[31] *Ant. J.* xxxix (1959), pp. 17–18, pl. i.

[32] Ibid. xl (1960), p. 17.

[33] Ibid. xxxix (1959), p. 13.

THE GROOVED WARE SITE AT LION POINT, CLACTON

RECENT discoveries have generated increased interest in, and criticism of, the concept of a single Grooved Ware tradition. It is hoped that the present paper will facilitate discussion by offering a more exhaustive account than was possible in the original pioneering publication by the Fenland Research Committee of 1936.[1] The paper is divided into three sections. The first describes the location and extent of the Grooved Ware site as far as this can now be determined, together with a critical description of how the material was collected and subsequently recorded. The second and third sections offer detailed descriptions and analyses of the pottery and associated flint industry recovered from the site, reallocated as far as possible to the original 'cooking-holes' described by the late Hazzledine Warren in his manuscript notes.

I

THE SITE

The Grooved Ware type-site about two miles south-west of Clacton, originally described as Lion Point but now known as Jaywick Sands, was first recognized by S. Hazzledine Warren and published by him in 1936.[2] His interest in this area was one of long standing since it was here that he discovered, in 1911, a wooden spear-point in association with the Palaeolithic flint industry for which his proposed name of Clactonian was adopted.[3] In the same year he was able to correlate the submerged forests and prehistoric land-surfaces at a number of places round the English coast-line, including Essex, and identify them as the Lyonesse surface, taking the name from an old Cornish tradition of a land beneath the sea.[4] Warren had always been active in geology. From 1903, when he left the family business at the age of thirty, he had devoted his life almost completely to Pleistocene geology and archaeology, serving for many years on the Council of the Royal Anthropological Institute and becoming President of the Geologists' Association in 1922–4.[5] The Pleistocene deposits at Clacton he recognized as filling a former channel of the Thames and therefore datable with reference to the gravel deposits of the Thames valley terraces. Warren was equally clear as to the context of his Neolithic discoveries. It was above the river gravel and marine deposit at Lion Point that the first Neolithic remains appeared in rainwash, but the main body of finds occurred above the rainwash on the Lyonesse surface which was overlain by a few inches of peat. A sheet of soft marine mud (*scrobicularia* clay) above the peat varied in thickness, as it built up to high-tide level or was scoured away by currents, but itself afforded evidence of submergence. That the original submergence was a rapid, rather than a very gradual, process is attested by the condition of the artifacts from the Lyonesse surface, which appear astonishingly fresh and lack the patination acquired by flint over a period of centuries in the surface soil. Moreover, the peat itself would have been washed away, and replaced by beach deposits, had it been exposed over a long period to erosion with every tide.[6]

On the submerged prehistoric surface, underneath the peat cover, Warren found a scatter of sherds and flints, but very little either in, or above, the peat. Also on this surface were concentrations of flint-work, sherds, pot-boilers, charcoal, etc., in occupation or camp sites, which were commonly 30 feet (more or less) in diameter. In addition he distinguished three other types of occupation site:[7]

(*a*) *Pit-dwellings*. Where the level of the occupation surface is not too low upon the foreshore, the lower part of the in-filling of pit-dwellings is sometimes revealed above low water. These pits are round or oval, measuring 10 to 20 feet across, with a flat floor on which is the debris from a wooden structure as well as sherds, pot-boilers, and bones, buried in black earth.[8]

(*b*) *Cooking-holes or earth ovens*—holes averaging 3 feet in diameter and 18 inches deep below the occupation surface. They were filled with black earth containing charcoal and pot-boilers and not infrequently yielded also worked flints and bones (sometimes calcined) and sherds.

(*c*) *Hearth sites*—small patches of charcoal and pot-boilers, often with lumps of burnt earth, that appeared to represent casual camp fires. They usually proved disappointing and yielded little useful evidence.

The best pottery examples came from occupation sites. Most of the best flint implements, on the other hand, were found in the surface scatter which, in general, may be regarded as being contemporary, although the strict evidence of a closed site is lacking. With reference to the material from occupation sites, however, Warren writes: 'I would emphasize that the groups marked are invariably close contemporary associations in pit-dwellings, cooking-holes or the like.'[9] Many such groups are recorded from the foreshore, i.e. between low-tide and high-tide levels, for 2 to 3 miles to the west of Clacton but only in the vicinity of Lion Point, Area 4 (Fig. 1), did they produce sherds of Grooved Ware. Here, within a distance of 150 yards, out of twenty-three cooking-holes not far below high-water mark, only two failed to produce some Grooved Ware. This area was bounded on the east, towards Clacton, by the silted-up bed of a creek, beyond which was one more cooking-hole also containing Grooved Ware. Apart from this series of cooking-holes there was no trace of Grooved Ware on the Clacton sites except at one point in Area 3, 400 yards beyond to the west of the main series, where more sherds were found, this time near to low-water level.[10]

The Hazzledine Warren bequest in 1958 brought to the Museum the whole of his extensive collection and also a number of records. These consist of a 'Partial emergency catalogue, including some general explanations' and a set of field notebooks giving the locations of the individual finds and their markings. There were no plans or sectional drawings of separate sites such as might have been expected, in ordinary circumstances, from a careful excavator. But the circumstances were not ordinary. Warren wrote: 'Work on the tidal sites has its own limitations and difficulties and is not infrequently in the nature of "snatch and grab" archaeology.[11] The state of one's digging on the following day, after two tides have been over it, can be readily imagined; it is often better to dig about a foot deep the first time and then leave it until the sea has swept away all the debris.'[12] From the notebooks and catalogue, however, we can learn something more of Warren's methods. It is clear that he numbered cooking-holes in the order of their discovery. It seems probable, but is not expressly stated, that the numbers ran from west to east. Unfortunately there are not many details of individual holes. No. 3 is stated to be the lowest and not far above half-tide level. (This was one of the two holes containing no Grooved Ware). No. 10 was 'particularly rich in flint work' and is dated October 1930. No. 12 is dated March 1931. No. 19 was 'very clearly defined, 3 ft. diam. 1 ft. 6 in. deep, with steep sides and a flattish bottom'. No. 20: 'The largest yet found—6 ft. × 4 ft. and 1 ft. deep—possibly two or more holes had run together.' No. 23: 'The last hole dug out up to October 1931. The coastal erosion then encountered the later silt of a creek, and no more cooking-holes were seen until the further bank of the creek was reached in 1937—then No. 24.'[13]

The 'partial emergency catalogue' that accompanied the bequest also records that Warren gave up numbering specimens in 1915 and adopted a system of 'abbreviation and special shorthand' to indicate not only the precise location but

also other information relative to his finds. For example, 'Lion Point Clacton' in one line is the location of a Neolithic find, while ' Clacton ' in two lines was
LionPoint

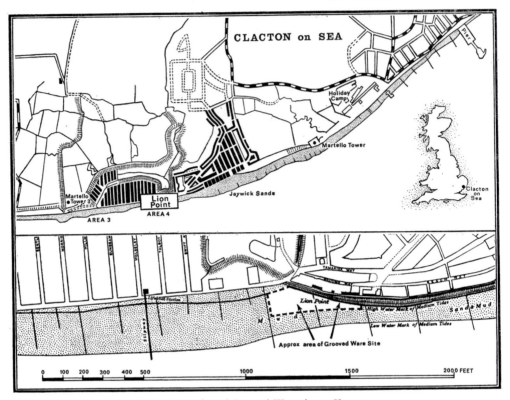

FIG. 1. Location of Grooved Ware site at Clacton.

used for the material from an earlier period. Five areas near Lion Point are distinguished by numbers, as follows:

1 from Clacton Jetty (not the pier) to the Martello Tower at Eastness, i.e. opposite Butlin's Holiday Camp

2 from Eastness to the east side of Lion Point (Jaywick Sands)

3 from the west side of Lion Point (towards the next Martello Tower)

4 is at Lion Point (Jaywick Sands) and therefore between 2 and 3

5 is at the western end of Jaywick, near Seawick (beyond 3).

To these numbers are added signs indicating the position on the foreshore with reference to the tides:

h.w.   is an abbreviation for 'high water' and h.w. 1 or h.w. 2 will be found on some objects from cooking-holes nos. 1 and 2. On other numbers up to 24, h.w. is omitted or replaced by $+$

96

$+$ $+$ is a little lower than h.w.

$+$ means above half-tide level

$\pm$ means about on half-tide level

$\cdots$ means below half-tide level but above low water of neap tides

—— means below low water of neap tides.

The above signs indicating level will be found with the number indicating area, e.g. Grooved Ware sherds from Area 3 are marked either $\cdots$ 3 or ——3 and in Area 4 the marking $\dfrac{\text{L.p.C.}}{4+}$ is used for a section occupied exclusively by the main Grooved Ware site and extending from above half-tide level right up to high-water mark. Every object marked with one of these level signs to give its location was necessarily found *in situ*, whether or not it bears, in addition, the marking Φ used to signify 'found *in situ*'.

Other signs and abbreviations are as follows:

s–b   means 'found on sea-beach', i.e. not *in situ*.

p   stands for 'peat' but is used exclusively for the older peat on the pre-historic surface and never for the peaty sub-soil of the saltings

$\overline{\text{O}}$ -o- $\underline{\text{o}}$ are used for top, middle, and bottom

$\overline{\overline{\text{O}}}$ means a higher level than the top, i.e. 'above'

$\underline{\underline{\text{o}}}$ similarly means 'below'

$\underline{\underline{\text{o}}}$ p   is a combination often used for 'below the bottom of the peat'

c–h   stands for 'cooking-hole' and can be shortened to 'h'. It is followed by a serial number

P–D   stands for 'pit-dwelling' and is followed by a serial number

L.p.C. is the usual abbreviation for Lion Point Clacton (in one line)

L   is a further abbreviation of L.p.C. used on small pieces

·IIA   is a marking applied to a few early finds at Lion Point when the pottery was erroneously attributed to the Iron Age.

This system of marking specimens, together with the explanations afforded by the catalogue, has enabled the original groupings of sherds, flint tools, and other material associated with individual cooking-holes to be reconstituted as the basis of the present study.

K. E. WILSON

II

THE POTTERY

(PLATES XXXIII–XXXVIII)[14]

Without exception, all the sherds recovered by Hazzledine Warren from 'Cooking Holes' 1, 2, 4–5, 6–21, 23, and 24, at Lion Point, can be attributed to the Grooved Ware tradition. These are considered along with Grooved Ware recovered from the old land surface, but having no precise location, in Area 4, and eighteen sherds from a single locality in Area 3.

Fabric

The vast majority of the 324 sherds are well fired and many show the addition of a small quantity of grog. Most of the sherds are weathered and slightly porous, showing the loss of some more soluble tempering, perhaps crushed shell. Exceptional are sherds from Area 3 of a much softer fabric, now in a badly decayed state.

Forms

In no case is more than a small proportion of each vessel represented in the sherd collection. Where it is possible to reconstruct the shape, the majority of vessels appear to be of more or less straight-sided, vertical or trunco-conic forms. However, some simple-rimmed open bowls with curving convex sides are also present, e.g. P10, P13, P23, and P36.

Of the forty-four rims represented, over half (twenty-seven) are of the simple rounded, flattened or pointed forms R1–4 (Fig. 2). A further two show only slight internal bevelling, R5. Three forms, R8–10, have well-developed internal bevels and a further two, R12 and R15, combine this feature with plastic decoration on the internal surface beneath. Plastic decoration also occurs in combination with a more simple rim form, R13, and with inturned forms, R14 and R16. Single examples are present of slightly everted, R6; externally bevelled, R7; and double internally moulded, R11, rims.

Bases are universally flat and in only three instances, P51, P65, and P69, is the junction with the wall emphasized into a slightly protruding foot.

Decorative techniques

A considerable variety of decorative techniques are used, but it is noticeable that neither cord nor comb is ever employed. The major techniques can be summarized:

1. *Incision*: lines drawn with a sharp implement, e.g. P47.

2. *Grooves*: narrow or broad lines of U-shaped section drawn with a blunt instrument, e.g. P74 and P77.

3. *Impressions*: a variety of impressions are employed, falling into three major groupings:
   (*a*) Oval to round, smooth, round-based, made in some cases perhaps with the edge of a small smooth pebble, e.g. P98–100.
   (*b*) Bone-end or twig-end impressions, e.g. P103.
   (*c*) Pointillé made with a small pointed implement, e.g. P47.

98

4. *Strokes*: small linear impressions made with a pointed implement, e.g. P31.

5. *Rustication*: five main varieties can be distinguished:
    (*a*) Finger-nail.
    (*b*) Finger-pinched, e.g. P118.
    (*c*) Finger-nail pushed sideways to produce a roughened surface, e.g. P89–92.
    (*d*) Finger-tipping, e.g. P112 and P113.
    (*e*) Finger-tipping to produce a wavy ridge, e.g. P87 and P88.

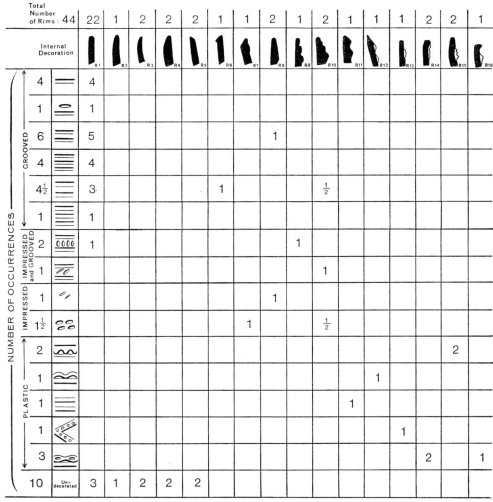

FIG. 2. Grooved Ware (Clacton). Correlation of rim forms (R1-R16) with internal decoration.

6. *Plastic*: in the form of:

    (*a*) Pellets, P36.
    (*b*) Straight cordons, e.g. P118.
    (*c*) Wavy cordons, e.g. P1.
    (*d*) Chain cordons, e.g. P2.

Internal decoration

A feature of the pottery is the high incidence of internal decoration. Of the forty-four rims from the site, no fewer than thirty-four carry this type of decoration (Fig. 2). Characteristic are simple rounded or flattened rims of form R1 combined with horizontal grooved decoration. In contrast the more pointed forms, R2–4, are left undecorated. Internal plastic decoration is another feature of the site occurring on seven of the rims, P1–2, 6–7, and 44–6. Only one vessel carries decoration on top of the rim, P31.

P8 is unique on the site in having decoration on the internal surface of the base.

External decoration

The main components used in the external decoration of the vessels are brought together in Fig. 3. The most commonly employed technique is broad or narrow grooving used either exclusively or in combination with other techniques. Sherds decorated with simple multiple horizontal grooves, e.g. P73–4, are frequent but it is likely that many of these represent small fragments from more complex schemes of the type represented, for example, by vessels P2 and P10. Zones of horizontal grooves are often employed to enclose or separate other motifs or alternate with rows of impressions, e.g. P1, or zones of finger-tip wavy ridges, e.g. P87–8. Zones of simple diagonal grooves are found, P2, as well as grooved herringbone, e.g. P96. Distinctive are sherds carrying multiple chevron and complex triangular and lozenge designs, e.g. P2, the geometric fields often being filled with impressions as in P1, 4, and 5. Incision, when it occurs, is used to create similar complex patterns, and on one vessel this is combined with pointillé decoration, P47.

While twig- and bone-end impressions are often used as subsidiary elements to fill geometric fields in complex patterns, or alternate with zones in a different technique, e.g. P1, regular oval impressions seem to be used either in rows or staggered in a pseudo-basketry effect to cover, perhaps, large areas of the vessel's surface. On a small number of sherds, e.g. P106–8, this type of pattern is further enhanced by transverse strokes on the intervening ridges.

Rusticated decoration appears on a number of sherds, sometimes in zones, e.g. P89–93, but few sherds are large enough to offer any precise indication as to the extent of the surface of the vessel covered by this type of decoration.

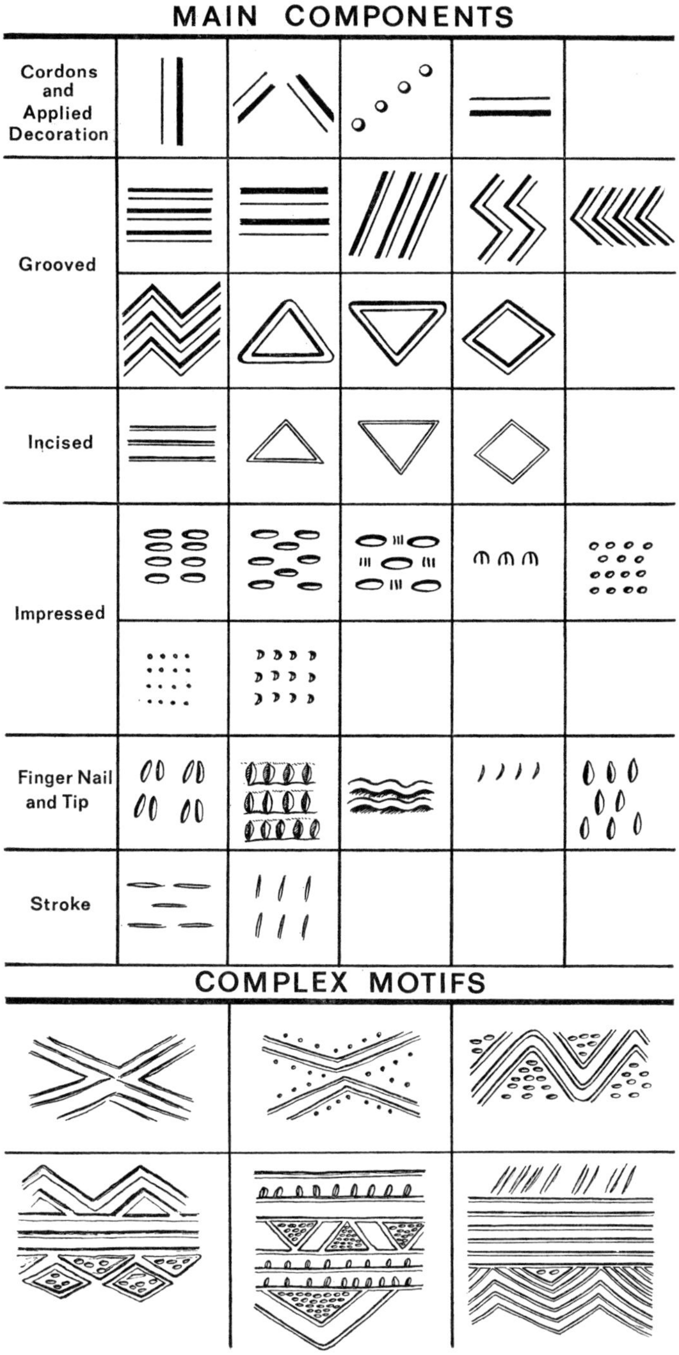

MAIN COMPONENTS

FIG. 3. Grooved Ware (Clacton). Main components and principal complex motifs used in external decoration.

Plastic decoration is rarely used on the external surface of vessels at Clacton. Only nine sherds are so decorated. Examples occur of vertical, P117–18, and diagonal cordons, P120, and one sherd carries a diagonal row of pellets, P36. The remaining sherds, all small, carry remains of horizontal cordons of which P110 and P112 show the cordon decorated with finger-tip or bone-end impressions.

Summary of Characteristics

This brief analysis is sufficient, perhaps, to highlight the main characteristics of the pottery from Lion Point. Positively, these can be summarized as: the extensive use of grooved decoration, often to create complex motifs incorporating lozenge and triangular shapes; the extensive use of a variety of simple impressions, employed repetitively, to cover the surface of the vessel, in rows or as a filling agent in the complex schemes; the frequent use of zoned decoration; the high incidence of internal decoration (77 per cent. of rims from the site carry internal decoration); the relatively rare (seven cases) but highly characteristic use of plastic decoration on the internal surface of the vessel, and incorporation of more than one form of finger-nail and finger-pinched rustication.

Negative characteristics are equally apparent: firstly, as was stressed in the original publication,[15] and subsequently,[16] the total absence of comb and corded techniques; the absence of curvilinear motifs, excepting plastic and finger-tip wavy cordons; the almost total absence of vertical panelling (one example, P118) and rim top decoration (one example, P31), and very rare use of external plastic decoration.

Contemporaneity of 'Cooking-holes'

In the absence of any positive stratigraphical data, the contemporaneity of the cooking-holes recorded by Hazzledine Warren can only be assumed. The sherd collection throws only a little light on this problem. The vessel, P3, is a reconstruction based on seven sherds, all apparently from the same vessel but found scattered in cooking-holes 4–5, 7, 10, and 11, suggesting that these at least are likely to have been in contemporary use. The sherd P6 is close, but not identical, in form and decoration to vessel P2. If this were to be accepted as being from the same vessel, then cooking-holes 8 and 19 were probably in contemporary use.

The only group which might, on stylistic grounds, be considered to fall outside the general run of sherds from the site, and therefore possibly not closely contemporary, are those from cooking-hole 16. The smoothed-out cordons, lightness of decoration, and combination of motifs on sherds P117, 119, and 120 stand out as a fairly distinct anomaly on the site.

Area 4

Cooking-hole 1 (3 sherds)

1. Three sherds from the same vessel including rim of hard compact paste.
Two sherds grey throughout; one
sherd brown externally, grey internally with some tempering. All
heavily weathered.

   Decoration: Internally, wavy applied
cordon above horizontal cordon. Externally, a pair of horizontal grooves
enclose a row of jabbed impressions.
This is separated by a plain band from
a zone of pendant and upright triangles
outlined and enclosed by grooved lines
and filled with impressions. Beneath
this further horizontal grooves enclose rows of impressions with a
double chevron beneath, the upper
triangular space being filled with impressions (Pl. xxxiii, P1).

   Reg. nos. 1958, 5–6, 921–2 and 687.

Cooking-hole 2 (2 sherds)

2. Wall sherd of compact paste tempered
with fine ?grog. Brown externally,
grey internally.

   Decoration: Horizontal grooves (Pl.
xxxvii, P74).

   Reg. no. 1958, 5–6, 690.

3. Base angle of compact paste, slightly
porous and weathered. Light brown
both faces with grey core.

   Decoration: Roughly horizontal grooves
with beginnings of jabbed decoration
above (Pl. xxxvi, P50).

   Reg. no. 1958, 5–6, 689.

Cooking-holes 4 and 5 (3 sherds)

4. Rim sherd of compact paste tempered
with fine ?grog. Brown both faces
with grey core. Heavily weathered.

   Decoration: External surface mostly
eroded but remains of applied cordon.

(Pl. xxxv, P29).

   Reg. no. 1958, 5–6, 695.

5. Rim sherd of compact paste, brown
externally, grey to brown internally.
Weathered.

   Decoration: Two grooves on the internal rim bevel. Externally, a triangular
motif filled with jabbed impressions
and outlined by grooved lines, above
horizontal groove (Pl. xxxiv, P3).

   Reg. no. 1958, 5–6, 694.

6. Wall sherd of slightly porous paste,
brown externally, grey internally.

   Decoration: Part of grooved flag motif
whose upper triangle is filled with
jabbed decoration beneath horizontal
grooved lines. (Pl. xxxvii, P83).

   Reg. no. 1958, 5–6, 693.

Cooking-hole 6 (2 sherds)

7. Rim sherd of compact paste, grey
throughout.

   Decoration: On the internal rim bevel
two horizontal grooves and two ridges,
the upper ridge carrying vertical
stroke decoration. Externally, double
grooved chevrons above horizontal
grooves with flag motif beneath, triangular elements of which are filled
with jabbed impressions (Pl. xxxiv,
P5).

   Reg. no. 1958, 5–6, 709.

8. Heavily weathered wall sherd with remains of grooved decoration (not
illustrated).

   Reg. no. 1958, 5–6, 710.

Cooking-hole 7 (6 sherds)

9. Rim sherd of slightly porous paste, grey
externally, brown internally.

   Decoration: Two horizontal grooves on
the internal rim bevel with two additional horizontal round-based impressions. Beginnings at one point of

transverse incised strokes on enclosed ridge. Externally, diagonal grooves with jabbed impressions above. (Pl. XXXIV, P3).

Reg. no. 1958, 5–6, 715.

10. Rim sherd of compact sandy paste tempered with some grit. Brown externally, grey internally.

Decoration: Internally, two shallow grooves: externally, remains of diagonal grooved ornament (Pl. XXXV, P18).

Reg. no. 1958, 5–6, 716.

11. Wall sherd of slightly porous paste, brown externally, grey internally.

Decoration: Incised chevron pattern above horizontal grooved lines (Pl. XXXVIII, P94).

Reg. no. 1958, 5–6, 717.

12. Wall sherd of slightly porous paste, grey externally, brown internally.

Decoration: Horizontal grooves beneath jabbed impressions (Pl. XXXIV, P3).

Reg. no. 1958, 5–6, 718.

13. Base angle of slightly porous paste, grey throughout with marine encrustation externally. Undecorated.

Reg. no. 1958, 5–6, 718a.

14. Fragment of thin flat base of fairly compact, slightly porous paste, grey to brown both faces (not illustrated).

Reg. no. 1958, 5–6, 719.

Cooking-hole 8 (9 sherds)

15. Rim and upper part of a vessel of compact slightly porous, paste, grey throughout.

Decoration: Internally, rim cordon above applied chain cordon with horizontal cordon beneath. Externally, diagonal incised lines above horizontal grooved lines with multiple grooved chevrons beneath, the upper triangular space filled with two jabbed impressions.

Reg. nos. 1958, 5–6, 725 and 923 (Pl. XXXIII, P2).

16. Rim sherd of slightly porous sandy paste, dark brown to grey both faces.

Decoration: Internally, thin cordon above short vertical strokes with partial groove beneath. Externally, remains of horizontal grooved lines (Pl. XXXV, P16).

Reg. no. 1958, 5–6, 735.

17. Rim sherd of compact sandy paste, brown externally, grey internally.

Decoration: Internally, two shallow grooves. Externally, remains of horizontal impression above horizontal grooves (Pl. XXXV, P21).

Reg. no. 1958, 5–6, 726.

18. Wall sherd of compact slightly porous paste, patchy grey to brown both faces.

Decoration: Remains of probable triangular grooved decoration filled with jabbed impressions above horizontal grooved lines (Pl. XXXVII, P80).

Reg. no. 1958, 5–6, 727.

19. Wall sherd of compact paste, grey throughout.

Decoration: Remains of grooved line and jabbed decoration.

Reg. no. 1958, 5–6, 728.

20. Wall sherd. Very heavily weathered, grey throughout.

Reg. no. 1958, 5–6, 729.

21. Wall sherd. Heavily weathered, grey throughout. Remains of grooved decoration.

Reg. no. 1958, 5–6, 730.

22. Small wall sherd of compact paste, grey throughout. Remains of grooved decoration.

Reg. no. 1958, 5–6, 732.

23. Small fragment of base angle of compact paste, brown externally, grey internally.

Undecorated (Pl. xxxvi, P67).
Reg. no. 1958, 5–6, 731.

Cooking-hole 9 (17 sherds)

24. Rim sherd of compact paste, heavily weathered, greyish brown both faces.
Decoration: Internally, horizontal grooved lines (Pl. xxxv, P20).
Reg. no. 1958, 5–6, 752.

25. Two sherds from base angle of a vessel of fine compact paste, reddish brown externally, grey internally.
Decoration: Remains of jabbed decoration (Pl. xxxvi, P53).
Reg. nos. 1958, 5–6, 744–5 and 938.

26. Base angle of compact slightly porous paste, brown externally, dark grey internally.
Decoration: Horizontal grooves (Pl. xxxvi, P59).
Reg. no. 1958, 5–6, 743.

27. Base angle of compact paste, grey both faces.
Undecorated (Pl. xxxvi, P66).
Reg. no. 1958, 5–6, 755.

28. Wall sherd of compact paste tempered with ?grog, brown externally, grey internally.
Decoration: Horizontal grooves and vertical strokes (Pl. xxxviii, P113).
Reg. no. 1958, 5–6, 741.

29. Wall sherd of compact paste tempered with ?grog, grey to brown externally, grey internally.
Decoration: Horizontal grooves.
Reg. no. 1958, 5–6, 746.

30. Wall sherd of flaky paste tempered with some grog, grey throughout.
Decoration: Horizontal grooves.
Reg. no. 1958, 5–6, 747.

31. Wall sherd of compact paste, reddish brown externally, grey internally.

Decoration: Horizontal grooves.
Reg. no. 1958, 5–6, 758.

32. Wall sherd of compact paste, grey both faces.
Decoration: Grooved line.
Reg. no. 1958, 5–6, 754.

33. Wall sherd of compact slightly porous paste, brown externally, grey internally.
Decoration: Remains of grooved line.
Reg. no. 1958, 5–6, 754.

34. Wall sherd of compact paste, brown externally, grey internally.
Decoration: Alternate short, deep, horizontal grooved impressions.
Reg. no. 1958, 5–6, 748.

35. Wall sherd of compact paste, grey externally, greyish brown internally.
Decoration: Rusticated.
Reg. no. 1958, 5–6, 742.

36. Wall sherd of compact paste, light brown externally, dark grey internally.
Decoration: Remains of grooves.
Reg. no. 1958, 5–6, 751.

37. Two wall sherds of slightly porous paste, light brown externally, light brown to grey internally.
Decoration: Large shallow impressions.
Reg. nos. 1958, 5–6, 749–50.

38. Two heavily weathered wall sherds.
Reg. no. 1958, 5–6, 754.

Cooking-hole 10 (16 sherds)

39. Rim sherd of compact paste, brown externally, grey internally.
Decoration: Internally, two wide grooves on the internal rim bevel. Externally, diagonal grooved lines with jabbed impressions above (Pl. xxxiv, P3).
Reg. no. 1958, 5–6, 769.

40. Rim sherd of compact paste, grey both faces.
Decoration: Internally, single grooved line. Externally, remains of horizontal grooved lines (Pl. xxxv, P35).
Reg. no. 1958, 5–6, 775.

41. Wall sherd of compact paste, brown throughout. Heavily weathered.
Decoration: Remains of jabbed impressions.
Reg. no. 1958, 5–6, 772.

42. Wall sherd of slightly porous paste with some grit and sand. Brown externally, dark grey to brown internally.
Decoration: Wide shallow grooves (Pl. xxxvii, P72).
Reg. no. 1958, 5–6, 768.

43. Wall sherd of hard compact paste, brown externally, grey internally.
Decoration: Alternate short horizontal oval impressions (Pl. xxxviii, P98).
Reg. no. 1958, 5–6, 767.

44. Wall sherd of compact paste, grey to brown both faces. Weathered.
Decoration: Probably part of grooved flag motif filled with impressions (Pl. xxxvii, P75).
Reg. no. 1958, 5–6, 770.

45. Wall sherd of compact, slightly porous paste, brown externally, grey to brown internally.
Decoration: Wide shallow grooves.
Reg. no. 1958, 5–6, 778.

46. Wall sherd of compact but slightly porous paste, grey externally, brown internally.
Decoration: Wide shallow grooves beneath a row of jabbed impressions.
Reg. no. 1958, 5–6, 771.

47. Four wall sherds with grooved decoration.
Reg. no. 1958, 5–6, 776.

48. Fragment of base and fragment of undecorated wall.
Reg. no. 1958, 5–6, 776.

49. Two wall sherds of compact, slightly porous paste, brown both faces with grey core.
Decoration: One with staggered oval impressions; the other, elongated oval impressions.
Reg. nos. 1958, 5–6, 773–4.

Cooking-hole 11 (17 sherds)

50. Rim and wall sherd of compact paste, grey throughout.
Decoration: Internally, three horizontal grooved lines. Externally, a grooved multiple chevron pattern, the triangular fields filled with jabbed impressions, enclosed between zones of horizontal grooved lines (Pl. xxxiv, P4).
Reg. nos. 1958, 5–6, 792 and 803.

51. Rim sherd of compact paste, grey both faces.
Decoration: Internally, deep oval impressions. Externally, diagonal grooves above jabbed impressions with broad shallow grooves beneath. Below this remains of rusticated decoration (Pl. xxxiv, P3).
Reg. nos. 1958, 5–6, 797 and 927.

52. Wall sherd of compact, slightly porous paste, brown externally, grey to brown internally.
Decoration: Broad shallow grooves enclosing zone filled with finger-nail rustication (Pl. xxxvii, P93).
Reg. no. 1958, 5–6, 794.

53. Wall sherd of compact paste, grey externally, brown internally.
Decoration: Grooved lines above incised or rusticated decoration (Pl. xxxiv, P3).
Reg. no. 1958, 5–6, 801.

54. Wall sherd of compact paste, brown both faces.
Decoration: Grooved lines with a row of jabs above and triangle outlined with grooves beneath filled with jabs (Pl. XXXVII, P79).
Reg. no. 1958, 5–6, 800.

55. Small fragment of wall of compact paste, brown externally, grey internally.
Decoration: Horizontal grooves enclose diagonal finger-nail impressions.
Reg. no. 1958, 5–6, 805.

56. Wall sherd of compact paste, greyish brown both faces.
Decoration: Broad grooved chevrons (Pl. XXXVIII, P95).
Reg. no. 1958, 5–6, 804.

57. Wall sherd of compact paste, reddish brown externally, grey internally.
Decoration: Rusticated.
Reg. no. 1958, 5–6, 795.

58. Wall sherd of compact, slightly porous paste, brown both faces. Weathered.
Decoration: Remains of horizontal and diagonal grooves.
Reg. no. 1958, 5–6, 796.

59. Four wall sherds with remains of horizontal grooves.
Reg. nos. 1958, 5–6, 798–9 and 806–7.

60. Base angle and fragment of base of compact paste, brown both faces with grey core (Pl. XXXVI, P68).
Reg. nos. 1958, 5–6, 793 and 807.

61. Undecorated fragment of base.
Reg. no. 1958, 5–6, 807.

Cooking-hole 12 (7 sherds)

62. Wall sherd of compact, slightly porous paste, brown both faces with dark-grey core.
Decoration: Two wavy bands above horizontal grooved lines. Beneath this, beginnings of grooved triangular pattern filled with impressions (Pl. XXXVII, P87).
Reg. no. 1958, 5–6, 823.

63. Wall sherd of similar paste, brown to grey externally, light brown internally.
Decoration: Horizontal grooved lines between wavy bands (Pl. XXXVII, P88).
Reg. nos. 1958, 5–6, 821–2.

64. Two wall sherds of compact paste, brown externally, grey internally. Heavily weathered.
Decoration: Remains of horizontal grooved lines.
Reg. nos. 1958, 5–6, 819–20.

65. Wall sherd of rather porous paste, brown externally, grey internally.
Decoration: Horizontal oval impressions.
Reg. no. 1958, 5–6, 824.

66. Wall sherd of hard compact sandy paste, brown externally, grey internally.
Decoration: Single horizontal grooved line.
Reg. no. 1958, 5–6, 825.

67. Heavily weathered undecorated wall sherd.
Reg. no. 1958, 5–6, 826.

Cooking-hole 13 (2 sherds)

68. Wall sherd of compact porous paste, grey to brown both faces.
Decoration: Finger-tip rustication (Pl. XXXVIII, P105).
Reg. no. 1958, 5–6, 838.

69. Wall sherd of compact paste, brown externally, dark grey internally.
Decoration: Remains of oval impressions.
Reg. no. 1958, 5–6, 839.

Cooking-hole 14 (10 sherds)

70. Rim sherd of compact paste, grey both faces.
    Decoration: On top of the rim, remains of transverse impressions. Externally, horizontal incised strokes (Pl. xxxv, P31).
    Reg. no. 1958, 5–6, 850.

71. Rim sherd of compact paste, grey throughout.
    Decoration: Internally, remains of horizontal groove above wavy cordon (Pl. xxxvi, P44).
    Reg. no. 1958, 5–6, 945.

72. Wall sherd of compact paste, brown both faces.
    Decoration: Horizontal grooved lines below rustication (Pl. xxxvii, P90).
    Reg. no. 1958, 5–6, 844.

73. Wall sherd of compact paste, light brown both faces with grey core.
    Decoration: remains of deep impressions.
    Reg. no. 1958, 5–6, 847.

74. Wall sherd of compact paste, grey throughout.
    Decoration: Internally, remains of broad groove and moulded pattern. Externally, remains of heavy moulding (Pl. xxxviii, P114).
    Reg. no. 1958, 5–6, 846.

75. Three wall sherds with remains of horizontal grooved lines.
    Reg. nos. 1958, 5–6, 843, 845 and 848.

76. Fragment of base angle of compact paste, brown externally, grey internally.
    Reg. no. 1958, 5–6, 849.

77. Wall sherd of compact paste, brown both faces.
    Decoration: Indefinite but appears to be remains of oval impression.
    Reg. no. 1958, 5–6, 1027.

Cooking-hole 15 (3 sherds)

78. Rim and wall sherd of vessel of compact slightly porous paste, patchy brown to grey both faces. Surface weathered.
    Decoration: Internally, horizontal grooved lines. Externally, jabbed impressions beneath the rim; elsewhere, horizontal grooves above triangular pattern outlined with grooves and filled with impressions (Pl. xxxv, P10).
    Reg. nos. 1958, 5–6, 856–7.

79. Rim sherd of compact paste, grey externally, lighter grey internally.
    Decoration: Internally, horizontal grooved lines. Externally, opposed grooves above horizontal grooved lines (Pl. xxxv, P22).
    Reg. no. 1958, 5–6, 854.

80. Wall sherd of fairly compact slightly porous paste, greyish brown both faces.
    Decoration: Horizontal grooved lines.
    Reg. no. 1958, 5–6, 855.

Cooking-hole 16 (3 sherds)

81. Wall sherd of compact paste, reddish brown to grey externally, dark grey internally. Surface heavily weathered.
    Decoration: Combines fine incised lines and slight cordons (Pl. xxxviii, P119).
    Reg. no. 1958, 5–6, 861.

82. Wall sherd of compact paste tempered with grit, dark brown to grey throughout. Weathered.
    Decoration: Combines diagonal grooved herringbone and incised lines with slight vertical and horizontal cordons (Pl. xxxviii, P120).
    Reg. nos. 1958, 5–6, 860 and 862.

83. Wall sherd of compact paste tempered with grit, reddish brown externally, grey internally. Weathered.

Decoration: Remains of grooved herringbone and slight plain cordon (Pl. XXXVIII, P117).
Reg. no. 1958, 5–6, 863.

Cooking-hole 17 (3 sherds)

84. Base angle of compact paste, grey throughout.
Decoration: Remains of grooved ?filled triangle pattern above roughly executed horizontal grooved lines (Pl. XXXVI, P55).
Reg. no. 1958, 5–6, 864.

85. Wall sherd of compact paste, brown externally, grey internally.
Decoration: Grooved herringbone (Pl. XXXVIII, P96).
Reg. no. 1958, 5–6, 865.

86. Heavily weathered wall sherd of compact sandy paste.
Reg. no. 1958, 5–6, 866.

Cooking-hole 18 (5 sherds)

87. Rim sherd of compact paste, brown externally, grey internally. Weathered.
Decoration: Internally, horizontal grooves. Externally, remains of horizontal grooved decoration (Pl. XXXV, P14).
Reg. no. 1958, 5–6, 868.

88. Wall sherd of compact paste with some coarse sand, brown externally, grey internally.
Decoration: Oval impressions, some of intervening ridges decorated with pairs of jabbed impressions (Pl. XXXVIII, P106).
Reg. no. 1958, 5–6, 869.

89. Wall sherd of compact paste, brown both faces.
Decoration: Horizontal grooves above beginnings of impressed decoration.
Reg. no. 1958, 5–6, 870.

90. Wall sherd of compact paste, brown externally, grey internally. Weathered.
Decoration: Remains of grooved decoration.
Reg. no. 1958, 5–6, 871.

91. Undecorated wall sherd of compact paste.
Reg. no. 1958, 5–6, 876.

Cooking-hole 19 (9 sherds)

92. Rim sherd of compact slightly porous paste tempered with some grit, grey throughout.
Decoration: Internally, applied chain cordon above shallow horizontal groove. Externally, groups of diagonal grooved lines above horizontal grooves (Pl. XXXIV, P6).
Reg. no. 1958, 5–6, 879.

93. Three sherds probably from the same vessel including the rim of compact porous paste, brown externally, grey internally.
Decoration: Horizontal incised lines above incised flag motif (Pl. XXXV, P17).
Reg. nos. 1958, 5–6, 877 and 880–1.

94. Rim sherd of compact paste, light brown both faces.
Decoration: Horizontal grooves above rows of horizontal oval impressions (Pl. XXXV, P11).
Reg. no. 1958, 5–6, 878.

95. Wall sherd of compact slightly porous paste, brown both faces.
Decoration: Staggered oval impressions, one ridge decorated with additional pair of jabbed impressions.
Reg. no. 1958, 5–6, 884.

96. Wall sherd of somewhat porous paste, brown externally, grey internally.
Decoration: Remains of grooved and ridged decoration, ridges being decorated with short transverse strokes (Pl. XXXVIII, P116).
Reg. no. 1958, 5–6, 885.

97. Two wall sherds with remains of grooved decoration.
Reg. no. 1958, 5–6, 882–3.

98. Wall sherd of compact paste, grey throughout.
Decoration: Widely spaced broad grooves (Pl. xxxvii, P77).
Reg. no. 1958, 5–6, 1007.

Cooking-hole 20 (5 sherds)

99. Rim sherd of compact slightly porous paste, brown internally, grey externally.
Decoration: Externally, horizontal grooved lines. Internally, traces of diagonal impressions (Pl. xxxv, P41).
Reg. no. 1958, 5–6, 897.

100. Base angle of compact paste, grey throughout. Undecorated (Pl. xxxvi, P64).
Reg. no. 1958, 5–6, 899.

101. Three wall sherds, not necessarily from the same vessel, carrying deep oval impressions (one illustrated, Pl. xxxviii, P104).
Reg. nos. 1958, 5–6, 896, 898 and 900.

Cooking-hole 21 (4 sherds)

102. Rim sherd of compact but slightly porous paste, grey internally, grey to brown externally. Weathered.
Decoration: Internally, converging cordons decorated with impressions above a grooved line. Externally, horizontal grooves enclose and separate double wavy bands (Pl. xxxiv, P7).
Reg. no. 1958, 5–6, 905.

103. Base angle of rather porous paste, brown externally, grey to brown internally.
Decoration: Horizontal grooved lines (Pl. xxxvi, P49).
Reg. no. 1958, 5–6, 907.

104. Wall sherd of compact paste, brown externally, grey internally.
Decoration: Horizontal grooved lines or impressions.
Reg. no. 1958, 5–6, 906.

105. Base sherd of rather porous paste, light brown externally, grey to brown internally.
Reg. no. 1958, 5–6, 908.

Cooking-hole 23 (3 sherds)

106. Rim sherd of compact paste, brown both faces with dark grey core.
Decoration: On the internal rim bevel, irregular stab-and-drag lines (Pl. xxxv, P40).
Reg. no. 1958, 5–6, 912.

107. Wall sherd of compact sandy paste, brown externally, grey internally.
Decoration: Part of a grooved triangular pattern filled with oval impressions (Pl. xxxviii, P102).
Reg. no. 1958, 5–6, 913.

108. Wall sherd of rather sandy paste, brown externally, grey internally.
Decoration: Grooved lines.
Reg. no. 1958, 5–6, 914.

Cooking-hole 24 (4 sherds)

109. Wall sherd of compact paste, grey to brown both faces.
Decoration: Finger-nail rustication.
Reg. no. 1958, 5–6, 916.

110. Three undecorated wall sherds.
Reg. nos. 1958, 5–6, 917–19.

Area 4: *General*

111. Two sherds including rim of vessel of compact paste tempered with much fine grit, brown both faces.
Decoration: Internally, two horizontal grooves. Externally, irregular opposed grooved-line decoration (Pl. xxxv, P13).

Reg. nos. 1958, 5–6, 928, 978, 1000 and 1041.

112. Rim sherd of compact paste tempered with fine grog, brown internally, grey externally.
Decoration: Internally, two horizontal grooved lines. Externally, horizontal grooved lines above staggered oval impressions (Pl. xxxv, P27).
Reg. no. 1958, 5–6, 1001.

113. Rim sherd of compact, slightly porous paste, brown both faces.
Decoration: Internally, wavy finger-tip cordon with groove above and ridge and groove beneath. Externally horizontal grooved lines (Pl. xxxvi, P46).
Reg. no. 1958, 5–6, 952.

114. Rim sherd of compact paste, grey internally, brown externally.
Decoration: Internally, single grooved line. Externally, remains of horizontal grooved lines (Pl. xxxv, P25).
Reg. no. 1958, 5–6, 968.

115. Rim sherd of compact slightly porous paste, grey internally, grey to brown externally.
Decoration: Internally, single horizontal grooved line. Externally, horizontal grooves (Pl. xxxv, P26).
Reg. no. 1958, 5–6, 1038.

116. Two rim sherds of compact rather porous paste, grey throughout.
Decoration: Internally, two horizontal grooves. External surface eroded (Pl. xxxv, P19 and P23).
Reg. nos. 1958, 5–6, 1030 and 1036.

117. Rim sherd of slightly porous paste, grey internally, brown externally. Heavily weathered.
Decoration: Internally, three shallow horizontal grooves. External surface lost (Pl. xxxv, P15).
Reg. no. 1958, 5–6, 1035.

118. Small rim fragment of compact porous paste, grey throughout.
Decoration: Internally, single horizontal grooved line. Externally, horizontal grooved line (Pl. xxxv, P24).
Reg. no. 1958, 5–6, 1040.

119. Rim sherd of compact slightly porous paste, brown both faces, grey core.
Decoration: Internally, remains of two wide grooves. Externally, diagonal grooves separate jabbed impressions (Pl. xxxiv, P3).
Reg. nos. 1958, 5–6, 937 and 951.

120. Rim sherd of compact paste, brown internally, external surface lost.
Decoration: Internally, wavy finger-tip cordon with grooved line above and ridge beneath (Pl. xxxvi, P45).
Reg. no. 1958, 5–6, 965.

121. Rim sherd of compact slightly porous paste, brown externally, grey internally.
Decoration: Internally, two horizontal grooves. Externally, remains of opposed diagonal incised lines above horizontal groove (Pl. xxxv, P39).
Reg. no. 1958, 5–6, 943.

122. Rim sherd of compact slightly porous paste, grey throughout.
Decoration: Internally, two horizontal mouldings (Pl. xxxvi, P43).
Reg. no. 1958, 5–6, 946.

123. Rim sherd of rather porous paste, grey both faces.
Decoration: Shallow finger-tip impressions (Pl. xxxv, P32).
Reg. no. 1958, 5–6, 1125.

124. Rim sherd of compact paste, grey both faces.
Decoration: Heavy vertical finger-nail rustication (Pl. xxxv, P37).
Reg. no. 1958, 5–6, 933.

125. Rim sherd of compact slightly porous paste, grey both faces.
Decoration: Remains of shallow oval impressions (Pl. xxxv, P30).
Reg. no. 1958, 5–6, 1101.

126. Rim sherd of compact paste, brown externally, grey internally.
Decoration: Internally, horizontal grooved line (Pl. xxxv, P34).
Reg. no. 1958, 5–6, 1073.

127. Rim sherd of compact slightly porous paste, grey to brown externally, grey internally.
Decoration: Internally, impression above grooved line. Externally, diagonal incised lines (Pl. xxxv, P12).
Reg. no. 1958, 5–6, 1100.

128. Rim sherd of compact paste, grey throughout.
Decoration: Internally single horizontal grooved line (Pl. xxxv, P38).
Reg. no. 1958, 5–6, 1061.

129. Rim sherd of compact paste, grey throughout.
Decoration: Diagonal row of applied pellets with beginnings of fine incised decoration (Pl. xxxv, P36).
Reg. no. 1958, 5–6, 1085.

130. Rim sherd of compact paste, brown externally, grey internally.
Decoration: Diagonal stab-and-drag line above diagonal cordon with impressions beneath (Pl. xxxv, P33).
Reg. no. 1958, 5–6, 1103.

131. Rim sherd of compact slightly porous paste, grey throughout. Weathered.
Decoration: Internally, three horizontal grooved lines (Pl. xxxv, P28).
Reg. no. 1958, 5–6, 992.

132. Base angle of compact slightly porous paste, brown externally, brown to grey internally.

Decoration: Multiple grooved chevrons and remains of impressions above horizontal grooved lines (Pl. xxxiv, P9).
Reg. no. 1958, 5–6, 920.

133. Two sherds including base angle of compact slightly porous paste, brown to grey both faces.
Decoration: Internally, finger-tip impressions. Externally, horizontal groove (Pl. xxxiv, P8).
Reg. nos. 1958, 5–6, 935 and 1298.

134. Base angle of compact paste, brown externally, black incrustation internally. Heavily weathered.
Decoration: Remains of horizontal grooved lines above short diagonal lines (Pl. xxxvi, P51).
Reg. no. 1958, 5–6, 931.

135. Three sherds including base angle of slightly porous paste, grey throughout.
Decoration: Incised flag pattern, with pointillé filling (Pl. xxxvi, P47).
Reg. nos. 1958, 5–6, 939, 969 and 1094.

136. Base angle of compact paste, brown externally, grey internally.
Decoration: Horizontal grooved lines (Pl. xxxvi, P63).
Reg. no. 1958, 5–6, 1003.

137. Base angle of compact paste, brown externally, grey internally. Heavily weathered.
Decoration: Remains of horizontal grooved line (Pl. xxxvi, P70).
Reg. no. 1958, 5–6, 1013.

138. Base angle of compact paste, grey throughout.
Decoration: Remains of horizontal grooved line (Pl. xxxvi, P52).
Reg. no. 1958, 5–6, 977.

139. Base angle of compact slightly porous paste tempered with some sand. Brown externally, grey internally.
Decoration: Remains of finger-tip impressions (Pl. xxxvi, P48).
Reg. no. 1958, 5–6, 1043.

140. Base angle of compact paste, brown externally, grey internally.
Decoration: Remains of horizontal grooved lines (Pl. xxxvi, P60).
Reg. no. 1958, 5–6, 1096.

141. Base angle of fine compact paste, brown to grey externally, brown internally with dark-grey core.
Decoration: Heavily weathered but appears to be remains of oval impressions (Pl. xxxvi, P54).
Reg. no. 1958, 5–6, 1012.

142. Base angle of compact slightly porous paste, light brown externally, dark grey internally. Weathered (Pl. xxxvi, P56).
Reg. no. 1958, 5–6, 1018.

143. Base angle of compact paste, light brown to grey externally, grey internally. Undecorated (Pl. xxxvi, P57).
Reg. no. 1958, 5–6, 1047.

144. Base angle of compact paste, light brown externally, grey internally. Undecorated (Pl. xxxvi, P69).
Reg. no. 1958, 5–6, 1019.

145. Base angle of compact paste, grey throughout. Heavily weathered (Pl. xxxvi, P58).
Reg. nos. 1958, 5–6, 1044–5.

146. Base angle of compact paste, brown both faces with grey core.
Undecorated (Pl. xxxvi, P65).
Reg. no. 1958, 5–6, 1020.

147. Base angle of compact slightly porous paste, brown externally, grey internally.

Decoration: Remains of grooved line (Pl. xxxvi, P61).
Reg. no. 1958, 5–6, 1286.

148. Base angle of fine compact paste, light brown externally, grey internally.
Decoration: Remains of grooved line (Pl. xxxvi, P71).
Reg. no. 1958, 5–6, 1049.

149. Base angle of sandy paste tempered with grog, brown externally, grey internally. Heavily weathered (Pl. xxxvi, P62).
Reg. no. 1958, 5–6, 981.

150. Two wall sherds of compact paste, grey externally, brown internally.
Decoration: Horizontal grooved lines. (One illustrated, Pl. xxxvii, P73).
Reg. nos. 1958, 5–6, 1017, 1028 and 1067.

151. Wall sherd of compact paste tempered with grog and a little grit, grey to brown both faces.
Decoration: Staggered elongated oval impressions (Pl. xxxviii, P99).
Reg. no. 1958, 5–6, 950.

152. Wall sherd of compact paste, brown both faces.
Decoration: Staggered stab-and-drag oval impressions (Pl. xxxviii, P100).
Reg. no. 1958, 5–6, 996.

153. Wall sherd of compact paste, grey throughout.
Decoration: Staggered oval impressions (Pl. xxxviii, P101).
Reg. no. 1958, 5–6, 1086.

154. Wall sherd of compact paste, brown externally, dark grey internally.
Decoration: Incised horizontal lines (Pl. xxxvii, P76).
Reg. no. 1958, 5–6, 995.

155. Wall sherd of compact paste, grey to brown externally, brown internally.
Decoration: Zone of finger-nail rustication enclosed, and each row separated, by horizontal grooved lines (Pl. xxxvii, P91).
Reg. no. 1958, 5–6, 926.

156. Wall sherd of similar paste.
Decoration: Zone of finger-nail rustication bordered above and divided-horizontally into rows by grooved lines (Pl. xxxvii, P92).
Reg. no. 1958, 5–6, 953.

157. Wall sherd of compact paste, brown internally, grey to brown externally.
Decoration: Zone of finger-nail rustication bordered above and divided horizontally into rows by grooved lines (Pl. xxxvii, P89).
Reg. no. 1958, 5–6, 962.

158. Wall sherd of compact paste, grey both faces with dark-grey core.
Decoration: Horizontal grooved lines above grooved triangle filled with jabbed impressions (Pl. xxxvii, P82).
Reg. no. 1958, 5–6, 929.

159. Wall sherd of compact paste, brown both faces with grey core.
Decoration: Vertical plain cordon separates panels of finger pinched rustication (Pl. xxxviii, P118).
Reg. no. 1958, 5–6, 1010.

160. Wall sherd of fine compact sandy paste, grey to brown externally, grey internally.
Decoration: Grooved triangle filled with rough diagonal strokes with jabbed impressions outside, above horizontal grooved line (Pl. xxxvii, P78).
Reg. nos. 1958, 5–6, 994 and 1083.

161. Wall sherd of compact paste, grey both faces.

Decoration: Grooved chevron above jabbed impressions (Pl. xxxvii, P84).
Reg. no. 1958, 5–6, 920a.

162. Wall sherd of compact paste, brown externally, grey internally.
Decoration: Horizontal grooved lines (Pl. xxxvii, P81).
Reg. no. 1958, 5–6, 1054.

163. Shoulder sherd of compact paste, brown externally, dark grey internally.
Decoration: Traces of shallow stab-and-drag lines (Pl. xxxviii, P115).
Reg. no. 1958, 5–6, 934.

164. Wall sherd of compact paste, greyish brown externally, grey internally.
Decoration: Large staggered oval impressions with short vertical transverse strokes on the intervening ridges (Pl. xxxviii, P108).
Reg. no. 1958, 5–6, 976.

165. Wall sherd of compact paste, brown both faces with grey core.
Decoration: Staggered oval impressions with short vertical transverse strokes on the intervening ridges (Pl. xxxviii, P107).
Reg. no. 1958, 5–6, 999.

166. Wall sherd of compact paste, grey externally, brown internally.
Decoration: Grooved chevron (Pl. xxxviii, P97).
Reg. no. 1958, 5–6, 924.

167. Wall sherd of compact paste, tempered with a little fine grit, grey throughout.
Decoration: Two cordons, upper decorated with finger-tip impressions, lower plain, from which descend beginnings of vertical cordons (Pl. xxxviii, P112).
Reg. no. 1958, 5–6, 990.

168. Wall sherd of compact sandy paste, brown both faces with dark grey core.

Decoration: Two horizontal grooved lines beneath row of short diagonal grooved lines (Pl. xxxviii, P109).

Reg. no. 1958, 5–6, 932.

169. Wall sherd of compact paste, grey throughout.

Decoration: Grooved lines with row of finger-nail impressions beneath (Pl. xxxviii, P111).

Reg. no. 1958, 5–6, 970.

170. Wall sherd of compact paste, grey to brown externally, grey internally.

Decoration: Rough incised triangular pattern, filled and enclosed by areas of stabbed impressions (Pl. xxxvii, P85).

Reg. no. 1958, 5–6, 1082.

171. Wall sherd of compact sandy paste, grey throughout.

Decoration: Wide, flat, ridge decorated with round impressions (Pl. xxxviii, P110).

Reg. no. 1958, 5–6, 1092.

172. Wall sherd of compact paste, grey throughout.

Decoration: Rows of bird-bone impressions (Pl. xxxviii, P103).

Reg. no. 1958, 5–6, 983.

173. Wall sherd of compact slightly porous paste, grey externally, brown internally. Weathered.

Decoration: Jabbed impressions above grooved lines (Pl. xxxvii, P86).

Reg. no. 1958, 5–6, 1002.

174. Wall sherd of compact paste, grey to brown externally, grey internally.

Decoration: Remains of grooved triangle, filled with jabs.

Reg. no. 1958, 5–6, 973.

175. Wall sherd of compact paste, grey throughout. Weathered.

Decoration: Internally, remains of groove on internal rim bevel. Externally remains of grooved triangular pattern filled with jabs.

Reg. no. 1958, 5–6, 1031.

176. Two wall sherds of compact paste, brown both faces with grey core.

Decoration: Finger-nail rustication divided into rows by horizontal grooved lines.

Reg. nos. 1958, 5–6, 985 and 1087.

177. Two wall sherds of fine compact paste brown to grey both faces.

Decoration: On one sherd internally, remains of horizontal grooved lines. Externally, deeply incised horizontal lines.

Reg. nos. 1958, 5–6, 958 and 1066.

178. Wall sherd of compact paste, brown externally, grey internally.

Decoration: Oval impressions, some of the intervening ridges decorated with pairs of jabbed impressions.

Reg. no. 1958, 5–6, 1084.

179. Wall sherd of fairly compact paste tempered with grit. Patchy brown to grey both faces.

Decoration: Large oval impression, ridges above and below decorated with short vertical strokes.

Reg. no. 1958, 5–6, 1033.

180. Wall sherd of compact paste, brown to grey externally, grey internally.

Decoration: Staggered oval impressions, intervening ridges decorated with jabbed impressions.

Reg. no. 1958, 5–6, 1091.

181. Wall sherd of compact paste, brown both faces with grey core.

Decoration: Remains of applied cordon.

Reg. no. 1958, 5–6, 982.

182. Wall sherd of compact slightly porous paste, brown externally, grey internally.
Decoration: Finger-nail impressions.
Reg. no. 1958, 5–6, 1080.

183. Wall sherd of compact slightly porous paste, grey to brown externally, grey internally. Heavily weathered.
Decoration: Horizontal grooves, one of the intervening ridges decorated with impressions.
Reg. no. 1958, 5–6, 1089.

184. Wall sherd of compact slightly porous paste, brown to grey both faces.
Decoration: Horizontal grooves above oval impression.
Reg. no. 1958, 5–6, 1024.

185. Wall sherd of compact, slightly porous paste, grey both faces. Weathered.
Decoration: Broad horizontal strokes.
Reg. no. 1958, 5–6, 1095.

186. Five wall sherds of compact slightly porous paste, light brown externally, grey internally. Weathered.
Decoration: Finger-nail rustication above horizontal grooved lines.
Reg. nos. 1958, 5–6, 972, 986, 998, 1023, and 1059.

187. Five wall sherds of compact paste, grey throughout.
Decoration: Deep vertical finger-nail impressions.
Reg. nos. 1958, 5–6, 930, 974, 988, 993, and 1105.

188. Five wall sherds from different vessels with remains of horizontal grooves with jabbed impressions above.
Reg. nos. 1958, 5–6, 942, 960, 1079, 1106, and 1299.

189. Six wall sherds from different vessels decorated with oval impressions of varying size.

Reg. nos. 1958, 5–6, 961, 979, 1021, 1088, 1093, and 1098.

190. Twenty-seven wall sherds decorated with narrow horizontal grooved lines.
Reg. nos. 1958, 5–6, 936, 955–6, 959, 963, 966, 984, 1005, 1008–9, 1022, 1034, 1050–3, 1055–7, 1062, 1064–5, 1072, 1074, 1104, 1299(2).

191. Four wall sherds with wide shallow horizontal grooved lines.
Reg. nos. 1958, 5–6, 987, 1026, 1060, and 1077.

192. Ten wall sherds with staggered oval impressions.
Reg. nos. 1958, 5–6, 925, 941, 949, 975, 980, 997, 1029, 1070, and 1096–8.

193. Twenty-eight sherds lacking decoration, too indefinite or too abraded to be classified.
Reg. nos. 1958, 5–6, 948, 954, 967, 971, 1025, 1032, 1058, 1063, 1069, 1071, 1075–6, 1081, 1090, 1102, 1107, 1113, 1121(2), 1123, 1127(2), 1284, 1287, 1297, and 1300 (3).

AREA 3 (18 sherds)

194. Rim sherd of compact rather sandy paste, grey throughout.
Decoration: Internally, two wide horizontal grooves. Externally, on the edge of the rim and forming a zone beneath, oval impressions. Beneath this, horizontal grooved lines (Pl. xxxv, P42)
Reg. nos. 1958, 5–6, 664 and 666.

195. Two sherds of soft sandy paste, dark grey throughout.
Decoration: Multiple grooved chevrons.
Reg. nos. 1958, 5–6, 647–8.

116

196. Wall sherd of soft paste. Dark grey throughout, much of external surface lost.
   Decoration: Zone of horizontal grooved lines.
   Reg. no. 1958, 5–6, 667.

197. Two wall sherds in a very decayed state. Dark grey throughout.
   Decoration: Remains of wide horizontal grooves.
   Reg. nos. 1958, 5–6, 649–50.

198. Three wall sherds from different vessels with remains of grooved line decoration.
   Reg. nos. 1958, 5–6, 651 and 666.

199. Wall sherd of compact, slightly porous paste, grey both faces.
   Decoration: Impressions above grooved lines.
   Reg. no. 1958, 5–6, 665a.

200. Four small wall sherds with remains of impressions.
   Reg. no. 1958, 5–6, 668a.

201. Undecorated base angle of compact paste, dark brown to grey externally, grey internally.
   Reg. no. 1958, 5–6, 645.

202. Undecorated base angle of compact paste, grey throughout.
   Reg. no. 1958, 5–6, 646.

203. Two small wall sherds, heavily weathered.
   Reg. no. 1958, 5–6, 664a.

I. H. LONGWORTH

III

THE FLINT INDUSTRY

A total of 522 flints were recorded from the pits on the foreshore at Lion Point. In general their condition is fresh and unrolled although the patination is rather variable. The raw material is good quality and of local origin. Of the total number of artifacts 365 are waste flakes (70 per cent.), 69 are cores (13 per cent.), and the remainder (88 or 17 per cent.) are implements or fragments of the same. Only 2 per cent. of the artifacts had been burnt. A noteworthy feature of the percentages is the very high proportion of cores and implements in relation to the waste flakes. At the earlier Neolithic site of Hurst Fen, for example, which was of a domestic character, cores numbered 3 per cent. of the total as opposed to the 13 per cent. at Lion Point.[17] Furthermore, the implement percentage on domestic sites is normally 3 per cent. or 4 per cent. in contrast to the 17 per cent. at the locality under discussion. One must assume that no selection process was employed when the flints were collected from the foreshore and therefore that this process took place in Late Neolithic times. If these pits contain the rubbish from a living area then one would expect a high proportion of implements, but this does not explain the relatively large numbers of cores. One is left with the possibility that the cores and implements were deliberately selected for inclusion in the pits but the reason for this procedure is obscure, unless the pits had played a part in some ritual which involved the deposition of selected artifacts. The evidence to support this possibility is slender but similar depositories have been recorded in a ceremonial context at Durrington Walls[18] and at Brackmont Mill, Fife.[19]

The implements

A number of flakes showed signs of edge abrasion but in many cases it was uncertain whether this was due to utilization in Late Neolithic times or to subsequent wear and they have been left out of account. The implement types are as follows:

Scrapers	55	62·5 per cent.
Flakes with edge retouch	11	12·5
Polished-axe fragments	9	10
Transverse arrowheads	3	3·5
Knives	3	3·5
Serrated flakes	3	3·5
Borers	3	3·5
Flaked axe	1	1
Total	88	100 per cent.

The total number of implements is too small to enable any statistical comparisons to be made. The scraper is the most common implement type—a usual characteristic in Neolithic flint assemblages. Amongst the much larger collection of Late Neolithic flint artifacts from Durrington Walls, for example, scrapers also comprise 62 per cent. of the total and the range of implement types is much the same. Amongst the other implements the transverse arrowheads (Pl. xxxix, 7–9) are noteworthy as being typical of the British Late Neolithic flint industries and the polished axe fragments, knives, saws, and borers can all be paralleled in similar contexts either individually or collectively. The small serrated flake with a lustrous working edge (Pl. xxxix, 13) and the small chipped axe (Pl. xl, 2) do not occur commonly with Late Neolithic associations. The importance of the collection is that although small it can be associated beyond doubt with an uncontaminated group of Late Neolithic potsherds of Grooved Ware type. Such clear associations are rare and the group of artifacts derives importance from this fact.

Scrapers (Pl. xxxix, 1–6)

Scrapers are the most common implement type and comprise 62·5 per cent. of the total complement. This figure does not include the scrapers on cores noted below (see p. 121).

Class A	End scrapers	(i) Long[20]	(Pl. xxxix, 1)	5	42
		(ii) Short	(Pl. xxxix, 2–3)	37	
Class C	Disc		(Pl. xxxix, 6)	5	
Class D	Side	(i) Long		—	
		(ii) Short	(Pl. xxxix, 5)	2	
Class E	On broken flakes			5	
Class F	Hollow		(Pl. xxxix, 4)	1	
Total				55	

The most common types of scraper are those on the ends of fairly short flakes (67 per cent.). This may be due to frequent resharpening of the implement but is more likely to reflect the average flake size in Late Neolithic industries. A similar phenomenon has been noted in the scraper complement from the occupation floor on the West Kennet Avenue; but the scrapers from Lion Point are too few to enable any metrical analyses to be made. Other scraper types are not numerous and the double-ended form (Class B) is not present.

Flakes with edge retouch

This category includes those flakes with deliberate retouch along one or both edges and which could have been employed for a variety of tasks. After the scrapers they are the most common implement type.

Polished-axe fragments

Small chips of polished axes were recorded from seven cooking-holes (nos. 4–5, 8, 9, 12, 18, 19, and 23). In no case could the form of the parent axe be determined from them and their patination was uniformly denser than that of the associated flints. On these slender grounds it is possible to suggest that they are older than the other flints but if so one must assume that the axe chips were deliberately acquired and included in the pits—presumably as part of a ritualistic function. The evidence is not conclusive but is given added weight by the unusually high percentages of implements and cores which may have been deliberately selected for inclusion in the pits.

Transverse arrowheads

Three transverse arrowheads were recorded from cooking-hole nos. 4–5 (Pl. xxxix, 8), 7 (Pl. xxxix, 9), and 11 (Pl. xxxix, 7). These arrowheads have been classified according to the scheme propounded by Professor Clark in 1934[21] into classes E (Pl. xxxix, 7, 9) and F (Pl. xxxix, 8). Such arrowheads are frequently found amongst Late Neolithic flint industries.

Knives

Three knives of varied types were recorded amongst the material:

Pl. XL, 1. A pointed blade with flat retouch along one edge and inverse flat retouch along the opposite edge. The basal portion of the blade was not worked but presumably left to act as a handle (cooking-hole no. 19).

Pl. XXXIX, 11. The medial fragment of a blade of plano-convex section with flat retouch over its domed upper surface. The piece is too fragmentary for certainty but it seems likely that the knife is one of plano-convex type (cooking-hole no. 10).

Pl. XXXIX, 10. The central portion of a thick, bifacially worked blade of slightly plano-convex section with some indication of polish on both surfaces. It seems likely that this is a fragment of a large laurel-leaf blade, of which ten more or less complete examples have been found on the foreshore (cooking-hole no. 12).[22]

Serrated flakes

Three serrated flakes were found; one each in cooking-hole nos. 4–5 (Pl. XXXIX, 13), 8 (Pl. XXXIX, 12), and 11. Of these, one possessed lustre along one edge from cutting a silica-rich substance.

Borers

Three borers were found; one each in cooking-hole nos. 4–5, 12 (Pl. XL, 3) and 20. All are on thick ridged flakes with steep retouch defining the tip.

Flaked axe

A small flaked axe or cleaver was recorded from cooking-hole no. 6 (Pl. XL, 2). It has no special preparation of the chopping edge.

The cores

The industry produced a large number of cores—69 or 13 per cent. of the artifact total, which can be classified as follows:

Class A	1 platform	
	1. Flakes removed all round	7
	2. Flakes removed part of way round (Pl. XL, 5)	17
Class B	2 platforms	
	1. Parallel platforms	3
	2. One platform at oblique angle	–
	3. Platforms at right angles	4
Class D	Keeled: flakes struck from two directions	9
Class E	Discoidal (Pl. XL, 4 and 6)	13
Unclassifiable		16
	Total	69

The discoidal cores are of some technical interest as they are bifacially worked and could have been utilized as small chopping tools. In fact they are cores prepared in 'Levallois' fashion for the removal of short, broad flakes. Several cores exhibit scars where such flakes have been removed (Pl. XL, 4) and the recognition of this careful preparation of the cores is of some interest. Nearly 4 per cent. of all the cores had been subsequently utilized as scrapers.

Stone

Small fragments of sandstone were recorded from four cooking-holes (nos. 7, 10, 12 and 19). In addition a small chip of a polished greenstone axe of group I was recorded from cooking-hole no. 10.[23] Stone of west country origin was utilized from earliest Neolithic times and axes of group I have been found in Late Neolithic contexts in association with Grooved Ware at Woodhenge and probably Durrington Walls.

Details of stone artifacts from the cooking-holes

COOKING-HOLE 1

Implements:

Scrapers	3

By-products:

Flakes	3
Total	6

COOKING-HOLE 2

Implements:

Scrapers	1

By-products:

Flakes	1
Total	2

COOKING-HOLE 4–5

Implements:

Scrapers	12
Polished-axe fragments	1
Transverse arrowheads	1
Serrated flakes	1
Borers	1

By-products:

Flakes	9
Cores	7
Total	32

COOKING-HOLE 6

Implements:

Flaked axe	1

By-products:

Flakes	7
Total	8

COOKING-HOLE 7

Implements:

Scrapers	1
Transverse arrowheads	1

By-products:

Flakes	17
Cores	3
Total	22

COOKING-HOLE 8

Implements:

Scrapers	2
Flakes with edge retouch	3
Polished-axe fragments	1
Serrated flakes	1

By-products:

Flakes	17
Cores	3
Total	27

COOKING-HOLE 9

Implements:

Scrapers   1
Flakes with edge retouch   1
Polished-axe fragments   2

By-products:

Flakes   10
Cores   1
Total   15

COOKING-HOLE 10

Implements:

Scrapers   7
Knives   1

By-products:

Flakes   159
Cores   15
Total   182

Stone: one chip of a polished axe of a dark-coloured greenstone exhibiting the visible characteristics of Group 1.

COOKING-HOLE 11

Implements:

Scrapers   8
Flakes with edge retouch   3
Transverse arrowheads   1
Serrated flakes   1

By-products:

Flakes   23
Cores   6
Total   42

COOKING-HOLE 12

Implements:

Scrapers   6
Flakes with edge retouch   2
Polished-axe fragments   2
Knives   1
Borers   1

By-products:

Flakes   69
Cores   9
Total   90

COOKING-HOLE 13

By-products:

Flakes   1
Cores   2
Total   3

COOKING-HOLE 14

Implements:

Scrapers   1

By-products:

Flakes   3
Cooking   3
Total   7

COOKING-HOLE 15

By-products:

Flakes   1
Cores   1
Total   2

COOKING-HOLE 16

Implements:

Scrapers   1
Total   1

COOKING-HOLE 17

By-products:

Cores   3
Total   3

COOKING-HOLE 18

Implements:

Scrapers   2
Polished-axe fragments   1

By-products:	
Flakes	1
Cores	1
Total	5

COOKING-HOLE 19

Implements:

Scrapers	6
Polished-axe fragments	1
Knives	1

By-products:

Flakes	30
Cores	5
Total	43

COOKING-HOLE 20

Implements:

Scrapers	3
Flakes with edge retouch	1
Borers	1

By-products:	
Flakes	13
Cores	6
Total	24

COOKING-HOLE 21

By-products:

Flakes	1
Cores	2
Total	3

COOKING-HOLE 22

By-products:

Flakes	2
Cores	2
Total	4

COOKING-HOLE 23

Implements:

Polished-axe fragment	1
Total	1

G. J. WAINWRIGHT

CONCORDANCE

Plate XXXIII.

Grooved Ware: P1 = no. 1; P2 = no. 15.

Plate XXXIV.

Grooved Ware: P3 = nos. 5, 9, 12, 39, 51, 53, and 119; P4 = no. 50; P5 = no. 7; P6 = no. 92; P7 = no. 102; P8 = no. 133; P9 = no. 132.

Plate XXXV.

Grooved Ware: P10 = no. 78; P11 = no. 94; P12 = no. 127; P13 = no. 111; P14 = no. 87; P15 = no. 117; P16 = no.16; P17 = no. 93; P18 = no. 10; P19 = no. 116; P20 = no. 24; P21 = no. 17; P22 = no. 79; P23 = no. 116; P24 = no. 118; P25 = no. 114; P26 = no. 115; P27 = no. 112; P28 = no. 131; P29 = no. 4; P30 = no. 125; P31 = no. 70; P32 = no. 123; P33 = no. 130; P34 = no. 126; P35 = no. 40; P36 = no. 129; P37 = no. 124; P38 = no. 128; P39 = no. 121; P40 = no. 106; P41 = no. 99; P42 = no. 194.

Plate XXXVI.

Grooved Ware: P43 = no. 122; P44 = no. 71; P45 = no. 120; P46 = no. 113; P47 = no. 135; P48 = no. 139; P49 = no. 103; P50 = no. 3; P51 = no. 134; P52 = no. 138; P53 = no. 25; P54 = no. 141; P55 = no. 84; P56 = no. 142; P57 = no. 143; P58 = no. 145; P59 = no. 26; P60 = no. 140; P61 = no. 147; P62 = no. 149; P63 = no. 136; P64 = no. 100; P65 = no. 146; P66 = no. 27; P67 = no. 23; P68 = no. 60; P69 = no. 144; P70 = no. 137; P71 = no. 148.

Plate xxxvii.

Grooved Ware: P72 = no. 42; P73 = no. 150; P74 = no. 2; P75 = no. 44; P76 = no. 154; P77 = no. 98; P78 = no. 160; P79 = no. 54; P80 = no. 18; P81 = no. 162; P82 = no. 158; P83 = no. 6; P84 = no. 161; P85 = no. 170; P86 = no. 173; P87 = no. 62; P88 = no. 63; P89 = no. 157; P90 = no. 72; P91 = no. 155; P92 = no. 156; P93 = no. 52.

Plate xxxviii.

Grooved Ware: P94 = no. 11; P95 = no. 55; P96 = no. 85; P97 = no. 166; P98 = no. 43; P99 = no. 151; P100 = no. 152; P101 = no. 153; P102 = no. 107; P103 = no. 172; P104 = no. 101; P105 = no. 68; P106 = no. 88; P107 = no. 165; P108 = no. 164; P109 = no. 168; P110 = no. 171; P111 = no. 169; P112 = no. 167; P113 = no. 28; P114 = no. 74; P115 = no. 163; P116 = no. 96; P117 = no. 83; P118 = no. 159; P119 = no. 81; P120 = no. 82.

Plate xxxix.

Flints: nos. 3, 4, 6, 8, and 12 from cooking-hole 4–5; no. 9 from cooking-hole 7; no. 13 from cooking-hole 8; nos. 5 and 11 from cooking-hole 10; no. 7 from cooking-hole 11; no. 10 from cooking-hole 12; no. 2 from cooking-hole 16; and no. 1 from cooking-hole 20.

Plate xl.

Flints: nos. 4 and 6 from cooking-hole 4–5; no. 2 from cooking-hole 6; nos. 3 and 5 from cooking-hole 12; and no. 1 from cooking-hole 19.

[1] S. H. Warren, S. Piggott, J. G. D. Clark, M. C. Burkitt, and H. and M. E. Godwin, 1936. Archaeology of the Submerged Land-Surface of the Essex Coast, *P.P.S.* ii. 178–210. [2] Ibid.
[3] S. H. Warren, 1926. The Classification of the Lower Palaeolithic with special reference to Essex, *Trans. S.E. Union Sci. Soc.* 38–50.
[4] W. A. E. Ussher, 1879. Historical Geology of Cornwall, *Geol. Mag.*, Dec. ii, vol. vi, 32.
[5] K. P. Oakley, 1959. The Life and Work of Samuel Hazzledine Warren, F.G.S., *Essex Naturalist*, xxx. 5, 143–7.
[6] S. H. Warren, 1919. The Dating of Surface Flint Implements, *P.P.S.E.A.* iii. 96.
[7] S. H. Warren, *et al.*, 1936. Op. cit.
[8] S. H. Warren and I. F. Smith, 1953. Neolithic pottery from the Submerged Land-Surface of the Essex Coast, *Inst. Arch. Annual Rep.* 1952–3, 26.
[9] S. H. Warren, 1958. Manuscript Partial Emergency Catalogue of Warren Bequests (at British Museum).
[10] S. H. Warren, *et al.*, 1936. Op. cit.
[11] Ibid.
[12] S. H. Warren and I. F. Smith, 1953. Op. cit.
[13] S. H. Warren, 1958. Op. cit.
[14] I am indebted to Mr. P. C. Compton of the Department of Prehistoric and Romano-British

Antiquities for all the pottery drawings in this report, and for executing Figs. 1–3. I should also like to record my grateful thanks to my wife, Clare, for her help in preparing the pottery catalogue.

[15] S. Piggott in S. H. Warren, *et al.*, 1936, op. cit., p. 191.
[16] S. Piggott, 1954. *The Neolithic Cultures o, the British Isles*, p. 344.
[17] J. G. D. Clark, E. S. Higgs, and I. H. Longworth, 1960. Excavations at the Neolithic site at Hurst Fen, Mildenhall, Suffolk, 1954, 1957 and 1958, *P.P.S.* xxvi. 214.
[18] Report forthcoming.
[19] I. H. Longworth, 1968. Further discoveries at Brackmont Mill, Brackmont Farm and Tentsmuir, Fife, *P.S.A.S.* xcix. 60–92.
[20] i.e. the length is more than 1·5 times the breadth.
[21] J. G. D. Clark, 1934. Derivative forms of the *Petit Tranchet* in Britain, *Arch. J.* xci. 32–58.
[22] S. H. Warren, *et al.*, 1936. Op. cit., p. 204, figs. 12, 21 and 22.
[23] E. D. Evens, L. V. Grinsell, S. Piggott, and F. S. Wallis, 1962. Fourth Report of the Sub-Committee of the South-Western Group of Museums and Art Galleries on the Petrological Identification of Stone Axes, *P.P.S.* xxviii. 260, Serial No. 892.

THE PIERCEBRIDGE PLOUGH GROUP

THE tiny bronze model of a man ploughing with a pair of oxen (Pls. XLI, XLII, and Fig. 1) found at Piercebridge, County Durham,[1] is well known to students both of Roman Britain and of ancient agriculture, but it does not appear to have been the subject of a full discussion before.[2] Apparently found early in the nineteenth century it passed through a number of hands before being bought at Lord Londesborough's sale at Sotheby's in 1879 by Augustus Wollaston Franks and presented by him to the British Museum.[3]

Although engravings and photographs of it have been published on a number of occasions they have often failed to do justice to the skill with which the group is modelled, partly because they usually make it appear larger than it actually is,[4] and partly as a result of the smooth, darkly patinated surface which makes it an extremely difficult subject for the photographer. Its condition is indeed remarkable for it is free of even the slightest trace of corrosion, and apart from the loss of the long goad originally held in the ploughman's right hand, it must be just as it left the workshop. Examining it one is at once struck by the skill of the artist, the tiniest details are rendered: the features of the ploughman and of the oxen, the man's thumb which curves around the butt of the goad, the cloven hooves of the animals—all are perfectly clear, though measuring only millimetres. Nor has corrosion marred and blurred this clarity; here we have a ploughman and his team with most of the details clear to see.

Method of manufacture

Technically the model is a *cire-perdue* casting, the original being modelled in wax.[5] With so small a piece it would not be necessary to have a clay or sand core and it is probably solid bronze. After casting it must have been cleaned up, probably by someone other than the original modeller, for he failed to remove the strip (originally of wax) which had served to support the right arm when the figure was encased in clay. This strip, which is now quite meaningless in the general design of the group, can be seen running from the man's right buttock to his right elbow (Pl. XLIII *a*); without it the extended arm and goad would have been in danger of distortion or of breakage when the clay mould was made. It would have had the additional advantage of acting as a riser through which the molten metal could flow during the casting process; but when the model was removed from the mould, of course, it should have been chiselled away before the final polishing. A drawing of the model with this strip removed can be seen in Fig. 1, and the arbitrary way in which it was squashed on can clearly be seen

125

in Pl. XLIII *a*. If the suggestion that the group was not finished by the original modeller is correct, and he would scarcely have left the strip in place, we may see in it some evidence for its being made in a workshop, in which individual workmen had their tasks, rather than by a single man. Whether it was made to order or not we cannot tell, but the mere fact that it is a *cire-perdue* casting indicates that it was probably a unique piece.

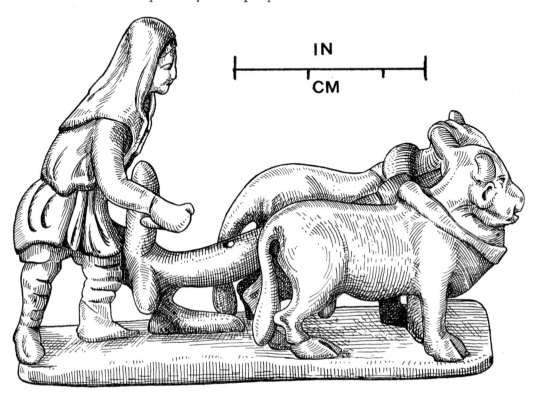

FIG. 1. The Piercebridge statuette with casting strip removed.

The ploughman

The skill of the modeller is seen nowhere more clearly than in the ploughman himself. He is pressing forward over the plough, with his left knee braced against the stilt while his left hand grasps its top. His right leg is pushed back, with the foot turned out to gain the maximum thrust. The tiny figure wonderfully conveys the sense of strain and physical effort which the man is putting into his work. His right hand is pushed forward in a way which now appears meaningless until one notices the butt which is projecting back from the palm (Pl. XLIV *a*), all that remains of the long ox-goad with which he was urging the beasts forward.[6] On both hands only the thumb is clearly modelled, but it gives sufficient form to the

126

hand to make the rendering of the fingers unnecessary. His face is slightly marred by the flattening of his nose (Pl. xLv), probably accidentally squashed when the original wax model was encased in clay. The eyes, and mouth, however, are carefully modelled, and just below the front of the hood there appears a slight fringe of hair. Although the size of the head makes the features little more than sketches, they are well proportioned and lack the distortions common in Celtic representations of the head. He is clean shaven. The rest of his body is concealed by clothing. The main garment is a loose tunic, caught in at the waist, no doubt by a belt, although this detail is hidden by the overhanging tunic, the easy folds of which show clearly that it is made of cloth. On the left forearm are a number of slight ridges which must represent the creases of a sleeve, presumably of the tunic. The skirt of this tunic ends just above the knees and his legs are protected by close-fitting garments indicated by a series of horizontal ridges around the legs (Pls. xLI and xLIII *b*). Although trousers would be a possibility these normally ended just below the knee and would scarcely hang in such unnatural folds as these. Rather the impression is of some form of leggings made by winding strips of cloth around the legs, an obvious and simple form of protection. They lack the regularity of the leggings made from a single piece of wide cloth which are seen on some continental reliefs.[7] His feet are merely indicated without any details of their covering, but the absence of toes, in contrast to the carefully modelled thumbs or the cloven hooves of the oxen, suggest that they are protected by shoes. His head and shoulders are covered by a hooded cape, with broad flaps at the front which are drawn across his chest and fastened at a single point below the neck (Pl. xLv). At the back the cape runs down to a point below his shoulders, and has a fold or seam along its midline. It has a rather stiff appearance, markedly in contrast with the free folds of the tunic, and there can be little doubt that the sculptor is indicating a leather garment, a material ideally suited for a protective cape. A careful examination of the figure and the details of his dress makes it even more clear that the strip running from the tail of his tunic to his right elbow has no place in the design. It cannot be part of his clothes and it cannot be anything else! Only as a support for the arm during casting does it make sense.

As Dr. J. P. Wild has recently pointed out a short hooded cape, tunic, and leggings were the common garments of the countryman in the north-western provinces of the Roman Empire.[8] Many examples could be quoted from a wide area; for example the mounted huntsman on a relief from Neumagen (Holland),[9] or the bronze figure from Trier, which is a very close match for our figure. There also the cape is clearly made of leather but with the stitching plainly marked along the edges and across the hood.[10] A similar hood, with a hole for fastening it immediately below the man's chin, can be seen on a deer-hunt relief on a Gallic sarcophagus.[11] A second man in the same scene is probably wearing a similar hood, though it is thrown back on his shoulders, while a third hunter wears leggings which may be formed of material wound around his calves, although the regularity of the turns, and the even finish at the top and bottom suggest that the strips may be sewn together. Another hooded figure is seen strolling in the foreground of a villa scene in a wall painting from Trier.[12] The costume appears again on Italian sarcophagi decorated with hunting scenes, and makes it clear that the farm worker was not the only person to favour this style of dress, for his master might wear it when in the country. Such detailed examples are less common in Britain, but this is the result, at least in part, of the relative rarity of reliefs. That hooded garments were common is shown by the figure of winter on the 'seasons' mosaics[13] and by the reliefs of the Genii Cucullati.[14]

The oxen

The oxen present a contrast to the ploughman; he is straining forward, pressing against the plough and urging them on with the goad, while they stand four-square and still, their heads turned slightly inwards (Pl. XLIV *b*). They seem to be eternally at the beginning of a furrow, at that moment when the ploughman has braced himself and is about to urge the beasts forward—all is ready and in a moment the ploughing will begin. The oxen themselves are rendered with almost as much care as the ploughman. The cloven hooves are carefully indicated, the heavy square faces and short horns, all are there; only in the exaggerated concave curve of the hind legs does reality waver. Their sex is clearly indicated; the right hand animal is male, not merely are the sexual organs carefully modelled, but it has the massive square face of the bull. The other animal lacks such obvious indications of its sex, but the absence of an udder need not make us doubt that it is a cow. Nor is its face as large and broad as the bull's.

The modelling of the inner side of the animals' faces, particularly of the cow, is very imperfect. Possibly they were intended to be seen from the side rather than the front, but more probably the inner face was damaged when the wax model was assembled, or encased for casting. Although one cannot be certain, it seems likely that the main elements of the group were modelled individually before being arranged and finished, and the sculptor might well feel that damage done at the last moment at a point where it was not clearly visible did not justify his dismantling the whole piece. If the damage was done as the piece was encased it might not be obvious until the casting was completed, in which event little could be done to remedy it.

With the yoke, however, the sculptor has abandoned minute realism and is content with a more generalized sketch. The yoke and the bands about the beasts' necks are all merged into one, with the yoke arching up over the necks of the oxen on either side of the draught pole to run straight into the bands (Pls. XLVI and XLVII *a*). The junction of the pole and yoke is equally generalized, and we cannot look to the Piercebridge model for the details of Roman yokes. All that one can safely say is the sculptor was not representing an elaborate yoke of the form seen on some continental reliefs but a simple piece of farm gear.[15] The method of yoking oxen to a plough or cart is shown in a number of models, reliefs and mosaics.[16] In each case the ends of the yoke project just beyond the necks of the animals and it is held by a band or strap which passes under the ox's throat. The outer end of this band is tied or fastened in some other way to the end of the yoke while the inner end goes around the yoke between the animal and the draught pole. There is no doubt that the collar-like appearance of our yoke and bands is largely the result of casting it in a single piece, and one may note that the detail of the Arrezzo model, for example, was achieved by casting the components separately and then assembling the group.

The plough[17]

It is when we turn to the plough itself that we reach the point of greatest interest and most difficulty (Pls. xlvii *b* and xliii *b*). Relatively little has been written about this plough. Gow mentioned it in passing;[18] the present writer once dismissed it as 'not modelled in detail', although 'there is little doubt that it is an ard';[19] while K. D. White commented that it 'looks more like the "one-piece" plough represented by the Arrezzo model',[20] but offered no further comment. In any discussion one must begin by deciding how far it represents an actual plough, and how far the sculptor has allowed himself the freedom of stylization. As we have seen, the ploughman and his oxen are modelled with considerable fidelity but the yoke is more stylized, though its main form is not distorted. Taking these facts into consideration it seems reasonable to assume that the plough is essentially a representation of an actual plough, but one lacking the finer details. It consists basically of three parts (Pls. xli, xlii, and xliii *b*): the plough-head or sole which curves up into the stilt; the beam which is straight and meets the stilt just above the curve of the plough-head and, on either side of this junction, a pair of forward curving arms. The end of the plough-head as we see it is square cut, but as it is sloping down into the ground it is probably not the true tip. The stilt has no separate handle, and the left hand of the ploughman is shown grasping it a little way from its top. The beam is straight and runs without a break up to the yoke, which is fastened to it just before its end. Where it passes between the flanks of the oxen it is fused to them (Pls. xlvi and xlvii *a*), probably as a result of a defect in the casting. The left leg of the ploughman is similarly fused to the stilt. About a quarter of the way along the beam from its junction with the stilt there is a round hole which runs vertically into it but does not appear on the lower side (Pls. xlvi and xlvii *a, b*). There can be no doubt that this hole is part of the design.

The interpretation of this plough presents a number of problems, but one must always remember that it is of minute size and that the artist probably did not regard it as the most important part of the composition; neither it nor the yoke are modelled with the same care as the man and his oxen. The detail is inevitably schematized; for example, one cannot say that the stilt passes through the beam or vice versa, for they merge in a general junction with the side arms (Pl. XLIII *b*).[21] The absence of a true handle is probably another simplification. Such a handle appears to have been normal on the Scandinavian ards[22] and it would have been difficult to control the plough by merely holding the almost vertical stilt. Although the plough models from Germany and Sussex lack a separate handle the end of the stilt is turned down to form one, and the angle of the stilt is by no means as severe as in our model (Fig. 3). Nor in reality are all the timbers of the plough likely to have been of rounded section. The Danish ards and the plough models all have squared timbers.

The common plough of north-western Europe in the Roman period appears to have been the bow-ard[23] (Fig. 2), while in the Mediterranean regions it was more commonly the sole-ard.[24] After a detailed examination of the Piercebridge statuette the present writer has concluded that it represents a modified form of the bow-ard. The original type is illustrated by a group of models from Germany and Sussex (Fig. 3), as well as by the actual examples from Scandinavian and Scottish peat bogs.[25] These have the stilt and plough-head made in one piece usually with a curve so that in use the stilt leaned towards the ploughman (Fig. 2*a*). The lower part of the stilt runs through the beam which is curved down at its rear end.[26] Most of the Danish examples were equipped with an arrow-shaped main-share and a bar-like fore-share, with the tangs of both running through the same hole in the beam as the stilt, and with their tangs wedged against the stilt (Fig. 2*a*). It is known that this general type of ard, but fitted with an iron fore-share and coulter, was used in Roman Britain in the fourth century A.D.[27] It would be very difficult, however, to argue that the plough represented on the Piercebridge model ever carried such a long fore-share. As far as one can tell the plough-head is almost rectangular and the curve of the stilt and position of the beam does not allow for a bar share. If then our plough lacked such a share it must either not have had an iron share, which seems improbable, or carried one of a different type. In fact a variety of share which would fit directly on to the plough-head is known from Roman contexts,[28] including London and Frindsbury, Kent.[29] They are heavy symmetrical shares, with a triangular blade and flanged socket (Fig. 4). When the plough was in operation the point of the share would be buried in the soil giving the rather square-cut appearance of the Piercebridge model.

Two main objections may be made to this suggestion that the Piercebridge plough is a modified form of bow-ard. The first is that the beam does not curve

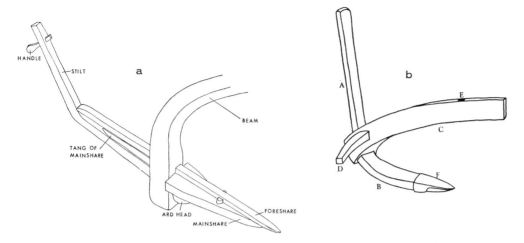

FIG. 2(a) Bow-ard (based on the Donnerup ard) after H. C. Bowen, *Ancient Fields*.
FIG. 2(b) Conjectural reconstruction of the Piercebridge plough.

- A Stilt.
- B Plough head.
- C Beam.
- D Support for earth-board.
- E Hole for coulter.
- F Iron share.

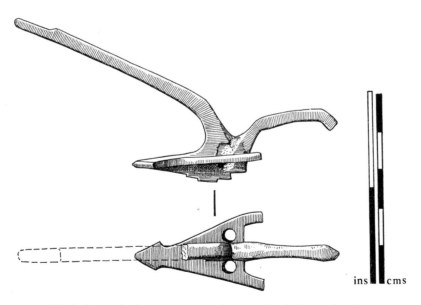

FIG. 3. Bronze model of a bow-ard with an arrow-shaped share and paired earth-boards. From Sussex (B.M.)

down sufficiently at its junction with the stilt; the second is that the stilt itself rises almost vertically rather than curving back towards the ploughman. In the normal bow-ard the beam must meet the stilt in such a way that the tanged shares can pass through it at the required angle and have room to lodge in the stilt, hence the pronounced downward curve of the beam and the space between

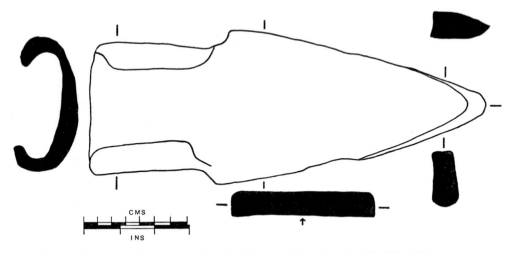

FIG. 4. Symmetrical flanged share from Bucklersbury House, London (Guildhall Museum).

the beam and stilt (Fig. 2*a*). If tanged shares are not used this is unnecessary, and the beam can meet the stilt without so pronounced a curve. It is unfortunate that our model shows least detail at precisely this point, for without greater delicacy of modelling a slight curve could not be indicated, even if it existed in the original plough. It is also possible that the angle of the stilt has been exaggerated, though it must have been quite steep in reality. One must remember that if it were to be sloped back, the length of the statuette would be markedly increased; and the artist may have preferred to sacrifice strict accuracy for a more compact general effect.

Two other features need to be discussed. The first is the pair of thick heavy arms which protrude and curve slightly forward at the junction of the beam and stilt (Pls. xlvii *b* and xliii *b*). Gow was of the opinion[30] that they could 'not be earth-boards as they point forwards. Possibly they are footrests to assist the ploughman in throwing his weight onto the share'. Against this suggestion is the fact that they are placed in such a position that if the ploughman were to throw his weight on them he would probably tilt the share out of the ground. The most probable explanation of their use is that they are not earth-boards in themselves but the supports for earth-boards.[31] All of the plough models from Germany as well as that from Sussex have these earth-boards which run back

132

from the tip of the share to the base of the stilt, where they are supported by arms (Fig. 3). The classical references, as well as common sense, indicate that they could be easily removed if they were not needed, and in the Piercebridge model we may see a plough in which this has been done. The other detail of note is the hole which runs into the top of the beam just above the tip of the plough-head (Pls. XLVI and XLVII *a, b*). If we accept this as an intentional feature, and it is difficult to do otherwise, it is most probably intended to receive a coulter.[32] Coulters like earth-boards could be removed with ease and were only used when the work required them.

If this reconstruction of the type of plough represented by the Piercebridge model is correct, it becomes of considerable interest as a unique, and reasonably detailed illustration of a type otherwise known only from the iron fittings: a bow-ard in its relationship of beam, stilt, and plough-head, but with a flanged share fitting directly on to the plough-head, and with detachable earth-boards and coulter. A tentative reconstruction is shown in Fig. 2*b*.

The date and origin of the model

The statuette bears no obvious stylistic or other indication of its date within the Roman period, and there is no reason to disagree with Professor Toynbee's suggestion of a date in the second or third century A.D.[33] The site at Piercebridge is best known as a fort, probably built at the end of the third century under Constantius and continuing in use throughout the fourth century, but many finds indicate earlier occupation dating back to the second century and lasting throughout the third.[34] There is thus no difficulty in reconciling the date of the site with the date proposed for the statuette.

The style of the statuette would accord with its being made in a provincial workshop in Britain, Gaul, or Germany, and without other evidence one cannot decide which, but as it was found in Britain a British origin would seem likely. There is of course no reason to suppose that it was made at Piercebridge.

Function and significance

Bronzes were not normally intended purely as ornaments in the Roman world, and the majority of small bronzes are representations of deities, or have some votive significance. A number of other models representing ploughing scenes are known from the ancient world, but the majority tend to be earlier in date than ours, and their relevance to it, if any, is uncertain.[35] In the writer's opinion the Piercebridge statuette carries clear evidence that it was of a religious nature. Whether the ploughman is himself divine is an open question. One may note that he appears to be quite disproportionately tall in comparison with the oxen, indeed were he standing upright instead of bending forward their flanks would scarcely reach his waist. If his height has been exaggerated it would strongly suggest that he is a divine being, but it is perhaps unwise to make too much of this comparison. Nor does his costume make his status clearer. As we have observed, he wears the usual clothes of a ploughman, and while his hood may make him comparable with the Genii Cucullati, and the statuette was certainly found in an area where those deities were worshipped,[36] one cannot divorce the hood from the remainder of his costume.

Of much greater significance is the use of a bull and a cow in the same team. This is not normal, nor is it a very suitable combination for they are matched neither in size nor strength. Yet the care with which the sculptor has indicated their sex shows that it was important. The use of such an odd team suggests the possibility of a religious significance and there is excellent literary evidence from the classical world to show that the combination of bull and cow in a single plough team was used for at least one major religious ceremony. This was in ploughing the furrow which marked out the line to be followed by the walls of a city—the *pomerium*. Plutarch in his life of Romulus[37] describes how a cow and bull were yoked together to plough the *pomerium* of Rome, but the most detailed description comes from Servius who was citing Cato:

VRBEM DESIGNAT ARATRO quem Cato in originibus dicit morem fuisse. conditores enim civitatis tauram in dexteram, vaccam intrinsecus iungebant, et incincti ritu Gabino, id est togae parte caput velati, parte succincti, tenebant stivam incurvam, ut glebae omnes intrinsecus caderent.[38]

'He marks out the city with a plough', which Cato in his Origins says was the custom. For the founders of a state used to yoke a bull to the right and a cow on the inside and girt in the Gabine manner, i.e. their heads covered with part of their togas, and with part drawn up, they held a plough handle curved so that all the clods fall inwards.[39]

One may note that our bull and cow are in the positions required by Cato, and although our ploughman is not wearing a toga it may be significant that his head is covered with a hood. It would be unwise, however, to suggest that the model necessarily represents the ploughing of the sacred *pomerium* around a city, although it could well do so, for other religious ceremonies may have required such a team. We are after all dealing with a Romano-Celtic statuette, with the ploughman dressed in Celtic rather than classical manner, and of the details of Celtic religion we know relatively little. But there can be no reasonable doubt that the Piercebridge statuette represents a religious or divine scene.[40]

W. H. MANNING

[1] The Roman name of Piercebridge was apparently *Magis*.

[2] Early in the nineteenth century it was described and illustrated in William B. Scott's *Antiquarian Gleanings in the North of England*, 10, pl. xviii. Cf. also Gow, 257, fig. 8; *Guide to the Antiquities of Roman Britain* (British Museum)

1964), 54, no. 13, pl. 16; Toynbee (1962), 149, no. 54, pl. 60; Manning (1964), 57, fig. 4B; White 143, pl. 11 *b*.

[3] It is now in the Department of Prehistoric and Romano-British Antiquities. Registration number 79. 7–10. 1.

[4] It is 6·9 cm. long and 4·5 cm. high.

5 This is the obvious method of making it, for although small bronzes were sometimes produced in piece-moulds (e.g. the bronze plough model from Sussex (Fig. 3) which was made in a mould of at least five pieces (Manning (1966), 55, fig. 1)) this would scarcely be practical for a group of this complexity. The complete absence of any sign of casting flashes confirms that it was not mould-made.

6 Men driving oxen were usually shown with such a goad, e.g. the ploughman on the St. Romain-en-Gal mosaic (G. Lafaye *Revue Arch.* 3ᵉ, ser. xix (1892), 323–47, no. 25), and the driver of the ox-cart on the Piazza Armerina mosaic (Pace, pl. 19).

7 e.g. the huntsman from Neumagen (Wild, 184, fig. 11, 1) and a bronze figure from Trier (Wild, 185).

8 Wild, 185.

9 Wild, 183, fig. 11, 1.

10 Wild, 185. I am indebted to Dr. Wild for showing me a photograph of this figure.

11 Pobé and Roubier, pl. 96.

12 Pobé and Roubier, pl. 167.

13 e.g. Lullingstone (Toynbee (1962), pl. 228), Bignor (Toynbee (1962), pl. 218), and Chedworth (Toynbee (1962), pl. 216).

14 Toynbee (1957).

15 Elaborate yokes are known from a number of sources, cf. *Germania*, xxiii (1939), 56.

16 e.g. the plough model from Arrezzo (Gow, pl. xviii) and the cart on the Piazza Armerina mosaic (Pace, pl. 19).

17 It would be correct to call it an *ard*, but this would probably be confusing. An ard in Scandinavian literature is a symmetrical plough without a mould board.

18 Gow, 257.

19 Manning (1964), 57.

20 White, 143.

21 The most recent classification of plough types (Sach, 1968) uses the relationship of the beam, stilt, and sole as a key criterion.

22 Cf. the Døstrup ard (Glob, fig. 37).

23 Manning (1964), 55 ff. The bow-ard (Fig. 2a) is a symmetrical type with a curved bow-like beam and stilt, the latter terminating in an inclined share (cf. Glob, 109). It is Sach's Type III (Døstrup type) (Sach, 12).

24 White, 127 ff., and Gow, 249 ff. The soleard has a narrow horizontal sole, with the share at its tip and with the beam and stilt separately mortised into it. The sole continues behind the stilt as a heel on which the ploughman can press

his foot to prevent the plough riding up. It is Sach's Type VIII (Triptolemus type) (Sach, 14). Sach includes the crook-ard of the Scandinavian archaeologists (Glob, 14 ff.) in this type, but one should note that in these the sole and beam are made in one, only the stilt being mortised in. Variants probably existed in both areas, but most of our knowledge is derived from reliefs, models, and mosaics with the result that the detail is often obscure or suspect.

25 For the German models cf. Haberey Abb. 2, 24 and Abb. 4, 1; for the Sussex model (Fig. 3) cf. Manning (1966), fig. 1; for the Scandinavian ards (Fig. 2a) cf. Glob, especially figs. 28–9 (Donnerupland ard) and fig. 37 (Døstrup ard). The Scottish examples are a plough-head and stilt from Milton Loch Crannog and a beam from Lochmaben, Dumfriesshire (Fenton, 269, pl. xliv, 1 and fig. 3).

26 The Danish examples form Sach's Type III; the German models his Type IV (Sach, 12).

27 Manning (1964), 60 ff.

28 They are known from Britain (note 29 below), Gaul (Manning (1964), 60, note 35) and Italy (from Pompeii—v. White, fig. 110a, after F. Petrie, *Tools and Weapons*, pl. 67, no. 34). They would fit a modified bow-ard or a sole-ard. It is possible that the share of the models from Sussex (Fig. 3) (Manning (1966), fig. 1), Rodenkirchen (Haberey, Abb. 2, 24) and another from an unknown German findspot (Haberey, Abb. 4, 2) are of this type. These models are not sufficiently detailed to make this point certain, but they could also be arrow-shaped tanged shares as the share of the Cologne model certainly is (Haberey, Abb. 4, 1).

29 London (Fig. 4) (Manning (1964), 60, fig. 5F); Frindsbury (*Arch. Cant.* lxv (1952), 156, pl. i). The asymmetrical shares from Brading, Folkestone, and Dinorben (Manning (1964), 64, fig. 5C) would also fit such a plough head.

30 Gow, 257.

31 Earthboards or ground-wrests are the *aures* (ears) of the Latin agricultural writers. They can be seen on the Sussex and German models (cf. note 25 above) as narrow boards which run back from the tip of the share to the base of the stilt (Fig. 3). They were used to ridge the earth and to make furrows to improve the drainage (Varro, *R.R.* 1, xxix, 2, and Pliny, *N.H.* xviii. xlviii).

32 Manning (1964), 64, note 65. A most unlikely alternative is that it received an arrow-shaped share of the type seen on a crook-ard from

Dabergotz (Glob, 23, fig. 16, and Sach, 14). It may be noted that the hole in our model is just above the front of the plough-head, a position far better suited for a coulter than an inclined share.

[33] Toynbee (1962), 149, no. 54.

[34] R. Harper, *Trans. Architect. and Archaeol. Soc. of Durham and Northd.* N.S. i. 33; and information from Dr. M. G. Jarrett.

[35] Several are illustrated in Gow.

[36] Toynbee (1957).

[37] Plutarch, *Romulus* 11.

[38] Servius, *ad Aen.* v. 755 (citing Cato, *Origines*, fr. 1. 18. Jord.).

[39] If the plough is tilted to one side during the ploughing it will turn the sod even if the plough is symmetrical and lacks a mould board. A photograph in F. Payne, 'The Plough in Ancient Britain' (*Arch. Journ.* civ (1947), pl. vii) shows this being done in the Himalayas. The importance of all the clods falling inwards is emphasized by Plutarch.

[40] In preparing this paper I have received help and information from Miss C. M. Johns, Mrs. M. O. Manning, Mr. D. Brothwell, Mr. P. T. Eden, Mr. A. Fenton, Professor F. R. D. Goodyear, Mr. K. S. Painter, and Dr. J. P. Wild. The photographs are the work of Mrs. G. Booth. Figs. 1 and 3 were drawn by Miss M. O. Miller.

BIBLIOGRAPHY

Fenton   Fenton, A.: Early and Traditional Cultivating Implements in Scotland, *Proc. Soc. Ant. Scot.* xcvi (1962–3), 264 ff.

Glob   Glob, P. V.: *Ard og Plov* (1951).

Gow   Gow, A. S. F.: The Ancient Plough, *Journ. Hellenic Studies*, xxxiv (1914), 249 ff.

Haberey   Haberey, W.: Gravierte Glasschale und sogenannte Mithrassymbole aus einem spätrömischen Grabe von Rodenkirchen bei Köln, *Bonner Jahrb.* cxlix (1949), 94 ff.

Manning (1964)   Manning, W. H.: The Plough in Roman Britain, *Journ. Roman Studies*, liv (1964), 54 ff.

Manning (1966)   Manning, W. H.: A Group of Bronze Models from Sussex in the British Museum, *Antiquaries Journ.* xlvi (1966), 50 ff.

Pace   Pace, M.: *I Mosaici di Piazza Armerina* (1955).

Pobé and Roubier   Pobé M., and Roubier, J.: *The Art of Roman Gaul* (1961).

Sach   Sach, F.: Proposal for the Classification of Pre-Industrial Tilling Implements, *Tools and Tillage* i. 1 (1968), 3 ff.

Toynbee (1957)   Toynbee, J. M. C.: Genii Cucullati: *Colln. Latomus*, xxviii (1957), 456–69.

Toynbee (1962)   Toynbee, J. M. C.: *Art in Roman Britain* (1962).

White   White, K. D.: *Agricultural Implements of the Roman World* (1967).

Wild   Wild, J. P.: Clothing in the north-west Provinces of the Roman Empire, *Bonner Jahrb.* clxviii (1968), 166 ff.

UPPER PALAEOLITHIC ENGRAVED PIECES IN THE BRITISH MUSEUM

A COMPARATIVE ANALYSIS OF TWO FRAGMENTS BY NEW METHODS

THE Upper Palaeolithic collections in the British Museum include almost 200 engraved and sculptured objects of bone and stone which have traditionally been categorized as objects of 'art' or 'decoration'. The majority of these pieces are found in three historically important century-old collections of French materials: that of Henri Christy, largely from the Magdalenian sites of La Madeleine (after which the period is named), Les Eyzies and Laugerie Basse, and those of the Viscount de Lastic-Saint-Jal and Peccadeau de l'Isle, containing materials from the Magdalenian sites of Trou des Forges and Montastruc at Bruniquel. The materials from these sites were crucial in the early development of the science of Old World Prehistory, and they still constitute basic collections in this field, but the pieces are now scattered; in addition to the British Museum they are found in the Musée des Antiquités Nationales (Saint-Germain-en-Laye), the Musée de l'Homme (Paris), the Musée d'Histoire Naturelle (Montauban), and in collections at Toulouse, Talence, Les Eyzies, Périgueux, and Cambridge. The British Museum materials are, therefore, important not only historically but as documents necessary for a comprehensive and comparative study of Upper Palaeolithic European engraving.

The British Museum collection has two engraved artifacts from the Aurignacian site of the Gorge d'Enfer, which are among the earliest engraved objects found and published by Lartet and Christy. These are among the few engraved objects known from this period. The Museum also has some pieces from Cresswell Crags and Church Hole in England, as well as single pieces from other sites on the Continent. An examination and analysis of these materials in the British Museum by a stereoscopic zoom microscope with a magnification range of 10 × to 60 × has significantly supplemented the research results obtained by the author during a five-year programme of microscopic and comparative analysis on the Continent.[1]

In the long-term programme the methods adopted were both internal and comparative. As part of the study, all of the available engraved pieces from a single site and a single level were subjected to microscopic analysis. The data from the different levels of one site were then compared with the data obtained from comparable levels in other sites that were regionally and temporally related.

Cross-cultural comparisons were then conducted among the different European Upper Palaeolithic engraving traditions: Franco-Cantabrian, the East Gravettian, and the Mediterranean. Finally, an evolutionary development was established for each of these regional and temporal traditions and an attempt was made to determine the common cognitive and stylistic characteristics and influences among them. Internal and comparative analysis revealed an unexpected *cognitive* and *symbolic* complexity, as well as technical and stylistic differences, in the engraving traditions of the late Upper Pleistocene. Since the methodology and results are new, I present here the analysis of two small, apparently insignificant fragments from the Aurignacian and Late Magdalenian in the British Museum collection to illustrate the scope of the findings and the nature of the analytical problems involved in the microscopic, comparative method.

AURIGNACIAN (*c.* 32,000–25,000 B.C.)

An engraved fragment (8 cm.) of shaped and flattened bone from the Abri Lartet in the Gorge d'Enfer in the Vézère valley of the Dordogne was described by Lartet and Christy as a 'Bone knife-like Implement, notched and scored'.[2] The fragment has a deteriorated surface, a heavy soil encrustation, and it has been additionally covered by a protective coat of shellac. This combination has made microscopic analysis somewhat more difficult than usual (Fig. 1 and Pls. XLVIII and XLIX), but at the same time it has highlighted the value and significance of the comparative method. The fragment belongs to a class of engraved mobiliary artifact which has been found in the earliest Upper Palaeolithic levels (the Chatelperronian of Arcy-sur-Cure) and with increasing frequency in the later periods. In Lartet and Christy's volume an essay was devoted to what were called these 'tally' pieces.[3]

Recently A. Leroi-Gourhan suggested that these marked objects should be differentiated from the art, symbolism, and signs of the caves: 'these . . . objects . . . were long ago named "marques de chasse", "hunting tallies". Needless to say, nothing has been discovered to support this designation: the idea of the hunter consistently making a notch on his small stick every time he brought down a mammoth is more entertaining than plausible. Whatever the purpose of these objects, their occurrence throughout the Upper Palaeolithic is a remarkable phenomenon. The earliest representation we have of a rhythmic arrangement with regular intervals, the beginning of the evolution that led to the ruler, the musical staff, the calendar . . .'.[4] In 1958 Karel Absolon, on the basis of the East Gravettian of Moravia, Czechoslovakia, tentatively suggested that they indicated the use of a 'decimal' system of numbers based on a finger count and the numbers '5' and '10'.[5] Despite a century of research, there has been no generally acceptable theory for an explanation of these marks and particularly no methodology or technology for their study. The piece in the British Museum, because of its condition, would, by itself, offer no opportunity for a clarification of the problem.

Fortunately the fragment in London from the Gorge d'Enfer may be related to a companion piece, a bone 'knife' at Saint-Germain-en-Laye[6] from the same site and level and made in the same style. This is a relatively unbroken artifact (10·1 cm.) without encrustation (Fig. 2 and Pls. L and LI). Comparative microscopic analysis of these two bones from a single level was carried out and they were then compared with similarly engraved French pieces from the same general period.

The 'knife' at Saint-Germain is engraved in the same manner as the London fragment, that is, with compositions that are different in form and detail on each face as well as being notched along the edges. On each face there are groups of linear marks. These are somewhat more carefully made and placed near the rim and towards the narrow, forward half of the bone on the example at Saint-Germain. A visual comparison of the two bones is sufficient to indicate that the linear groups on the London fragment were engraved in a freer, looser manner and with a larger use of space but, nevertheless, in the same basic tradition.

Microscopic examination of the Saint-Germain example indicated that the so-called 'knife' showed no evidence of use in cutting nor any primary area of wear or polish along the edges or faces of the forward, narrow half of the bone, towards the point, as would occur if this were a knife or a polisher. Instead, it is towards the wider rear and along the back that one finds evidence of a generalized polishing, an equal rounding of the notches, as though the object had been subjected to persistent handling. This evidence of handling at the rear and lack of evidence for cutting, scraping, or polishing towards the point was found to be true of other Aurignacian bones of this type. It may hint at a non-frictional usage of the object as a pressure flaker or perhaps as a regularly handled ceremonial or ritual object. It was certainly not used as a *knife*.

Of more significance, the microscope revealed that the groups of linear marks on both faces were made by different points which engraved lines with distinctive cross sections. Each group was also made at a different angle, to a different rhythm and spacing, with a different pressure cutting to a different depth, and to a different length. The process is clear both in the macrophotographic detail and in the schematic line illustration of the first face (Fig. 2 and Pls. L and LI). These results show that the groups were intentional rather than random and, because of the complex changes, suggest they were neither conceived nor engraved as a single scheme of decoration. Instead, they had been differentiated as 'sets' which had been put down, or accumulated, sequentially in time. The microscopic evidence for the lengths of time involved in this sequential notational process will be discussed in a monograph devoted to methodology.[7]

On the British Museum fragment, despite the deterioration, the encrustation, and the shellac, the microscope was able to pick up the intentionally engraved marks on both faces and to establish that they were made in the same fashion, in groups, at varying angles, rhythms, positions and, as far as could be determined, by different points. These point differences were established with certainty for at least three sets on the faces and for three sets on the edges, which were also spatially separated into groups. Such accumulations of 'sets' on the faces and edges of a bone plate or *slate* are common in this period. Significantly, microscopic analysis will usually reveal differences between such groups and the markings that accumulate on a cutting or hammering surface or those engraved on the flattened bases of bone points and intended for 'gripping' purposes. Such practical marks show a random arrangement, they are all made by one point or they show a random mixing of marks by many points.

The example at the Musée des Antiquités Nationales provides additional data concerning the sequence of making and offers us a clue as to the general cognitive nature of these cumulative compositions.

Reconstruction of the probable sequence of composition revealed that *after* each face had been marked with linear sets made in horizontal sequence, groups of dots were added within the areas remaining, but this time in *vertical* sequence, each dot being made by a twist of the point. This can be verified in the enlarged detail of (Pls. L and LI) where it can be seen that the series of dots are fitted between the unmarked upper border and the linear markings near the lower border. A similar sequential distribution of lines and dots appears on the reverse face. These dots, therefore, represent a terminal use of the *slate* engraved in an intentionally differentiated style.

What we seem to have on these two Aurignacian examples, and in this class of Upper Palaeolithic objects, is a *visual-kinesthetic* system of differentiating accumulating sets or groups of marks by the style of stroke, the angle of stroke, the pressure of stroke, the direction of accumulation, and the area of distribution of different groups on the edges and faces of the *slate*.

In addition, the microscope demonstrated that the bone at Saint-Germain had been ochred red *after* the engraving, since the colour is found deep in each mark on both faces. This perhaps indicates that the bone had a symbolic or narrative content beyond that which would normally apply to a daily, utilitarian object, such as a polisher or knife, or even to a gaming tally.

The example in the Saint-Germain museum, then, reveals a complex series of cognitive, visual, and *kinesthetic* differentiations. The very complexity allows us to make certain tentative deductions concerning the process involved. If we assume a beginning on a blank *slate*, and accept the fact that there are notational groups, then each group of marks would establish and maintain its identity as the accumulation proceeded. When the maker looked at his 'slate' at any point in that accumulation, he would apparently have been able to reconstruct the sequence of making, know at which point he was, and evaluate the whole as a series of sets or a 'sum'. When either the bone was completed or a set was finished, the sum or the slate was additionally 'signified', or given a meaning, by ochring. The composition, therefore, must be understood as a time-factored process, rather than as a form of decoration.

If this interpretation be valid, then the microscopic analysis of such a notational slate, particularly when the slate is relatively whole and provides the clues for a sequential reconstruction, will show a series of fixed counts made in a limited number of possible orders. It is relatively easy to perform arithmetical and statistical tests on these examples to determine whether arithmetical or calendric periodicities occur in the small, separated sets or in the combined sequential sets. The problems involved in such analyses are discussed, in terms of the Gorge d'Enfer bone at the Musée des Antiquités Nationales, in the above-cited monograph.[7]

In terms of this analysis the fragment in the British Museum seems to represent *two* early stages of notational accumulation and differentiation: an edge notching and a primary linear marking of the faces.

A third example will help to clarify this identification of a specific engraving tradition. Engraved pieces from Aurignacian levels are occasionally found with only edge marks or face marks. Though these are almost always divided into 'sets', they represent only one stage of accumulation and do not serve analytical purposes as well as the more complex pieces. Aurignacian pieces engraved on both edges and faces with marks subdivided into smaller sets, as on the Gorge d'Enfer pieces, are quite common.[8] Microscopic analysis of these pieces has revealed that, in every case, the markings and their divisions into sets were made in the manner just described and that the description of these pieces in the literature is inadequate, being indicative and approximate rather than precise and analytical.

One of the most important examples of this tradition, comparable in its complexity to the accumulations on the plaques from the Gorge d'Enfer in the collection at the Musée des Antiquités Nationales, comes from the same Dordogne region. It is a flattened plaque of roughly the same size and shape. The piece is in the reserve collections of the Musée National de Préhistoire at Les Eyzies.[9]

By its style of engraving this piece is apparently from the same Aurignacian period as the bone from the Gorge d'Enfer; it certainly represents an example and a development of that tradition. The fragment (6.5 cm.) is engraved on both faces and the edges (Figs. 3–5, Pls. LII and LIII).[10] It is in a better state of general preservation than either bone from the Gorge d'Enfer, has not been coated with preservative, and is therefore more explicit in its microscopic data.

Microscopic analysis of the bone revealed that it had been made into a 'slate' out of a larger object by a long deep intentional cutting along one face after

141

which the fragment was cracked and broken off. Whatever the original purpose of the whole flattened bone, the fragment was then used as a 'slate'. Analysis of the markings revealed that they consisted of variations in the notational manner just described. Because of the complexity and the analysis that it makes possible, the bone can serve admirably as the 'type' for the developing Upper Palaeolithic tradition.

Both faces are engraved with groups of linear marks made near the rim or border. The marks on face number one are longer and somewhat further from the edge than those on face number two (Figs. 3 and 4 and Pls. LII and LIII). On the first face, where there is little space left for central marking, two groups of lightly engraved linear marks at bottom right are over-engraved at an angle by later sets of deeper linear marks, resembling but not quite forming the well-known 'hatched effect'. The numerical count of these over-engraved lines does not quite match that of the original series.

On the second face the linear marks are shorter and a secondary engraving is, therefore, made *between* the rows, a process that is cognitively comparable to the tertiary use of dots on the 'slate' from the Gorge d'Enfer. In addition, there is one sequence of nine light marks along the top border which is over-engraved by a set of three deep marks made by another point and rhythm and at another angle. Both edges are notched with groups of marks that are intentionally separated by blank spaces and are also made by different points, at different angles and rhythms, and by different pressures (Fig. 5 and Pl. LIV).

It is obvious from internal and the comparative analysis that this marking is part of a non-decorative, visual-kinesthetic system of notational accumulation. The author has shown elsewhere that this system of accumulating groups persists and develops through the Magdalenian and into the Mesolithic[11] and he has been able to document the stylistic and technical steps in the development.

LATE MAGDALENIAN (*c.* 15,000–10,000 B.C.)

In the early stages of the Upper Palaeolithic, the animal representations and notations were usually engraved separately on different artifacts. Beginning in the Late Aurignacian and Perigordian, however, and increasingly as one moves up the stratigraphic levels, one finds compositions in which engraved notational groups are intentionally associated with the representations of animals, human figures, and abstract signs and symbols.

In the British Museum there is the fragment of a point or rod (5·8 cm.) excavated from a Late Magdalenian level at the site of Trou des Forges, Bruniquel (Pl. LV). It contains the engraved forepart and head of an insect, apparently an ant. The marks are made in a manner common to the period and have been traditionally termed decorative or symbolic.[12] Each mark is made by a double stroke which creates an image resembling the apex of an angle: ◣.

142

If the composition, including the marks and the insect, is accepted as 'decorative', it remains an odd, curious piece. But when the marks are analysed in terms of the evolved tradition of which it is a part, and when the 'insect' image is put within the repertoire of representations associated with this particular late form of marking, new data and relevancies appear. The fragment is one of the simplest examples of a class of composition that has been found in Late Magdalenian Franco-Cantabrian levels at Teyjat, Laugerie-Basse, Gourdan, Mas d'Azil, and La Vache, as well as Bruniquel.[13] In every example there is a comparable block of notational marking in the same, general angular style which is associated with, but separated from, the image. The repertoire of representations includes an insect, plants, a possible 'feather', a fish head, seals, the rear flippers of a seal, the legs of a frog, an anthropomorphic figure, conventionalized horse heads, and a composition with four stag heads whose antlers are in various stages of development. In every case the notations have been added to or over-engraved by later groups of marks made by other points in a tradition whose simple origins lie in the Aurignacian/Perigordian. In each example the associated representational images are different not only from each other but also from the body of representational images found on the engraved bones and pebbles of the same period, often containing 'killed' food animals and no associated notations. The class here under discussion was apparently composed with another, specialized symbolic intent.

Microscopic analysis of the Bruniquel fragment reveals that the angular marks are multiple, made by at least one but often two or more strokes added at an angle to the primary stroke (Pls. LVI–LVIII). In this late tradition a block of notation often begins or ends with a set of three or more long strokes made by a different point and at a different angle. One of these is shown in the detail, Pl. LVIII. In addition, after the primary border sequences have been engraved, a third series of marks is often added between these rows by another point and at a different angle, a technique whose origins we have also seen in the Aurignacian examples. One of these mid-way marks made by a different point is shown in Pl. LVIII. The full, schematic rendering of the fragment is presented in Fig. 6.

To show the complex nature of such marking, which may be deduced only from microscopic and comparative analysis of examples in this class, I illustrate a comparable fragment of a bone rod recently excavated from the Magdalenian VI levels of La Vache (Fig. 7). It shows the legs of a frog or an anthropomorph, three long deep strokes that separate the image from the area of notation, and then a notational grouping made by adding groups of strokes by other points and other angles to the primary series.[14] Exactly this style of multiple angular marking is found also on a piece from Bruniquel.[15]

As we have seen, notation by its nature consists of sequential and therefore 'time-factored' seriation. The representations that are associated with the notation in this class of Late Magdalenian composition may thus also be considered 'time-factored', though the nature of that relation will require exhaustive analysis. To begin with, the one aspect common to these images, representing plant, antlered herbivore, sea mammal, fish, feather, insect, and amphibian, is an apparent seasonality or periodicity in their habits of appearance or disappearance from the environment. If statistical and arithmetical analyses of the notations can determine their intent and significance, as has been suggested by the author, the relation of a 'time-factored' repertory of images to a 'time-factored' notation will make possible a still higher level of comparison and interpretation.

SUMMARY

By internal and comparative analysis of two fragments, Aurignacian and Magdalenian, the author has attempted to indicate certain aspects of the range and complexity of Upper Palaeolithic engraving and the possibilities inherent in a new methodology and technology. The presence of a developing tradition of notation has been indicated from the earliest to the terminal stages of the Upper Palaeolithic, essentially a visual-kinesthetic form of accumulation and differentiation. Associated with and related to these symbolic groups of unit marks are images and symbols.

A. MARSHACK

1 The research was supported by the Wenner-Gren Foundation, New York; the National Science Foundation, Washington, D.C.; and the Peabody Museum of Archaeology and Ethnology, Harvard University, Cambridge, Mass. Photographs and illustrations copyright © Alexander Marshack 1971.

2 Edouard Lartet and Henry Christy, *Reliquiae Aquitanicae*. Edited by T. R. Jones, 1875, B, pl. xxv, 2*a*, *b*, *c*.

3 Ibid., T. R. Jones, 'On some bone and other implements from the caves of Périgord, France, bearing marks indicative of ownership, tallying, and gambling', pp. 183–201.

4 André Leroi-Gourhan, *Treasures of Prehistoric Art*, trans. Norber Guterman, 1967, p. 40. Alexander Marshack, 'Lunar Notation on Upper Paleolithic Remains', *Science*, vol. 146, (6 Nov. 1964), pp. 743–5.

5 Karel Absolon, 'Dokumente und Beweise der Fähigkeiten des Fossilen Menschen zu Zählen im Mährischen Paläolithikum', *Artibus Asiae*, xx—2/3 (1957), pp. 123–50.

6 Lartet and Christy, op. cit., B, pl. xiii, 1 3*a*, *b*.

7 Alexander Marshack, *Notation in the Upper Palaeolithic*. To be issued as Mémoire no. 7 by the Laboratoire de Préhistoire, Université de Bordeaux.

8 They have been found in Aurignacian levels at Arcy-sur-Cure, Aurignac, Blanchard, Isturitz, Lartet, Téoulé, Pair-non-Pair, Le Poisson, La Souquette.

9 The piece seems to have entered the museum collection early in the pioneering period of excavation in this area of the Dordogne, and it is without adequate coding or indexing so that the site, excavator, and publication, if any, are difficult to ascertain.

10 Musée National de Préhistoire, Les Eyzies-de-Tayac, A212.

11 Alexander Marshack, *Discovering Man*. To be published in London by George Weidenfeld & Nicolson Ltd. in 1970. Alexander Marshack, *Mesolithic Notation*. Paper to be issued by the Centro Camuno di Studi Preistorici, Capo di Ponte, Italy.

[12] Étienne Patte, 'Remarques sur quelques figurations préhistoriques', *Revue anthropologique*, nos. 1–3, Jan.–Mar. 1934, pp. 43–60.

[13] Henri Breuil, 'Les subdivisions du paléolithique supérieur et leur signification', *Compte rendu de la XIV session du Congrès International d'Anthropologie et d'Archéologie Préhistoriques*, (1913; 2nd ed., 1937), Fig. 29: 5, 6, 7, and 13. Capitan *et al.* 'L'Abri Mège', *Revue anthropologique*, vol. xvi (1906), p. 209, fig. 71: 1, 2, 5*b*. Édouard Piette, *L'Art pendant l'Âge du Renne*,
1907, fig. 92 (complete bone) and pl. lxiii.

[14] Romain Robert et Louis-René Nougier, 'Baguette demi-ronde gravée du Magdalénien final de la grotte de La Vache', *Bulletin de la Société Préhistorique de l'Ariège*, vol. xxii (1967), illusts. pp. 13 and 15. Photographs by A. Marshack.

[15] Émile Cartailhac, 'Les stations de Bruniquel sur les bords de l'Aveyron', *L'Anthropologie*, vol. xiv (1903), p. 146, fig. 53.

A GROUP OF LATER IRON AGE COLLARS OR NECK-RINGS FROM WESTERN BRITAIN[1]

THE precise identification and dating of regional 'schools' or workshops amongst the surviving products of Early Celtic art in Britain, despite the pioneering studies of E. T. Leeds,[2] Sir Cyril Fox[3] and, in more recent years, Professor E. M. Jope (see p. 61) remains largely an uncertain task if not an unattainable ideal. The purpose of the present note is to list and briefly comment on a group of metal collars or neck-rings whose distribution, style, and, where present, datable associations point to the existence in the west of England during the first century A.D. of a small, local and not particularly accomplished school of metalworkers specializing in the production of a type of object which, though playing an important role in continental Iron Age art and society is, save for undecorated rings and the gold torcs of the East Anglian, Snettisham-Belstead class,[4] not otherwise well represented in the British Isles.[5] The individual neck-rings of what might be termed the 'Wraxall class', after the finest extant example, are as follows:

1. Tower House, Birdcombe Court, Wraxall, Somerset. Bronze collar. Internal diameter 12·5 cm. Swivel joint at rear, hooked tenon catch or 'joggle joint' at front. Ornament cast, provision for fifteen circular insets on either half. Discovered without further association in 1837. City Museum, Bristol, Inv. no. E. 1784. (Pl. LIX *a*.)

   H. Ellacombe in *Archaeologia*, xxx (1844), 521 and pl. 61 *a*; A. W. Franks in *Archaeologia*, liv (1895), 495–6 and pl. xlvii; *PP*, 106, 126; A. Fox, *South West England* (1964), 134 and pl. 77; S. Thomas, *Pre-Roman Britain* (1965), pl. 27.

2. Pen-coed-foel, Llandyssul, Cardiganshire. Half of cast bronze neck-ring with provision for hinge and pin fastening. Internal diameter *c.* 12 cm. Five large raised bosses separately riveted to the main plate. Found during ploughing within small hillfort *c.* 1895. City Museum, Bristol, Inv. no. E. 1789. (Pl. LIX *b*.)

W. R. Barker, *Proc. Clifton Antiq. Club*, iii (1896), 210; E. T. Leeds, *Celtic Ornament in the British Isles* (1933), 56, 59–60; W. F. Grimes, *The Prehistory of Wales* (1951), 122, 226, no. 702 and pl. xviii; *PP*, 106 f., 150 and pl. 12 *d*; H. N. Savory, *Early Iron Age in Wales* (1968), 21 and fig. 16.

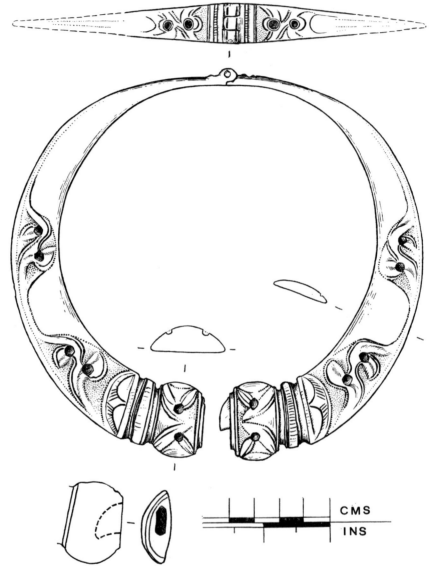

FIG. 1. Portland Island, Dorset. List no. 3. Collar with detail to show joggle joint mechanism. Scale $\frac{2}{3}$.

3. Portland Island, Dorset. Cast bronze collar. Internal diameter 12 cm. Hinge at rear, joggle joint at front. Provision for sixteen circular settings. Said to have been found in

stone coffin with pear-shaped bead-rim pot of dark smooth ware, a second-century A.D.
Samian platter and riveted bronze knife. British Museum, Reg. no. 89. 7–15. 1. (Pl. LX
and Fig. 1).

A. W. Franks in *Archaeologia*, liv (1895), 496; R. A. Smith, *Early Iron Age Guide*
(British Museum, 1925), 150; *PP*, 106–7 and pl. 62*a*; J. V. S. Megaw in *Cornish
Archaeology*, vi (1967), 6 ff. and pl. 1*b*.

FIG. 2. Unprovenanced. List no. 4. Collar. Solid triangles show area where red enamel survives. Scale ⅔.

4. Unprovenanced, ? Dorset. Cast brass collar. Internal diameter 12·2 cm. Hinge at rear,
joggle joint at front. Provision for twenty-six circular insets and eight triangular red enamel

147

settings some only of which survive. Supposed to have been obtained in the region of Portland and closely related stylistically to Portland. British Museum, Reg. no. 1963. 4–7. 1. Purchased from the son of the original owner and not previously published. (Pl. LXI and Fig. 2).

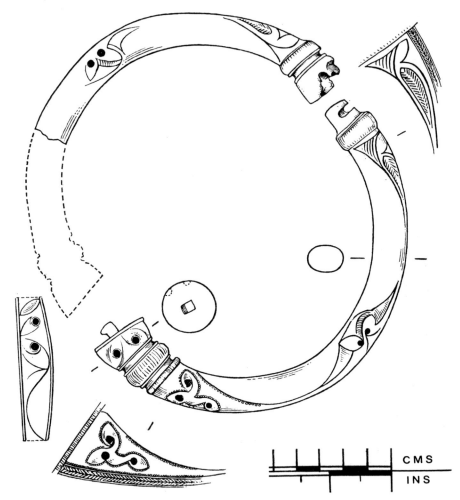

FIG. 3. Dorchester, Dorset. List no. 5. Bronze collar. Scale $\frac{2}{3}$.

5. Dorchester, Dorset. Fragmentary cast bronze collar. Internal diameter 11·7 cm. Constructed in two separate pieces joined at rear with swivel joint, at front with joggle joint. Two empty setting holes on surviving terminal: ? cast ornament. Found by labourers in levelling meadow between River Frome and the North Walk and associated with several human skeletons and 'two vases of bowl form', one black, one brown and porous. Dorset County Museum, Dorchester, Inv. no. 1902. 1. 37.[6] (Pl. LXIII and Fig. 3).
   Gentleman's Magazine (Sept. 1841), 303.

6. Greenhill, Weymouth, Dorset. Fragment of ?penannular bronze ring with one spatulate terminal. Length of surviving chord *c.* 10 cm. Some engraved ornament, terminal drilled for two circular glass settings of which one (green) survives. Associated with bronze 'nail cleaner', bone pins, ? tankard hold-fast, ivy-leaf horse pendant and bronze plaque with niello decoration (see p. 153 below). British Museum, Reg. no. 92. 9–1. 1707. (Fig. 4).

R. A. Smith, *Early Iron Age Guide*, 151; E. T. Leeds, *Celtic Ornament*, 62, n. 1.

7. Trenoweth, St. Stephen-in-Brannel, Cornwall. Bronze and brass collar with lead core. Internal diameter 11·7 cm. Incised decoration with provision for at least twenty glass insets of which twelve survive, the smaller clear glass, the larger brown; originally hinged. British Museum, Reg. no. 95. 7–25. 35. (Pl. LXII).

R. Pole Carew in *Archaeologia*, xvi (1912), 137–8 and pl. x; H. O'N. Hencken, *Archaeology of Cornwall and Scilly* (1923), 109, 133, 166 and fig. 2*g*; *PP*, 107 and 126; A. Fox, *South West England*, 134 and pl. 78; J. V. S. Megaw in *Cornish Archaeology*, vi (1967), 5–8 and pl. 1*a*.

Despite differences of detail and quality of decoration, as well as, more interestingly, striking differences in their metallurgical composition to be noted below, there are a number of linking features which make it possible to regard the above seven rings as variations on more or less the same local themes. Excluded from this group are two Scottish

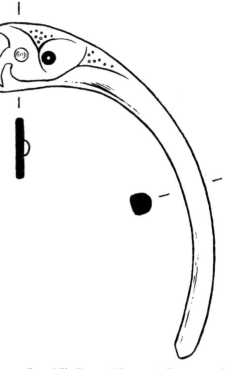

FIG. 4. Greenhill, Dorset. List no. 6. Fragment of bronze penannular ring. Scale $\frac{1}{1}$.

collars, that from Lochar Moss, Dumfriesshire, now in the British Museum[7] and one from Stichill, Roxburghshire, found, probably, with a pair of massive armlets of a type restricted to central and eastern Scotland and the subject of a recent detailed study.[8]

Both Scottish rings do have points of similarity to examples in our southern group; Lochar Moss with its cast relief ornament of what Leeds first termed 'broken-back S coils' has the same (though punched, not cast) ornament of toothed or wavy lines decorating the edge as Wraxall and Dorchester (Pls. LIX *a* and LXIII) and raised bosses and squaring off of the flat section like Llandyssul; the raised bosses may imitate enamel. Lochar Moss has been included amongst a class of mainly first century A.D. 'beaded torcs'[9] and, despite a more western than north-eastern English distribution of the beaded torc, a good case may be made out for Lochar Moss being a product of the Brigantian area, a region which seems to have influenced considerably the motifs used on the Scottish massive armlets. It may not be insignificant that the most westerly found of the beaded torcs, that from Lambay Island, Co. Dublin, was found with other objects of almost certain Brigantian manufacture.[10]

Stichill (or Stichel), on the other hand, has the same general shape as Portland and the unprovenanced collar from the Portland region. However, Morna Simpson is surely correct in following Leeds and seeing a link with Roman finds from the north of England in the separately stamped or repoussé front panels with their variant of what Leeds called the 'swash N'.[11] The decoration on the remainder of the horizontal surface and at the rear of the Stichill collar is quite different; the spindly spirals and trumpet features recall only vaguely the much tighter, three-dimensional forms of Llandyssul and definitely southern pieces. Again Dr. Simpson indicates a general non-southern 'decorative atmosphere' as a source for such ornament—significantly enough with Lambay Island in mind —comparing the Bann disc, the Petrie 'crown' and, one may add, the Cork horns, examples all it is now suggested of tooled, not cast, ornament;[12] in the absence of a recent technical examination of the Stichill collar one might consider an Irish link far from out of the question.

Mention has been made once more in the last paragraph of Llandyssul; and Llandyssul, over which Sir Cyril Fox had no doubts as to its southern or 'Dobunic' origin, may in fact stand as a link piece between certain stylistic traditions of the north and of the south and west (Pl. LIX b). The versions of the comma-spirals or 'Llyn Cerrig trumpets' and elongated S curves which take the place of the northern broken-back coils, no less than the basic form of the ring with flattened cross-section and hinge and pin joint on the main diameter, similar to Wraxall and Trenoweth, in my view do point to the south and west.[13]

Returning now to our main group of Wraxall neck-rings, the type piece sets the pattern for all save perhaps Dorchester and Greenhill which, however, still exhibit a partial hooked scroll; a basic design of interlocking S curves and scroll-and-trumpet forms is followed on the other two cast rings with plastic decoration, Portland and its near-twin. Here, as with the Ipswich find, is one of the few examples of British Iron Age metal-work where one can be really certain that one is studying pieces which, though not identical, came from the same hand. Even on the two crudest rings, Trenoweth and the Greenhill fragment (Pl. LXII and Fig. 4, which last almost looks like part of a post-Roman penannular brooch[14]) where the decoration is incised or a combination of repoussé and incision and not cast, there is a similar elaboration of scroll-work and provision for insets at the joint points—a feature seen to a lesser degree on the Llandyssul half-collar. The flattened D cross-section with its lack of ornament on the rear, the 'joggle' or catch joints with a hooked tongue push-fitted into a slot, the use save in one detail of the decoration of Portland, of stippling or punching rather than hatching to give a 'background' design and the plentiful use of insets themselves are all features which give a morphological and stylistic unity to the Wraxall group. The much-rubbed design of the Dorchester ring appears also to be cast and is restricted to the one side of the ring which, with its circular cross-section, looks like a crude local attempt to produce in cast bronze the general form of the tubular gold torcs of the Broighter–Snettisham types, actually imports from northern France as recent evidence has tended to confirm:[15] in the same way the terminals of the Portland 'twins' might be considered as two-dimensional imitations of eastern ring-terminal torcs. The joggle joints may also reflect a link with the Broighter type of torc.

The use of a dotted background for curvilinear motifs of the cruder form as those in the centre of the twin arcs of the Trenoweth ring (Pl. LXII) can be seen on south-western pottery and elsewhere in the west country. One of two enamelled two-link bits in the Knowle Hill, Bawdrip, Somerset hoard—better known as the Polden Hills find—has a similar pattern below one of the side rings;[16] another parallel is the decoration of one of the several bronze 'dress fasteners' or strap terminals from the Melsonby (Stanwick), North Riding, Yorkshire metal hoards. This terminal, with provision for insets as well as crude comma elements, has been dated to the third quarter of the first century A.D., and is one of several pieces from the Brigantian capital considered to show south-western influence.[17] It should be admitted, though, that the use of stippling can also be seen on material from East Anglia, for example, on a fragmentary mount from Lakenheath, Suffolk.[18] Crude stippling filling in arcs in the manner of Trenoweth and Greenhill is also to be seen on a Leeds Class 2 terret with red enamel enrichment from Cawston, Norfolk, and a quadrilobe harness mount with yellow as well as red enamel from Norton, Suffolk,[19] and was clearly a technique also followed in eastern England at the time of the Roman conquest.

One possible link between the widespread group of harness bronzes of the first century A.D. from southern and eastern Britain and our Wraxall neck-rings is the four triangular depressions for enamel, not glass, settings flanking the pseudo-knobs of the unprovenanced twin to the Portland collar (Pl. LXI); similar 'dragon's teeth' settings can be found again in the Polden Hills find[20] and an unassociated and also enamelled mount from Chepstow, Monmouthshire.[21] Such provision for triangular insets, which seems to reflect Belgic or provincial Roman practice,[22] in place of the cruder glass settings which may be intended to imitate enamel, is something different however, from the pendant triangle bordering the Trenoweth ring; here a more valid comparison would be the edging of the mirror from a female grave in the Trelan Bahow, St. Keverne, Cornwall cemetery, possibly introduced into Cornwall in trading up the Helford River: the motif goes back to the Wisbech scabbard mount.[23] The pelta design of both this mirror and one from the Stamford Hill, Plymouth, Devon cemetery[24]—another piece comparatively late in what (excepting these two) should, *pace* Fox, be considered a south-eastern rather than 'Dobunic' mirror style—offers a source for the hatched, not dot-filled, peltas flanking the knobs of the Portland ring (Pl. LX *a*), though the hatching also recalls the enamel 'keying' of such pieces as the Waterloo helmet.[25] One other piece which combines elements to be found in the mirror style with details of the Wraxall group's ornamentation is the fragmentary ? shield-mount from Carloggas hill-fort, St. Mawgan-in-Pydar—yet another Cornish find.[26] Here is the dot-filled background design, comma spirals with cut-out centres to be filled with nail-heads rather than insets, and a stamped back-bone like the beaded, toothed or cable edging of Wraxall, Dorchester, and the Portland 'twins', though Dorchester's 'herring bone' can also be found on south-western pottery.

One other piece relevant to the present discussion combines dot-infilling and incised triangles. This is the hold-fast from Greenhill, roughly beaten up from what appears to be tin-plated bronze and published in Dr. Corcoran's list of definite and possible tankard handles.[27] The grip has a simple row of scribed zigzags or continuous triangles either side of, and bordered by, deeply incised grooves. On the now single surviving terminal plate is a lightly incised Maltese cross figure infilled with dots in the manner of the penannular fragment; the layout is, like the ring fragment, reminiscent of details of Trenoweth.

Such comparative eclecticism of motifs as this brief analysis suggests is to be expected in the territory of the Durotriges and Dumnonii—hardly the centre of skilled metal-working traditions yet important for its contiguity to the tin resources of the far west, which in turn explain the occasional imports into this region. The south-west in fact may be compared with the north-east of Britain not only for its debts to specific and more developed regional styles but for drawing upon a common pool of artistic ideas, albeit with a touch of provincial archaism. No less varied is the metallurgy exhibited by those few of the Wraxall group of neck-rings which have so far been examined.[28]

The analysis of the Trenoweth ring has been previously published in the present writer's recent brief account.[29] It could hardly be more of a composite; the core is a lead-tin alloy, the back plate bronze, and the decorated front plate is a copper alloy containing zinc, lead, and some tin—a brass which may explain its apparent gilded surface. The widespread use of brass, usually considered as a technological innovation resulting from the introduction of Roman alloying methods, has recently been a turning-point in the arguments concerning the date of the Tal-y-Llyn, Merionethshire, hoard.[30] However this may be, zinc alloying does occur with one pair of the Scottish massive armlets, that from Aboyne, Perthshire, one with 1·4 per cent. zinc, the other with no less than 9·13 per cent. zinc.[31] What is really interesting, however, is the result of the analyses of the Portland 'twins' (Appendix, p. 154 below) which shows that, despite the close stylistic similarities, the two rings are made from quite dissimilar alloys, one being a leaded bronze, the other a leaded brass. Both, however, have suitable properties for casting; the points of similarity with the metal of Trenoweth are the use of lead alloying and particularly a copper-zinc alloy, but exactly what significance should be placed on this apparent lack of metallurgical consistency —for example, to what degree it reflects local ignorance of the most suitable casting process or local lack of necessary raw materials—must await a much-needed expansion of the number of available analyses of British Iron Age metal-work.

Two final points remain; the date of the Wraxall group of collars and their possible reason for manufacture. As to dating, the Portland ring's supposed discovery with a knife which on other grounds would be considered Late Bronze Age throws some doubt on the genuineness of the whole association, though the bead-rim pot would not be out of place in a Durotrigan context.[32] Stichill, with the same general form as the Portland 'twins' and, like them, probably borrowing from Roman collars the jointed hinge mechanism, must be post-conquest in view of the repoussé plates' resemblance to enamelled seal-boxes (one from Castle Hill, Nottinghamshire, with a firm Flavian date).[33] Dr. Simpson would compare what she considers to be the cast ornament of Stichill to the spacer plates of Roman multi-strand necklaces and, if valid, the same parallel at a further stylistic remove would apply at Llandyssul. The Greenhill fragment would seem to be the most closely dated of all the Wraxall rings; other pieces from the find are identifiable as Roman horse-trappings and mountings, datable to the first campaigns of the Roman conquest and the decades following. The bronze plaque with niello decoration has parallels from Leicester, Verulamium, and Wroxeter;[34] the pendant is a common form found not only on the Continent at sites like Carnuntum but at Cirencester, Colchester,[35] and amongst the Roman material from Hod Hill, Dorset, which, like the Greenhill finds, once formed part of the Durden collection: material from Richborough Castle dated between A.D. 65 and 80 is considered a good dated parallel for the Hod Hill piece.[36] In brief, having in mind also the strictly balanced layout of their ornament, it seems that a mid- or later first-century date for all the Wraxall rings would not be unreasonable.

Mention has been made in the introductory paragraph of the comparative rarity of richly decorated neck-rings in the British Iron Age. Unlike the majority of the East Anglian gold work, which seems to have formed part of traders' or workshop hoards, the Wraxall torcs have mainly isolated findspots. Apart from Greenhill, one was found within a hill-fort, one possibly from a burial, two close to rivers—Trenoweth being not far north from Castle Gotha, a hill-fort occupied in the first two centuries A.D. and with evidence for local bronze working—and the rest are single finds. Several are of very considerable weight; Portland weighs 299 gm., the unprovenanced 'twin' 503 gm., Trenoweth 717 gm., and Wraxall 1,268 gm. The flat **D** cross-section would make these rings uncomfortable for any but the briefest period of wearing. For once the word 'ritual' would seem more than the archaeologist's usual easy way out and Lady Fox, writing of Wraxall and Trenoweth, has suggested that such rings may have had as part at least of their purpose the decoration of wooden cult figures such as have, in fact, been found in the West Country.[37] It is certainly noticeable that, despite the universal importance which the torc had in the Celtic world, wooden figures, particularly those of the simple 'column-statue' type meant for temporary siting at local cult centres,[38] are only on the rarest of occasions carved with a torc. Yet the custom of bedecking sacred trees and idols, no less than the deposition of objects in isolated areas and especially in water, is too well known to need further comment here. It may be that the Wraxall group of collars, with their distribution largely beyond the Belgic sphere of influence, may represent a residual and material memory of long-established western Celtic practices, practices which we know from other evidence continued even in Belgic Britain, undeterred by the Roman conquest.[39]

J. V. S. Megaw

APPENDIX

Metallurgical examination of the Portland 'twins' (British Museum, Registered nos. 89. 7–15. 1 and 1963. 4–7. 1).

1. *Sampling*. In order to avoid visible damage, and to cut down actual damage to the minimum, the samples of metal were taken in both cases from the projecting metal tongue, visible only when the collars are opened. The samples were in the form of micro-drillings, a total of about 25 mg. being taken from each torc. This allowed for qualitative spectrographic analysis and duplicate quantitative polarographic analysis.

2. *Qualitative spectrographic analysis*. This showed that the two collars are made from quite different alloys. The Portland torc is a copper-tin alloy containing lead and a trace of silver, i.e. it is essentially a leaded bronze, whereas the 1963 collar is a copper-zinc alloy containing lead and tin and traces of iron, silver, and silicon, i.e. it is a leaded brass.

3. *Quantitative polarographic analysis*. This gave the following results:

Portland torc		1963 torc	
Copper	81·8 per cent.	Copper	83·7 per cent.
Tin	4·5	Zinc	13·0
Lead	11·3	Lead	3·2
		Tin	0·8
	97·6		100·7

The figures are the average value obtained from duplicate experiments in each case and, although they do not add up exactly to 100 per cent. are regarded as quite satisfactory in the circumstances, for the samples used for each analysis were very small, ranging from 6·6 mg. to 12·3 mg., and the presence of so much lead, particularly in the Portland torc, implies a non-homogeneous alloy. A further point of interest in the case of the Portland torc was that hydrogen sulphide was detected when the sample was dissolved in acid, indicating the presence of sulphides in the alloy. This could account at least in part for the low total analysis in that case.

A. E. A. Werner
H. Barker
Research Laboratory, British Museum.

[1] This study is offered to the Keeper and staff of the Department of Prehistoric and Romano-British Antiquities with the author's best wishes and grateful thanks for much past and continuing assistance without which a European prehistorian resident in Australia could not survive. The line drawings are the work of the Department's Illustrator, Mr. Philip Compton.

[2] E. T. Leeds, *Celtic Ornament in the British Isles down to AD 700* (1933).

[3] Sir Cyril Fox, *Pattern and Purpose: Early Celtic Art in Britain* (1958)—abbreviated here *PP*.

[4] R. Rainbird Clarke in *Proc. Prehist. Soc.* xx (1954), 17 ff.; Elizabeth Owles in *Antiquity*, xliii (1969), 208.

[5] Miss Jean Burns of the University of Glasgow has recently completed a catalogue of Iron Age neck-rings in the British Isles and I am much indebted to her for access to her notes; I have also benefited from discussions with Mr. M. G. Spratling.

[6] The Curator and Secretary of the Dorset County Museum, Mr. R. Pears, kindly made the torc available for study and analysis.

[7] A. Wray in *Archaeologia*, xxxiv (1852), 83–7 and pl. xi; Leeds, op. cit. 53, 60 and 110; *PP*, 107 and pl. 29 *b*; Morna Simpson in (ed.) J. M. Coles and D. D. A. Simpson, *Studies in Ancient Europe: Essays presented to Stuart Piggott* (1968), 248 f.

[8] Simpson, op. cit. 233–54.

[9] R. B. K. Stevenson in *Proc. Soc. Antiq. Scot.* lxxxii (1947–8), 293–5; id. in (ed.) A. L. F. Rivet, *The Iron Age in Northern Britain* (1966), 26 ff.

[10] R. A. S. Macalister in *Proc. R.I.A.* 38 C9 (1928–9), 240–6 esp. pl. xxiv. 3.

[11] Leeds, op. cit. 110 f.; Simpson, loc. cit. in n. 7.

[12] M. J. O'Kelly in *J. Cork Hist. and Ant. Soc.* lxvi (1961), 1–12.

[13] Compare the running scrolls on Glastonbury pottery: W. F. Grimes in *Proc. Prehist. Soc.* xviii (1952), 166–7 and fig. 6.

[14] E. Fowler in *Proc. Prehist. Soc.* xxvi (1960), 149–75, esp. 169 ff. and class Aa (= I–III A.D.) and derivatives of Dark Age date.

[15] R. Rainbird Clarke, op. cit., 36–42 and pls. i–v; *PP*, 48 and pl. 32 *b*; R. Joffroy in *Comptes rendus de l'Académie des inscr. et belles-lettres: juillet-oct. 1967* (1968), 479–85.

[16] C. J. Hartford in *Archaeologia*, xiv (1803), 92, no. 3 and pl. xix. 1 = British Museum, Reg. no. 46. 3–22. 69.

[17] Morna MacGregor (Simpson) in *Proc. Prehist. Soc.* xxvii (1962), 34 and fig. 7 = set D, no. 24.

[18] R. Rainbird Clarke in *Arch. J.* xcvi (1939), 71 and pl. xiv. 2.

[19] Rainbird Clarke, op. cit. in n. 18, 70 and fig. 12. 3.

[20] *PP*, 129 and pl. 72 *c*.

[21] *PP*, loc. cit. and pl. 70 *c*; H. N. Savory, *Early Iron Age Art in Wales* (1968), 23 and fig. 24.

[22] Leeds, op. cit. 28 ff.

[23] Wisbech: *PP*, 1–2 and fig. 2; E. M. Jope in (ed.) S. S. Frere, *Problems of the Iron Age in S. Britain = Inst. Arch. Univ. London Occ. Paper* xi (n.d.), 74 and pl. iv *a*. Trelan Bahow: *PP*, 98; A. Fox, *South West England* (1964), pl. 76.

[24] *PP*, 97, pl. 56*b* (K) and fig. 60 = Stamford Hill I.

[25] *PP*, 49 and pl. 27 *b*.

[26] Sir Cyril Fox in *Arch. J.* cxiii (1956), 80–1, pl. xl and fig. 40; *PP*, 115–16 and pl. 67 *b*; A. Fox, op. cit. 134 and fig. 39.

[27] British Museum, Reg. no. 92. 9–1. 1706. J. X. W. P. Corcoran in *Proc. Prehist. Soc.* xviii (1952), 99, no. 11 '? II A.D.'.

[28] The ready co-operation of the Keeper of the British Museum's Research Laboratory and his staff in what it is hoped will be a continuing programme is here gratefully acknowledged.

[29] J. V. S. Megaw, *Cornish Archaeology*, vi (1967), 6.

[30] M. G. Spratling in *Antiquity*, xl (1966), 230; Savory in *Bull. Board Celtic Studies*, xxii (1966), 101–2.

[31] Simpson, op. cit. 234.

[32] R. E. M. Wheeler, *Maiden Castle, Dorset = Soc. Antiq. Res. Report*, xii (1943), 204–10.

[33] F. Oswald, *Nottingham Castle: City of Nottingham Art Gallery and Museum* (1927), 28, fig. 2 and pl. vi. 7.

[34] For Greenhill see G. Webster in *Arch. J.* cxv (1960), 95, and fig. 8 = no. 233 (B.M. Reg. no. 92. 9–1. 1705); compare nos. 134, 197, 254.

[35] Webster, op. cit., nos. 25, 35, 62.

[36] J. W. Brailsford, *Hod Hill*, i (1962), 3, fig. 3 and pl. i = A 43; I am grateful to Mr. K. S. Painter, Assistant Keeper, Department of Prehistoric and Romano-British Antiquities, for his assistance with the Greenhill material.

[37] A. Fox, op. cit. 134.

[38] Anne Ross, *Pagan Celtic Britain* (1967), 35; Simone Deyts in *Rev. arch. de l'Est et Centre-Est*, xvii. 3–4 (1966), 199–202.

[39] Ross in *Studies in Ancient Europe*, 255–85.

VILLAS AND CHRISTIANITY IN ROMAN BRITAIN

THERE is very little literary evidence for Christianity in Roman Britain; but what evidence there is does point to the existence of the cult from an early date. No weight can be attached to legends such as those about the coming to Britain of St. Paul and of St. Peter and of Joseph of Arimathea, who is said to have planted the sacred thorn at Glastonbury;[1] and about a king Lucius, who is said to have sent to Pope Eleutherus in the second half of the second century A.D. *obsecrans ut . . . Christianus efficeretur*;[2] but it may have been as early as A.D. 208–9 that St. Alban was martyred at Verulamium, and Aaron and Julius at a town which may be Caerleon, and if so this would be good evidence that Christianity was introduced to Britain as early as the second century, perhaps by the time of Severus.[3] Tertullian, in any case, writing about A.D. 206 of the spread of Christianity, speaks of *Britannorum inaccessa Romanis loca, Christo vero subdita*.[4] Origen, too, writing at some date earlier than A.D. 230, mentions Britain as Christian several times.[5] From the fourth century there is more satisfactory testimony. The names of three British bishops who attended the Council convened at Arles by Constantine in A.D. 314, the first such assembly convened by a Roman emperor, are preserved among the signatories to the acts of the Council:[6]

> *Eborius episcopus de civitate Eboracensi provincia Britannia.*
> *Restitutus episcopus de civitate Londiniensi provincia suprascripta.*
> *Adelphius episcopus de civitate Colonia Londiniensium.*
> *Exinde Sacerdos presbyter, Arminius diaconus.*

These are the bishops of York, London, and a third perhaps from Lincoln or Colchester.[7] Then, in a passage of Sulpicius Severus are to be found three British bishops attending the Council of Ariminum in A.D. 360.[8] Finally there is the story, from the *Life of St. Germanus* written by Constantius, who lived in the second half of the fifth century, of how Germanus came in A.D. 429 to convert the Britons from their Pelagian heresy and not only achieved his object, but won the Alleluia victory.[9]

The literary evidence thus leaves no doubt that Christianity was firmly established in Britain in the Roman period. The important Cirencester cryptogram most probably belongs to the second or third century;[10] but the quantity of archaeological evidence for these two centuries is so small that it may be taken as certain that Christianity was a minority religion confined for the most part to foreign traders and immigrants. Even after Christianity became recognized as the official religion throughout the empire in A.D. 312 relics of the faith are curiously rare in the towns of Britain, the most substantial being the little church built about A.D. 360 at Silchester. Professor Toynbee has demonstrated that there is more material evidence than Collingwood probably realized when writing in 1930 and 1936, to which must be added some important discoveries made since 1939; but it remains true that the small size of the Silchester church and the general paucity of evidence suggest small numbers and a lack of wealth, and this is supported by the record that poverty compelled three of the British bishops attending the Council of Ariminum in A.D. 359 to accept Constantius' offer of free transport by the imperial posting service on their journey.[11]

If Christianity had in fact taken root in town or country one might have hoped to find some archaeological evidence of popular Christianity in town and country, a decline of paganism, continuity from the Roman into the post-Roman periods, and some parallel cultural developments in the province such as an increase in literacy and in practice of Roman law. Almost the opposite seems to be the case.

First, no large Christian sites are known, while there is, on the other hand, copious evidence for paganism. There are, for example, fourteen temples known where sufficient numbers of coins have been found to suggest that they are votive offerings rather than chance losses, and at all of them the coins are either all or very largely late:[12]

Temple	*Number of coins*
Frilford 2, Berkshire	150
Weycock Hill, Berkshire	Numbers unknown, but large
Bourton Grounds, Buckinghamshire	200+
Jordon Hill, Dorset	192+
Maiden Castle 2, Dorset	123
Lydney, Gloucestershire	6,000+
Wycomb, Gloucestershire	500+
Verulamium, Hertfordshire	151+
Hockwold, Norfolk	345
Woodeaton, Oxfordshire	2,730+
Brean Down, Somerset	468
Bruton, Somerset	About 1,500

| Pagans Hill, Somerset | 237+ |
| Farley Heath, Surrey | 1,022+ |

Two particular cases are Frilford and Pagans Hill. At Frilford, in the thin layer of darkish earth on the latest pathway leading up to the temple were found some seventy-eight coins, all of the fourth and early fifth centuries. Of these the main incidence was of coins minted between about A.D. 350 and 400.[13] At Pagans Hill eighty-three coins were found, all ranging from Gallienus (A.D. 253–68) to Arcadius (A.D. 383–408).[14] Similarly, although the temples should have been closed after the death of Constantine,[15] there was considerable building after that date. At Pagans Hill in Somerset and at Worth in Kent there were substantial structural repairs.[16] At Maiden Castle the temple was not built until after A.D. 367 and was repaired at some date after A.D. 379.[17] Most striking of all is Lydney in Gloucestershire, where the great temple dedicated to Modens was founded not earlier than A.D. 364.[18] The temple was well planned and constructed, and it was surrounded by a well-laid-out settlement which included a guest-house for pilgrims, baths and apartments for worshippers, all paved with mosaic floors. From an inscription on one of the pavements it is clear that local officials had taken an active part in this expensive enterprise. An interpreter on the staff of the governor had acted as clerk of the works, and the officer in charge of the supply depot of the Roman fleet based on the Severn estuary had laid a mosaic pavement, which was paid for out of fees or money offerings to the god. More than 6,000 coins, excluding hoards, were found on the site, and these, as well as the great profusion of trinkets, must be the offerings of the faithful.[19] In the towns, too, the vigour of paganism is attested, by the remodelling after A.D. 380 of the Romano-Celtic temple at Verulamium, by the restoration, probably in the reign of Julian (A.D. 360–3), of the Giant Column in Cirencester (Corinium) dedicated by the governor of Britannia Prima to Jupiter and mentioning the *prisca religio*, and by the use at least until the 370s of two of the temples at Silchester.[20] Indeed, it is important that almost the only significant archaeological evidence for Christianity in London, the chief city of the province, is the negative fact, about the middle of the fourth century, of an attack on the Walbrook Mithraeum drastic enough to compel the adherents to hide the sacred images of the cult.[21] It seems likely that the Christians were responsible; but in this and the other towns of Britain the positive archaeological evidence for Christianity is negligible.[22]

Second, there is no significant evidence of continuity from Roman to post-Roman Britain. The early bishoprics of the English Church, for example, apart from a few exceptions such as Canterbury, were based not on the great Roman towns, as in Gaul, but on royal villas and other places of later and entirely English significance.[23] There is, on the other hand, a considerable body of early Christian funerary inscriptions in Latin from Celtic Britain,[24] which might be thought to give linguistic evidence of a corrupt continuation of the monumental tradition of the Roman province, particularly since the 'tyrants' of the fifth and sixth centuries seem to have wished to adopt an outward appearance as inheritors of the Roman power.[25] Jackson has demonstrated, however, that if parallels are wanted we must turn to contemporary Gaul:[26]

All through the period of the fifth to seventh century the British and Gaulish *inscriptiones Christianae* show certain close epigraphic similarities, though with a natural time-lag in Britain. For instance, the common use of vulgar and cursive forms in fifth-century British inscriptions agrees with the practice in the early inscriptions of Gaul and the Rhineland rather than with the pagan monumental tradition of the Roman Empire, and the appearance of epigraphic uncial letters in the sixth century, and of book letters by the late sixth and seventh, is a reflection of what happened in Gaul. Further, the formulae which are found on the British tombstones are not those of pagan Roman Britain but of fifth- to sixth-century Christian Gaul. Thus the use of *hic iacet*, originating in Italy in the later fourth century, and specifically Christian, came into fashion in Gaul in the first half of the fifth century, particularly in the Lyons-Vienne area, and in the Rhineland above all at Trier. Again, *in hoc tumulo* is especially characteristic of Gallic Christianity in the fifth and following centuries, and so with *in pace*, mostly in southern Gaul. The chi-rho monogram of the earlier type with the chi over the rho was largely replaced in southern Gaul at the end of the fifth century by the later type with a mere cross-bar, which is found there between about 400 and 540. The former type never occurs with post-Roman monumental inscriptions in Britain, whereas the latter is not rare. As a kind of negative parallel, Gallic inscriptions do not usually bear any date until the second half of the fifth century, though they then became common; and this agrees with the practically universal absence of dates in Britain.

Third, there is no evidence of widespread knowledge of Latin or of widespread practice of Roman law. The importance of Latin comes from the fact that Christianity demanded at least a minimum of lettered culture.[27] As a religion of the book it depended on a written revelation, the holy books of the Jewish religion, which it gathered and claimed as its own, and to which came to be added those of the New Testament. The biblical character of the prayers of the liturgy, and the place given to readings, made the presence of the book constant and necessary. The whole life of the church came to depend more and more not on an oral tradition, but on a tradition enshrined in literature. First there were all the rules and ordinances which later made up canon law; then the spiritual literature, the apologetics, and, after the appearance of heresies, polemic and dogma.[28] Thus, from the most immediate demands of piety to the most elevated ambitions of religious thought, everything conspired to demand from Christians a type of culture, and consequently an education, where literacy occupied a favoured place. For any Christian in the west a knowledge of Latin was therefore essential.[29] In Africa this was one of the specific qualities for which Bishop Valerius recruited Augustine to his church at Hippo:[30]

159

He [Valerius] used to tell people how the Lord had heard the prayers he had so often sent up to Him that heaven would send him just such a man as this [Augustine], who would help him to build up the Lord's Church by his invigorating teaching of the Word of God. For this was a work for which he knew himself to be less fitted, being a Greek by birth and less versed in the Latin language and literature.

The assumption of literacy in or a knowledge of Latin also lay behind all Augustine's work, as is clearly demonstrated in the summary of his sources by Augustine's biographer, Possidius:[31]

As for all that he dictated and published, and all the debates in the cathedral that were taken down and revised, some were against heretics of various kinds, others were expositions of the canonical books for the instruction of holy sons of the Church, but there are so many that there is hardly a student who has been able to read and get acquainted with them all. However, not to be thought in any way to fail those who are particularly eager for the words of truth, I have decided, if God furthers it, to append to this little work of mine a catalogue of these books, pamphlets, and letters. Anyone who reads it, and who cares more for God's truth than for earthly riches, will be able to pick out for himself the book he wants to read. If he wants to make himself a copy of it, he should apply to the Church at Hippo, where the best texts can generally be found. Or he may make inquiries anywhere else he can and should make a copy of what he finds and preserve it and not grudge lending it in his turn to someone else asking to copy it.

The importance of books in relation to Augustine and Christianity is summed up at the end of the *Life* in these words:[32]

To the Church he left an adequate body of clergy, as well as convents for men and women, full of celibates under their appointed superiors. He also left a library with books containing writings by himself and other holy men. It is through these, thanks be to God, that his quality and stature in the Church is known to the world; and in these he will always live among the faithful.

In Gaul a similar situation existed. St. Martin achieved a good many conversions by means of opportune miracles;[33] but religious life in the province was based as firmly on the written word as elsewhere in the empire. This is easily seen in the story of the election of Martin as Bishop of Tours:[34]

Particularly strong resistance was offered [to his election], it is said, by one of the bishops present, named Defender. It was much remarked, therefore, that he received unpleasant mention in the reading from the Prophets on that occasion. For it so happened that the Lector whose turn it was to read had been held up by the crowd and was not in his place and, in the confusion among the ministers during the wait for the absentee, one of the bystanders picked up a psalter and plunged into the first verses he saw. It was: 'Out of the mouths of babes and sucklings thou hast brought praise to perfection, to destroy the enemy and defender.' When these words were read, the congregation raised a shout and the opposition was put to shame and it was generally thought that God had prompted the reading of this particular psalm in order that Defender should hear its condemnation of his proceedings. For while the praise of the Lord had been brought to perfection out of the mouths of babes and sucklings in the person of Martin, he himself had been exposed as an enemy and destroyed at the same time.

In evangelizing Ireland St. Patrick, each time he chose or had brought to him a child to be made a monk, 'baptized him and gave him an alphabet'.[35] Throughout the West the newly formed monasteries, the schools which grew at the episcopal centres, and the schools which in the sixth century the parish priests of the countryside were ordered to form, all taught reading and writing in order to give access to the sacred literature and to provide an ever-increasing number of priests to explain and interpret the text to their flock. For all this, for conversion, for admission, for participation, and for understanding, some knowledge of Latin was a basic necessity. Britain, however, except for the aristocracy, was a Celtic-speaking country, and there is almost no trace of the Vulgar Latin which was the normal speech of the masses on the Continent. Conditions in Britain, therefore, were linguistically unsuitable for the propagation of Christianity.[36]

It is the same with Roman law, as Stevens has shown.[37] Caracalla's edict of A.D. 212, giving citizenship to virtually all the empire, should, Stevens argues, have brought the *ius civile* into everyone's life. Yet in A.D. 224 it was prescribed that a governor might try cases at his own discretion under local law and in any event should be prudent in tampering with it.[38] But the process of simplifying Roman law for the common man into what moderns have called a 'Vulgar Law' should have made this regulating act of A.D. 224 virtually superfluous. In late Roman Britain, however, Celtic law was still being applied and sometimes conflicted with Roman principles.[39] In A.D. 410 the Britons, in ejecting the Roman administrators, ejected the 'Laws of the Romans' with them.[40] The minority of Britons who practised Roman law will have been those whose Celtic system of land-tenure most nearly matched the Roman norm.[41] Only they will have been able to amass estates large enough to profit from Britain's inclusion within the empire and to become the province's aristocracy; but their way of life and their class will have been destroyed when Britain left the empire and lost her markets. The small number of those practising Roman law in Britain is demonstrated by the fact that after the Roman period there were on the Continent practitioners to draft codes of law for barbarian tribes along Roman lines and in the Latin language; but in Britain there were no practitioners of Roman law and few speakers of the Latin language.[42] Consequently Anglo-Saxon laws are unique among barbarian law codes both as written in the vernacular and as owing nothing to Roman law, while in Wales much of the original Celtic law survived from the pre-Roman period to be codified for the first time at the end of the tenth century A.D.[43]

The evidence thus far is that Christianity was certainly established in Roman Britain, but that, while there is evidence for the bulk of the population practising paganism, there is no evidence for their practising Christianity. The parallel evidence of language and laws confirms that the society of Roman Britain was not one in which Christianity was likely to flourish, while the linguistic evidence of the post-Roman funerary Latin inscriptions of the fifth and sixth centuries seem to show connections with new missionizing from Gaul rather than with surviving influence from Britain.[44] The Christianity of post-Roman Britain, then, may perhaps be seen as a new product, having nothing to do with the Roman period, when the province was essentially pagan. To represent Britain, however, as being strongly pagan in the fourth century is not to give a complete picture, for a number of major Christian finds since 1939 have forced scholars to reassess carefully the position of Christianity in the province. The most spectacular of the finds are the silver treasure from Mildenhall in Suffolk, the series of lead tanks from sites such as Icklingham in Suffolk, the painted wall-plaster from Lulling-stone in Kent, and the mosaic from Hinton St. Mary in Dorset.[45]

What is the significance of these important finds? The Christian nature of the Mildenhall silver is demonstrated by the Christian symbols on the spoons (Pls. LXIV, LXV). In addition, however, it is not mere chance that the great dish and two of the small platters have scenes which are Dionysiac in nature. From the time of the revival of his cult in Rome and Italy under Trajan down to the middle of the fourth century Dionysus and the members of his entourage enacted an ever-expanding role as the prime sources of pagan eschatological expectations. There is almost infinite variety of the themes proclaiming faith in Dionysus as lord and protector of the dead, conqueror of death, and cause of bliss in the after-life, and of his attendants—Centaurs, Victories, Cupids, Seasons, and so forth—as purveyors of his gifts and as conveyors of the souls of the departed to a better world. Accordingly it was relatively easy, in view of the number of ideas held in common, superficially at least, by the followers of Christ and Dionysus, for the early Christians to absorb into their art several elements of Bacchic imagery—notably the vine, along with vintaging and wine-pressing episodes; Victories, Cupids, Psyches, and Seasons as heralds of the soul's immortality in bliss and triumph over death; and even, very occasionally, the figure of Dionysus himself as a type of the life-giving, saving, and victorious Christ.[46] The scenes on the Mildenhall dish and platters must be seen as specific examples of this absorption of the Dionysiac cult by Christianity, with the marine symbolism of Oceanus in the centre of the great dish implying, as on the Dionysiac sarcophagi, the notion of the soul's journey across the ocean to a blissful further shore.[47] A large portion, then, of the Mildenhall treasure holds together not only as part of one of the largest hoards of silver plate in the late empire, but also as being specifically Christian in character.

The uses to which the lead tanks were put have been the subject of much speculation (Pls. LXVI, LXVII).[48] Their capacity ranges from about ten gallons in the case of the Ireby example to sixty-five gallons in the case of one of the tanks from Bourton-on-the-Water, and Sir Ian Richmond suggested that they might have been water-troughs or steeping-vats for dyeing, fulling, or brewing. Yet, as Professor Toynbee has pointed out, the comparatively elaborate external decoration which they bear makes the idea that they served such completely utilitarian purposes improbable.[49] They might have been ornamental; but all are most likely to have served religious purposes, some for pagan ritual ablutions, those with Christian symbols for liturgical usage, as fonts or baptisteries.[50] To this suggestion Professor Toynbee added a further point.[51] From representations on works of early Christian art it is clear that at this period baptism was administered by affusion, not by total immersion. Since the Icklingham and Wiggonholt tanks are 32 and $30\frac{1}{2}$ inches respectively in diameter, a neophyte could have stood in them with his feet in water, while the officiant poured water over his head from a *patera*. It may well be that the figured scene on the fragment of a tank from Walesby in Lincolnshire shows the first part of such a ceremony of baptism, with a man and woman disrobing and waiting for the baptism itself, which might have formed the subject of the scene in the left-hand portion of the frieze that is lost. If so, this would help confirm the baptismal function of the tanks; but whether religious or merely ornamental or purely practical in character, it is clear that the tanks with Christian emblems were made in the first instance for Christian owners, and it is of course not impossible that even the tanks without Christian symbols fulfilled a Christian religious function. All are likely to be of the same date and possibly the products of the same workshop, in view of their close similarity to one another.[52]

The interpretation of the Christian rooms in the Roman villa at Lullingstone has been well summed up by Professor Toynbee (Pls. LXVIII, LXIX *a*, *b*).[53] It is probable that the Christian wall-paintings mean that the Christian owners of the house had installed a domestic oratory there or had even converted this part of their home into a multi-cellular house-church or chapel-complex. In the latter case the room with the frieze of figures would have been the chapel proper, while the room leading out of it could have been the ante-chapel or narthex, approached through the lobby to its west, of which the only door led out of the villa on the north. The structural alterations made the four rooms in this part of the villa a self-contained entity in the fourth century, distinct in purpose from the other portions of the villa. In towns, after the Peace of the Church, multi-cellular house-churches were gradually superseded by independent 'basilicas'; but in country districts, such as that which surrounded the Lullingstone villa, house-churches are likely to have remained in use for many years, or even to have been installed *de novo*, in post-persecution times.[54] There is in fact evidence for churches and chapels built on the great country villa estates of late Roman Gaul.[55] At any rate, whether used as a church proper for Mass, or simply as an oratory for family prayers, comparable to the *sacrarium* on one of Ausonius' estates in Aquitaine, or even merely as a living-room occupied by Christians, the room with the frieze of figures at Lullingstone can claim to be either the first predominantly Christian room or the first certainly Christian place of worship discovered in Britain since the excavation of the church at Silchester; and the Christians to whom it belonged were clearly persons of wealth and importance. It has been wondered whether the six persons on the frieze of the main room represent members of the family which owned the villa; whether the group consists of a combination of dead and living Christians, the former curtained and the latter uncurtained; and whether, if this was a chapel, dead members of the family were commemorated there. In fact, however, the figures can now be seen to be so similar to each other that there is no likelihood that they are meant to be portraits, and we have no evidence for an alternative hypothesis, that this villa, remote from any urban ecclesiastical centre, contained the shrine or *memoria* of a well-known martyr. The absence of any heating apparatus below the fourth-century mosaic pavement of the dining-room suggests that at this period the house was used only as a summer residence. But the chapel complex may well have been kept open all the year round for the benefit of the Christians of the district. Hence its isolation from the rest of the villa. There is no proof that a secular life did not continue in other parts of the house after the installation of the Christian paintings, at least until the filling-in of the bath-block about A.D. 380.[56]

The main feature of the pavement at Hinton St. Mary now cannot be doubted to be a bust of Christ with the Chi-Rho monogram behind his head (Pl. LXX).[57] The tree of life, hunting-scenes, rosettes, and pomegranates are ubiquitous funerary symbols, and there is no reason why they should not bear a Christian interpretation in this context, in just the same way as do the pagan motifs in the undoubted Christian context of the mosaics of the fourth-century cathedral at Aquileia.[58] Similarly there is no difficulty in interpreting the Hinton St. Mary Bellerophon as a Christian ideal of victory over evil and death.[59] What is not yet possible, because of the fragmentary nature of the site, is to interpret the function of the building to which the pavements belong.[60] By analogy, however, something can be said, for there is on a site at Frampton in Dorset a series of pavements which were laid in three linked rooms at the same time and by the same firm as the Hinton St. Mary pavements (Pl. LXXI). The most famous of these is the Neptune and Chi-Rho mosaic, a pavement that consists of two figured squares, one larger than the other. From the side of the larger square projects an apse, with a chalice in a panel at its apex and across its chord a border, of which the sacred monogram in a roundel forms the central feature, while a floral scroll runs on either side of it. The square is framed all round by a border, in each of the four lengths of which is a dolphin-procession; while on the side adjacent to the apse, but within the square, is an inscription running to right and left of a centrally placed head of Neptune facing towards the apse and with a pair of dolphins issuing from his mouth. The head breaks through the dolphin procession at this point, as does also, in the centre of the side adjacent to the smaller square, a figure of Cupid, flanked by birds and, above them, by the remnants of another text. In the centre of the larger square is a roundel containing probably the remains of a Bellerophon and Chimaera scene.[61] Outside the roundel, in the corners of the square, are small square panels, each with a figure-group, one of which is lost, illustrating the story of Venus and Adonis. Between these squares are four lunette-shaped sectors, the decoration of three of which has disappeared, while in the fourth we can detect remains of water-birds. Beyond the linking geometric strip, in the smaller main square of the pavement, Bacchus is seated on a leopard in a large roundel, which is flanked on two sides of the square by rectangular panels, one showing a hunter in pursuit of a stag and what may be a bear, the other a second hunter attacking a lion. The large and centrally placed Chi-Rho in the apsed compartment of this pavement would seem to indicate that whoever had the Frampton mosaic laid was a Christian or had close Christian contacts. If that were so the pagan motifs of the two main squares, including the Neptune and the verses in his honour, do not appear to have troubled him. He would no doubt have interpreted them, as his pagan contemporary neighbours would have done, as symbols of the after-life, of death, rebirth, and paradise. The buildings to which this pavement and its companions belong have often been called a villa; but they lie in low, wet ground, unsuitable for a house, and, although Lysons's excavation did not recover the whole plan, his account suggests that he did not miss much of what remained. The plan is peculiar and cannot as it stands represent a villa-site. Lysons was quite sure, and his conclusion was:[62]

What is described above appears to ascertain the whole extent of the buildings to which these pavements belong: it will be seen by the plan that they bear no resemblance to a Roman house, nor do the rooms appear to have been adapted to domestic purposes; they seem rather to have been intended for purposes of religion: indeed the form of the pavement marked (B) in the ground plan pretty clearly indicates it to have been the floor of a temple. These edifices were probably dedicated to different deities, but the principal attention appears to have been paid to Neptune.

The motifs were less pagan than Lysons supposed. Indeed they may be taken as positively Christian. But there seems no reason to dispute his argument that the buildings at Frampton are religious and not domestic. Indeed, similar structures of the same date are to be found, for example, in the two Christian chapels found in 1957 and 1958 at Aquileia.[63] It is not known if the Hinton St. Mary mosaic was in an independent building or part of a larger structure; but the close connection of the mosaic with those at Frampton does suggest that, whichever is the case, the room that contained the mosaic may well have been a Christian chapel.[64]

Professor Frend has pointed out that the significance of the distribution of these finds and all earlier finds seems to be that the majority were associated with Roman villas or their owners.[65] Pewter dishes from Welney and Appleshaw, spoons from the Mildenhall hoard and the Chedworth villa, engraved silver table ware from Traprain Law, and gold signet-rings from the Fifehead Neville villa point to this conclusion.[66] So, too, do the Christian monograms scratched on freestone slabs at Chedworth before the final phase of its occupation.[67] The evidence of language and of law strengthens the hypothesis that it was only this class of society which was able, by changing from Celtic to Roman law, to accumulate the wealth which made possible the leisure and the literacy to be open to conversion to Christianity. The failure of this group to produce a missionary such as St. Martin of Tours resulted in their losing the leadership of British society when the central government of the empire withdrew its support. The church could have remained as a binding structure by which the population could eventually have dominated its new masters; but the lack of interest by the British aristocracy in proselytizing the masses to the new religion left the unromanized people completely open to domination by the new invaders and led to the disappearance of the aristocracy. Their own position had depended on Britain being part of the social and economic structure of the empire, and it had no support based on religion to fall back on within the island once the troops and administrators had departed. Consequently the estate names of their villas disappeared. Such names in Roman Gaul, very commonly adjectives in -acum formed from the name of the original owner, have survived in their hundreds in the present nomenclature of the villages of France.[68] This is not so in Britain.

Yet in spite of the end, and in spite of its small numbers, the Christian community was nevertheless important during its existence. Its beginning is doubtless to be seen in such villas as those in the Cirencester area with mosaics showing the theme of Orpheus and the beasts (Pl. LXXII).[69] Professor Toynbee has gone so far as to suggest that all or some of them may be crypto-Christian.[70] There is nothing hidden about these pavements, however, and they can without difficulty be accepted as an expression of a trend in Britain, as elsewhere, towards belief in an after-life and salvation for the initiate. Once Christianity became orthodox, however, there was obviously no difficulty in giving the Orpheus theme a Christian interpretation, and the moment is perhaps marked by the addition of a Hinton St. Mary type mosaic to the floor of the hall of the villa at Withington in Gloucestershire, and a similar conversion is demonstrated by the deliberate christianizing of the basin of the nymphs at Chedworth.[71] The dating of the Dorset group of mosaics soon after the Peace of the Church, the creation of house-churches possibly at Hinton St. Mary and Frampton and certainly at Lullingstone, and the use of expensive services of silver at Mildenhall and of pewter at Appleshaw, all demonstrate the early conversion and material wealth of these fourth-century villa-owners.[72] As for the intellectual vigour of the group, their religious thought was active enough to foster one of the great early Christian heresiarchs, Pelagius, who left the country about A.D. 380.[73] Later, between A.D. 420 and 430, Fastidius composed in Britain the work, *On the Christian Life*, addressed to a British woman.[74] Bede's description of the occasion in A.D. 429, when St. Germanus met the *immensa multitudo* at St. Albans and converted it from Pelagianism to orthodox Catholicism, and the evidence of the cemetery at Ancaster in Lincolnshire, if it is late Roman, may point to the cult making some headway in the towns as a popular movement in the early fifth century.[75] Yet there is little to set against the view that Christianity in Britain was almost entirely a religion practised by some of the richer landowners, and that, when the social and economic circumstances of the empire destroyed their class and way of life, the cult died with them.

The Christian discoveries since the war show that in the Roman period Britain was sharing fully in the main stream of Christian art in the West. One can find parallels to the Lullingstone wall-paintings, for example, in a sarcophagus and wall-paintings in the catacombs at Rome, in a fourth-century mosaic representing a church from a coffin found in a church at Tabarka on the north coast of Tunisia, and on the sarcophagus of Saint-Cannat.[76] With the other two major discoveries of the last thirty years, the Mildenhall treasure and the Hinton St. Mary mosaic, they have completely changed our conception of Christianity in Roman Britain, and they have enabled us to appreciate that Christianity in Britain was both distinctive in character and important out of all proportion to the quantity of remains it has left behind. Yet it was the failure of the villa-owners to establish Christianity as the basis of the new social order that led to the disappearance of their own order. The conversions could have been made, as the success of the missionizing of the fifth and sixth centuries shows.[77] The conversion of the Celtic areas in the west and north, however, is to be credited to missionaries trained in the Schools of Gaul.[78] This post-Roman phase continues with the arrival in A.D. 597 of the mission led by St. Augustine, whose two main tasks were the conversion of the Saxon kingdoms and the bringing of the church established in the Celtic areas into the Catholic unity.[79] The ending of the phase came in A.D. 663 at the Synod of Whitby when the problem of unity was finally resolved.[80] The members of the church throughout this period were of course the direct descendants of the population of the Roman period; but their faith seems to have been an entirely new affair, the result of post-Roman conversion, unconnected with the fourth-century Christianity of the upper-class, educated, landed owners of the Icklingham, Mildenhall, Lullingstone, and Hinton St. Mary estates, whose tenants in town and countryside were almost all pagan.[81]

K. S. PAINTER

[1] Williams (1912), pp. 54 ff. The stories about Paul and Peter are neither tradition nor even fiction but late conclusions drawn from words used by Paul and from words written by ancient writers about the two saints. The story of Joseph is connected with the story of the founding of Glastonbury and is found first in the writings of William of Malmesbury (died A.D. 1142). It is part of the cycle of literary romances that centre on the quest for the Holy Grail.

[2] Williams (1912), pp. 60 ff.; Bede, *H.E.* i. 4, who goes on '. . . susceptamque fidem Britanni usque in tempora Diocletiani principis inviolatam integramque quieta in pace servabant'. The story also appears in Nennius, *Hist. Brittonum*, c. 22. Both Bede and Nennius derive their accounts from the *Liber Pontificalis*.

[3] The best recent discussions about Alban are by Frend and Morris. Frend (in Barley and Hanson (1968), p. 38) summarizes the evidence as follows, 'The first tangible evidence for Christianity in Britain may well be the traditions surrounding the martyrdom of the soldier Alban at Verulamium. Alban's death is attested in four independent sources, namely his *Acta Martyrum*, the *De excidio Britanniae* of Gildas, the *Vita Germani* of Constantius, written in Gaul *c.* 475 (*Vita* 16: *MGH, Merov,* vii. 262), and a reference in the sixth-century Gallic poet, Venantius Fortunatus (see Levison (1941), pp. 337 ff., and Morris (1968), and Stevens (1941), p. 373). If the last two entries are too late to carry conviction, the *Acta* have the merit of showing detailed knowledge of the topography of Verulamium and must be taken seriously. The cult of Alban can also be traced back at least to 429. The martyrdom, however, can hardly have occurred as Bede suggests (*H.E.* i. 7) in the Great Persecution under Diocletian and his associates (A.D. 303–12), for contemporaries were unanimous that Constantius I, in whose dominions Britain lay, took practically no part in the persecution (Augustine, *Ep.* 88. 2, citing a letter from Donatist bishops to Constantine in 313, Lactantius, *De Mortibus Persecutorum*, 15, and Eusebius, *H.E.* viii. 13. 12). Levison's tentative arguments in favour of the period Decius-Valerian (A.D. 250–60) are not supported by anything much more tangible than inherent probability. Recently, Dr. John Morris has pointed

to the description in the *Acta* of Alban's judge as "Caesar" in the earliest manuscript. This could be merely fantasy on the part of the author designed to increase the importance of the martyr in the eyes of his readers, but it could also refer to Geta Caesar who in 208–9 was left as the governor of the civil province of Britain while his father Septimius Severus and his elder brother Caracalla were campaigning against the Picts. The view that a governor might order the cessation of persecution on the ground that it was simply aiding the spread of Christianity could correspond to an early third-century situation when "the blood of martyrs" was "seed", and when the lot of Christians was very much at the mercy of individual governors (as shown by cases quoted by Tertullian in *Ad Scapulam* written in 212–13). We would be wise however to admit with Levison, "*ignoramus* and *ignorabimus*" (Levison (1941), p. 350).' The martyrdom of Aaron and Julius, *legionum urbis cives*, has been credited to Chester, to Carlisle, and to Caerleon. The ancient sources are Bede, *H.E.* i. 7; Gildas, *DEB* 10: 31. 14–22; Geoffrey of Monmouth; Giraldus Cambrensis. For modern discussions see Toynbee (1953), p. 2; Levison (1941), pp. 340–4; Davies (1968), pp. 136 and 144. For the date, *c.* A.D. 250–60, see Williams (1912), p. 102.

[4] *adv. Iudaeos,* 7.

[5] e.g. *Hom. iv in Ezek, Quando enim terra Britanniae ante adventum Christi in unius dei consensit religionem?*

[6] The Corbey MS. Mansi, *Conciliorum nova et amplissima collectio,* ii, p. 476.

[7] Mann (1961) has suggested that the priest and deacon formed a fourth delegation, their bishop for some reason being unable to attend. Sir Ian Richmond, however, took them to be the attendants of Bishop Adelphius, their attendance perhaps indicating his primacy (*Archaeological Journal*, ciii, 1947, p. 64). Mann's hypothesis, that the three bishops and the other two priests represented the churches of the capitals of the four British provinces of the day (York, London, Lincoln, or Colchester, and perhaps Cirencester) is attractive. Mann's argument is (1) that four of the five provinces of the diocese of the Gauls were each represented by one bishop, or his appointees, only, (2) that a comparison

with the *Notitia Galliarum* shows that in each case the bishop, or his appointees, came from the Metropolis or capital of the province, (3) that circumstances in Gaul and in Britain are likely to have been similar, and that the pattern visible in the diocese of the Gauls is probably relevant for comparison with Britain, (4) that the Verona List shows that in A.D. 312–14 there were four provinces in Britain, and (5) that the delegations from Britain are therefore probably four in number, one from each of the capitals of the provinces. Against this, (1) as Mann himself points out, the same pattern of delegations does not emerge from the dioceses of Viennensis or the Spains, and the fifth of the provinces of the diocese of the Gauls, Lugdunensis Prima, was represented by two delegations, that from the Capital Lugdunum being supported by another from Augustodunum, (2) Richmond's suggestion seems to account more satisfactorily for the force of *exinde* in the last item, making Sacerdos and Arminius dependent on Adelphius, than does Mann's interpretation of the word as 'also from Britain', (3) similarity between Gaul and Britain is assumed and not proved, (4) Mann is attempting to locate the four provinces of Britain and their capitals on the evidence of the delegation-list, not to interpret the delegation-list on the basis of known provinces and capitals, and for him, therefore, the assumption that the delegations come from the capitals is basic. Mann's argument turns on the similarity of the Church in Gaul and Britain. In other ways this paper tries to show that they were not.

8 *Sacr. Hist.* ii. 41.

9 Constantius, *Vita S. Germani*, 13–18. Constantius was born at Lyon about A.D. 415, and probably wrote the *Life* about A.D. 480. Bede repeats the story, *Historia Ecclesiastica*, i. 17, 18, 20.

10 This was found in 1868, scratched in rustic capitals on a fragment of red wall-plaster from a Roman house, reading ROTAS/OPERA/TENET/AREPO/SATOR, and generally translated, 'the sower Arepo holds the wheel carefully'. In 1926 Grosser published his discovery that all the letters can be rearranged to form a cross, of which the vertical and horizontal limbs are each composed of the words PATER NOSTER, with the single N at the central point of intersection and A and O (alpha and omega) before and after each PATER NOSTER. See Toynbee (1953), pp. 2–3. For the date see Frere (1967), p. 332.

11 Collingwood (1930), pp. 145, 176; Collingwood and Myres (1936), p. 273; Toynbee

(1953). For the three bishops see Sulpicius Severus, *Sacr. Hist.* ii. 41.

12 This list is adapted from Lewis (1966), p. 47, where detailed references are given.

13 Bradford and Goodchild (1939), especially p. 32; also C. E. Stevens, 'The Frilford Site—A Postscript', in *Oxoniensia*, v (1940), p. 166.

14 Rahtz (1951), especially p. 117 and pp. 127–35 for the coins.

15 T. Mommsen and P. Krüger, *Theodosiani Libri XVI*, i. 2 (Berlin, 1905), xvi. 10, 4 (346 [354?] Dec. 1): *IDEM AA. AD TAVRVM (PRAEFECTVM) P(RAETORIO). Placuit omnibus locis adque urbibus universis claudi protinus templa et accessu vetito omnibus licentiam delinquendi perditis abnegari. Volumus etiam cunctos sacrificiis abstinere. Quod si quis aliquid forte huiusmodi perpetraverit, gladio ultore sternatur. Facultates etiam perempti fisco decernimus vindicari et similiter adfligi (or puniri) rectores provinciarum, si facinora vindicare neglexerint.* A. H. M. Jones, *The Later Roman Empire I* (1964), i, p. 113.

16 Pagans Hill: see above, note 14. Worth, *Antiquaries Journal*, viii (1928), pp. 76 ff.; xvii (1937), p. 310; xx (1940), p. 115.

17 Wheeler (1943), pp. 72 ff., 120 ff., 131 ff.

18 Wheeler (1932), p. 31.

19 Ibid. For the inscription, p. 102. The inscription is lost, but is recorded in a drawing: *D . . . TILVIVS SENILIS PR REL EX STIPIBVS POSSVII/O. . . . ANTE VICTORINO INTER . . . l . . . E.* This was restored by Collingwood as *D(eo) N(odenti) T(itus) Flavius Senilis, pr(aepositus) rel(iquationi), ex stipibus possuit; o[pus cur]ante Victorino inter-[pret]e.* 'To the god Nodens, Titus Flavius Senilis, officer in charge of the supply-depot of the fleet, laid this pavement out of money offerings; the work being in charge of Victorinus, interpreter on the governor's staff.' For the coins see pp. 104–31. For the trinkets, see pp. 68 ff.; there are, for example, fragments of about 270 bronze bracelets, a number too large to be accounted for by accidental loss, and surely therefore to be accounted for as votive offerings of the poor deposited in the temple (pp. 82–4).

20 *Verulamium*: Wheeler (1936), pp. 31, 131 ff.; *Cirencester*: Collingwood and Wright (1965), no. 103, Face, '*I(ovi) O(ptimo) [M(aximo)]/ L(ucius) Sept(imius) [. . ./ u(ir) p(erfectissimus) pr(aeses) B[r(itanniae) pr(imae)] resti[tuit]/ ciuis R[emus]*', Back, '*[Si]gnum et/[e]rectam/[p]risca re/[li]gione co/[l]umnam*', Left side, '*Septimius/*

169 z

renouat/primae/provinciae/rector'; *Silchester*: Boon (1957), p. 120.

[21] London Mithraeum: W. F. Grimes (1968), pp. 109, 117.

[22] *London: B.M. Guide to Early Christian and Byzantine Antiquities* (1921), fig. 38, *JRS*, xliii (1954), p. 107, and Merrifield (1965), pp. 61–2; *Exeter*: Fox (1952), p. 92; *Canterbury*: Painter (1965), Jenkins (1965); *Catterick*: *JRS*, l (1960), p. 239.

[23] Rice Holmes (1911), pp. 346–8; Jackson (1953), p. 230; Collingwood and Myres (1936), p. 437; Ordnance Survey, *Map of Britain in the Dark Ages* (1966), pp. 23 and 54.

[24] There are close on 200 inscriptions dating between the fifth and twelfth or thirteenth centuries. For the numbers and distribution see Jackson (1953), p. 151.

[25] Jackson (1953), p. 162.

[26] Ibid. pp. 163 ff. See also Nash-Williams (1950), pp. 3–16.

[27] Brown (1968), pp. 90–1, points out that Augustine's vast output in Hippo demonstrates the pressure of the need to extend religious literacy as widely as possible. The recruitment of the clergy, the introduction of the monastic life, the consequent growth of a piety based on the *Lectio Divina* —all these changes of the late fourth century placed more and more weight on the Latin language. See also Marrou (1965), p. 476.

[28] The relationship between Judaism and Christianity: Sulpicius Severus (*Chronicon*, ii. 30, 6) records that, after the burning of the Temple, the Emperor Titus turned over in his mind the possibility of destroying both Judaism and Christianity: '*Quippe has religiones, licet contrarias sibi, isdem tamen ab auctoribus profectos Christianos ex Judaeis extitisse, radice sublatam stirpem facile perituram.*' See Frend (1965), pp. 178 ff. The literary nature of Christianity: Marrou (1965), pp. 453 ff.

[29] Brown (1968), pp. 90–1. There were some translations of the Bible in antiquity into the language of non-classical, sometimes non-literate peoples, such as the Ethiopians, Armenians, Georgians, Huns, Germans, and, in the ninth century, Slavs; but these were exceptions from the rule of trying to draw the pagan out of the confines of his language into a culture which (for the west) could only find adequate expression in Latin. See Brown (1968), pp. 90–1, and Marrou (1965), p. 456.

[30] Possidius, *Sancti Augustini Vita*, v: *Preces quas frequentissime fudisset suas exauditas a Domino fuisse narrabat, ut sibi divinitus homo concederetur talis, qui posset verbo Dei et doctrina salubri Ecclesiam Domini aedificare: cui rei se homo natura Graecus, minusque Latina lingua et litteris instructus, minus utilem pervidebat.*

[31] Possidius, *Sancti Augustini Vita*, xviii: *Tanta autem ab eodem dictata et edita sunt, tantaque in ecclesia disputata, excepta atque emendata, vel adversus diversos haereticos, vel ex canonicis libris exposita ad aedificationem sanctorum Ecclesiae filiorum, ut ea omnia vix quisquam studiosorum perlegere et nosse sufficiat. Verumtamen ne veritatis verbi avidissimos in aliquo fraudare videamur, statui Deo praestante in huius opusculi fine etiam eorundem librorum: tractatuum et epistolarum Indiculum adiungere: quo lecto qui magis Dei veritatem quam temporales amant divitias, sibi quisque quod voluerit ad legendum eligat, et id ad describendum, vel de bibliotheca Hipponensis ecclesiae petat, ubi emendatiora exemplaria forte potuerint inveniri, vel unde valuerit inquirat, et inventa describat et habeat, et petenti ad describendum sine invidia etiam ipse tribuat.*

[32] Possidius, *Sancti Augustini Vita*, xxxi: *Clerum sufficientissimum, et monasteria virorum ac feminarum continentibus cum suis praepositis plena Ecclesiae dimisit, una cum bibliotheca et libris tractatus vel suos vel aliorum sanctorum habentibus, in quibus dono Dei qualis quantusque in Ecclesia fuerit noscitur, et his semper vivere a fidelibus invenitur.*

[33] Sulpicius Severus, *Life of St. Martin*, xiii, xiv, xv, etc.

[34] Ibid., ix.

[35] Stokes, tr. of *Life of St. Patrick*, ii. 326, 29; 328, 27; 497, 24. See also Marrou (1965), p. 476.

[36] For the extent to which Latin was spoken in Britain see Jackson (1948); Jackson (1953), pp. 94 ff., 107 ff., 247; and Jackson (1954), pp. 61–3.

[37] Stevens (1947), pp. 132–4; Stevens (1966).

[38] For the edict of Caracalla see Jones (1960), pp. 129–40. Its date may be A.D. 314; see *Journal of Egyptian Archaeology*, xlviii (1962), pp. 124–31. For the law of A.D. 224 see *Cod. Just.* viii. 53, 1.

[39] See Stevens (1947).

[40] Zosimus, vi. 5, 2.

[41] Stevens (1966).

[42] For the practitioners of Roman law drafting codes for the barbarians, see Stevens (1966), p. 110, quoting Levy, *West Roman Vulgar Law*,

pp. 14–17. For the extent to which Latin was spoken in Britain see Jackson (1953), pp. 94 ff., 107 ff., 247.

43 Stevens (1966), especially pp. 110–11.

44 See Jackson (1953), ch. V. 'The Early Christian Inscriptions', especially pp. 190 ff.

45 Toynbee (1953), pp. 1–24; Frend (1955), pp. 1–18. *Mildenhall*: Brailsford (1947); *Lead Tanks*: Toynbee (1953), pp. 15–16; *Lullingstone*: Meates *et al.* (1951); Meates *et al.* (1953); Meates (1954); Meates (1955); Meates (1956); *Hinton St. Mary*: Toynbee (1964a); Toynbee (1964b); Painter (1967); Taylor (1967).

46 Turcan (1966); Lehmann-Hartleben and Olsen (1942).

47 Turcan (1966), p. 508.

48 Toynbee (1953), pp. 15–16.

49 Ibid., p. 16.

50 Cabrol and Leclerq (1903–50), 'Baptême'; 'Baptistère'; 'Immersion'.

51 Toynbee (1953), p. 16.

52 Ibid., Toynbee (1964c), pp. 353–5. For scenes of fourth- or fifth-century baptism showing the neophyte standing in a small tank or basin, while water flows upon his or her head, see Brusin (1936), pp. 12, 45, fig. 26, and Cabrol and Leclerq, I. ii (1924), col. 2672, fig. 871.

53 Toynbee (1964c), pp. 221–7 (with bibliography).

54 Toynbee (1953), p. 12.

55 Mâle (1950), pp. 62–4.

56 Meates (1955), pp. 159–61.

57 Toynbee (1964b).

58 Brusin (1964), pp. 24–39.

59 For detailed accounts and bibliographies of the known Bellerophon pavements see Aymard (1953); Toynbee (1955); Toynbee (1964c). The Bellerophon mosaic at Hinton St. Mary is the thirteenth such representation to be discovered, or the fourteenth if the damaged central roundel at Frampton is similarly identified, as it probably should be (Toynbee (1968), pp. 182–3). The other mosaics are at Olynthus in Greece, at Autun, Avenches, Nîmes, and Reims in France, at Herzogenbuchsee in Switzerland, at Parndorf in Austria, at Coimbra in Portugal, at Gerona in Spain, at Lullingstone and Frampton in England, at Ravenna in Italy, and at Istanbul in Turkey. Chronologically they range from the fifth century B.C. in Greece to the sixth century A.D. at Istanbul. The majority, however, seem to fall into a group in the western provinces, to be dated between the second and fourth centuries A.D., and the popularity of

the theme may well date from the time of Hadrian. There can be no doubt about the Christian significance of the Bellerophon scene in spite of a recent vigorous statement to the contrary by Brandenburg (1968). Brandenburg admits that the Chi-Rho must represent Christ; but he assumes that the owner was chiefly interested in motifs suggesting well-being and good food. He takes Bellerophon to represent the ideal hunter who provides food for the table, and he thinks that the Chi-Rho bust is not Our Lord as Saviour, but as a sort of 'magical' provider of the good things of this life. Brandenburg wants all the motifs in the mosaic to be 'status-symbols' of the owners' wealth and abundance of the good things of this life. There is surely, however, as Professor Toynbee has pointed out to me, no more difficulty in interpreting the Hinton St. Mary Bellerophon as an 'ideal' of victory over evil and death than as an 'ideal' hunter. And since winds, hunting-scenes, rosettes, and pomegranates are ubiquitous funerary symbols, there is no reason why they should not be symbolic on the Hinton St. Mary mosaic. It seems, moreover, to create unnecessary difficulties if one insists on taking the clear motif as being not Christian but merely the representative symbol of a kind of magical all-provider of material goods. The prominence of the Chi-Rho bust seems in fact to put the truly Christian character of the Hinton St. Mary mosaic beyond all doubt. If parallels are wanted for traditional pagan motifs in a Christian context, and therefore bearing an undoubted Christian interpretation, one needs only to look, for example, at the mosaics of the fourth-century cathedral at Aquileia.

60 Painter (1967).

61 Lysons (1813); Toynbee (1968), pp. 182–3.

62 Lysons (1813).

63 Brusin (1961).

64 Lysons (1813); Farrar (1957); Painter (1967), p. 24.

65 Frend (1955), p. 7.

66 *Welney*: *Cambridge Antiq. Soc. Proc.* xli (1949), p. 79; *Appleshaw*: Engleheart (1898), and Haverfield (1900); *Mildenhall*: Brailsford (1947); *Chedworth*: *Archaeological Journal*, xxvi (1869), p. 225, St. Clair Baddeley, *Chedworth Roman Villa* (1934), p. 25, Richmond (1960); *Traprain Law*: Curle (1923); *Fifehead Neville*: *Proc. Soc. Ant.*, ser. 2, 1881–3, p. 68, *Ant. Journ.* ii (1922), p. 89, Toynbee (1953), p. 19, and *B.M. Guide to Early Christian and Byzantine Antiquities* (1921), figs. 33 and 34.

[67] *Chedworth slabs*: Toynbee (1953), pp. 14–15; Richmond (1960), p. 22; H Scarth, *J.B.A.A.* (1869), xxv. 217–18.

[68] Jackson (1953), p. 233.

[69] Smith (1965).

[70] Toynbee (1968), pp. 188–9.

[71] Richmond (1960), p. 22.

[72] Dating of Dorset mosaics: Smith (1965).

[73] Myres (1960).

[74] The career of Fastidius was described briefly at the end of the fifth century by Gennadius of Marseille (*De Scriptoribus Ecclesiasticis* 56: *Patrologia Latina* 58. 1094). See Frend (1968).

[75] Constantius, *Vita Sancti-Germani*, 12–18.

[76] *Sarcophagus from Rome*: Toynbee (1964c, pp. 225–6) points out that, 'A notable parallel to the scheme of design of this monogram is provided by the carving in the central panel of a marble-columned sarcophagus of the mid-fourth century, found in the Domitilla Catacomb near Rome and now in the Lateran Christian Museum (no. 171: C. van der Meer and C. Mohrmann, *Atlas of the Early Christian World*, 1958, pp. 142–3, 145, figs. 466–7). There, in the lateral panels, are scenes from Our Lord's Passion, His encounter with Pilate in the two panels on the right, His crowning with thorns (for which a wreath of bejewelled laurel is actually substituted), and the carrying of the Cross by Simon the Cyrenaean on the left. The two innermost colonettes support a shell-shaped semi-dome, from the crown of which emerges the head of an eagle holding in its beak a laurel wreath that encircles a large-scale, very prominent chi-rho monogram. The ends of the *taenia* that binds the wreath fly out on either side, carved in low relief against the background. The bottom of the wreath rests on the top of the vertical stem of a cross-like feature, on each of the horizontal arms of which is perched an inward-facing bird, pecking at the wreath. Beneath the arms of the Cross two sleeping soldiers are seated. The monogram, wreathed in victor's laurel, does, in fact, represent Our Lord rising from the Holy Sepulchre, the place of which is taken by the Cross. Life is triumphant over death, Easter Sunday over Good Friday. The Cross has become the banner of the Victor; and it has been suggested (van der Meer and Mohrmann, o.c.) that the soldiers' attitudes were intended to recall those of conquered barbarians crouched beneath a pagan Roman trophy. The birds are Christian souls feeding on the life-giving garland, just as at Lullingstone the birds eat seeds or berries falling from the wreath; and the busts of Sun and Moon in the angles above the springs of the semi-dome represent the vault of Heaven, into which the eagle is carrying the wreath and monograph. It may well be that at Lullingstone the main-room monogram, at any rate, symbolised the Resurrection and that, if there really were, say, two columns below the wreath, they suggested the architecture of the Tomb.' *Catacombs*: Wilpert (1903), e.g. pls. 88, 174; *Tabarka*: H. Leclerq, 'Eglise', in Cabrol and Leclerq, iv. 2, cols. 2231–3, Gauckler (1906), Ward-Perkins and Goodchild (1953), pp. 57–8; *Saint-Cannat Sarcophagus*: Leclerq in Cabrol and Leclerq, iv. 2, col. 2229.

[77] For surveys of Wales and the north see Davies (1968) and Thomas (1968).

[78] Frend (1968), pp. 43–4.

[79] Bede, *H.E.*, i. 26.

[80] Ibid. iii. 25.

[81] I have received help with this paper, directly or indirectly, from many people. I must thank especially J. W. Brailsford, Mrs. I. Cotton, S. S. Frere, W. H. C. Frend, D. B. Harden, P. Compton, Miss M. Salisbury, and Miss J. M. C. Toynbee.

BIBLIOGRAPHY

Aymard (1953) Jacques Aymard, 'La Mosaïque de Bellérophon à Nîmes', in *Gallia*, xi (1953), pp. 249–71.

Barley and Hanson (1968) M. W. Barley and R. P. C. Hanson (edd.), *Christianity in Britain, 300–700* (Leicester University Press, 1968).

Bede, *H.E.* Bede, *Historia Ecclesiastica*.

Boon (1957) G. C. Boon, *Roman Silchester* (Max Parrish, London, 1957).

Bradford and Goodchild (1939) J. S. P. Bradford and R. G. Goodchild, 'Excavations at Frilford, Berkshire, 1937–8', in *Oxoniensia*, iv (1939), pp. 1–70.

Brailsford (1947) J. W. Brailsford, *The Mildenhall treasure* (British Museum, 1947).

Brandenburg (1968)   Hugo Brandenburg, 'Bellérophon Christianus? Zur Deutung des Mosaiks von Hinton St. Mary und zum Problem der Mythendarstellungen in der kaiserzeitlichen dekorativen Kunst', in *Römische Quartalschrift*, lxiii (1968), pts. 1/2, pp. 49–86.

Brown (1968)   P. Brown, 'Christianity and Local Culture in Late Roman Africa', in *JRS*, lviii (1968), pp. 85–95.

Brusin (1936)   G. Brusin, *Il Reale Museo Archeologico di Aquileia* (itinerari dei musei e monumenti d'Italia, no. 48, 1936).

Brusin (1961)   G. Brusin, *Due Nuovi Sacelli Cristiani di Aquileia* (Aquileia, 1961).

Brusin (1964)   G. Brusin, *Aquileia e Grado* (Padua, 1964).

Cabrol and Leclerq   F. Cabrol and H. Leclerq, *Dictionnaire d'archéologie chrétienne et de liturgie* (Paris, 1903–50).

Collingwood (1930)   R. G. Collingwood, *The Archaeology of Roman Britain* (Methuen, 1930).

Collingwood and Myres (1936)   R. G. Collingwood and J. N. L. Myres, *Roman Britain and the English Settlements* (Oxford, 1936).

Collingwood and Wright (1965)   R. G. Collingwood and R. P. Wright, *The Roman Inscriptions of Britain*, i (Oxford, 1965).

Curle (1923)   A. O. Curle, *The treasure of Traprain* (1923).

Davies (1968)   W. H. Davies, 'The Church in Wales', in Barley and Hanson (1968), pp. 131–50.

Engleheart (1898)   G. H. Engleheart, 'On Some Buildings of the Romano-British Period, Discovered at Clanville, near Andover, and on a deposit of Pewter Vessels of the same period found at Appleshaw, Hants.', in *Archaeologia*, lvi (1898).

Farrar (1957)   R. A. H. Farrar, 'The Frampton Villa, Maiden Newton', in *Proceedings of the Dorset Natural History and Archaeological Society for 1956*, vol. lxxviii (1957), pp. 81–3.

Fox (1952)   Aileen Fox, *Roman Exeter* (1952).

Frend (1955)   W. H. C. Frend, 'Religion in Roman Britain in the Fourth Century', in *JBAA*, xviii (1955), pp. 1–18.

Frend (1965)   W. H. C. Frend, *Martyrdom and Persecution in the Early Church* (Blackwell, Oxford, 1965).

Frend (1968)   W. H. C. Frend, 'The Christianisation of Roman Britain', in Barley and Hanson (1968), pp. 37–49.

Frere (1967)   S. S. Frere, *Britannia, A history of Roman Britain* (Routledge & Kegan Paul, London, 1967).

Gauckler (1906)   P. Gauckler, in *Monuments et mémoires Piot*, xiii (1906), pp. 188–97, pl. xviii.

Grimes (1968)   W. F. Grimes, *The Excavation of Roman and Mediaeval London* (Routledge & Kegan Paul, London, 1968).

Haverfield (1900)   F. Haverfield, 'Romano-British Hampshire', in *A History of Hampshire and the Isle of Wight* (Victoria History of the Counties of England), vol. i, (1900), pp. 297–8.

JBAA   *Journal of the British Archaeological Association*.

JRS   *Journal of Roman Studies*.

Jackson (1948)   K. Jackson, 'On the Vulgar Latin of Roman Britain', in U. T. Holmes and A. J. Denomy (edd.), *Mediaeval Studies in Honor of J. D. M. Ford* (Cambridge, Mass., 1948).

Jackson (1953)   K. Jackson, *Language and History in Early Britain* (Edinburgh, 1953).

Jackson (1954)   K. Jackson, 'The British Language during the Period of the English settlements', in N. K. Chadwick (ed.), *Studies in Early British History* (Cambridge, 1954), pp. 61–82.

Jenkins (1965)   F. Jenkins, 'St. Martin's Church at Canterbury: A Survey of the Earliest Structural Features', in *Medieval Archaeology*, IX (1965), pp. 11–15.

Jones (1960)   A. H. M. Jones, *Studies in Roman Government and Law* (Oxford, 1960).

Jones (1964)   A. H. M. Jones, *The Later Roman Empire* (Blackwell, Oxford, 1964).

Lehmann-Hartleben and Olsen (1942)   K. Lehmann-Hartleben and E. C. Olsen, *Dionysiac Sarcophagi in Baltimore* (New York and Baltimore, 1942).

Levison (1941)   W. Levison, 'St. Alban and St. Albans', in *Antiquity*, xv (1941), pp. 337 ff.

Lewis (1966)   M. J. T. Lewis, *Temples in Roman Britain* (Cambridge University Press, 1966).

Lysons (1813)   S. Lysons, *Reliquiae Romanae-Britannicae*, i (London, 1813).

Mâle (1950)   E. Mâle, *La Fin du paganisme en Gaule* (Paris, 1950).

Mann (1961)   J. C. Mann, 'The Administration of Roman Britain', in *Antiquity*, xxxv (1961), pp. 316–20.

Marrou (1965)   H.-I. Marrou, *Histoire de l'éducation dans l'Antiquité* (6th ed., Paris, 1965).

Meates *et al.* (1951)   G. W. Meates, E. Greenfield, and E. Birchenough, 'The Lullingstone Roman Villa', in *Archaeologia Cantiana*, lxiii for 1950 (1951), pp. 1–49.

Meates *et al.* (1953)   G. W. Meates, E. Greenfield, and E. Birchenough, 'The Lullingstone Roman Villa, Second Interim Report', in *Archaeologia Cantiana*, lxv for 1952 (1953), pp. 26–78.

Meates (1954)   G. W. Meates, 'The Lullingstone Roman Villa, Third Interim Report', in *Archaeologia Cantiana*, lxvi for 1953 (1954), pp. 15–36.

Meates (1955)   G. W. Meates, *The Lullingstone Roman Villa* (Heinemann, London, 1955).

Meates (1956)   G. W. Meates, 'Lullingstone Roman Villa', in R. L. S. Bruce-Mitford (ed.), *Recent Archaeological Excavations in Britain* (Routledge & Kegan Paul, London, 1956), pp. 87–110.

Merrifield (1965)   R. Merrifield, *The Roman City of London* (Ernest Benn Ltd., London, 1965).

Morris (1968)   J. R. Morris, 'The date of St. Alban' in *Hertfordshire Archaeology*, i (1968), pp. 1–8.

Myres (1960)   J. N. L. Myres, 'Pelagius and the End of Roman Rule in Britain', in *JRS*, l (1960), pp. 21–36.

Nash-Williams (1950)   V. E. Nash-Williams, *The Early Christian Monuments of Wales* (Cardiff, 1950).

Painter (1965)   K. S. Painter, 'A Roman Silver Treasure from Canterbury', in *JBAA*, xxviii (1965), pp. 1–15.

Painter (1967)   K. S. Painter, 'The Roman Site at Hinton St. Mary, Dorset', in *British Museum Quarterly*, xxxii (1967), pp. 15–31.

Rahtz (1951)   P. Rahtz, 'The Roman Temple at Pagans Hill, Chew Stoke, N. Somerset', in *Proceedings of the Somersetshire Archaeological and Natural History Society*, xcvi (1951), pp. 112–42.

Rice Holmes (1911) T. Rice Holmes, *Caesar's Conquest of Gaul* (Oxford, 1911).

Richmond (1960)   I. A. Richmond, 'The Roman Villa at Chedworth', in *Transactions of the Bristol and Gloucestershire Archaeological Society*, lxxviii for 1959 (1960), pp. 5 ff.

Smith (1965) D. J. Smith, 'Three fourth-century schools of Mosaic in Roman Britain', in *La Mosaïque gréco-romaine* (Éditions du Centre national de la recherche scientifique, Paris, 1965).

Stevens (1941) C. E. Stevens, 'Gildas Sapiens', in *English Historical Review*, lvi (1941), p. 373.

Stevens (1947) C. E. Stevens, 'A Possible Conflict of Laws in Roman Britain', in *JRS*, xxxvii (1947), pp. 132–4.

Stevens (1966) C. E. Stevens, 'The Social and Economic Aspects of Rural Settlement', in C. Thomas (ed.), *Rural Settlement in Roman Britain* (Council for British Archaeology, Research Report 7, London, 1966), pp. 108–28.

Taylor (1967) C. C. Taylor, 'The Later History of the Roman Site at Hinton St. Mary, Dorset', in *British Museum Quarterly*, xxxii (1967), pp. 31–5.

Thomas (1968) A. C. Thomas, 'The Evidence from North Britain', in Barley and Hanson (1968), pp. 93 ff.

Toynbee (1953) J. M. C. Toynbee, 'Christianity in Roman Britain', in *Journal of the British Archaeological Association*, xvi (1953), pp. 1–24.

Toynbee (1955) J. M. C. Toynbee, 'Mosaïques au Bellérophon', in *Gallia*, xiii (1955), pp. 91–7.

Toynbee (1958) J. M. C. Toynbee, 'Encore des mosaïques de Bellérophon', in *Gallia*, xvi (1958), pp. 262–6.

Toynbee (1964*a*) J. M. C. Toynbee, *The Christian Roman Mosaic, Hinton St. Mary, Dorset* (Dorset Monographs no. 3, published by the Dorset Natural History and Archaeological Society, 1964; also printed in volume 85 of the Society's *Proceedings*).

Toynbee (1964*b*) J. M. C. Toynbee, 'The Christian Roman Mosaic, Hinton St. Mary, Dorset', in *JRS*, lxiv (1964), pp. 7–14.

Toynbee (1964*c*) J. M. C. Toynbee, *Art in Britain under the Romans* (Oxford, 1964).

Toynbee (1968) J. M. C. Toynbee, 'Pagan Motifs and Practices in Christian art and ritual in Roman Britain', in Barley and Hanson (1968), pp. 177–92.

Turcan (1966) R. Turcan, *Les Sarcophages romains à Représentations dionysiaques; Essai de chronologie et d'histoire religieuse* (Bibl. des écoles françaises d'Athènes et de Rome, 210: Paris: E. de Boccard, 1966).

Ward-Perkins and Goodchild (1953) J. B. Ward-Perkins and R. G. Goodchild, 'The Christian Antiquities of Tripolitania', in *Archaeologia*, xcv (1953), pp. 1–84.

Wheeler (1932) R. E. M. Wheeler and T. V. Wheeler, *Excavation of the Prehistoric, Roman and Post-Roman Site in Lydney Park, Gloucestershire* (Reports of the Research Committee of the Society of Antiquaries of London, ix, 1932).

Wheeler (1936) R. E. M. Wheeler and T. V. Wheeler, *Verulamium, A Belgic and two Roman Cities* (Reports of the Research Committee of the Society of Antiquaries of London, xi, 1936).

Wheeler (1943) R. E. M. Wheeler, *Maiden Castle, Dorset* (Reports of the Research Committee of the Society of Antiquaries of London, xii, Oxford, 1943).

Williams (1912) Hugh Williams, *Christianity in Early Britain* (Oxford, 1912).

Wilpert (1903) G. Wilpert, *Roma sotterranea, le pitture delle catacombe romane* (1903).

Wilson (1968) D. R. Wilson, 'An Early Christian Cemetery at Ancaster', in Barley and Hanson (1968), pp. 197–9.

THE EXAMINATION OF USE MARKS
ON SOME MAGDALENIAN END SCRAPERS

THE traditional terminology used to describe prehistoric stone tools often reflects their presumed usage—e.g. scrapers, burins, awls, axe-heads, knives. Their use was deduced largely by making analogies with present-day practices, for instance the identification of stone axe and adze heads for working wood, or of stone scrapers for cleaning hides. The most systematic work in this field is that by Pfeiffer (1912) who draws his analogies as much from European crafts as from ethnographic practices. A few experiments with stone tools, such as skinning a carcass with a simple flake knife, showed what can be achieved but they are inconclusive as to the original function of the tool in question. Some 'obvious' inferences have been drawn from the shape and characteristics of the tools, for instance, the identification of stone awls. Some terms have clearly turned out to be misnomers and these traditional terms are now increasingly regarded merely as names, descriptive of a particular type of flint or stone artefact, without prejudice to its intended function.

For purely classificatory typological analyses such as those used by Bordes and others for characterizing archaeological 'cultures' such a formal description of stone artefacts is useful and adequate. However, for the fuller cultural interpretation of prehistoric artefactual assemblages a functional identification of the artefacts is essential. In addition, the characteristic association of certain different 'function-associated' tools (e.g. butchering tools, bone-working tools, etc.) will have to be established in order to interpret the significance of some of the proportional variations in tool types within a 'culture' revealed by the classic typological analyses (see L. R. Binford and S. R. Binford, 1966). For instance, S. R. Binford's (1968) explanation of the different tool assemblages of contemporary Mousterian sites in the Near East is based on assumptions about the different activities carried out at these sites, deduced from the probable functions of the tools. More refined analyses of such 'activity-specialized' sites would have required more detailed knowledge of the function of these tools.

A knowledge of the function of stone tools is thus an essential basis for the more interpretative analytical methods employed in modern prehistoric archaeology. Semenov (1957 [1964]) is the first to have attempted to do so on more objective criteria than those used hitherto. His method is based on the identification of traces of wear and of damage caused during use. Reference to such use marks had already been made by Pfeiffer in support of some of his identifications, particularly of the use of bone tools, but Semenov undertook a systematic examination of stone tools from Palaeolithic and Neolithic sites. He was able to identify use marks consisting of scratches and polished surfaces on tools of various types, and on this evidence has suggested how they had been used. In the English language edition of his book the magnifications used in his photographs are not always stated, but it is clear that in the majority of cases he used low magnifications up to about 20×, with occasional higher magnifications, generally around 100× to 200×, for detailed examination of the polished surfaces. Such higher magnifications can reveal whether the polish was caused principally by unidirectional movement of the tool, or by movement in several or random directions. More recently, M. Brézillon (1966) has examined flints from the late Magdalenian site of Pincevent, with a view to elucidating the apparently randomly distributed fine retouch on many blades and on scrapers. He concluded that the fine retouch resulted from the use of these blades for scraping or whittling hard resilient material, such as bone or antler, and he confirmed this possibility by experimentation. He also observed that a certain amount of rounding off of the edges by abrasion followed prolonged use in this way. Brézillon used magnifications of up to *c.* 10×. Recent experiments using obsidian choppers and blades to work wood (Keller, 1966) showed that they developed a characteristic flaking pattern which varied both according to the manner in which the tool was used, and the hardness of the material on which it was used (in this case different woods).

It is clear, therefore, that for the identification of the function of stone tools it is necessary to examine both the chipping caused by use and the abrasion and scratch marks.

Recent examination of use marks on late Magdalenian end scrapers from La Madeleine in the British Museum collections revealed some interesting features which have not been discussed in connection with similar tools either from the Russian Palaeolithic sites or from Pincevent. These are:

1. Chipping and abrasion of the working edges as two distinct forms of wear.
2. The use of both the scraper end and the sides of the blades on ochreous material.
3. Damage to the butts of the blades.

The end scrapers were examined with a binocular microscope with zoom magnification ranging from 4× to 80×. At higher magnifications with a metallographic microscope the structure of the cherty flint and numerous fine cracks and fissures became visible. This showed the whole surface as very irregular and seriously complicated the identification of the fine scratch marks which had been caused by usage or by natural soil abrasion. The lower magnification is sufficient to resolve those scratches which were caused by 'dirt' of the sand or silt grades trapped on the tool or on the worked surface during use, and these show the direction of movement during use.

A a

The scraper edge

It was found that chipping is largely confined to the upper surface, whereas the removal of flakes from the under surface was extremely rare. It is, therefore, important to differentiate between the flaking which results from the manufacture of a scraper and that which results from its use.

The scraper edges were formed by the removal of small flat lamellar flakes more or less radially from the circumference of the edge. In most cases the lamellar retouch was followed by the removal of short hinged flakelets along the ridges between the lamellar flakes in order to make the curvature of the edge more regular.

It is the scars from these latter flakelets which resemble the chipping due to wear. In cases where the scraper edge had been intensely damaged by chipping through use, the edge became chipped along its entire periphery by two, three, or more rows of hinged flakelets, forming a miniature step-flaked edge (Pl. LXXIII *a*), and blunting the scraper edge to approximately right angles with the under surface. The original scraping angle, which may be determined as the angle between the under surface and the lamellar retouch, rarely exceeds 75°. On a scraper with only incipient scraping damage it is difficult to ascertain the extent of wear. In such cases only chips which cover the central depressions of the lamellar scars have been identified as due to wear. The first chipping damage along the edge consisted of small scalar flakelets, similar to those described below for the blade edges. Further damage to the scraper edge resulted in the removal of the hinged flakelets. On many scrapers wear formed a discontinuous row of scars along the periphery of the edge, with distinct concentrations on any projections such as the ridges between the retouch scars.

The edge damage was most marked in the central region of the scraper edge, and tended to decrease towards each side. Wear therefore tends to increase the radius of curvature of the scraper end. Such flattening of the tool may be symmetrical about the axis of the blade, or it may be lopsided to the right or to the left. The sample of thirty-four scrapers examined in this study is too small to confirm Semenov's observation that wear tends to be heaviest on the right-hand side of the tools.

Chipping-edge damage with hinged flakes must have resulted from pressure exerted on the underside of the scraper edge at an acute angle to the edge of the tool. It follows that the scraper was used on a rigid surface held with the plane of the tool approaching a right-angle to this surface as illustrated by Semenov (fig. 31). The occasional flat scars on the under surface of the scrapers must have resulted from resistance to irregularities on the scraped surface. The scarcity of these inverse scars indicates that either the surface to be worked was already fairly smooth, or that the tools were used to scrape off comparatively soft material from a rigid surface. It is evident both from the hinged flaking and from the frequent occurrence of snapped scraper ends that considerable downward pressure was sometimes applied during use. Only one instance, however, was found where the damage was such as to have caused irregular bruising of the edge instead of the hinged chipping.

Abrasion of the scraper edge began with a slight rounding off of projections, especially at both corners of the scraper. Stronger abrasion resulted in the formation of a lightly cambered, flattened band around the periphery of the scraper (Pl. LXXIII *b*). This band makes a wide angle with the under surface of the tool, and truncated the flake scars of the upper surface. Edge wear by abrasion always followed after some damage by chipping which was sometimes quite extensive.

On a few of the abraded specimens there were some more or less parallel grooves perpendicular to the scraper edge (Pl. LXXIII *c*). In most cases magnification of about 20 × or more is necessary to identify these striations. Striations of this nature imply a fairly consistent back and forth movement of the tool, at least in the final stages of its use, and the presence of fine grit (in the sand or silt grades) on the worked surface. In the majority of cases, however, such striations are not visible at magnifications of up to 80 × . In these cases, as on the striated specimens, the abraded surface is seen to be irregularly pitted, but the abrasion is too fine to be resolved even at 80 × . Unless abrasion is very extensive indeed, traces of the earlier edge damage by chipping are still visible in the form of crescentic hollows in the abraded surface, aligned more or less parallel to the scraper edge. A few facets with a high glossy polish do occasionally occur, but these are rare and always small. On only two of the group of thirty-four scrapers did the abrasion extend over the upper surface of the tool. In both cases it affected only the ridges between the lamellar scars.

Thus the first traces of wear on a scraper edge are small flake scars which blunt the tool edge, and these are followed by rounding off by abrasion which, in some cases at least, was principally unidirectional.

There is, however, some evidence to suggest that chipping and abrasion may result from somewhat different conditions of use. In the first place, the extent to which scraper edges have been chipped prior to abrasion varies considerably, from a single discontinuous row of scars to extensive step flaking. Secondly, the abraded band usually makes a wide angle with the under surface, suggesting that the tool was held at a somewhat less wide angle with the scraped surface than when hinged flakelets were removed. Finally, three specimens showed that the abraded edge had subsequently been rechipped. In each case part of the abraded edge survived intact, varying in extent from *c*.⅓ to *c*.⅔ of the periphery. The remaining part of the edge was chipped over the abraded band. In two of these cases this secondary chipping gave rise to a markedly asymmetrical curvature of the scraper. It is unlikely that this secondary phase of chipping could have been due to an attempt to resharpen the tool, since in each case its distribution was asymmetrical and on one scraper it was confined to a small stretch on one side of the tool only, and did not affect the centre of the scraper front.

The blade edges

The blade edges for nearly half of the thirty-four scrapers considered here show clear signs of use. Wear damage consisted of chipping and/or abrasion. The chipping was as described by Brézillon for the Pincevent blades. It consisted of small flat scars of fairly regular size removed obliquely across the edge. In several cases the first series of scars was covered by a second (or third) row of shorter scars (Fig. 1). The distribution of these flake scars tended to cover part of the blade only and rarely extended down the entire length on any one side. These flake scars occurred on either the ventral or dorsal surfaces, but rarely on both surfaces along the same stretch of the edge. Independent series of oblique scars occurred on different parts of the edges of the same tool.

A number of blades also have part of their edges rounded by abrasion. There is no correlation between the extent of wear on the scraper edge and the extent of wear on the blade edges on any one tool. Brézillon suggests that this type of wear results from whittling bone or antler. It remains to be shown by experiment whether similar traces of wear would also result from scraping a tightly stretched hide, hide on a block, or wood.

The fact that wear damage on the blade sides as well as on the scraper edge was of frequent occurrence strongly suggests that these objects were intended as composite tools for scraping with a blunted scraper edge and for scraping (or whittling) with a sharp edge. Furthermore, it is reasonable to suppose that the two working edges performed related functions and were used on the same material, whether hide, bone, antler, or wood.

The blade butt

Examination of the butt end of the blades showed that in the majority of cases (twenty-one) the butt was either naturally tapered or it was lightly retouched to a taper on one or both sides. The butt end of six tools was snapped. Of the twenty-eight whole specimens, twenty showed traces of wear on the butt. The wear consisted of abrasion, chipping, and battering marks. Most of the damage was concentrated on projecting parts, on edges (including the edges of the striking platform) and on ridges of the upper blade surface. Abrasion was the most frequent and most marked form of wear and extended for up to *c.* 10 mm. along the blade, becoming weaker away from the butt. Chipping was confined to sharp edges, such as the blade side and actual butt edges. Battering extended all round the butt where it was abraded: it could be identified from the small incipient cones of percussion at magnifications of around 10× or more. No striations were identified on any butts.

The intensity of the damage varied from a faint rounding of the edges to intense abrasion and bruising which almost obliterated the original shape of the butt. This damage suggests that both pressure and battering were applied *around* the butt of some of the blades, as might have occurred if the blade had been fitted with a loose-fitting haft. However, the distribution of edge damage along the lower butt part of the blade on some of these same specimens shows clearly that these blades were also sometimes used unhafted as 'sharp' scrapers or whittling knives. It is, therefore, very likely that instead of being used with hard hafts of materials such as bone or wood, the tools were sometimes used with impermanent hafts such as a pad of fibrous material held in the palm of the hand.

Ochre

Clear traces of red ochre were observed on twelve of the scrapers examined.

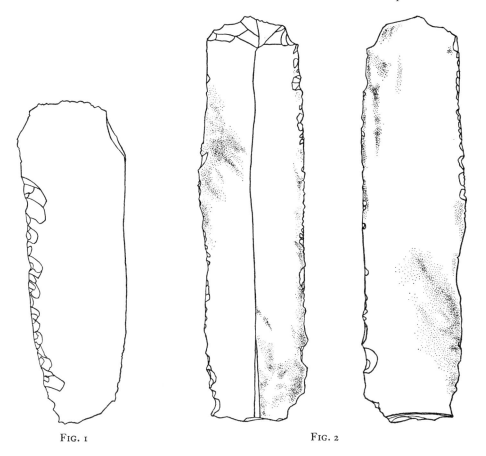

FIG. 1   FIG. 2

Fig. 1. Scraper MS 15, illustrating a first row of scalar flake scars, followed by a discontinuous series of smaller flakelets. Scale 4:3.
Fig. 2. Scraper MS 6, illustrating the relative distribution of edge damage through chipping and streaking with red ochre (stippled). Scale 4:3.

181

The amount and distribution of the ochre was very variable. On some specimens it was confined to small specks in cracks or pits on the abraded surfaces. On others the ochre is clearly visible to the naked eye as streaks of red near the blade edges and/or on the butt end. Ochre always occurs with traces of wear whether by chipping or abrasion. It is found most strongly along the blade edges where it sometimes covers the edge and part of one surface as if an object covered in a red ochre paste had been scraped (Fig. 2). On the scraper edges it usually occurred as mere traces in cracks on the upper scraping edge. On one strongly abraded scraper, however, the flint surface was markedly impregnated with ochre on either side of the abrasion band, clearly indicating its use on an ochreous surface. On the butt it may be streaky along the edges or irregularly distributed around the butt, as mere traces in cracks and pits.

The sparse and irregular distribution of the ochre around the butt is difficult to associate with any particular type of movement, and it could have arisen merely as 'dirt' if considerable amounts of ochre were used on the site. On the blade and scraper edges, however, it is clear that the distribution of the ochre directly reflects the use of the tool. It could have been used directly on a lump of ochre, for example to prepare facets on an ochre crayon; this could, however, have been done more easily on a stone rubber. Alternately, it could have resulted from the use of the blade on material covered in ochre or an ochre paste, for instance on hide, bone, antler, or wood. Since there is no direct evidence for the coloration of antler or bone objects with ochre, the two other alternatives, hide or wood, are perhaps more probable. In view of their perishable nature, it is here that the more traditional approach to the use of tools retains its usefulness. The use of ochre in connection with the decoration of hides and wood is well documented, particularly among Australian aborigines, but Sollas (1924), p. 275, further claims that in southern Australia skins were rubbed with a fat and ochre mixture to make waterproof cloaks. It is likely that the ochre acted merely as a pigment for it is not known to have any tanning or softening action on hide.

ANDRÉE ROSENFELD

BIBLIOGRAPHY

BINFORD, L. R., and BINFORD, S. R., 1966. A Preliminary Analysis of Functional Variability in the Mousterian of Levallois Facies. *American Anthropologist. Recent Studies in Palaeoanthropology,* lxviii (2), part 2, pp. 238–95.

BINFORD, S. R., 1968. Early Upper Pleistocene Adaptations in the Levant. *American Anthropologist,* lxx (4), pp. 707–17.

BRÉZILLON, M., *in* LEROI-GOURHAN, A., and BRÉZILLON, M., 1966. L'Habitation magdalénienne no. 1 de Pincevent près Montereau (Seine et Marne). *Gallia préhistoire,* ix (2), pp. 279–304.

KELLER, C. M., 1966. The Development of Edge Damage Patterns on Stone Tools. *Man,* i (1966), pp. 501–11.

PFEIFFER, L., 1912. *Die Steinzeitliche Technik,* xliii. Allgemeinen Versammlung der Deutschen Anthropologischen Gesellschaft, Jena.

SEMENOV, S. A., 1957. (English translation 1964.) *Prehistoric Technology,* London.

SOLLAS, W. J., 1924. (3rd edition.) *Ancient Hunters and their Modern Representatives,* London.

A GROUP OF INCISED DECORATED ARMRINGS AND THEIR SIGNIFICANCE FOR THE MIDDLE BRONZE AGE OF SOUTHERN BRITAIN

IN 1965 Briard published a corpus of incised decorated armrings from Brittany which he termed the 'Bignan type' and emphasized their similarities to a number of armrings from the Somme/Seine basin area of northern France.[1] Examples of armrings of this type had been known since Breuil's paper on the hoard from Villers-sur-Authie[2] and Marsille's original publication of the hoard from Bignan.[3]

Interpretations as to the date of the armrings and their original source have differed widely. Breuil assigned a 'Halstatt influence' for the origin of the armrings from Villers-sur-Authie. Hawkes gave a Halstatt B date to this same hoard, in his discussion of the group of Picardy pins.[4] He considered these pins and armrings represented a late Tumulus culture tradition surviving in a predominantly Urnfield context. Sandars, on the other hand, agreed with Hawkes's dating but considered these armrings to be a north French variant of Halstatt B Urnfield armrings found in eastern and central France.[5] Briard has suggested a slightly earlier date (i.e. Middle to Late Bronze Age transition) for the armrings of his Bignan type and agrees with Hawkes's interpretation of a late Tumulus culture survival. But he also emphasizes a contribution to the decoration from the earlier Tréboul phase in Britanny.

Smith discussed both Hawkes's Picardy pin group and a few examples of the decorated armrings in southern Britain but was chiefly concerned with establishing an earlier dating to the Middle Bronze Age for these continental finds.[6] She isolated the decorative motif of the outlined pointed ellipse and compared it to the decoration on the D-sectioned armrings both of the Ilmenau culture of north-west Germany, and on armrings from north-eastern France. These armrings contributed to her overall impression of north-eastern France forming an 'eclectic region' wherein the elements of her 'Ornament Horizon' were collected and transmitted to southern Britain.

It has now become possible with Briard's documentation and illustration of the decorated armrings in the Breton hoards, to re-examine the specimens found in southern Britain, and to evaluate their significance afresh. The purpose of this paper is to document the British examples of this armring type and to establish their origin and relationship to other imports of metalwork from the Continent.

This paper will attempt to show that elements of the decorative style found on these armrings attracted wider attention in southern Britain and were reproduced on metalwork of purely native origin. It will also be suggested that a particular style of decoration is not necessarily limited to any particular metal type and that analysis of decorative styles must be undertaken separately from formal type classification.

Conditions of discovery and association

Fourteen decorated armrings have been found in southern Britain, of which two from the Portsmouth hoard were lost in bombing during the last war. The associations of eight of these armrings, together with the similarities in size, section, and decoration, have led to their being treated as pairs. Three other armrings have been found in hoard associations which also contain other ornaments. Only the remaining three armrings were single finds.[7]

The two armrings from Ramsgate (Kent)[8] are reputed to have been found with a skeleton, indicating that these should be considered as part of a grave-group. The armrings were found in association with a ribbed bracelet which had squared plain terminals, a type that has been assigned a north European origin and dated to Montelius III. The British Museum register implies that a third armring from the grave-group not acquired by the museum was similar to these two. Two armrings discovered by the author in Canterbury Museum are unfortunately unprovenanced but are almost exact parallels to the Ramsgate pair. Their museum location and close similarity to the Ramsgate armrings would most probably indicate a Kent provenance. Another decorated armring in the same museum, also unprovenanced, may also have come from Kent but there is no evidence to substantiate this.

The hoard from Portsmouth (Hants) originally contained two decorated and two plain annular armrings plus a side-flanged looped palstave. The only evidence that now remains of these is a note and illustration by Wheeler and Crawford.[9] The two decorated armrings from Liss (Hants), however, received attention by Evans in 1881, where he mentions the possibility that they had been found with a decorated cast flanged axe of the same provenance. This suggestion was discounted by Wheeler and Crawford and, as Butler has said,[10] the discrepancy in archaeological dating is quite considerable. The most recent discovery from Hampshire is in a hoard from Hayling Island where a single decorated armring was found in association with a plain annular armring, twenty-seven looped and unlooped palstaves, and a fragmentary quoit-headed pin.[11]

A hoard containing three palstaves, a decorated annular armring, and a lozenge-sectioned penannular armring was found whilst erecting a 'Dutch barn' at Grimstone in Dorset.[12] Another decorated armring originally in the Hall collection, is said to have been found at Milton Abbas (Dorset) possibly with a plain oval-sectioned penannular armring. The association, however, cannot be confirmed either from the original publication[13] or in the records of Dorchester Museum and it is treated in this article as a single find.

One of the seventeen ornaments in the Ebbesbourne Wake hoard is an armring with incised multi-ribbed lozenge decoration.[14] It was found with fifteen other armrings and a broken spiral-twisted bronze torc in the top of a lynchet of a 'Celtic field system' on Elcombe Down, Ebbesbourne Wake (Wiltshire). This hoard contains the largest and most representative selection of ornament types available in southern Britain during the later Middle Bronze Age.

Finally a single find of a penannular decorated armring was found in the Thames, possibly at Southwark. This is the northernmost find-spot for this type of decorated armring.

This summary demonstrates the limited distribution of these armrings in southern Britain. Two general conclusions can be made as to their associations. Firstly, these decorated armrings are found in association with other 'native' ornament forms in four of the hoards, namely Ebbesbourne Wake, Portsmouth, Hayling Island, and Grimstone, and with a possible import at Ramsgate. And secondly, the other most common association is with palstaves as at Portsmouth, Hayling Island, and Grimstone. Similar hoard compositions have been described by Briard for Brittany. It will be shown later that a number of the palstaves in the Hayling Island and Grimstone hoards are of north French origin.

Formal variation

All the armrings are fully cast but vary to the extent that post-casting work has been used to modify their shape. The armrings from Ebbesbourne Wake, Grimstone, Hayling Island, Portsmouth, Milton Abbas, and unprovenanced are annular solid cast rings and completely circular in shape. The remaining armrings are penannular (i.e. with open terminals), a technique associated with a slightly oval shape where the terminal lengths have been flattened to meet each other. The presence or absence of terminals will be shown later to contribute to the style and pattern of decoration used.

A distinction in the cross-section of these armrings also serves to differentiate the two main forms represented in southern Britain. The six armrings from Kent, Liss and Ramsgate, were cast with a rounded section, and the internal faces of the Liss armrings have been subsequently flattened by hammering. They are all penannular and the terminals of the four armrings from Ramsgate and Kent are set wide apart. Four of the seven remaining armrings were cast with either a semicircular or concavo-convex section with the convex face carrying the decoration on the outside and the flat or concave face on the inside. The three exceptions are the armrings from Ebbesbourne Wake, Hayling Island, and Portsmouth, which have both convex internal and external faces. All six

B b

annular armrings possess one of the variant sections of this last category and are included within this group of seven armrings (Fig. 1).

The greatest internal diameters of those armrings that can be measured all fall within 6–7 cm., with the greatest face width between 1–2 cm. The bodies of the penannular armrings taper slightly towards the terminals producing a

	annular	penannular	section				internal diameter	museum location
			●	◗	◖	❶		
Ramsgate		●	●				6·4 cms	BM 1900 7-19 7
Ramsgate		●	●				6·6 cms	BM 1919 10-14 2
Kent		●	●				6·8 cms	Canterbury Museum No 477
Kent		●	●				6·7 cms	Canterbury Museum No 478
Liss		●	●				6·5 cms	BM 61 8-21 3
Liss		●	●				6·5 cms	BM 61 8-21 4
Portsmouth	●					●	?	Lost · formerly in Portsmouth Museum
Hayling Island	●					●	6·5 cms	Portsmouth Museum
Grimstone	●				●		6·3 cms	Dorset County Museum 1963·15·4
Milton Abbas	●				●		6·3 cms	Dorset County Museum 1902·1·12
Ebbesbourne Wake	●					●	6·2 cms	Salisbury Museum
Thames–Southwark ?		●		●			6·4 cms	London Museum A11029
Unprovenanced	●				●		6·7 cms	Canterbury Museum No 479

FIG. 1. Inventory and typology of decorated bronze armrings.

constriction before the slightly expanded terminals. The face width is more or less constant on the annular armrings.

Manufacture

Without a full metallographic study it would be impossible to state categorically the manner in which these armrings were made. The distinction between penannular and annular armrings most probably reflects a difference of manufacturing technique rather than any attempt at a deliberate

formal/functional effect. There is no question of an open armring of such proportions being easier to remove from the arm or the leg than a solid cast ring. The
casting of fully formed solid armrings, however, is known from the Early Bronze
Age with the stone mould matrices of Britton's Migdale-Marnoch tradition.[15] The
complex sections of some of the armrings, e.g. that of Grimstone, would certainly
indicate that a clay mould was used. Penannular armrings were probably bent
into their present form from a specially shaped bronze rod or bar.[16] The ingot
bar in the Burgess Meadow hoard could have been intended for such a purpose.[17]
It would seem likely that this was done before the decoration was applied, since
the working involved would have been considerable and would have incurred
a risk of damage to the external faces.

As already mentioned, the internal faces of the armrings from Liss (Hants)
show signs of extensive hammering (probably cold worked) in order to flatten
the surface. The outer faces which were to be decorated would presumably have
received more careful treatment, probably limited to smoothing and polishing
the surface. It would also seem reasonable to suppose that the hammering on the
inner face was carried out before the decoration was applied.

Examination of the incised lines on the Liss armrings shows that the decoration in these two cases was executed with a small, sharp-pointed, triangular or
lozenge-sectioned tool. There is no sign of 'stitching' or unequal cutting depths
which would indicate use of an indirect tracer technique; from which it may be
concluded that the tool was held in the hand and that the individual lines were
produced with a single stroke. Kersten illustrates a woman's grave belonging to
the Ilmenau culture in north-west Germany (Hügel 7 at Juliusburg).[18] It contained a decorated round sectioned neckring with plain unhooked terminals
and what Kersten described as a pin cast in a bronze handle. The similarities
between armrings of the Ilmenau culture and those from northern France
and southern Britain will be discussed later but this 'pin' is probably the type
of tool used to produce the decoration on the armrings.

Only two analyses are available to give some idea of the metal composition
of this group of decorated armrings. These are for the two Ramsgate armrings
and show a very high tin content and a low lead content even for the Middle
Bronze Age lead range (i.e. $<$ 1 per cent.).[19] This agrees with the proportion of
tin generally used as an alloy in northern France at this time, not only for armrings (of which only two analyses exist) but for palstaves as well. It should also
be mentioned that a high tin content (i.e. $>$ 14 per cent.) is found in the hoards
in the Sussex/Isle of Wight region at this time.

Decoration—analysis

Any discussion of these decorated armrings should include the typologically
similar plain annular armrings, such as those found in the Ebbesbourne Wake,

Eglesham Meadow (Dorset), Hayling Island, and probably in the Portsmouth hoards. The reasons for the application of decoration on certain armrings should be considered separately from the factors that produced similarities in shape, size, and individual features. Briard's assertion that armrings of his 'Bignan type' must be decorated is therefore open to doubt. This is emphasized by the fact that typologically similar armrings have been found in the same hoard associations in Brittany and yet have been separately treated on the basis of the presence or absence of decoration. However, most of Briard's general conclusions as to position and type of decorative motif used also apply to the English examples.

Decoration is exclusively on the external curved face of the armrings. It is divided up into panels separated by columns of vertical lines which are sometimes themselves divided by a single band of horizontal or diagonal lines or a vertical line of *pointillé*. Each panel contains a carefully integrated scheme, using a number of the motifs shown in Fig. 5. The decorative pattern differs according to whether the armring is annular or penannular in shape. On annular armrings a repetition of one or two particular motifs tends to be used around the whole circumference, each panel being divided from the next by one of the column variants. It would appear, however, that the presence of terminals tended to influence the style and position of the panels on the penannular armrings. The same decorative style is used, starting from both terminals and converging on a distinctive motif used for the centre face of the armring. The terminal ends are usually elaborately decorated with vertical incised bands of lines.

The decorative style is purely geometric, comprising, for example, pointed multi-ribbed and cable-line pointed ellipses (Fig. 5. I, J, and M), multi-rib chevron and lozenge shapes (P, Q, R, S), cable-lining (N and O), hatched triangles (U), herring-bone patterns (V and W), bands of cross-hatching and vertical and horizontal lines (A–H) and *pointillé*. Most of these elements can be found in the earlier decorative traditions of western Europe, as, for example, on Irish gold and bronze metalwork of the Early Bronze Age, on the spearheads of the Tréboul phase in Brittany and especially in the decorative styles used on ornaments of the Tumulus culture in central and western Europe. Briard has loosely termed this 'le vieux style géométrique européen'. The distinguishing characteristics of these armrings are the complexity and the arrangement in the design of these motifs and the high quality of the work.

The number of decorated panels on the British examples of this armring type varies from four to six. The two pairs from Ramsgate and Kent possess the least complex decoration (Fig. 2. 1 and 2). The panels are decorated with only two parallel or slightly diverging cable-lines. One of the armrings from Ramsgate[20] shows that the incised decoration was begun from both ends and was meant to meet in the middle. On this particular example the spacing was misjudged and

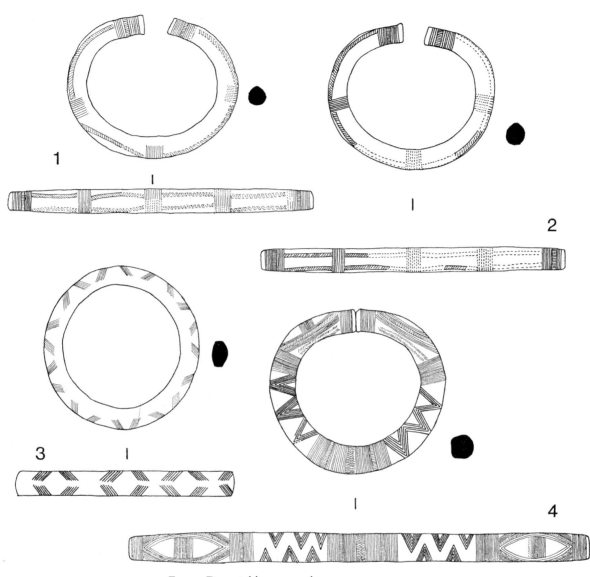

FIG. 2. Decorated bronze armrings:

1. Kent (Royal Museum, Canterbury, no. 477)
2. Kent (Royal Museum, Canterbury, no. 478)
3. Ebbesbourne Wake, Wilts. (Salisbury Museum)
4. Liss, Hants. (B.M. Reg. no. 61, 8–21, 3)

a hasty but rather clumsy adjustment had to be made. The annular armring from Ebbesbourne Wake (Fig. 2. 3) possesses only multi-rib lozenges with no defined panels or partitions of vertical lines. The pointed ellipse motif occurs on the armrings from Milton Abbas, Portsmouth, Hayling Island, and Liss (Figs. 2. 4 and

3. 5); cable-lining was used on the first, multi-ribbing on the second and third together with *pointillé*, and a combined cable-line and multi-rib motif on the very elaborate Liss armrings. It should be mentioned here that the decorative styles of the one Portsmouth armring and the Hayling Island armring are almost identical. Multi-ribbing and *pointillé* appear to be associated as a motif, as seen on the armrings from the Thames (Fig. 3. 6), from Portsmouth, from Hayling Island and on the unprovenanced armring (Fig. 3. 7). Herring-bone patterns occur on the armrings from Liss both as a side decoration in the panels and also, on one, as a vertical column in the partition. It is also reported to be a rare feature on the Breton armrings. The use of *pointillé* presents difficulties for interpretation since it is used both as an outlining device (as are single and double lines) and as an integral part of a motif that is repeated on other armrings.

A large number of separate motifs are used in the decorative style displayed by these armrings. However, only a small proportion of these are found on any particular armring. Fig. 5 shows that nine out of the surviving thirteen armrings have five motifs or less. Yet, apart from pairs, very few of the armrings from northern France or southern Britain can be said to be identical. The nature of their variation seems to depend principally on the differing combinations that the arrangement of these motifs can produce. This variation indicates a flexible decorative tradition in which the motifs used are standardized but the manner of their association is allowed marked individuality. The skill of execution and the complexity of the use of these standard elements indicates specialized skill and knowledge.

Continental comparisons

With the possible exception of the two pairs of armrings from Ramsgate and Kent, it is unlikely that any of the fourteen decorated armrings known to have been found in southern Britain were actually made there. This supposition is based on their limited number and distribution, the style of decoration and the apparent absence of a similarly complex 'native' tradition of incised decoration, and on a comparison with contemporary imports of north French metalwork that have been found. Since the variety of typological and decorative features would not suggest evidence of selection, these imports of decorated armrings should constitute a random, but not necessarily representative, sample of the possible variety of forms available in their area of origin.

The closest parallels to the British armrings are the more numerous examples of decorated armrings found in northern France both in hoard contexts, with palstaves and plain armrings, and as single finds. The use of *pointillé* and the pointed ellipse as decorative motifs appears to be frequent on armrings from north-eastern France and the Seine basin area. The Breton group, by which

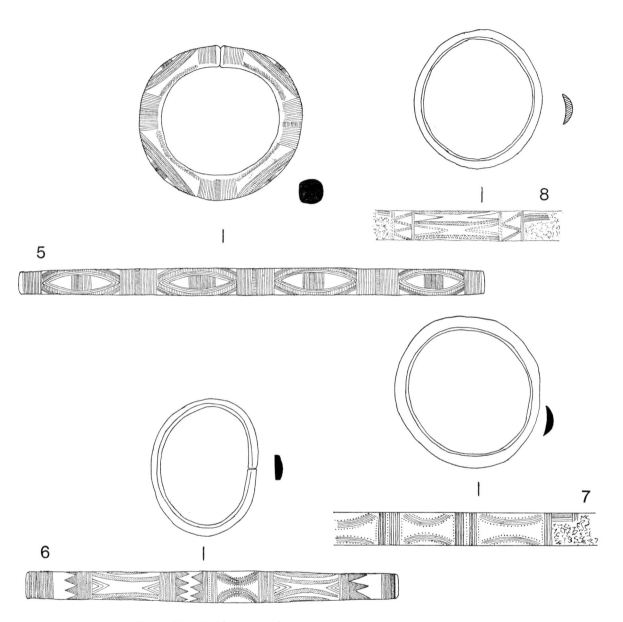

FIG. 3. Decorated bronze armrings:

5. Liss, Hants. (B.M. Reg. no. 61, 8–21, 4)
6. River Thames, possibly Southwark (London Museum no. A. 11029)
7. Unprovenanced (Royal Museum, Canterbury, no. 479)
8. Grimstone, Dorset (Dorchester Museum)

Briard's Bignan type was defined, shows a greater preference for simpler geometric motifs mainly within the decorative tradition of the spearheads dated to his earlier Tréboul phase. *Pointillé* and the cable-line and multi-rib pointed ellipse motifs, and combined *pointillé* and semicircular motifs rarely appear. The absence of these elements appears to be the basis for Briard's distinction of the armrings of his Bignan type from 'les bracelets massifs incisés proches de ceux du type de Bignan'.

The two armrings from the Thames and Grimstone (Fig. 3. 6 and 8) are the most closely comparable in decoration to the examples given by Briard as belonging to his Bignan type.[21] The distinctive cross-section and the simplicity of decoration of the Ramsgate and Kent armrings cannot be fully paralleled in northern France. The double cable-line pattern is found on the D-sectioned armring in the first hoard from Sermizelles (Yonne).[22] But both the rounded cross-section and a decorative style similar to the Liss armrings is found on one of the armrings from the Rosay hoard (Seine Inferieure).[23] The simple multi-rib lozenge decoration of the Ebbesbourne Wake armring and its distinctive cross-section are found on one of the armrings in the Villers-sur-Authie (Somme) hoard[24] and also on one of the armrings in the Carlipa (Aude) hoard.[25] The unprovenanced armring is very similar to a single find from the River Seine at Villeneuve-St-Georges (Seine et Oise)[26] and to two armrings in the Villers-sur-Authie hoard.

The three armrings from Portsmouth, Hayling Island, and Milton Abbas specifically use the pointed ellipse or semicircular motif for decoration. The Portsmouth and Hayling Island armrings also display an extensive use of *pointillé* both within the motifs and for bordering and partitioning the panels. Preference for this type of decoration has been interpreted by Sandars as due to the increasing influence of Urnfield decorative styles especially on armrings in eastern and central France.[27] A number of armrings in the hoards from Longchamps près Entrepagny (Eure),[28] Villers-sur-Authie, Carlipa, the second hoard from Sermizelles (Yonne),[29] Le Hanouard (Seine Inferieure),[30] and Rougemontiers (Eure)[31] are all characterized by this distinctive use of multi-rib motifs plus *pointillé* for decoration.

Sprockhoff first drew attention to the relationship between the Ramsgate armrings and the decorated armrings of the Ilmenau culture of north-west Germany.[32] This similarity was further considered by Smith[33] who postulated a direct link between the French and British decorated armrings and armrings of the Ilmenau culture dated by Sprockhoff to Montelius III. Butler, on the other hand, merely emphasized the relationship between all the three regional groups without postulating the direct origin of one from another.[34] In form the Ilmenau armrings are usually penannular with a semi-circular cross-section but with a narrower face than that found on the British and French armrings. The decoration also tends to be restricted to the motifs D–F, I, and M in Fig. 5, but their arrangement can be complex. The closest analogy to the decoration on the Liss armrings, for example, is to be found on an armring from Lauenburg[35] and the rounded cross-section of the Kent, Liss, and Ramsgate armrings, although not typical of the Ilmenau type, is found on two armrings in the Spindlersfeld hoard.[36]

The Ilmenau culture would appear to be the source of a tradition in decorated armrings that was adopted and developed in northern France. The appearance in north-west Germany in Montelius II–III of the plain narrow-bladed palstave has been interpreted by Butler as showing that the north French metalworking industries were having some influence in northern Europe at this time. The evidence of the decorative motifs used would suggest that the three or four basic Ilmenau motifs were added to considerably when used in northern France. The line of diffusion would also be indicated by the decline of the appearance of these Ilmenau motifs from north-eastern to north-western France, and their replacement by an earlier and differing geometric style. That remnants of the Ilmenau style were still incorporated in the far west is shown by the presence of small hatch-filled ellipses on the armrings from Saint Just (Îlle-et-Vilaine) and Barre en Crossé-le-Vivien (Mayenne).[37]

The relatively small number of finds for a limited area of southern Britain do not support a postulated separate tradition there but suggests rather that they were a small group of imports representative of a wider influence involving other metal types.

Chronology

Briard has dated the armrings of his 'Bignan type' to the transition from Middle to Late Bronze Age in Brittany. By his acceptance of Hatt's chronology for eastern France, Briard sets this between 1,100 and 900 B.C. in northern France and more generally to the beginning of the 1st millennium B.C. The developed broad-bladed palstaves in the hoards containing decorated armrings in north-eastern France suggest a similar date. Sprockhoff originally dated the hoards and grave groups of the Ilmenau culture to Montelius III, possibly extending into Montelius IV. This would give a slightly earlier date for decorated armrings of the Ilmenau type in north-west Germany than for the derived forms in northern France.

There is independent evidence for the date of the decorated armrings of southern Britain. The looped side-flanged palstave in the Portsmouth hoard closely resembles a looped palstave in the Billingshurst hoard (Sussex),[38] that can be dated to Middle Bronze Age 2 in Hawkes's chronology. Similarly the hoard from Hayling Island contains two side-flanged palstaves with median ribs and crinoline-shaped blades that can be paralleled in the Burgess Meadow and Leopold St. hoards, and two side-flanged palstaves with groups of short vertical lines as decoration below the stopridge similar to palstaves in the Billingshurst and Blackrock hoards.[39] The Hayling Island hoard also contains a fragmentary quoit-headed pin similar to those found at East Dean and Hanley Cross (Sussex).[40] The Ebbesbourne Wake hoard contains other ornaments of native origin that can be paralleled in hoards such as Edington Burtle, Taunton Union Workhouse, Monkswood (Somerset), Brading (Hants), and Barton Bendish (Norfolk). All these hoards were placed by Smith in her 'Ornament Horizon' and dated by Hawkes to his MBA 2. The Grimstone hoard contains a lozenge-sectioned penannular armring and a broad-bladed palstave that Smith would place in her 'high-flanged' class. This palstave is of a type most commonly found in the south-west of England in hoards such as Edington Burtle and Taunton Union Workhouse and has been dated to MBA 2. There is therefore a consistent association, either direct or indirect, with material dated to MBA 2 in Hawkes's scheme. The proposed span of this chronological period has been set at between 1,200 and 1,000 B.C., but it is quite feasible that the forms of metalwork that were used to define this period were still being produced after 1,000 B.C.

The association of 'Picardy pins' and decorated armrings in the hoard from Villers-sur-Authie implies contemporaneity with the decorated armrings for this pin type in southern Britain and this view is supported by their similar decorative motifs. As Hawkes has established that the five pins of his Picardy group in southern Britain were derived from north-eastern France,[41] it can be shown that two established groups of ornaments were contemporary imports into southern Britain from northern France. The Grimstone and Hayling Island hoards also contain nine narrow-bladed looped palstaves (one from Grimstone and eight from Hayling Island) that are almost certainly north French in origin. Their distinctive features are convex flanges, a curved stopridge, a flat septum floor, and a long blade in proportion to the septum length. The associations of these palstaves with two decorated armrings implies contemporaneity with other imports or copies of north French narrow-bladed palstaves that have been found in the hoards from Pear Tree Green, Southampton, and Swanwick (Hants), Marshall Estate, Bognor,[42] and Sidlesham (Sussex), Dewlish (Dorset), and Wantage (Berks.). In Brittany, Briard has dated the looped narrow-bladed palstave of this type to his Rosnoën phase, contemporary with swords of his Rosnoën type. It would now seem reasonable to suggest that the similar swords or rapiers that have come from the Thames and which have been classed as the Lambeth type should also be considered as imports, rather than as mere British equivalents to the Rosnoën sword.[43] Briard's date for the Rosnoën phase in northern France would overlap the transition from MBA 2–3 in southern Britain and would make Rosnoën swords contemporary with north French decorated armrings of the Bignan type. The MBA 3 associations for Rosnoën swords in Britain (i.e. in the Penard and Ambleside hoards), in contrast to a MBA 2 date for decorated

194

armrings, would suggest either a possible earlier date for the first imports of Rosnoën swords or more likely a later date for MBA 2 type material in southern Britain.

A clearly defined series of imports of north French metalwork into southern Britain can therefore be shown to be contemporary with one another. This range

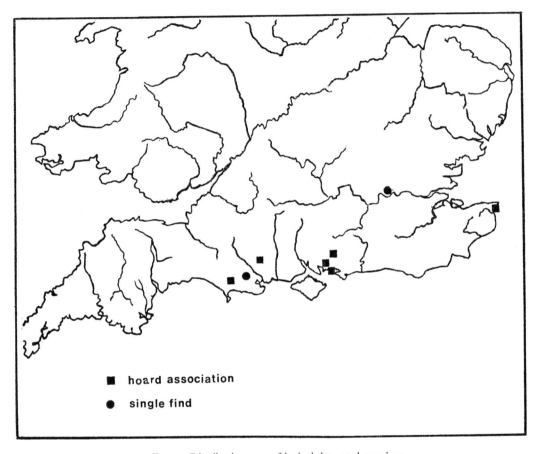

FIG. 4. Distribution map of incised decorated armrings.

of metalwork includes decorated armrings, decorated and undecorated pins, narrow-bladed looped palstaves, and Rosnoën type swords. The distribution of these imports is limited in the main to the south-eastern counties of southern Britain, roughly on a line along the Thames valley and then south to Dorset. The native metalwork of this area displays two other distinctive characteristics. The first is the appearance of large palstave hoards often containing more than ten implements, e.g. Pear Tree Green, Southampton; Fairlee, I.O.W.; and Marshall Estate, Bognor. The second is the use of a high tin bronze (i.e. > 14 per cent.).

Both these features are also characteristic of the north French metalworking industries at this time.

Decorative analogues on native metalwork—Postscript

The group of decorated armrings described above and the five pins forming Hawkes's Picardy pin group represent the first appearance in southern Britain since the end of the Early Bronze Age of an incised decorative style. As such it would be of interest to establish whether this stimulated the use of a similar decorative style on native metalwork.

Any such influence would most reasonably be expected to be found within the area where these pins and armrings have been found. Various examples may be cited. The pin from the Hanley Cross barrow (nr. Lewes)[44] has a lozenge-shaped plate set on the side of the shaft which is decorated with a multi-rib lozenge surrounded by a cable-line lozenge. There is also a bronze, spiral finger-ring in the Blackrock (Sussex)[45] hoard that has a semicircular section and is decorated with panels of multi-rib lozenges separated by bands of vertical lines. Undecorated spiral finger-rings can be paralleled elsewhere in southern Britain. Yet, on the basis of the decoration, Piggott, Smith, and Butler have asserted that the Blackrock finger-ring could be matched only in Montelius III graves in Mecklenberg. It seems more likely that the influence of the armring and pin decorative tradition is represented in the ornamentation of this ring. The bronze dirk-handle in the same hoard is decorated with a cable-line pattern and herring-bone motifs on the hilt-plate and horizontal bands of lines on the grip, all of which are outlined by *pointillé*. Coles has recently compared this solid-hilted dirk-handle to those found on the Ambleside and Salta Moss rapiers.[46]

Two of the quoit-headed pins in the Barton Bendish and Boughton Fen hoards (Norfolk) have incised decoration on the loop faces. The Barton Bendish pin[47] has a series of hatched triangles (motif υ) on the face between the slight flanges that rim the loop. The Boughton Fen pin is decorated with a multi-rib chevron device (motif s) bordered on the two rims of the loop with horizontal lines. A type of fern-leaf motif decorates the flat space where the stem of the pin meets the loop. This multi-rib chevron device is found again on a small wire bracelet with hooked terminals from Icklingham in Suffolk.[48]

A decorated neckring with plain hooked terminals is reputed to have been found at Billingham House near Ryde (I.O.W.) with a spiral-twisted bronze torc and possibly a palstave. The association and provenance is by no means confirmed and the presence of the neckring could be explained as a mislaid collector's piece. The decorative style is composed of cable-line and multi-rib pointed ellipses, panels of herringbone and cross-hatching motifs separated by columns of vertical lines. Proudfoot[49] has reconstructed a gold neckring from the Downpatrick gold hoard with a partially similar decoration, which Eogan[50]

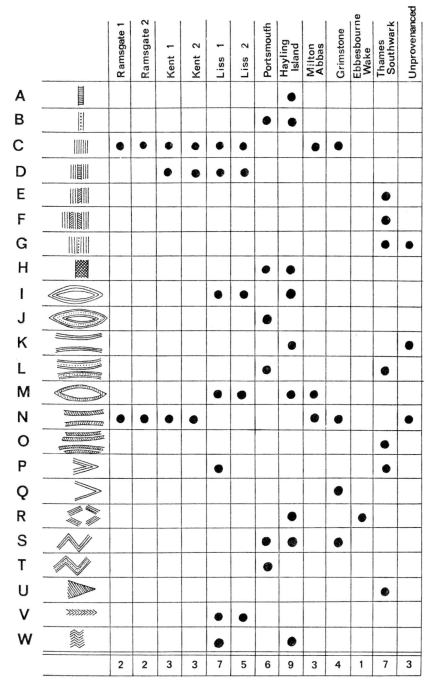

FIG. 5. Decorative motifs on bronze armrings.

has dated to his Bishopsland phase in Ireland. Eogan also quotes four bronze decorated neckrings from Saint-Viâtre as a parallel to the Downpatrick gold find.[51]

Examples of decoration on native tool and weapon types of the British Middle Bronze Age are both extremely rare and limited in the complexity of motifs used. The basal looped spearhead from Brigmerston Down (Wilts.)[52] has a multi-rib lozenge motif on the loop plate and the socket is decorated with a line of multi-rib chevrons around the base above two bands of horizontal lines. The decoration is crudely scratched on the surface and lacks regularity in the number of lines executed and their linking up with one another. *Pointillé* is also found on the blade in the angle between the mid-rib and the blade faces. One other heavily decorated spearhead is of the side-looped form from Sparsholt (Berks.).[53] The decoration on its socket is divided into three panels, the lowest containing motif U, the next motif B, and a hatched zigzag pattern on the third panel. Each panel is separated by a horizontal band of three lines. Two converging lines of motif B are set on the blade face in the angle between the blade and the mid-rib.

The only relevant decorated palstave known is from Dorchester (Dorset) and has a multi-rib lozenge set on both flange sides. This is not incised, however, but hammered out, probably with a round-based punch.

The evidence for a native tradition of incised decoration is therefore rather meagre. Furthermore, the pin from Hanley Cross and the solid bronze hilt from Blackrock may be imports rather than native in origin. However, if the above examples are accepted, it can be seen that the decoration on the native metalwork displays a tendency to abstract certain motifs, especially hatched and multi-rib chevron and lozenge shapes and uses them without any of the complex arrangements found on the imported armrings and pins. It should also be noted that the established native preference for manufacturing ornaments of massive proportions would appear to be at variance with the acceptance of an incised decorative tradition in Britain.[54]

M. J. ROWLANDS

ACKNOWLEDGEMENTS

The author wishes to thank the following museums for allowing material in their collections to be published: the Royal Museum, Canterbury; Portsmouth City Museum; the Dorset County Museum, Dorchester; the Salisbury and South Wiltshire Museum; and the London Museum.

Grateful thanks are are also extended to the following who kindly read and criticized this article: Dr. J. Alexander, Professor J. D. Evans, Dr. I. H. Longworth, R. Mercer, G. de G. Sieveking, and Dr. Peter J. Ucko.

1 Briard, *Les Dépôts bretons et l'âge du bronze atlantique*, 1965, chap. viii.

2 Breuil, *L'Anthropologie*, xxix (1918), pp. 251 ff.

3 Marsille, *Catalogue du Musée archéologique de la Société polymathique du Morbihan*, 1921, p. 77, pl. vi.

4 Hawkes, 'The Deverel Urn and the Picardy Pin . . .', *PPS*, viii (1942), pp. 26–47.

5 Sandars, *Bronze Age cultures in France*, 1957, pp. 279, 280–1.

6 Smith, *PPS*, xxv (1959), pp. 159–62.

7 See inventory (Fig. 1).

8 *Inventaria Archaeologica*, GB 48.

9 Wheeler and Crawford, *Archaeologia*, lxxi (1920–1), p. 139, fig. 4. Only the armring illustrated was used for analysis.

10 Butler, *Palaeohistoria*, 1963, ch. xiii, p. 157.

11 The Curator of Antiquities at Portsmouth Museum hopes to publish this hoard in the *Proc. Hants. Field Club* in the near future. Publication has been delayed because of the conservation treatment required.

12 *Proc. Dorset Nat. Hist. and Arch. Soc.* 1964, p. 115.

13 Woolls, *Barrow diggers*, p. 74, pl. 5, fig. 14.

14 Shortt, *Wilts. Arch. Mag.* 1949, pp. 104–12.

15 Britton, *PPS*, xxix (1963), p. 268, fig. 9.

16 Both Courtois (*Gallia Préhistoire*, 1960, p. 75) and Briard (1965, p. 130) reiterate Müller's (*Rhodana*, 1925) misuse of ethnographic data to suggest that these armrings were made from bars cast in simple open sand moulds.

17 *Inventaria Archaeologica*, GB 6, fig. 7.

18 *Die Vorgeschichte des Kreises Herzogtum Lauenburg*, Kersten, 1951, p. 62 and Abb. 39, figs. 8 and 9.

19 Brown and Blyn-Stoyl, *PPS*, xxv (1959), p. 208 and *Archaeometry*, supplement 1959, analyses 466 and 467.

20 *Inventaria Archaeologica*, GB 48, fig. i.

21 Briard, op. cit., 1965, figs. 38 and 40. Briard, 1961: *Travaux-Rennes*, hoard from Guipry.

22 Sermizelles 1st hoard, *Gallia Préhistoire*, 1959, p. 107, fig. 19.

23 Coutil, *Assoc. franç. avanc. sciences—Congrès de Rouen*, 1921, pl. 6.

24 Breuil, op. cit. 1918, fig. 4. 5.

25 Carlipa Aude, *Gallia Préhistoire*, 1964, p. 16, figs. 5 and 6.

26 Gaudron, *BSPF*, 1951, p. 564, fig. 1.

27 Sandars, op. cit. 1957, p. 190.

28 Coutil, *BSPF*, 1925: Cachette de l'âge du bronze de Longchamps.

29 Sermizelles 2nd hoard, *Gallia Préhistoire*, 1959, p. 107, fig. 20.

30 Coutil, op. cit. 1921, pl. 6.

31 Ibid.

32 Sprockhoff, Niedersachsens Bedeutung für die Bronzezeit westeuropas, *BRGK*, 1941, p. 82.

33 Smith, op. cit. 1959, p. 160.

34 Butler, op. cit. 1963, chap. xiv, sect. v, p. 157.

35 Kersten, op. cit. 1951, Taf. 40, Fig. 9.

36 Sprockhoff, *Marburger Studien*, 1938, 'Die Spindlersfelder-Fibel', Taf. 82.

37 Briard, op. cit. 1965, fig. 40:2 and fig. 41.

38 *Sussex Arch. Coll.* xxvii, p. 183.

39 Piggott, C. M., 'A Late Bronze Age Hoard from Blackrock . . .', *PPS*, xv (1949), pp. 107 ff.

40 Curwen, *The Archaeology of Sussex*, fig. 49 and Appendix to chaps. vii and viii.

41 Hawkes, op. cit. 1942, p. 40.

42 *Sussex Arch. Coll.* lxvi, pp. 225 ff., pls. 1 and 3.35.

43 As, for example, Burgess implies: *Bronze Age Metalwork in Northern England*, note 38, p. 43.

44 Curwen, op. cit., fig. 49.

45 Piggott, C. M., op. cit. 1949, fig. 1.3a, b, c.

46 Fell and Coles, 'Reconsideration of the Ambleside hoard . . .', *Trans. Cumb. West. Antiq. and Arch. Soc.* lxv (1965) p. 48.

47 *Inventaria Archaeologica*, GB 7, 2 (1).

48 Moyses Hall Museum, Bury St. Edmunds—F117.

49 Proudfoot, *The Downpatrick Gold Find*, Arch. Research Public. No. 3, 1955.

50 Eogan, 'The later Bronze Age in Ireland . . .', *PPS* (1964), p. 281.

51 Saint-Viâtre, *Gallia*, xix (1961), p. 338.

52 Brigmerston Down, *British Museum: Bronze Age Guide*, 1920, fig. 20.

53 Sparsholt, Ashmolean Museum NC 407.

54 Since this article was written, a new hoard of bronze metalwork with four incised decorated armrings has been found in the excavations of the Iron Age hill-fort at Norton Fitzwarren, Somerset (Langmaid, N. G., *Proc. Som. Arch. Soc.* 1970, 114).

The hoard, found concealed on the inner face of the outer ditch of a Middle Bronze Age enclosure underneath the hill-fort, contained eight armrings, two 'high-flanged' palstaves and a 'slender socketed axe'. Four of the armrings are incised decorated and form two pairs, one annular and one penannular. A third pair is 'rib decorated' and the two remaining single armrings appear to be 'boss decorated' and plain lozenge-sectioned. [Personal communication: N. G. Langmaid.]

THE CONSERVATION AND RESTORATION
OF ROMANO-BRITISH WALL-PLASTER

THE fragments of decorated wall-plaster excavated from Romano-British villas present problems of reconstruction to the conservator, but provide important evidence for the archaeologist. Because the plasters can be up to 25 feet long and 8 feet high, there is often a vast number of fragments to treat and identify, followed by difficulty of handling as the pattern is established; but the larger and more complete the area, the more evidence will be provided of the taste and skill of Romano-British villa-owners and their craftsmen. Conservation and exhibition must be planned together from the beginning of the work, in conjunction with the closely related problem of transport of the completed sections. None of these problems can be solved haphazardly.

In 1957 the first large ancient wall-plaster to come into the Museum's care was placed on loan by Lord Verulam and the Gorhambury Estate Company. This was the scroll plaster from St. Albans, described by Miss J. Liversidge (p. 87). It appeared at the British Museum ingeniously mounted on a framework by Dr. N. Davey, sometime Director of the Building Research Station, and ready for exhibition. The plaster itself is about 12 feet long by 3 feet high, with an uneven outline. In order to minimize the problem of carriage, Dr. Davey made up the fragments into seventeen sections of about 12 inches by 18 inches. The aggregate behind the plaster rendering had been removed in order to reduce weight, and the sections were then fixed to expanded aluminium mesh by a mixture of sand and nitro-cellulose adhesive. A strip of aluminium was secured to the mesh, by which the pieces were bolted to a lattice frame. The spaces between the fragments were filled with the mixture of sand and nitro-cellulose, and coloured to follow the pattern of the original design. The seventeen pieces were mounted on to the lattice frame, and a surrounding facia board completed a rectangle 14 feet long by 4 ft. 6 in. high. With a leg at each end and a support in the centre, this became a screen easily transported for short distances. For longer journeys, the pieces were quickly unscrewed. The conservation and construction is still sound after twelve years' exhibition. The only technical criticism came from Dr. Davey himself, who suggested that instead of sand and nitro-cellulose, a filling of Polyfilla should be used, and also that the colour could be matched a little nearer to the tones of the original.

Such criticisms were borne in mind when the work on the second, red, wall-plaster, which is also from Verulamium, was carried out. This plaster was mounted by Dr. Davey during 1968. The fragments had previously been assembled into pieces of about 24 by 18 inches at the Institute of Archaeology before the plaster was placed on loan at the Museum. During January 1968 the plaster was measured in order to assess its eventual area, so that a suitable position could be allocated to it in its mounted form. The pieces of wall-plaster, in their storage trays, were then transported to Lacock, Wiltshire, where the necessary laying-out area was available. Here the aggregate backing to the rendering and the plaster of Paris backing applied at the Institute of Archaeology during the earlier reconstruction were removed. This was a laborious and dusty process, carried out with a circular saw on an electric drill operated like a bacon slicer, set to cut to a predetermined depth with the wall-plaster face down. To ensure that the fragments would not separate during this operation, a sheet of tissue was stuck to the surface with Polycell. The flexibility of the tissue allowed the fragments to be adjusted to fit closely. The wall-plaster was laid face down on a sheet of glass which ensured a level surface, and allowed the correctness of the positions to be checked through the glass. Scrim and Polyfilla were then applied to the back of the wall-plaster.

To hold the wall-plaster pieces in position for exhibition, several wooden frames were made with expanded aluminium on one surface. The frames together made up the area of plaster to be exhibited, but their individual measurements were dictated by the size of the vehicle available for conveyance. The wooden frames were laid flat and the wall-plaster pieces arranged to cover them. Those pieces which were clear of any joins between the frames were attached to the expanded aluminium with Polyfilla. After their return to the Museum the frames were fitted to a board of resin-bonded laminated wood 10 ft. 6 in. long by 8 feet high, which had previously been secured to the north wall of the Roman Britain gallery. The pieces which covered joins were left to be secured in the Museum, using blobs of plaster of Paris within a circle of Polyfilla on the back of each piece, which was then held against the expanded aluminium until set. The plaster of Paris set quickly, and so held the piece in position, while the Poly-filla set at a slower rate, but more strongly. So, gradually, the area of the frame-work was almost covered. To make the finished effect more presentable, the area of the framework had been extended beyond the unevenly contoured edge of the wall-plaster to form a rectangle. This area was now filled in, using a plaster-board as a filler and then a skimming of Polyfilla to level off the surface. The joins between the plaster-board and wall-plaster, and the wall-plaster to wall-plaster, were filled in with Polyfilla. In order to simplify the final colouring, various powder pigments were mixed with the Polyfilla. Powder pigments mixed with P.V.A. emulsion were used to paint the made-up surface. The principle followed in colouring was not to match the original exactly, but to give the impression of completeness over a large area, while allowing the restoration to be distinguished as such.

The third wall-plaster treated for exhibition was discovered in 1949–51 in the Roman villa at Lullingstone, Kent, in a collapsed state within a basement room. This plaster should properly be described as a collection, because there may be fragments from eight walls and two ceilings. The collection has been worked on at various times at the Institute of Archaeology and at Lullingstone Castle. Various details and designs came to light, but owing to inadequate laying-out space, little advance has been made for some years.

During a week in September 1967 the entire collection of wall-plaster fragments in boxes and trays was packed and transported to London, and there arranged as it had been at Lullingstone Castle. As sufficient space was now available, the recognizable designs on the wall-plaster fragments were laid out on tables arranged to match the walls of the room from which they came. This brought to light a number of gaps in previous reconstructions and descriptions. Almost all information about the plaster—not only the designs and patterns, but also details of the height, length, and position, and evidence of doors, windows, and returns, and from which walls the various features came—had to be deduced from the plaster itself. After two months' concentrated effort in the summer of 1968, sufficient progress had been made for it to be necessary to check various conclusions about the plaster at Lullingstone villa itself. Study of the remains of the building and examination of the features of the wall-plaster remaining *in situ* answered many questions.

The need for factual information was increased by the decision that two areas of the wall-plaster should be exhibited in 1969. These two areas are the Chi-Rho panel and the standing figure, both now on exhibition. At the time when the decision to exhibit was made, the Chi-Rho was only half formed, with the columns wrongly positioned and the spandrel and base uncertain. The position of the figure was also uncertain, as were the dado and the extent of the design details (see Pl. LXIX *a* and *b*).

Although only two areas were required for immediate exhibition, it proved more rewarding to place all the fragments in their groups as they were identified, thus diminishing the number still to be placed. In this way many areas of pattern have been worked out by following through the design and types of feature recognized. Building features such as windows, niches, and returns all provide measurements which can be taken into consideration. To ensure correct relationships of verticals and horizontals to the circular wreath of the Chi-Rho, a sheet of Perspex was scored to provide a network of lines at right angles and several circles of different diameters. This sheet was laid over the fragments, which were then correctly positioned.

The problem of mounting the panels required for exhibition was overcome by using foaming polyurethane resin. It was necessary to support a number of fragments in the correct position in such a way that they could be applied to a screen for exhibition without obscuring or damaging the backs, and yet easily be removed.

EXHIBITING THE LULLINGSTONE WALL-PLASTER

The exhibition area used to display the Lullingstone plaster is a three-sided room 18 feet long, 15 feet deep, and 12 feet high. One 18-foot side is open. A reconstruction of the wall-plaster was carried out consisting of a frame containing original wall-plaster of an area of each of two walls. The west wall decoration had six figures over a dado and was 14 feet long. This fitted conveniently into the dimensions of the 18-foot side. The south wall decoration included a magnificent Chi-Rho with surrounding wreath and flanking columns. As its actual position along the wall has not yet been proved, the Chi-Rho motif was arranged into the centre of the left 12-foot side, which brought the two wall-plasters into correct orientation. The correct positioning and measurements are adhered to wherever they are known, as there is always a danger that inaccuracies or suggestions made in good faith may become accepted as fact and cause needless confusion. The Chi-Rho wall represented should probably be about 21 ft. 6 in. long.

In order to attach the frames containing the wall-plaster into their respective positions, it was necessary to design a suitable wooden framework. The details of the wall-plaster indicated that the walls may have been about 8 feet high. The figures on the west wall seemed to require 4 feet height from the top of the dado to the return for the ceiling. The dado was allocated the remaining 4 feet, and for the sake of uniformity, and measurements not proving otherwise, the Chi-Rho panel and its dado were each allocated 4 feet height. The remaining area of the west and south wall space is covered with canvas panels painted by Mr. Philip Compton, the departmental Illustrator. These panels are accurate reconstruction drawings for the remaining fragments of wall-plaster which will eventually be restored and exhibited. They give an impression of the manner in which this room, and probably the villa, was decorated.

To the top of the framework has been added a 3-foot projection to represent the ceiling, and containing illumination for the wall-plaster, so that a viewer may observe the decoration as if within a room (see Pl. LXVIII).

The manner in which the wall-plaster fragments are secured into the wooden frame for exhibition was decided after discussion and experiment using fragments without decorative detail.

The materials used in the reconstruction were as follows: one frame of aluminium angle supporting a wooden frame 3 inches deep, the size of the frame being 3 ft. 6 in. by 4 feet; a sheet of plate glass 4 by 5 feet in a wooden frame;

a plate glass mirror 2 by 2 feet in a wooden frame; a sheet of hardboard $\frac{1}{8}$ inch thick, and a sheet of expanded polystyrene $\frac{1}{16}$ inch thick, each to fit into the first wooden frame; Polyfilla; polyurethane foaming resin; G-cramps, various hand-tools, anglepoise lights, acetate sheet and polythene sheet.

The area 3 ft. 6 in. by 4 feet high was decided upon in order to include a column each side of the figure and the height from the top of the dado to the return of the ceiling. The fragments were carefully laid out on sawdust so that their positions could be adjusted. The various vertical and horizontal lines were noted, and other lines in the decoration were seen to continue from one fragment to another so that the decoration could be distinguished and identified on appropriate pieces even though there were spaces where fragments were missing. When the plaster was in position, a sheet of acetate $\frac{1}{25}$ inch thick was placed on top and the detail drawn on with wax pencils. Particular attention was paid to the vertical and horizontal lines, as it is essential to get the picture square.

The sheet of plate glass in its wooden frame was placed on the edges of two benches to leave a space beneath. The acetate sheet was placed upside-down on the plate glass in the appropriate position, and secured with Sellotape. The wooden frame was placed on top of the acetate sheet with the aluminium frame uppermost. G-cramps were used to hold the frame firm and avoid accidental displacement. The fragments of wall-plaster were now positioned face down to conform with the lines and details on the acetate sheet; to facilitate the correct positioning of the fragments, the mirror was placed on the floor beneath the plate glass, and anglepoise lamps were used to illuminate the decorated surface. It then became possible for the operator to look from above through the acetate sheet at the reflection in the mirror of the decorated surface of the wall-plaster as it lay face down on the plate glass.

When all the fragments were in their correct positions, a sheet of expanded polystyrene $\frac{1}{16}$ inch thick was marked out with the contours of the fragments. The contours were also traced on to the hardboard sheet. The contour areas were then cut out, and the polystyrene sheet placed on to the acetate sheet between the fragments. This formed a spacer to ensure that the wall-plaster would stand proud of the resultant reconstruction to avoid confusion. The hardboard was then placed on to the polystyrene sheet, smooth surface down, as this would become the surface presented for painting-in the design to complete the reconstruction. The spaces between the wall-plaster and the hardboard were then filled with Polyfilla, care being exercised to avoid movement of the fragments. The backs of the fragments were afterwards covered over with modelling clay. This was done first of all by forming a continuous wall upon each fragment and then placing in a piece of polythene sheet to avoid more clay touching the wall-plaster than was necessary. The clay was used in order to prevent the polyurethane foam from covering the back of the wall-plaster, which contained details of building construction.

The backboard was then measured and a sheet of polythene cut to a similar size. The polyurethane resin PP1/a was mixed according to the instructions and poured between the clay-covered fragments. As the resin began to foam, the sheet of polythene was laid over the contents of the wooden frame and then the backboard placed as nearly in position as the G-cramps would allow. As the resin foamed, so the backboard restricted its progress upwards and ensured all crevices were filled. Only light pressure should be applied to the backboard initially, as too much restraint can cause disruption of the frame. After the foam had ceased to expand, a wait of twenty minutes ensured satisfactory curing and rigidity, and the excess foam which had exuded above the limits of the wooden frame was cut off with a carpenter's saw.

The clay was then removed from the back of the fragments and the foam tidied to form neat holes. The G-cramps were removed from the wooden frame and the entire reconstruction lifted carefully from the plate glass. The acetate sheet prevented adhesion, and the polystyrene sheet could then be removed to expose the wall-plaster fragments surrounded by a hardboard sheet, which was ready to be coloured as required. The backboard was finally screwed in place.

It was difficult to estimate the amount of polyurethane resin required. One pound weight of each of two components provides approximately $1\frac{1}{2}$ cubic feet of foam, but it is not easy to assess the volume of the space in the wooden frame to be filled with foam, so that in practice three mixes were needed. As the foam sticks to itself as well as to everything else with which it comes in contact, the second reconstruction was done using clay walls to confine the foam into areas, the clay being removed as the next mix of resin was poured.

The reconstruction was then held up to its space in the framework representing the west wall, and adjustments were made to ensure an easy fit. Holes were drilled and screws secured it in place. The canvas panels were then added each side and beneath to complete the reconstruction of the six figures and marbled dado.

The method used for this exhibition is a prototype for the remainder of the wall-plaster. It is intended that the fragments will be contained within frames which will join together to form the areas of the walls from which they came.

P. H. T. SHORER

PALAEOLITHIC DECORATED BONE DISCS

MINIATURE carved or engraved objects of bone or stone, usually depicting animals, are found in west European Upper Palaeolithic living sites of all dates, but in the earlier stages they are few and simple in character. They become more frequent in the Magdalenian of France and have a sudden and spectacular development in Magdalenian IV. Almost every *belle pièce* that one can think of belongs to this cultural stage and the greater number of them come from the caves in the Pyrenees, such as Mas d'Azil, Lourdes, and Isturitz. These French Pyrenean sites are extremely rich in *Art Mobilier* pieces and they are rich not only in the number of pieces that they contain, but in the variety of these. In the stage of Magdalenian IV new techniques are used, new objects made and the aesthetic quality of the work is astoundingly high. It is a brilliant episode, but comparatively short lived; many of the forms are abandoned by the stage of Magdalenian V and workmanship and ability have almost everywhere declined by Magdalenian VI. It is a phenomenon that has a limited geographical distribution also, being confined to the Pyrenees and the Dordogne, with a few outliers in central Europe: it is not found in the Vienne and Poitou areas, nor in Cantabria.

Briefly, the characteristics of Magdalenian IV miniature art are marked in the technical field by a great development in the carving of reindeer antler and of bone, ivory, and stone. Animal statuettes were sculptured in the round, figures were carved in high and low relief, in *champlevé*, or cut as *contours découpés*. The term *champlevé* is used by Breuil to describe a piece where the background has been cut out around a figure to give it a low relief, as in a cameo, and was used on bone where the spongy central tissue made deeper carving impracticable. The *contours découpés* are rather like these *champlevé* pieces, but freed from their background to make a two-dimensional model, with very little thickness. Plain outline drawings have no place in the Magdalenian IV stage; almost every animal has its coat and muscles marked by carefully incised engraving, often of a rather schematic type such as chevrons to mark its mane, and although the pieces are very naturalistic they are not individualized. If a bison is shown, it is an ideal bison, rather stylized, very fierce, but somehow static. As with the polychrome paintings of Altamira, the effect is very sophisticated.

Magdalenian IV art in living sites is not limited to freestanding objects, however; tools and weapons are also carefully decorated and among these the spear throwers now reach a great importance; they are of two main types, weighted and unweighted, the second group of which were evidently hafted to give them greater length and propulsion. Both they and the pierced batons of this stage are beautifully and elaborately decorated with carving in relief and with engraving. In fact it is a characteristic of Magdalenian IV that decoration overruns the surface of the tools; fish knives and spatulae are often appropriately decorated with fish and the half rods have a quantity of highly schematic decoration lavished on them. There are a great variety of pendants in this stage, ranging from little horseheads cut from a hyoid bone, to polished stones such as jet, and pierced teeth and shells. There is also a group of very distinctive objects, small discs usually made from a circle of bone cut out of the scapula of horse or deer, or very occasionally made of stone. These discs are flat, often very thin and delicate, the majority of them have a hole in the centre, and they vary in size from about 3 to 8 cm. in diameter. A few are plain but most of them are decorated with either a schematic design or with drawings of animals. They are perhaps the most definitive object of the Magdalenian IV *Art Mobilier* complex for none are known in western Europe before or after this cultural stage.[1] They are not very common—in France 155, including fragments, have been recorded from nineteen different sites—but they are interesting, not only intrinsically but on account of their distribution both in and outside western Europe. They are found in central Europe, in European Russia, and in a related form in Siberia, which is a remarkable distribution (see map, Fig. 1). In central Europe where other elements of the Magdalenian IV complex occur, these discs are associated with it but further to the east their dating is far more diverse.

The west European discs are a very pleasing synthesis of the two main elements of Magdalenian art, having both naturalistic and schematic decoration (see Fig. 2). There are relatively few pieces with animals drawn on them but even these few give quite a comprehensive inventory of beasts. Two complete discs from Mas d'Azil (Pl. LXXVII, No. 8)[2] and Laugerie-Basse (Pl. LXXVII, No. 11) show, respectively, a cow on one side of the disc with a calf on the reverse and a chamois lying down, with a young one, standing, on the reverse. A broken disc from Raymonden (Pl. LXXVII, No. 9) has a mammoth on each side; another piece from Isturitz shows a bison's head with that of a horse on the reverse; there is a very fine reindeer's head on a fragment from Mas d'Azil (Pl. LXXVII, No. 10), and to complete the ecological picture there is, also from Mas d'Azil, another fragment with a man threatened by a bear's paw (Pl. LXXVIII, No. 12). As one might expect in the context of west European Palaeolithic art the man is ill-drawn, ithyphallic, and has a prognathous face. He is deliberately ill-drawn too, for on the same disc, beneath his feet, there is a horse's head, perfectly observed and carefully drawn. Reindeer are represented again on a number of fragments from Isturitz, which is interesting because reindeer, having disappeared from the archaeological record in the early and middle Magdalenian, do not become important again until the end of Magdalenian IV, thus confirming a probable late Magdalenian IV date for these discs.³ Perhaps the piece which is most delicately engraved, and most characteristic of Magdalenian IV technique, is a fragment from La Tuilière (Pl. LXXVI, No. 1) with the forepart of a horse on each side, showing a carefully shaded mane. This is in the British Museum,⁴ as is one of the most beautiful, if not the most typical, of the schematically decorated discs, from Bruniquel.

The naturalistic decoration on these discs is representative of much of Magdalenian IV work found in the Dordogne and in the Pyrenees, but the schematic decoration is unique. There are basically two motifs, one a pattern of lines radiating from the central hole (pattern A), the other composed of a line encircling the disc near the edge and of incisions between this and the edge, or notches on the edge (pattern B). In that the incised hatching of the second pattern is often arranged radially from line to edge, these two motifs have something in common, but the first is a central pattern, the second an edge pattern. In the first pattern (A), with lines radiating from the central hole, the lines may be single and few, as on the stone disc from Lourdes (Pl. LXXIX, No. 19); in multiple bunches, as on a bone disc from Laugerie-Basse (Pl. LXXIX, No. 20); or very numerous and close-packed, as on a second bone disc from this same site (Pl. LXXIX, No. 21). Very unusually the radiating pattern may be built up from something more elaborate than a simple straight line, for example, the larger of the two discs from Le Portel has this pattern drawn with both straight and wavy lines (Pl. LXXIX, No. 17). The first motif (A) is the more common, however, and there are examples of it in western Europe from Gourdan, Isturitz, Le Portel, Mas d'Azil, La Madeleine, and Bruniquel.⁵ The second, edge pattern (B), is basically as described above, that of a line incised around the disc near its circumference with the gap between line and edge filled with incised lines (Pl. LXXX, No. 22), but may have many variations. There may be a number of encircling lines, as on a fragment from Mas d'Azil (Pl. LXXX, No. 26), or none. In fact a number of discs, including some of those with animal decoration, have incisions around the edge. The fragment with a reindeer's head from Mas d'Azil (Pl. LXXVII, No. 10) has apparently continuous notching around the edge, while the chamois disc from Laugerie-Basse (Pl. LXXVII, No. 11) has a group of deep notches on the edge of the disc below and above the animal. Among other examples of Pattern B there are two disc fragments from Isturitz that are plain, except for hatching around the edge;⁶ one from Mas d'Azil decorated with a pattern of concentric lines drawn as though with a compass around the central hole, but no hatching; and a fragment from Isturitz on which the incised lines from the edge cross over the encircling line, reaching towards the centre (Pl. LXXX, No. 25). Patterns A and B may occur together: for example, the smaller of the two from Le Portel (Pl. LXXIX, No. 16) has the first pattern (A) of lines radiating from the centre, with incised hatching at the edge, while Mas d'Azil has a disc with radiating lines (A) and encircling line and hatching (B) (Chollot (1964), 289, No. 47224). Sometimes the centre of the disc is filled with another pattern, as on another disc from Mas d'Azil which has a pattern of broken dashes in parallel lines on one side, and of wavy lines, also in parallel, on the other (Pl. LXXVIII, No. 15). There is, in fact, an infinite variety of transitional decorations and combinations, but perhaps the most pleasing is that on a disc from Bruniquel, in the Betirac collection in France, which has the radiating line decoration (A), the encircling line and hatching decoration (B), a delicately scalloped edge, and an engraving of the head and shoulders of an ibex (Pl. LXXVI, No. 7).

From this confusion it is possible to isolate one or two more categories of decoration, the most distinctive of which is a barbed-line motif. This is best seen on the famous Bruniquel disc in the British Museum (Pl. LXXIV a) which has a denticulated edge, a notch at one end, a broken lug at the other, and a line with barbs drawn down the centre. A fragment from Mas d'Azil (Pl. LXXXI, No. 29) has the same barbed line, running apparently from the edge towards the centre, as has a fragment of a disc from Gourdan (Pl. LXXXI, No. 31) and a fragment from Kesslerloch in Switzerland shows two barbed lines radiating from the central hole (Pl. LXXXI, No. 30). There is another group of discs that connects with this Bruniquel piece. One of the peculiarities of this disc is that it has no hole, or trace of one, in the centre. It is not unique in this but apart from plain discs, which are presumably unfinished, a lack of central hole is rare. The Bruniquel piece may, however, have had a hole in the lug, which is now broken. There is a plain bone disc from Isturitz (Pl. LXXVIII, No. 14), which has a pierced lug; and three such, made of ivory, were found by Lartet and Christy at Cro-Magnon, two of which have a single hole and one of which has two (Pl. LXXVIII, No. 13). Strictly speaking, these pieces with a lug are pendants proper and not bone discs which, diagnostically, are circular with a central perforation; but if one includes the Bruniquel piece in the disc group, which it is imperative to do on account of its method of manufacture and decoration, then it is permissible to mention the Isturitz and Cro-Magnon lugged pieces, particularly that from Isturitz which is more nearly circular (the Cro-Magnon pendants are more ovoid in shape). There are four bone discs proper with a single hole at the side, two of which are particularly relevant in this context, for not only have they no central hole, like the Bruniquel disc, but one of them is the fragment **from** Mas d'Azil (Pl. LXXXI, No. 29) which has the barbed line motif—the second is a disc from Gros Roc (Charente-Maritime), which has an edge design reminiscent both of Pattern B, the edge line with incisions, and of the barbed line decoration of the Bruniquel piece itself. The decoration on the Gros Roc disc is, in so far as one can tell from the poor drawing published, a line with barbing that is drawn around the circumference of the disc. The last two pieces with side holes have central holes as well. They are the piece from La Tuilière (Pl. LXXVI, No. 1), in which the side

	Number of discs	PATTERN A — Decoration on the Face						PATTERN B — Edge Decoration				Suspension			
		Naturalistic decoration	Radial line pattern	Arrow design	Wavy line decoration	Curved parallel lines not related to centre of disc	Concentric circles, simple, multiple or combined with other decoration	Denticulated edge	Very fine all-round notching	Irregular notching	Notching with encircling line inside	No hole	Central hole	Side hole	Lug
WESTERN EUROPE															
ARUDY	5		×				×				×		×		
AURENSAN	2		×				×						×	×	
BRUNIQUEL	8	×	×	×				×	×		×	×	×		×
COMBARELLES	2												×	×	
CRO-MAGNON *	3														×
ENLÈNE	2												×		
GOURDAN	2		×	×					×				×		
GROS ROC	1			?							?			×	
ISTURITZ	68	×	×				×		×		×		×		×
LAUGERIE-BASSE	8	×	×							×			×		
LORTHET	3		×			×						×	×		
LOURDES	1		×										×		
LA MADELEINE	2		×										×	×	
MAS D'AZIL	41	×	×	×	×	×	×	×	×		×	×	×	×	?
PORTEL	2		×		×		×		×				×		
RAYMONDEN	1	×								×			×		
TROIS-FRÈRES	2												×		
TUC D'AUDOUBERT	1												×		
LA TUILIÈRE	1	×											×	×	
CENTRAL EUROPE															
ANDERNACH	1												×		
BRNO	14								×			×	×		
HOLLENBERG	1												×		
KESSLERLOCH	3			×									×		
KŘÍŽOVA JESKYNĚ	1		×										×		
PEKÁRNA	2											×			
PETERSFELS	9		×		×							×	×		
RUSSIA and SIBERIA															
AFONTOVA GORA II	2								×				×		
AFONTOVA GORA III	1		×				×					×			
ANOSOVKA II *	2												×		
BURET	1												×		
IRKUTSK HOSPITAL *	1					×						×			
KOSTENKI IV *	2												×		
MAL'TA *	3				×								×		
MEZIN *	1												×		
MOLODOVA V	4		×					×				×	×		

FIG. 2. Motifs employed on decorated bone discs
*= Atypical discs and other related pieces

210

hole is broken, and one of the discs from Combarelles, which in fact has three holes, one in the centre and two diametrically opposed at the sides.

In addition to these few discs and fragments with a single hole at the side for suspension there are a number with holes around the edge used in a decorative manner. One of the two discs from La Madeleine has a group of four holes near the edge as well as a central hole, and there are four such examples from Mas d'Azil. Three are only fragments, but the fourth is complete; it has a central hole and sixteen additional holes spaced around the circumference (Pl. LXXX, No. 28). The effect is not particularly decorative but it is a considerable technical achievement.

The position of a hole in a disc is relevant to its use; most usually these Magdalenian IV bone discs are described as buttons and to support this idea there is a spatula from Bruniquel with a man engraved on it who has a line of buttons down his stomach.[7] However, in spite of this figure there are reasons for questioning whether bone discs were buttons. Some of the stone discs, which are very few, are strong but the bone discs are very thin and delicate and are not robust enough to button a garment made of skin or fur. Also some discs are unnecessarily large; for example, the incomplete piece showing a man and a bear's paw from Mas d'Azil has a height of 8 centimetres and its diameter when complete must have been greater than this. Needles with an eye are known from the Solutrean period onwards, so one can suppose that late Upper Palaeolithic people wore laced or stitched garments; but is one to suppose that they used buttons only in the period of Magdalenian IV, or that in other periods they used buttons of a perishable material? It seems more likely that their clothes were usually fastened with laces or toggles, of which there are plenty in the archaeological record, and that the discs were a special form of pendant. If this were so it would not matter (as it would in a button) if the hole were at the side or in the centre; in fact one may wonder if the central hole was an incidental by-product of the method of cutting discs from a shoulder-blade and was used because it was usually already there. In the schematically decorated discs the central hole is fundamental to the design; but whether the hole determined the design, or the design the hole, one cannot say. Bone discs occur at a period in which a great many varieties of pendant were made and they are often found in sites that have a great number of these. Their decoration suggests that they had a particular value which, while it does not invalidate the idea of their being buttons, does allow the possibility that they might be pendants instead. Considering that many discs are decorated on both sides it seems much more likely that they were hung as pendants,[8] in which case either face could be seen, than used as buttons.

In general, it is difficult to group the decorative motifs on the bone discs according to distribution. Naturalistic decoration is known only from six sites, Bruniquel, Laugerie-Basse, Isturitz, Mas d'Azil, Raymonden, and La Tuilière;

but the schematic decoration occurs almost everywhere, seems to have almost no geographic grouping, and virtually every motif is combined with every other in a great variety of permutations. Pattern A (the radiating line design) is the most common and widespread motif, but it has many forms and no one of these is much more common than any other. Any site may have any combination of motifs and, as one might expect, the sites with the greatest number of discs show the most variations, that is Mas d'Azil and Isturitz. There are only two variations that have a local distribution: they are the use of holes as an edge decoration, found only at La Madeleine and Mas d'Azil, and denticulate notching on the edge of a disc. The disc with the barbed line pattern and another small fragment from Bruniquel (Pl. LXXVI, No. 3) have very carefully cut denticulate edges and look as though the same hand had made both, and the disc with the Ibex head, also from Bruniquel (Pl. LXXVI, No. 7), has a scalloped edge. Such notching is not found at any other site in western Europe except at Mas d'Azil, where there is one similar fragment. This is the third instance of a close link between Bruniquel and Mas d'Azil, the other two being the use of a single side hole and the occurrence of the arrow design, neither of which are, however, exclusive to these two sites as is denticulate edging.[9]

The schematic decoration of the Magdalenian IV bone discs is unlike anything else in Palaeolithic art and, with the exception of a pierced baton from Gourdan[10] which has a design related to Pattern B and another from Arene Candide in north Italy,[11] with a radiating line pattern (type A) around the hole, such decoration does not occur on any other objects. For this reason, and because their dating in western Europe is so tight, their distribution outside this area is the more interesting.

There are 155 fragmentary and whole discs recorded in France,[12] in central Europe there are thirty-one, that is thirty-one referred to in publications. With the exception of the group from Brno these are entirely comparable to the west European discs. They come from seven different sites: Andernach on the Rhine near Coblenz, Petersfels in south Germany, Hollenberg and Kesslerloch in Switzerland, and Pekárna, Brno, and Křížova Jeskyně in Czechoslovakia. The now broken disc from Andernach is plain with a central hole and was found associated with uni- and bi-serial harpoons which suggest a Late Magdalenian date, and the Hollenberg disc was also found with a characteristic Late Magdalenian assemblage. There are six complete discs from Petersfels and three fragments: one complete disc is made of ivory, one of bone, and the others of lignite, and all but one have a central perforation. Three are decorated, and it is one of these decorated pieces that has no central hole. The ivory disc from Petersfels (Pl. LXXXI, No. 32) is unique in its decoration: it has the radiating line pattern (A) covered with a concentric pattern of wavy lines, wavy lines such as were used on the disc from Mas d'Azil (Pl. LXXVIII, No. 15), although there arranged in straight lines rather than in a circular pattern. The two ornamented lignite discs also show the radiating line pattern, one with a few lines drawn from the hole (Pl. LXXXI, No. 33), one with numerous lines drawn towards the centre (Pl. LXXXI, No. 34), but no central hole. The Magdalenian industry at Petersfels was all of one age and showed a mixture of traits that in the Franco-Cantabrian region are all of various Late Magdalenian age. Petersfels is a rich site: toggles of bone and ivory were found and a necklace of twelve lignite pendants, each of which is a miniature stylized female figure.

There is one complete disc from Kesslerloch made of lignite and two fragmentary bone discs, one of which is of particular interest (Pl. LXXXI, No. 30) as it has the barbed line decoration known elsewhere only from Bruniquel, Gourdan, and the Mas d'Azil. On this piece there are two barbed lines drawn from the central hole towards the circumference, which suggests that here the barbed decoration was arranged in radiating lines (A).[13] There were apparently three archaeological horizons at Kesslerloch but the stratigraphy was not preserved. There are a number of objects, though, of typical Magdalenian IV type, such as a half-rod with pimple decoration (a motif that occurs in the Dordogne and Pyrenees in a late Magdalenian IV context), five unweighted spear-throwers with horse-head decoration, and a weighted thrower with two deer heads. Presumably the discs may be associated with these.[14]

Pekárna in Moravia has a Late Magdalenian industry with some beautifully decorated horse mandible knives, a stylized Venus, and plain bone discs without holes. A further disc, which came from the nearby cave of Křížova Jeskyně (Pl. LXXIVb), also with a Magdalenian industry,[15] has a central hole and a pattern of radiating lines, in fact the basic Pattern A design, paralleled in many Pyrenean sites. The discs from Brno, the third Moravian site, were found in 1891, interred with the skeleton of an adult man. The grave also contained an incomplete male statuette made of mammoth ivory, and two big discs of stone with large central holes, but no flint or bone tools. Recent geological work[16] has dated the deposit in which the burial occurred to Würm II, but it is not absolutely conclusive to ascribe the burial to this stage since it may have been dug into the deposit from above. However, the cranial characteristics of the skeleton are described as 'strikingly' similar to the Combe Capelle skull and the Gravettian date suggested for the burial may be correct. Fourteen discs were found at Brno (Pl. LXXV). They are made from a variety of materials: quartzite, sandstone, chalk, ivory, bone, and chips of mammoth molar. One relatively large disc has a central hole; five small discs have a hole begun in the centre, but apart from these the discs are without holes. The large round disc, one squarish and one oval disc all have notching round the edge, and so have two of the three small discs with a vulva line drawn on them, while two further small discs have exceedingly fine edge notching. The three discs with vulva lines have no parallel among other objects

213

of this type, but there are numerous semicircular medallions at Kostenki I with a similar vulva marking. The largest round disc, with a central hole, is the only piece from this site with any further decoration. It has four lines drawn out from the centre that divide the face into four equal segments. This design is perhaps another variant of the radiating line pattern (A), although this criss-cross form is unique to the Brno disc.[17] The Brno discs are highly polished and at least seven of them are so perfectly circular that one is prompted to think that they must have been turned mechanically. Jelínek (1958) suggests that the large stone discs in the burial were flywheels for a drill, and the fact that the ivory statuettes were drilled through from end to end supports this idea.

As a group, these Brno discs have certain features in common with the west European discs, such as their size, shape, central holes, and notched decoration on the edge; and certain dissimilar characteristics, such as the fact that they are all more than usually thick in section, and a number have vulva markings on them.[18] However, before trying to determine the relationship of this group to the West one must consider the Russian and Siberian material.

Three thin-sectioned discs (Pl. LXXXII, Nos. 35–7), one with a central perforation, were found at Molodova V in the Dniestr valley in European Russia; and also an object described as a slab of sandstone, although it measures only $8 \times 6 \cdot 5 \times 1 \cdot 4$ centimetres. This is semicircular in shape, perhaps broken, and has a denticulated edge (Pl. LXXXII, No. 38). Abramova (1967a), also describes from this site 'a very unique piece of sandstone slab on which were bands painted a bright red, extending radially'. This may well be the radiating line design found in the Pyrenees and central Europe, but there is no illustration of it available. The dating of these pieces is of great interest, particularly as Molodova is one of the few sites in the east for which there is a reliable series of absolute dates. The three discs were found in Layer VII in association with a Gravettian industry which has been dated by C[14] to 23,000 B.P. and the denticulated and painted slabs in Layer VI, dated a little prior to 16,000 B.P., comparable to the Early Magdalenian of western Europe.[19] These two layers are separated by a sterile band, so there is no possibility of admixture.[20]

Still further to the east there is a very small mammoth-ivory disc with a broken central perforation found at Mezin on the Desna river; two equally small objects of marl from Anosovka II; and one similar, one larger, of slate from Aleksandrovka (Anosovka and Aleksandrovka are sites in the Kostenki group, south of Voronezh). In addition to the two discs with perforations at Anosovka there were fifty similar pieces without holes, and at Aleksandrovka there were ten 'spindle-whorl' pendants and thirty unpierced slate discs. These two sites and Mezin are relatively late, that is of Late Gravettian date, for although they may contain Magdalenian elements (in addition to the discs, Mezin and Aleksandrovka have perforated batons), their industry is of an advanced Gravettian type. The discs from Mezin and the Kostenki sites are much less convincing than either the central European or Siberian examples, but they are included as a possible link because they lie between the two areas.[21]

The most easterly discs are those found in sites near Lake Baikal in Siberia; that is at Mal'ta, Buret, and Afontova Gora II and III. These are open-air stations. The Palaeolithic level at Mal'ta represents the first stage of the Siberian Upper Palaeolithic and geological evidence places it in the Zyrianka glaciation prior to the Karginsk interglacial which has its optimum about 26,000 or 27,000 B.C. Buret and the Irkutsk Military Hospital site are of the same date as Mal'ta, while Afontova Gora I and II are usually placed a little later and Afontova Gora III is equated with the upper horizon at Mal'ta, which is considered to be contemporary with the west European Mesolithic.[22] Afontova Gora is the most westerly of these three stations: it lies on the Yenisei river. There are two discs from Afontova Gora II, one very small, one of a more conventional size (4·2 centimetres in diameter). The small one, which is very thin in section, is plain with a not quite central perforation; the larger one is also perforated and its edge is decorated with notches (Pl. LXXXIII, No. 42). On one side there are two or three deep gashes, but they seem not to form any pattern, and in section it is rather thick. A baton came from this same site. There is one disc from Afontova Gora III (the later site): it is thin in section, 6 centimetres in diameter and, like those from Afontova Gora II, made of stone. It has no perforation but both sides are decorated with lines radiating from the centre, and both have a single encircling line near the edge (Pl. LXXXIII, No. 39). The Afontova Gora disc is the only illustrated example of this motif from Russia but according to Abramova[23] it is quite commonly found, although she does not say at what stage. The disc from Buret, made of nephrite, is very like the plain one from Afontova Gora II: it is small and plain with a central hole, but those from Mal'ta are atypical. However, since they are made of mammoth ivory, are decorated, have a central hole and, with one exception, are of a size to fall into the disc category, they should perhaps be described. None of them is circular: the largest, which is 13·6 × 8·2 centimetres, is oblong with a design of wavy-line snakes on one side and elaborate dotted line spirals on the other (Abramova (1967 a), pl. l, fig. 2); another smaller piece is nearly circular, has one smooth side and a deeply cut wavy-line pattern on the other (Pl. LXXXII, No. 41); a third, now broken, is sub-quadrangular, again decorated with wavy lines (Pl. LXXXIII, No. 40), and a fourth has two square and two notched corners, with a design of crescentic punctuations in lines. They were found in a child's burial with a beautiful necklace with decorated pendants. The wavy-line decoration on these four objects from Mal'ta is reminiscent of that on the bone disc from Petersfels and, although the Mal'ta pieces are not strictly discs, they have some affinity to such a group, in that they are very carefully decorated in a schematic manner and have central perforations.

These early Russian and Siberian discs, and also those found at Brno, although they have clear affinities to those in western Europe, are not exactly similar: they are often thick-sectioned or eccentric in shape and decoration, as at Mal'ta. The only disc in east Russia or Siberia that is really similar to the west European group is that from Afontova Gora III, which is a late site. In view of the fact that Abramova says that the radiating line motif is quite commonly found in this (eastern) area, one need not suggest that this piece owes its derivation to the West, but it is interesting that the disc in the Eastern group that is most similar to the west European Magdalenian examples is itself late. In the matter of dating, although the dates for Siberian and Russian Palaeolithic material are not yet well substantiated, it is clear that the Eastern group cannot derive from a French Late Magdalenian source.

In western Europe decorated bone discs are associated with a very characteristic art complex, that of Magdalenian IV. This complex is best represented from a small group of sites in the Pyrenees and Dordogne that show a very close relationship to one another. As we have seen, there is a very close connection between the bone disc types of Bruniquel and Mas d'Azil, and there are further similar instances: for example, half-rods with a wavy serpentine line decoration are known only from Laugerie-Basse, La Madeleine, Bruniquel and Isturitz; those with a spiral decoration, only from Lespugue, Lourdes, Arudy, and Isturitz. Such close associations suggest that the people living in these sites must have been, if not related, then very friendly; or that such sites mark the northerly and southerly limits of nomadic groups who moved to and fro seasonally. Within a small area this is quite easy to accept, but when a related group is found at Kesslerloch in Switzerland it is more interesting. The affinities that Kesslerloch has to La Madeleine, for example, are very close;[24] contact, at least in Magdalenian IV, can hardly have been only accidental or sporadic. A style of engraving links Pekárna to Kesslerloch and Petersfels: for example, a horse's rib from Pekárna, engraved with three bison, has very close parallels at both the latter sites. A pattern of distribution for the bone discs from the Pyrenees and Dordogne region to central Europe, therefore, at some time around 11,000 B.C. has supporting evidence. The distribution of the bone discs within this area seems, without any doubt, to be a distribution from west to east. Bone discs are very numerous in the Pyrenean region;[25] they have a great variety of forms there and are closely confined to one archaeological stage. Fewer varieties of decoration are found outside this area, fewer actual discs, and their dating is less exact. At Kesslerloch they are in a Magdalenian IV context, but in other central European sites, where such fine divisions are not represented, they occur in Late Magdalenian assemblages, or simply in a late stage of the local record. Such a west to east distribution is of great interest, because it is in a direction contrary to much of the traffic in art forms in this period; that is, during the Upper Palaeolithic in general.

This is an incomplete picture however. The dating of the Russian and Siberian discs compels one to acknowledge the fact that discs occur earlier in the eastern area than they do in the west and that not only the form, but one of the basic motifs also, that of radiating lines, may have originated in this area. Together with many other 'East Gravettian' innovations, the practice of making discs must have spread to western Europe, but have been little employed until, for some reason we cannot explain, it was suddenly appreciated and exploited by a particular group of people living in the south French and Pyrenean region about 11,000 B.C. From here the idea was rediffused with a number of other Late Magdalenian traits at least as far as Central Europe. The later discs in the East, such as those from Mezin and Afontova Gora III, may be a continuation of the local tradition or, more arguably, the fringe results of Magdalenian expansion, but they do not invalidate this explanation: that of a primary distribution from European Russia to France and a secondary distribution back again. That disc manufacture was first known in the east, and later spread west, is supported by the pattern of distribution of a number of other traits. For example, the Gravettian Venuses occur earlier and in greater numbers in the central European and European Russian area, and later spread, as a cult, into Italy and Franco-Cantabria. It appears that the idea of wounding the replica of an animal to obtain the same effect upon a live one was also current in eastern Europe at an earlier date than in the west. The East Gravettian (Pavlovian) sites in Moravia have numerous clay figurines of animals that have been gashed before firing. This, and perhaps other ideas related to sympathetic magic, must have spread in a simple form to western Europe, where they were developed and elaborated in the art of both caves and living sites. Discs appear to follow much the same pattern of development. They start as a simple form with a little schematic decoration which, when handled by a group of imaginative and skilful people, becomes more varied, more elaborate, and more delicate. To the basic schematic decoration are added a number of variations, and naturalistic decoration is used as well.

It is this marvellous use of naturalistic decoration that is the principal difference between the art of West and East; the fact that it is used so prolifically in the West and so sparingly in the East conceals the fact that the art forms of these two areas have much in common. In both areas tools are decorated; in both areas naturalistic animal statuettes were made, and often broken with apparently deliberate intent (this is particularly noticeable at Isturitz and Kostenki);[26] in both areas human figures are, with the exception of the Venuses, shown distortedly, and the distortions are much the same. The sculptured faces from Kostenki, for example, are very like the prognathous engravings at La Marche, and late stylizations of the female form shaped like the pendant from Pekárna are known from the Pyrenees to Siberia. In both areas, replicas are made of the animals most wanted for food, and of some predators, and are sometimes gashed or marked with arrows. Certain motifs of schematic decoration have unexpectedly close parallels outside their own context.[27] Parallels to the Afontova Gora III disc can be found almost anywhere in central and western Europe; and the wavy-line decoration from Mal'ta is reminiscent of the decoration on the Petersfels disc, and even of that from Mas d'Azil. Some, though not all, of these similarities are too close to be fortuitous. They suggest either that all these ideas were fundamental to Palaeolithic art and were reproduced whenever people produced art of any form, or that there was far more contact and communication between groups than the industrial assemblages suggest. It is true, as Leroi-Gourhan has said elsewhere in reference to the Upper Palaeolithic, that in a primitive society weapons change often, tools less often, social forms less often again, and that religious observances persist longest of all; so that the flint assemblages which represent weapons and tools have a great diversity, and the art which represents religion, a great continuity; but nevertheless the second explanation, that of contact, is probably the better in this instance. The spread of a particular and *new* group of objects must depend on contact between *contemporary* people. The Gravettian Venuses, for example, are one such instance and the Magdalenian bone discs are another. The pre-Magdalenian distribution of discs from the east (perhaps even from Siberia) by way of central Europe to the west is more problematic, and may have taken a very long time. It is put forward here because it is supported both by dating and by the distribution of some other innovations in Palaeolithic art. However, the second distribution of Magdalenian discs in a contrary direction is very rapid, and does suggest that communication among Upper Palaeolithic people must have been far more fluid than a study of cultural distributions suggests; art forms, in fact, crossed industrial boundaries with comparative ease.

The distribution of the discs, and the fact that they are very accurately duplicated in areas very distant from one another, suggests they were objects with some emotive importance. Piette thought that the radiating-line pattern represented the rays of the sun; it seems a hazardous guess, but no one has made any other. All one can say is that their schematic decoration is unique and that they must have been valued highly, for many of them are beautifully made.

ANN SIEVEKING

APPENDIX

Bibliographical List of Palaeolithic Decorated Bone Discs and Related Pieces

ABBREVIATIONS

Abramova, 1967(*a*)   Abramova, Z. A., Palaeolithic Art in the U.S.S.R. *Arctic Anthropology*, IV, no. 2 (1967), 1–179.
    A translation of Abramova's fundamental work on this subject, published by the Soviet Academy of Sciences in 1962. The original illustrations

	(which have the same numbers) are better than those accompanying the translation, and should be referred to for purposes of study.
Abramova, 1967(*b*)	Abramova, Z. A., L'Art mobilier paléolithique en U.R.S.S. *Quartär*, xviii (1967), 99–125.
Chollot, 1964	Chollot, M., *Collection Piette. Musée des antiquités Nationales*. Paris, 1964.
Chollot-Legoux, 1962	Chollot-Legoux, M., *Arts et techniques de la préhistoire*. Paris, 1962.
Graziosi, 1960	Graziosi, P., *Palaeolithic Art*. London, 1960.
Lartet and Christy, 1865	Lartet, É., and Christy, H., *Reliquiae Aquitanicae*, Parts I and II, 1865.
Leroi-Gourhan, 1965	Leroi-Gourhan, A., *Préhistoire de l'art occidental*. Paris, 1965.
Müller-Karpe, 1966	Müller-Karpe, H., *Handbuch der Vorgeschichte*, Band I, München, 1966.
Piette, 1907	Piette, É., *L'Art pendant l'âge du renne*. Paris, 1907.
Sonneville-Bordes, 1960	Sonneville-Bordes, D. de, *Le Paléolithique supérieur en Périgord*, 2 vols. Paris, 1960.
Zervos, 1959	Zervos, C., *L'Art pendant l'âge du renne en France*. Paris, 1959.

CATALOGUE

An asterisk (*) following the name of a site indicates atypical discs and other related objects.

FRANCE

ARUDY

(A) Saint-Michel d'Arudy

Piette, 1907, pl. lxxxviii, fig. 11, 11*a*.
Broken disc with regular notch edge-decoration and concentric circles.

For this site see Mascaraux, La Grotte de Saint-Michel d'Arudy, Basses-Pyrénées. *Rev. de l'École d'anthropologie*, 1910, 357.

(B) Grotte d'Espalungue

1. Chollot, 1964, cat. no. 49140.
   Broken disc with regular edge-decoration and concentric circle, decorated with oblique lines
2. Chollot, 1964, cat. no. 49122 (*a*).
   Plain disc D. 32 mm.
3. Chollot, 1964, cat. no. 49122 (*b*).
   Plain disc D. 25 mm.
4. Chollot, 1964, cat. no. 47116.
   Broken disc. Unfinished.

For this site, which is that called La Grande Grotte d'Arudy in Piette, 1907, see discussion in Chollot, 1964, 187.

Also from Saint-Michel d'Arudy: A shoulder blade (Omoplate), unidentified but probably of reindeer, pierced with three holes from which bone discs have been cut, is published in Piette, 1907, pl. xc. 6; Chollot-Legoux, 1962, fig. 116; Chollot, 1964, cat. no. 56401.

AURENSAN

Several bone discs, including one broken disc decorated with a concentric circle near the edge, and radial ornament; also one plain ivory disc, diameter 25 mm. with a single perforation near the circumference (illustrated). Frossard, E. and C. L., 1870, 'Notes sur la grotte d'Aurensan', *Matériaux*, vi, 215–16 and pl. xi.

BADEGOULE

Féaux, M., 1905. Musée du Périgord catalogue no. 1707 (p. 69).

Disc decorated with ray ornament. The provenance of this piece is uncertain. It may have come from Laugerie-Basse (see note 1 below, p. 226).

BRUNIQUEL

(A) Abri Montastruc

1. Smith, R. A., *Stone Age Guide, British Museum*, 1926, 141 and fig. 154; also Cartailhac, E., 1889. *La France préhistorique*, fig. 24.
2. Fig. 30. 2. British Museum.
3. Fig. 30. 3. British Museum.
4. Fig. 30. 4. British Museum.
5. Fig. 30. 5. British Museum.
6. Fig. 30. 6. British Museum.
7. Betirac, B., L'Abri Montastruc à Bruniquel. *L'Anthropologie*, lvi (1952), 213–31; also Leroi-Gourhan, 1965, 345, fig. 248.
   Naturalistic decoration.

(B) Abris du Château

8. Cartailhac, E., Les Stations de Bruniquel. *L'Anthropologie*, xiv (1903), 136, fig. 18, no. 21.
   Perforated disc with radial decoration.

COMBARELLES (LES) 1 and 2

Rivière, E., Nouvelles Recherches anthropologiques dans la Dordogne. *Ass. française pour l'avanc. des sciences* (Caen) (1903), 709–22, especially p. 712.

One specimen with a side and a central hole is illustrated in pl. x. 3; but this report mentions 'several bone discs, engraved with numerous lines, drawn in every direction'. The specimen with two holes is also illustrated in Sonneville-Bordes, 1960, 425, fig. 244, 12, and is now in the Vesignié collection in the Musée de l'Homme.

CRO-MAGNON*

Lartet and Christy, 1865, B. pl. xi, 2. 4.
   3 oval pendants. Undecorated.

ENLÈNE

1. de Mortillet, G. and A., 1900. *Le Préhistorique*, p. 215. Cau-Durban, *Bull. de la Société ariégeoise des lettres, sciences et arts*, Tom. i (1882), 210.
   Disc unfinished. Small central hole; polished and scratched surface.
   Believed to be in Foix Museum.

2. Begouen, H., Sur une sculpture en bois de renne provenant de la caverne d'Enlène. *Anthropologie*, xxiii (1912), 289.

   Begouen, H., L'Art mobilier dans la caverne du Tuc d'Audoubert. *IPEK* for 1926, 223 and pl. 4, fig. 13, no. 2.
   Undecorated disc with central hole.

GOURDAN

1. Chollot, 1964, cat. no. 47067.
   Broken disc with arrow decoration and regular edge-decoration.
2. Chollot, 1964, cat. no. 47232.
   Disc with central hole and radial line decoration.
   Also illustrated in Chollot-Legoux, 1962, fig. 118. É. Piette, Études d'ethnographie préhistorique iii. *L'Anthropologie*, vii (1896), 385–427, especially 403, fig. 39.

Clouet, M., 1934. Médaillon et pierres à dessins du paléolithique supérieur santongenois. *Congrès préhist. de France*, xi. 176, fig. 1.

Reindeer antler disc with side hole. Decorated with regular edge-decoration and circumferential line.

ISTURITZ

A total of 68 discs from various excavations are documented by the following publications. Many are not described.

Saint-Périer, R. de, 1930. La grotte d'Isturitz I. *Archives I.P.H.* Mémoire 7, especially pp. 93–5, fig. 78 and pl. vi, nos. 15–17, 19, 21–3, 25.

8 specimens illustrated.

Saint-Périer, R. de, 1936. La grotte d'Isturitz II. *Archives I.P.H.* Mémoire 17, especially pp. 69–70, figs. 42, 62–3 and pl. vii, nos. 9, 20, 24–5, 30.

40 bone discs and 4 sandstone discs are recorded. From layer II.

Passemard, E., Les Rondelles percées d'Isturitz (Basses-Pyrénées). *C.R. Assoc. française pour l'avanc. des sciences* (Montpellier), 1922, 476–9.

7 discs recorded also described in Passemard, 1944.

Passemard, E., 1944. La Caverne d'Isturitz. *Préhistoire*, ix, 7–95, especially pp. 47, 66, fig. 33 and pl. xxv. 2.

13 bone discs illustrated and discs of ivory and stone mentioned. (Müller-Karpe, 1966, illustrates discs from the above publication, pls. 71 and 73.) Ornament complex and unusual, including ray and ladder ornament and naturalistic animal decoration.

Saint-Périer, 1930, fig. 77, illustrates a reindeer shoulder blade pierced by removal of a bone disc. Several further fragments are recorded.

LAUGERIE-BASSE

8 bone discs listed below have been recorded from different excavations at this site. (A further specimen mentioned in the literature—*Matériaux*, ix, p. 79, pl. iv, no. 2—is probably not a bone disc.)

1. Girod, P., and Massénat, E., 1900. *Les Stations de l'âge du Renne*, i, pl. vi. 12. Also illustrated in Girod, P., 1900, *Les Invasions paléolithiques dans l'Europe occidentale*, pl. 20. 5; Müller-Karpe, 1966, pl. 78C (1). Also Zervos, 1959, pl. 388 (wrongly attributed to St-Marcel).
   Broken disc with ray ornament.
2. Girod and Massénat, 1900, pl. xxi, no. 6a, b.
   Broken disc with naturalistic ornament including bison.
3. Girod and Massénat, 1900, pl. xxii, no. 5a, b.
   Unfinished piece with concentric circles described as a disc in the text.
4. Girod and Massénat, 1900, pl. xxiii, no. 7a, b.
   Broken disc with regular notched-edge decoration and arrow decoration.
5. Hardy, M., 1889. Gravures sur os de l'âge du renne trouvées à Laugerie-Basse. *Bull. Soc. hist. et arch. Périgord.* xvi, 185–8, fig. 2.
   Also de Mortillet, 1880, Une Gravure sur os de l'âge du renne, *Matériaux*, xv. 247; de Martillet, G. and A., 1903, *Musée préhistorique*, 2nd edn., pl. xxiii, nos. 191–2; de Mortillet, G. and A., 1900, *Le Préhistorique*, 215, fig. 67, where it is shown as in the Périgueux Museum. Modern illustrations, Leroi-Gourhan, 1965, fig. 48 (wrongly attributed to Raymonden in the text, p. 417). Müller-Karpe, 1966, pl. 79, no. 11.
   Disc with naturalistic decoration showing a chamois, standing on one side, sitting on the other.
   Now in the Périgueux Museum (Collection Hardy).
6. Féaux, M., 1905. *Musée de Périgord*, cat. no. 1675, p. 67.
   Plain disc pierced for suspension.

7. Peyrony, D., and Maury, J., 1914. Gisement préhistorique de Laugerie-Basse. *Rev. anthrop.* xxiv, 138, fig. 2, no. 5.
    Broken disc with radial ornament.
8. Müller-Karpe, 1966, pl. 78 C (2) (?).
    Complete disc with radial ornament.
    The original illustration of this piece has not been traced. It may come from a different site.

LORTHET
1. Chollot, 1964, cat. no. 48246.
    Broken disc, central hole, decorated with radial decoration and perhaps an animal head.
2. Chollot, 1964, cat. no. 48232.
    Disc, plain, unfinished, no central hole.
3. Chollot, 1964, cat. no. 48247.
    Disc, broken, decorated with chevrons and radial lines.

LOURDES (GROTTE DES ESPÉLUGUES)
Piette, 1907, pl. c, figs. 4 and 4*a*.
    Stone disc with radial ornament.

MADELEINE (LA)
1. Capitan, L., and Peyrony, D., 1928. *La Madeleine*, 39, fig. 18, 1.
    Also illustrated in Sonneville-Bordes, 1960, 352, fig. 184, no. 1; Müller-Karpe, 1966, pl. 102, fig. 16.
    Broken disc with radial decoration, central and side holes.
2. Capitan and Peyrony, 1928, 39, fig. 18, 2.
    Plain disc (broken) with central perforation.

MAS D'AZIL (LE)
A total of 41 discs from different excavations at this site are referred to in the following publications:
(A) Piette Excavations
1. Piette, É., 1902. Gravures du Mas-d'Azil et statuettes de Menton, *Bull. Soc. d'anthrop. de Paris*, v, vol. 3, 771–9, figs. 1 and 2.
    (Drawn by H. Breuil) also Chollot, 1964, cat. no. 48120.
    Leroi-Gourhan, 1965, fig. 50; Graziosi, 1960, pl. 85 (*a*).
    Broken disc with drawing of a human figure (both sides) and bear's paw (one side).
2. Piette, 1907, pl. xcvii, figs. 7 and 7*a*; also Chollot, 1964, cat. no. 47218.
    Broken disc decorated with antlered reindeer (both sides).
3. Chollot, 1964, cat. no. 47241.
    Broken disc with central hole and some decoration.
4. Chollot, 1964, cat. no. 47230.
    Broken disc with side hole, regular edge-decoration, with encircling line inside and radial arrow decoration.
5. Chollot, 1964, cat. no. 47238 (page 289). Cat. nos. duplicated in error by Chollot.
    Broken disc with radial zoned decoration.
6. Chollot, 1964, cat. no. 47224.
    Broken disc with regular edge-decoration and encircling line inside, and also radial line decoration.
7. Chollot, 1964, cat. no. 47225.
    Broken disc with perforation slightly off centre. Engraved with regular edge-decoration with hatched encircling line inside.
8. Chollot, 1964, cat. no. 47229. Also Chollot-Legoux, 1962, fig. 117.
    Disc with central perforation and regular edge-decoration with encircling line inside.

9. Chollot, 1964, cat. no. 47231.
   Broken disc with concentric circle decoration.
10. Chollot, 1964, cat. no. 47237.
   Broken disc with concentric circle decoration and regular edge-decoration.
11. Chollot, 1964, cat. no. 47235.
   Broken disc with central hole and concentric circle decoration on a larger arc than the disc.
12. Chollot, 1964, cat. no. 47228.
   Broken disc with radial line decoration and encircling line at the circumference.
13. Chollot, 1964, cat. no. 47239.
   Plain disc with central perforation.
14. Chollot, 1964, cat. no. 47597.
   Broken disc undecorated.
15. Chollot, 1964, cat. no. 47596.
   Broken disc decorated with irregular curved lines.
16. Chollot, 1964, cat. no. 47234.
   Broken disc with central perforation, decorated with irregular lines.
17. Chollot, 1964, cat. no. 47238 (page 293). Cat. nos. duplicated in error by Chollot.
   Broken disc with central hole decorated.
18. Chollot, 1964, cat. no. 47233.
   Broken disc with central hole.
19. Chollot, 1964, cat. no. 47236.
   Broken disc with central hole.
20. Chollot, 1964, cat. no. 47227.
   Broken disc with central hole.
21. Chollot, 1964, cat. no. 47226.
   Broken disc with central hole decorated with curved lines.
22. Chollot, 1964, cat. no. 47240.
   Broken disc with central hole.

(B) Péquart Excavations

Péquart, M. and St-J., 1962.

Grotte de Mas-d'Azil (Ariège), Une Nouvelle Galerie magdalénien, Part III. *Annales de paléonto-logie*, xlviii, 195–286 (page numbers at foot of page), esp. 222–32, figs. 144–50.
   20 specimens recovered. All illustrated.
   An unusual disc (above, fig. x) was published by Péquart, 1962, fig. 146; and is also illustrated by Chollot-Legoux, 1962, 119–20; by Leroi-Gourhan, 1965, fig. 247; and Graziosi, 1960, pl. 96C.
   Another celebrated example from the Péquart excavations at Mas d'Azil has a cow drawn in profile on one side and its calf (?) on the other side. Péquart, 1962, fig. 149, 3 (*a*) and (*b*) and fig. 150, 3 (*a*) and (*b*). This specimen is also illustrated by Graziosi, 1960, pl. 63 (*b*); Leroi-Gourhan, 1965, fig. 49 (also in Chollot-Legoux, 1962, 91, figs. 121–2); and Müller-Karpe, pl. 79, fig. 3. (In every case wrongly attributed to Laugerie-Basse).
   Péquart 1962, fig. 142, illustrates a shoulder-blade of reindeer with a perforation caused by cutting out a bone disc.

PORTEL (LE)

Breuil, H., and Jeannel, R., La grotte ornée du Portel à Loubens (Ariège), *L'Anthropologie*, lix (1955), pl. xxvii, 1, 2. Also Beltran, A., Robert, R., and Vezian, J., 1966, *La Cueva de le Portel*, Zaragoza, 1966, pl. viii, figs. 1 and 2.
   2 discs decorated with ray ornament.

RAYMONDEN (CHANCELADE)

Hardy, M., 1891. La Station quaternaire de Raymonden à Chancelade IV. Sculptures et gravures sur os. *Bull. Soc. hist et arch. du Périgord*, xix. 121–35, esp. pl. III. 4, and pl. 131.

Also Breuil, H., Nouvelles Figures de mammouth. *Revue d'École d'anth.* x, 1905, 154, fig. 78.

Carthailac, E., and Breuil, H., 1906. *La Caverne d'Altamira*, 124, fig. 101, nos. 1 and 2.

Broken disc, naturalistically decorated with figure of a mammoth on two sides.

TROIS-FRÈRES (LES)

Begouen, H., L'Art mobilier dans la caverne de Tuc d'Audoubert. *IPEK* for 1926, 223 and pl. 4, fig. 13, nos. 3 and 4.

2 broken discs, undecorated, each pierced with a central hole. One of them highly polished, the central hole and edge much worn by use.

TUC D'AUDOUBERT (LE)

Begouen, H., L'Art mobilier dans la caverne de Tuc d'Audoubert. *IPEK* for 1926, 223 and pl. 4, fig. 13, no. 1.

1 undecorated disc also 'several' fragments, all with central holes.

TUILIÈRE (LA)

Smith, R. A., 1937. *The Sturge Collection (Foreign)*, 43, cat. no. 723 illustrated. First published in Reverdit, 1878. Stations et traces des temps préhistoriques. *Bull. Soc. hist. et arch. du Périgord*, lvi, 384–419, esp. 398–9.

See also Delage, F., Les Roches de Sergeac. *L'Anthropologie*, xlv (1935), 281–317, esp. 302–3 and fig. 12 (H. Breuil), where this specimen in attributed wrongly to Abri Reverdit, as also in Sonneville-Bordes, 1960, 411 (see note 4 below, p. 227).

Disc with side and central holes decorated with horses on two sides.

CENTRAL EUROPE

ANDERNACH

Schmidt, R. R., 1912. *Die diluviale Vorzeit Deutschlands*, 88–90 and pl. xxxviii, no. 10.

Narr, K. J., 1955. *Das Rheinische Paläolithikum*, 91 ff., pl. 15, no. 8.

Broken stone disc with central perforation.

BRNO (BRÜNN)

Makowsky, A., Der diluviale Mensch im Löss von Brünn. *Mitt. Anthrop. Gesell. in Wien*, xxii (1892) 73–84, esp. 81–2 and pl. iii, nos. 4–9.

Breuil, H., Notes du voyage paléolithique en Europe centrale II. *L'Anthropologie*, xxxiv (1924), 515–52, esp. 548–51 and fig. 27, nos. 1–4.

Obermaier, H., 1924. *Fossil Man in Spain*, 127 and fig. 57, nos. 1 and 2.

Also illustrated in: Müller-Karpe, 1966, pl. 219C, nos. 1–6; Jelínek, J., Pelisek, J., and Valoch, K., 1959. Der fossile Mensch Brno II. *Anthropos* (Brno), ix (N.S. i), pl. iii and pp. 23–5.

2 large stone rings (Müller-Karpe, pl. 219C, no. 8), and 14 discs, as follows: 3 stone discs, 3 bone discs, 5 ivory discs, 3 discs of mammoth tooth. Many of these are decorated (see discussion in text).

HAVEL, N. GERMANY

Stimmung, R., 1917. Die Renntierzeit in der märkischen Havelgegend. *Mannus*, viii, 233–40, fig. 165A. See also Clark, J. G. D., 1936. *The Mesolithic Settlement of Northern Europe*, 164–5, 248, fig. 57, 6.

Bone disc with starfish pattern in *Bohrornament* attributed to the Maglemose culture.

HOLLENBERG, SWITZERLAND

Bay, R., 1953. Die magdalenien station am Hollenberg bei Arlesheim (Kanton Baselland). *Tätigkeitsberichte der Natur. Gesell. Baselland*, xix. Liestal (1950/1), 164–78.

   Disc with central perforation.

KESSLERLOCH

Mestorf, J., 1876. La caverne ossifère dite Kesslerloch à Thayngen près Schaffhouse. *Matériaux* 2nd ser. vii. 97–114, fig. 49.

Merk, C., 1876. *Excavations at the Kesslerloch, near Thayngen, Switzerland*, London, 1871, pl. xiii, nos. 76–7, pl. xiv, no. 82.

Sonneville-Bordes, D. de, Le paléolithique supérieur en Suisse. *L'Anthropologie*, lxvii (1963), 205.
   Broken bone disc with radial arrow decoration; one other, bone, broken; one lignite, complete.

KŘÍŽOVA JESKYNĚ

Valoch, K., 1960. Magdalenien na Moravie. *Anthropos*, N.S. 4, pl. xxx, no. 3.
   Bone disc with radial decoration.

PEKÁRNA

Absolon, K., and Czižek, R., 1932. Die paläolithische Erforschung der Pekárna-Höhle in Mähren. *Mitt. aus der Palaeo. Abteil. am Mähr. Landesmuseum*, no. 26, pl. xviii, no. 10, and p. 104.
   2 bone discs, not perforated. One fragmentary.

PETERSFELS

Nine discs, as follows, are illustrated in Peters, E., 1930. *Die altsteinzeitliche Kulturstätte Petersfels*. Augsberg.
   1. Pl. xxi, no. 29.
      Perforated bone disc with radial and concentric ornament.
   2. Fig. 8 and pl. xxv, no. 4.
      Perforated ivory disc with radial and wave ornament. Also illustrated Graziosi, 1960, pl. 86 (*d*).
   3. Pl. xxii, 31.
      Perforated lignite disc with radial ornament.
   4. Pl. xxii, 32.
      Unperforated lignite disc with radial ornament.
   5–9. Pl. xxii, nos. 33–7.
      Perforated lignite discs, except 37 (perforation unfinished).

RUSSIA AND SIBERIA

AFONTOVA GORA II
   1. Abramova, 1967(*a*), pl. lx, no. 2.
      Small disc, perforation at centre.
   2. Abramova, 1967(*a*), pl. lx, no. 3.
      Agalmatolite stone disc with regular edge-decoration.

AFONTOVA GORA III

Abromova, 1967(*a*), pl. lix, no. 12.
   Agalmatolite stone disc with radiating line decoration and circumferential line.

ANOSOVKA II*

Abramova, 1967(*a*), pl. xxiii, nos. 24, 25.
   2 small perforated marl discs, one broken.

BURET

Abramova, 1967(*a*), pl. lvii, no. 7.

Perforated nephrite disc. Also Abramova, 1967(*b*), 100. 'Some discs and pendants in stone and horn'.

IRKUTSK HOSPITAL*

Abramova, 1967(*a*), pl. xliii, no. 2.

Flattened ellipsoid ivory disc decorated with rows of parallel curved lines.

Also Abramova, 1967(*b*), 100. In the Irkutsk region in 1871, 'discs in ivory decorated with concentric lines'. This statement is apparently incorrect; the objects referred to are not discs, see Abramova, 1967(*a*), 51, for a more detailed description.

KOSTENKI IV (UPPER HORIZON) (ALEKSANDROVKA)*

Abramova, 1967(*a*), pl. xxi, nos. 3 and 4 (and pl. xx, no. 16).

Also Rogačev, A. N., Kostenki IV, *Materiali* 45 (1955), pl. xxii, nos. 1–2.

1 marl disc with central perforation; one larger of slate with central biconical hole.

MAL'TA*

Abramova, 1967(*a*), pl. l, nos. 5–7.

3 decorated ivory plates of rounded or sub-quadrangular shape with central perforation.

MEZIN*

Abramova, 1967(*a*), pl. xxxiii, no. 8.

Ivory disc with broken central perforation.

MOLODOVA V (SEVENTH HORIZON)

Abramova, 1967(*a*), pl. xl, nos. 13–15.

3 polished stone discs, one perforated.

Also Chernysh, A. P., 1957. Mnogosloinya Stoyanka Molodova V. *Kratkie Soobshcheniya IIMK*, 67, fig. 15, 25–7.

[1] Many come from nineteenth-century excavations where levels were not properly recorded, but in these cases it is possible to date them by their associations.

There are claims for earlier dates for the discs in the older French literature on the subject. Four separate examples have been cited:

(i) A disc with radial ornament in the typical Magdalenian IV style was published by Feaux in 1905 as from the Solutrean site of Badegoule (see Appendix for reference). Its associations in the catalogue are not necessarily Solutrean and, since its publication antedates any controlled excavations at Badegoule, it may well have been found on or near the surface and be of Magdalenian IV date. An alternative explanation is that the collection described by Feaux came from the collections ceded to the Périgueux Museum by the heirs of M. Hardy after his death, and may have been confused and belong to a different site, possibly Laugerie-Basse. In any case the associations and date of the piece cannot be established. The piece has not been included in the distribution map and table (Figs. 1 and 2).

(ii) Two discs from the lowest level (*couche inférieure*) of La Madeleine, sometimes said to be Magdalenian III in date. This level is now recognized as belonging to Magdalenian IV (Sonneville-Bordes, 1960, 348–50).

(iii) A single broken disc with radial ornament from the lower level at Laugerie-Basse (Appendix, Laugerie-Basse, no. 7). This archaeological level is stratified below a Magdalenian IV layer and was therefore thought to be Magdalenian III by the excavator. Sonneville-Bordes (1960, 379) now recognizes that the bone industry from this level is more likely to be Magdalenian IV, or at the most Magdalenian IIIb, a rather hypothetical industry, different in character and later than the classical Magdalenian III industry.

(iv) Certain discs are said to have been re-covered by Passemard from the lowest Magdalenian level which he recognized at Isturitz, for which a Magdalenian III date was once claimed. It seems that in this case also the level need be no earlier than Magdalenian IV.

One disc which is apparently much *later* in date than the Magdalenian IV examples has been found in the Havel district of north Germany (see Appendix). [A pierced baton resembling the Magdalenian implements and decorated with Mesolithic style ornament has also been published from the Havel district (Zotz, L. F., *IPEK*, 13–14 (1941), 1–22).] This is quite a large disc, 10 centimetres in diameter, with a central perforation and a design described as a 'complete starfish pattern' which is basically one of lines radiating from a central hole, carried out in the *Bohrornament* (drilled-hole) technique. This technique has close parallels in the eastern Palaeolithic art group, but in west and northern Europe it is usually restricted to the Maglemose period (Clark, J. G. D., 1936, *The Mesolithic Settlement of Northern Europe*, 163–5).

[2] This piece is often wrongly ascribed to Laugerie-Basse, for example in Leroi-Gourhan's *Préhistoire de l'art occidental* and in Müller-Karpe's *Handbuch der Vorgeschichte*, 1966.

[3] There are a number of disc fragments show-ing a part of an animal, such as its legs or rump, that is insufficient for identification; the species that can be clearly distinguished, however, occur as follows:

Bruniquel	1 ibex
Laugerie-Basse	2 ibexes: 1 bison
Raymonden	2 mammoths
La Tuilière	3 horses
Isturitz	1 horse: 1 bison: 5 reindeer
Mas d'Azil	1 horse: 2 bovids: 2 reindeer: 2 bears: 2 men.

[4] This piece, which is in the Sturge collection in the British Museum, is sometimes ascribed to the Abri Reverdit, Sergeac, for example, by Breuil, Delage (1935) and Sonneville-Bordes (1960). It was purchased from Reverdit with a collection from sites in the Dordogne including the group of rock shelters known as Les Roches at Sergeac, one of which is now called the Abri Reverdit, after its excavator. Breuil came across the disc in the Sturge collection, and wrongly thinking that it came from the Abri Reverdit, sent Delage a drawing of it with this provenance to include in his report *Les Roches de Sergeac* (Delage, 1935). In fact, the Sturge collection does contain many flints from Les Roches (Abri Reverdit), but the bone disc does not come from this site. The original label still on the disc is marked 'La Tui-lière, St-Léon-sur-Vézère' *in the handwriting of Reverdit himself*, of which other examples exist in the British Museum in the form of inscriptions in publications addressed to Dr. Sturge. This label is also marked with the printed initials of Reverdit's collection *A.R.* The station of La Tuilière is quite separate from Les Roches (see Peyrony, D., 1949, *Le Périgord préhistorique*, pp. 37–8). The piece is correctly attributed, Cat. no. 723 in the British Museum catalogue *The Sturge Collection of Flints (Foreign)*, 1937, published after Delage's report of 1935. This provenance is confirmed by a study of Reverdit's contemporary publications, where the piece is described. There are two publica-tions. In the first, Reverdit, 1878, 398–9, occurs a description of the finds from La Tuilière (St-Léon-sur-Vézère), which include a 'fragment of engraved bone—a disc with a hole for suspen-sion in the centre and a second hole on the edge, and presenting on both faces a large number of fine and regular lines . . .'. Reverdit sup-posed them to be drawings of a fish's fin, a barbed line, and so on. The lines on the present disc are difficult to make out and we can under-stand that until Breuil was able to study the piece the correct interpretation of the lines as horses could not be established. But it is clear from the description of the position of the central per-foration and the second, marginal, perforation that we are dealing with a piece of unusual design, which must undoubtedly be the specimen in the Sturge collection, here illustrated (Pl. LXXVI, No. 1) by a new drawing from the original specimen. No trace of a disc of any kind was found by Reverdit at Les Roches, as far as can be seen from his pub-lication, Reverdit, 1878, or from the later report, *Station des Roches, commune de Sergeac* (Dor-dogne), published separately by Reverdit in Toulouse in 1882. This is fortunate since La Tuilière, a small shelter on the opposite side of the river to Sergeac, though poorly excavated, did contain some late Magdalenian artefacts (Sonne-ville-Bordes, 1960), while the industry from the Abri Reverdit is Magdalenian III, which would provide rather a problematic context for a bone disc.

5 One disc with a radial pattern from the Abris du Château, Bruniquel, has been published. There are also five small bone discs from Montastruc Bruniquel in the Peccadeau collection at the British Museum (Pl. LXXVI, 2–6). These have not previously been published. Four of the five bear the simple radial decoration.

6 St-Périer, 1936, fig. 42, nos. 2 and 3: for bibliography and references to further illustrations of specimens discussed in this paper, see Appendix.

7 Leroi-Gourhan, 1965, 342, and fig. 214.

8 However, St-Périer has suggested that the discs may be a form of primitive musical instrument. He reports that if a string is passed through the central perforation of a number of bone discs, and they are shaken rapidly, they make a dry rattling sound not unlike castanets.

9 That is, exclusive within the context of western Europe; such a denticulate edge is found on a stone slab from Molodova V in European Russia (see p. 214 above).

10 The decorated baton from Gourdan was published by Piette and its decoration was not unnaturally interpreted as a representation of the solar disc (Piette, E., 1896, Études d'ethnographie préhistorique III, les galets coloriés du Mas-d'Azil, L'Anthropologie, vii, 404–5). The cutting of the solar disc representations is noticeably shallower than the heavy grooves outlining the perforations on the batons, and for this reason it is considered suspect by Chollot (1964 Cat. no. 47436). However, a very similar form of decoration is found on a notched bone fragment from Laugerie-Basse (Massénat, E., 1874, Dessins géométriques gravés sur les os recueillis à Laugerie-Basse, Matériaux, ii, serie 5, pl. iv and p. 79). This specimen is apparently genuine. It has been incorrectly described as a disc fragment (Passemard, 1924). As it is notched all the way round its outer edge, it seems to be still nearly complete, and its original shape appears to have been pointed and not circular. It should therefore not be described as a disc.

11 This baton is illustrated in Graziosi, 1960, pl. 105a. The burial from which it came is published and the batons described in Cardini, L., 1946, Gli strati mesolitici e paleolitici della caverna delle Arene Candide, Rivista di studi liguri, xii, nos. 1–3, pp. 29–37. The position of the batons is illustrated in the photograph of the burial, fig. 2.

12 One specimen from Belgium cited by Passemard (1922) is not a disc. (Dupont, M.-E., 1872,

L'Homme pendant les âges de la pierre, 157, fig. 31).

13 Merk, 1876, says that this piece has 'branch-like ornaments in a radiating form' on both sides, but only one side has been illustrated.

14 Cf. Sonneville-Bordes, D. de, 1963, Le paléolithique supérieur en Suisse, L'Anthropologie, 205–68, for a discussion of the Magdalenian IV character of the Kesslerloch assemblage and also Feustel, R., 1967, Remarques sur le Magdalenian Suisse, Arch. suisse d'anthrop. Générale (Geneva), 26, 29–39, for further discussion on the chronological position of Kesslerloch and the related sites, based on the few radiocarbon dates available. Feustel described Kesslerloch as Magdalenian IV/V, and would place it at approximately 11,000 B.C. in the Bølling oscillation; Petersfels is placed around 10,500 B.C. in the older Dryas; Pekárna and Andernach after 10,000 B.C. at the beginning of the Allerød. This scheme is rather too rigid, though the relative dating may well be correct.

It is not possible to relate the proposed dates for central European assemblages with discs with those from France as no French Magdalenian IV radiocarbon dates are available. Late Magdalenian radiocarbon dates in France are limited to those at Pincevent, near Paris (Leroi-Gourhan, A., and Brézillon, M., L'Habitation No. 1 de Pincevent, Gallia Préhistoire, ix (1966), part 2, 382, Appx. iv, Report by E. Gilot) which are presumably Magdalenian VI, and Magdalenian V and VI, dates from Angles-sur-l'Anglin in the Touraine and the La Vache cave in the Pyrenees (late Magdalenian VI), produced by the Groningen laboratory in the early 1950s, all of which produced dates between 10,500–9000 B.C. These dates would give some support to the proposed central European scheme.

15 Photographs of the Magdalenian disc from Křížova Jeskyně, and of the discs from the Brno II burial are illustrated (Pls. LXXIV, LXXV) by courtesy of Dr. Karel Valoch and of the authorities of the Brno Museum.

16 Jelínek, J., La nouvelle datation de l'homme fossile Brno II, L'Anthropologie, lxi (1957), 513–15, also idem, Proc V. Internationaler Kongress für Vor-und Frühgeschichte, Hamburg, 1958, 436.

17 The criss-cross pattern on the large disc from Brno does not show on Pl. LXXV, or on Jelínek, Peliseck and Valoch's (1959) illustration of the same piece, but both Obermaier, 1924, and Makowsky, 1892, show it clearly. See also Müller-Karpe, pl. 219, C(1).

18 Müller-Karpe, pl. 219, C(6).

[19] Charcoal from Molodova V layer 7 was dated by radiocarbon analysis Mo-11 to 23,000±800 B.P. (21,050 B.C.) by the Moscow Vernadsky Institute. Two further dates, obtained by the scintillation method for charcoal from the same horizon were 23,950±980 and 23,680±400 [Vinagradoff et al., 1966, Radiocarbon, 8, 318–19] and a further date GIN-10 on humus from layer 7 provides a date of 23,700±320 (21,750 B.C.) [Cherdyntsev et al., 1968, Radiocarbon, 10, no. 2, 421]. A date for charcoal from horizon 6 at this site is GIN-105 16,750±250 (14,800 B.C.). A long and chronologically consistent series of radiocarbon dates is available for different horizons at this site. [Arctic Anthropology, iv, no. 2, 1967, 224–5.] A good general description of the stratigraphy is available in Ivanova, I. K., and Chernysh, A. P., 1965, Quaternaria, vii. 197–215.

[20] Abramova, 1967(a), 49.

[21] The double male burial at Sungir' (Vladimir), published since the present paper was written, contains two perforated discs of mammoth ivory decorated with radial ornament in the classic manner. Judging from the photograph these are about 8–9 cm. in diameter. The disc accompanying the younger of the two boys has been impaled at shoulder height on the point of the mammoth-ivory lance by his side, the second disc is laid horizontally upon the long mammoth-ivory spear close to the head of the older boy. [Bader, O. M., Ill. Lond. News, 256 (1970), 24–5, esp. fig. 1.]

Bader states that the latest radiocarbon dates for the Sungir' settlement are around 22,000–23,000 B.P., though these cannot be used to date the burials directly. Earlier published dates include a date for bones from the settlement GIN-14 14,600±600 B.P. [12,650 B.C.] and another date based on humus underlying the camp site GIN-15 16,200±400 [14,250 B.C.] (Cherdyntsev et al., 1968, Radiocarbon, 10, no. 2, 422).

[22] Conflicting radiocarbon dates for Mal'ta include GIN-97 14,750±120 [12,800 B.C.] and other dates reputed to vary between 10,000–30,000 B.P. all for fossil bone material. Afontova Gora II include GIN-117 20,900±300 [18,950 B.C.] for charcoal from the camp site and Mo-343 for charcoal found between the middle and lower layers of the site dated 11,335±270 [9,385 B.C.]. It is generally accepted that Mal'ta is attributed to the last interstadial of the Zyrianka glaciation. [Cherdyntsev et al., 1968, Radiocarbon, 10, 2, 435–6; Vinagradoff et al., 1961, Radiocarbon, 8, 319.] All discussions of the Siberian settlement suggest that the Mal'ta site (claimed to be a single period site by the excavator, cf. Gerassimov, in Michael, H. N., The Archaeology and Geomorphology of N. Asia, 1964) is much the earlier of the two sites on geological grounds. [Adelksenov, M. V. and Medvedev, G. I., 1968, Arctic Anthropology, v. 1, 221; Ravskii, E. I., and Tseitlin, S. M., Geological periodization of the sites of the Siberian Palaeolithic, Arctic Anthropology, v, no. 1 (1968), 76–82.]

[23] Abramova, 1967(a) states that 'special interest is aroused by the presence of various discs and circles in all local regions of Upper Palaeolithic art, including the little known East Asiatic region. They have centrally located openings and in some instances radials extended out from the centre'.

[24] Unweighted spear-throwers with a horse-head decoration are known from many sites in south-west France, but the three sites with the greatest number are La Madeleine, Bruniquel, and Kesslerloch, and the Kesslerloch and La Madeleine pieces are very similar.

[25] In addition to the sites in the Pyrenees on the map a further disc has been described as coming from Enlène (see Appendix).

[26] Deliberate breaking is perhaps not confined to animal or human statuettes. M. and St-J. Péquart commented at Mas d'Azil that it was curious that in spite of careful searching they were always unable to find the second half of many broken discs and that such fragments showed a neat and symmetrical break, in almost every case, through the central perforation.

[27] For example, there is a slip of bone from Isturitz with notching round the edge and a little protuberance at each top corner that is astonishingly like a piece from Kostenki I, or two more from Avdeevo; and a piece from Le Placard, that has a hatched line with zigzags against it, is very like a piece from Predmost in Moravia.

THE KENDRICK'S CAVE MANDIBLE

PREHISTORIC decorative art in Great Britain is rare before the Bronze Age. One of the most important among the handful of pieces known from before this period is the decorated horse mandible fragment from Kendrick's Cave, Llandudno. Yet this piece and the site of its discovery are virtually unknown. Published in 1880, the mandible was lost to sight between 1885 and its acquisition by the British Museum in 1959, and other important finds from the excavation in which it was discovered have gone unrecorded. The circumstances of the excavation, the subsequent history of the collection from Kendrick's Cave, and the cultural affinities of the decorated horse mandible are the subjects of the present paper.

The investigation of Kendrick's Cave

Kendrick's Cave is a small natural cavern on the south side of the Great Orme (or Great Orme's head), a limestone massif on the seaward side of Llandudno, North Wales (O.S. Ref. SH 78008284). The entrance to the cave lies close to and immediately above the Tygwyn road, in the garden of Ardwy Orme (Fig. 1), the residence of the late Dr. G. A. Humphreys. The site is described by the Royal Commission as *Monument 365* in the Caernarvonshire Inventory—a natural cavern about 50 ft. deep and 16 ft. wide at the entrance, at about 200 ft. O.D. The first published description is in the combined papers by Eskrigge and Boyd Dawkins (1880). Eskrigge makes it quite clear that the discovery of antiquities in the cave was accidental and had only just taken place. The cavern had 'for many years been occupied by Mr. Kendrick, the lapidary. Some weeks since desiring to enlarge his accommodation he commenced excavation further back into the mountain.' Eskrigge continues with a description of the stratigraphy and the archaeological relics recorded in the course of this enlargement, to which is appended a footnote dated 5 August (1880), stating 'further excavations have since been made'. An independent description of some of the archaeological finds by Canon Ingram, published in 1885, describes the cave as having 'been in the gradual process of excavation by a person called Kendrick' and 'recommends that further researches seem most desirable, as they might settle any doubts which may have arisen as to the accuracy of the present explorer's statement, on which the truth of the discovery of the above mentioned remains in that particular cave rests'. The *Shrewsbury Chronicle* for 24 September 1880, which contains a summary of the Boyd Dawkins report, states that the finds 'might probably have been consigned to the *debris* from which they had been removed had it not been for a medical gentleman of Bangor, who recognised in them the remains of human beings and the work of human hands'.

It seems clear that Kendrick had little education,[1] and at first took little interest in his discoveries. When these appeared to be of scientific importance he placed them at the disposal of Mr. Eskrigge for scientific examination, retaining their

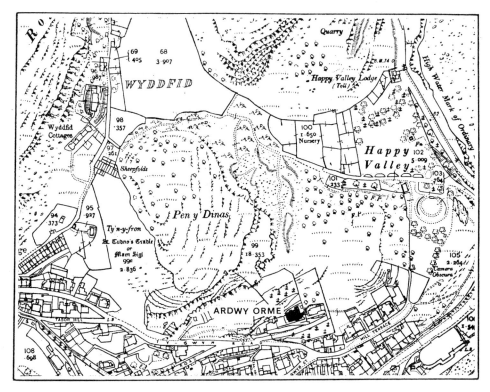

Fig. 1. Great Orme's Head, Llandudno. The entrance to Kendrick's Cave is in the garden of Ardwy Orme. (Reproduced by permission of the Director General, H.M. Ordnance Survey).

possession for himself.[2] It appears that Kendrick afterwards exploited the scientific interest aroused by the site to make the relics into a public exhibition at the cave entrance, and also added to these attractions a tunnel, which he excavated into the back of the cave and lit by lanterns hanging from the roof.[3]

As the archaeological relics appear to have aroused little interest at first, very little can be stated with certainty about the relative position and associations of the finds themselves. Eskrigge's statement of the stratigraphy is quite clear and appears to be accurate in general terms. He recognized a basal cave earth or clay, which Kendrick had penetrated to the depth of 2–3 ft., surmounted by 4–6 ft. of loosely cemented breccia made up of angular limestone blocks, and succeeded

231

in places by a layer of stalagmite. It is this breccia or 'limestone rubble' which contained the archaeological finds, and also some apparent burials of human skeletons. The cave earth contained bones identified by Boyd Dawkins as bison, said to be 'in a different mineral condition from the rest of the bones, and broken to extract the marrow'. These are said to be Pleistocene in date. The succeeding breccia contained, at a level thought to be approximately 1 ft. above the clay, portions of four human skeletons, two portions of horse mandibles (one decorated), two upper canine teeth of brown bear decorated and perforated for suspension, and at a point 2–3 ft. above the human skeletons were further animal remains including horse, sheep, and ox. Dawkins regarded the skeletons as burials and the archaeological relics as associated grave goods, which he would assign to the Neolithic period on anatomical grounds, and in contradistinction to the earlier Pleistocene remains in the cave earth. 'The general impression left in my mind by the whole series of remains is that the interment is of Neolithic age and that the cave was used as a sepulchral vault by a family of small Iberic cave dwellers in the neighbourhood.'

We have no evidence at the present time of the nature of the deposits as the cave has been much altered since the excavation, and all traces of breccia and cave earth appear to be lacking.[4] Modern opinion would certainly not support Dawkins's confident argument, nor does it seem necessary to assume that the contents of a deposit 4–6 ft. in thickness are all of the same date. In view of the lack of evidence for properly associated finds, the discoveries from Kendrick's Cave have to be treated on their own merits.

Archaeological specimens from the cave

It appears that when the remains from the cave then in possession of his relatives were purchased by the committee of the Llandudno public library, after the death of Thomas Kendrick, they were 'not as complete as when submitted to Professor Boyd Dawkins'.[5] Some of the most important pieces had already been dispersed to private collectors. Some human remains and a few unworked animal bones are now in the Llandudno public library, as are a small series of incised bones possibly of sheep or deer, stained with haematite, believed to be from this cave but unlabelled and not mentioned in any contemporary account.

Certain of the collections dispersed by Kendrick have turned up on the market in recent years. A small polished stone axe-head of typical British Neolithic type bearing the label, Kendricks Cave, Llandudno, was presented to the British Museum in 1956 by Mr. Weinreb the London bookseller, into whose hands it had come with a miscellaneous collection. The following year a further group of antiquities, all labelled as from the same source, were brought to the Museum for examination by Mr. J. R. Wright, a young collector in Worcester, who had purchased them from a dealer in that locality. This collection, which included the decorated jawbone fragment, and a number of previously unpublished pieces, were purchased by the Christy Trustees from Mr. Wright in 1959.

Among the outstanding specimens mentioned in the contemporary reports are two bear's teeth, and a further group of 'swine' teeth, decorated with transverse cut marks and perforated for suspension as part of a necklace. Both these groups appear to have passed through the local dealers' hands in the 1930s. The two bear's teeth are thought to be referred to in the entry 'Part of a necklace of bear's claws of prehistoric type'—in a catalogue of a sale at Glynllifon, Caernarvonshire[6] in 1932, located by the Royal Commission. The catalogue unfortunately gave no indication of the provenance of these pieces, and their present whereabouts are unknown. It seems likely that they will turn up on the market in the future, when they may be identifiable from the illustration published by Boyd Dawkins. A collection of nine bovid and deer teeth, decorated and perforated in the appropriate manner, but again unlabelled, were acquired by Mrs. Dowler of Penrhyn Bay as part of a local purchase of prehistoric antiquities at approximately the same period, and were presented by her in 1964 to the Rhôs-on-Sea Museum, Colwyn Bay, North Wales. There is reason to believe on internal evidence, and on general grounds, that these are the 'swine teeth' from Kendricks Cave. They have been lent to the British Museum for examination, and are described here by kind permission of the Rhôs-on-Sea Museum.

Miscellaneous pieces

In addition to the important finds mentioned by the contemporary accounts, the Museum collections include the following specimens labelled as from Kendrick's Cave, and belonging to various periods between the Neolithic and the Roman occupation.

1. A stone axe-head polished over-all, but with slight traces of chipping. It has a lenticular cross-section and a pointed butt. Length 88 mm.

   The specimen is made of a grey rock at present awaiting geological examination. It is a typical British Neolithic product. B.M. Reg. no. 1956, 2–2, 1.

2. Stone spindle-whorl, perforated. Diameter 46 mm. B.M. Reg. no. 1959, 12–3, 3.

3. A small flint axe-head or knife of black stone, roughly flaked round three sides and polished at the blade (Fig. 2. 2*a* and *b*). Length 81 mm. B.M. Reg. no. 1959, 12–3, 4. The specimen is made on a flat piece of stone flaked on both sides in a disc form, flat on one side and convex on the other, but with a typical balanced axe-blade termination made from two converging polished surfaces. Though it is formally in the axe clan, Mr. Houlder regards these pieces as allied to knives, and has published

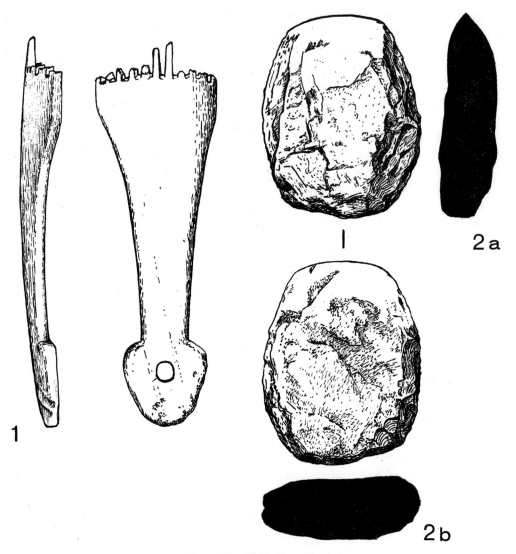

FIG. 2. Kendrick's Cave, Llandudno:
1. Bone comb.
2. Edge-ground axe.
Scale 2 : 3

comparable specimens from the Mynydd Rhiw Neolithic factory site in the same county.[7]

This specimen has been examined by the Geological Survey who find that it is made of an Epidiorite, best matched in the United Kingdom by specimens from Cornwall (see Appendix II).

234

4. A bone weaving-comb of Bulleid and Gray's Glastonbury type 2, with an oval or round enlargement at the butt end,[8] and with two teeth complete. The original number of teeth was eleven. The comb is polished over its upper surface, and has traces of two diagonal grooves which may result from use. At the comb-end the bone follows its natural curve and the inner surface is concave. Length 155 mm. (Fig. 2.1), B.M. Reg. no. 1959, 12–3, 2. This is plainly a variety of the long-lived Early Iron Age type, appearing notably at All Cannings Cross, Maiden Castle, and at Glastonbury and Meare Lake Villages.[9]

The comb is of importance here, as it has been used to give a comparative dating to the decorated horse mandible from the same site (see Appendix I).

There is also a series of six fragments of animal bones, including two with articular ends with lengths 70 mm., 71 mm., respectively, probably metacarpals of sheep or deer,[10] incised with a number of separate lines or groups of lines and showing traces of haematite staining (Fig. 3). These are now in the collections of Llandudno Public Library, and are kept in a case with the animal and human bones from Kendrick's Cave. Though they are not labelled, or mentioned in any contemporary publication, they have been preserved at Llandudno with the antiquities from the cave and are generally accepted as such. It has not proved possible to obtain an identification of the animal bones, which may be deer or goat, but are most likely to be sheep. The incisions appear to be some form of tally mark, but do not closely resemble the well-known Palaeolithic bone tallies or *Marques de Chasse* from France,[11] or the similar objects found in the Mesolithic period in Denmark. Nor do they resemble published Medieval examples. It has not been found possible to find any close parallels for these incised bones, and it may be that they are of modern manufacture. If they are accepted as genuine, and the bones prove to be of sheep, then they are likely to belong to a period later than the Neolithic. Nitrogen analysis would show the age of the *bones* (as distinct from the incisions) relative to the Iron Age bone comb found on the same site (see Appendix I).

The decorated teeth

The teeth in the Dowler collection at Rhôs-on-Sea Museum[12] illustrated here (Fig. 4) are thought to come from Kendrick's Cave since they are described in two independent contemporary publications in 1880 and 1885. Eskrigge writes (1880):

August 5th. Further excavations have been made resulting in the discovery ... (of) ... a number of small teeth with holes drilled through them, probably used as a necklace.

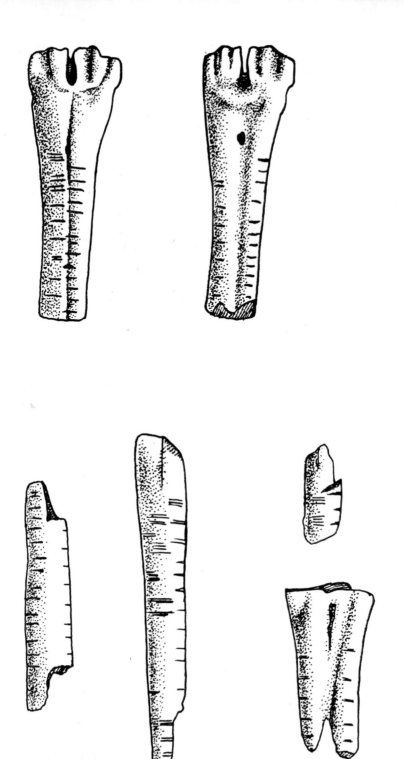

FIG. 3. Kendrick's Cave, Llandudno. Incised deer or sheep bones. (Llandudno Public Library.) Scale 1:1

In 1885 Ingram writes:

There have also been found a considerable quantity of swine's teeth, each marked on the fang with from four to six transverse lines, and perforated at the extremity with a hole through which ran probably a tendon of a reindeer, or some other ligament stringing them together as a necklace.

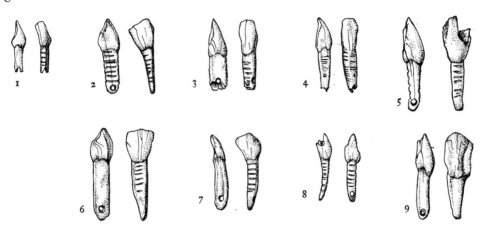

FIG. 4. Decorated bovid and deer teeth, believed to be from Kendrick's Cave. Rhôs-on-Sea Museum. Scale 1:2. 1, 7, 8: *C. Elaphus*. 2, 5, 6: Bovid. 3, 4. *C. Megaceros* or *Alces*. 9. Atypical

Though the teeth are of bovid and deer, they bear some resemblance to swine teeth, and it is evident, from the contemporary accounts, that the Kendrick's Cave teeth were never examined by a specialist. But the real significance of this quotation lies in the description of the decoration. Eight of the nine teeth, here illustrated from the Dowler collection, are decorated precisely in the manner that Ingram describes, and though 'from four to six' transverse lines is not accurate for all the teeth, it is the general impression given by the teeth as a whole. In addition to this decoration, each illustrated tooth is perforated in the extremity of the 'fang', rather than in a more central position, as is often the case with perforated teeth of later prehistoric periods. Some, though not all, of the teeth are slightly stained red with ruddle, or haematite.

Perforated teeth of wild animals are a common prehistoric antiquity in Britain[13] and western Europe, and it is not perhaps appreciated how restricted are the decorated examples. These are virtually confined to the classic Magdalenian stations of Franco-Cantabria, though one Upper Perigordian (Gravettian) and a possible Solutrean example can be quoted. Even among the French Magdalenian stations teeth decorated in this manner are comparatively rare. The total number of published sites containing such teeth is probably between fifteen and twenty, and in almost all cases only two or three decorated teeth are illustrated.[14] Though simple perforated teeth are a feature of the British Upper Palaeolithic, for example at Paviland,[15] no British decorated example is known to the author.

237

French collectors' pieces of such rarity are unlikely to have been available in the British antique market at any time, and the appearance of more than half a dozen specimens, closely resembling those described from Kendrick's Cave, at a local saleroom a generation after the dispersal of the finds is strong evidence that they came from this locality. The specimens themselves are undoubtedly authentic, and closely resemble French examples. It is reasonable to suppose that the teeth were either imported in Middle or Late Magdalenian times from south-west France, or are of British manufacture in the same general Palaeolithic tradition. A handful of other specimens (usually of carved bone or antler), equally close to their continental models, have been found in British caves.[16]

The decorated horse mandible

The most important piece acquired by the Christy Trustees for the British Museum in 1959 was the fragment of decorated horse mandible, Length: 135 mm., B.M. Reg. no. 1959, 12–3, 1, labelled as from Kendrick's Cave.[17] It is illustrated here in Pls. LXXXIV and LXXXV, taken respectively before and after cleaning by the Research Laboratory. When the fragment was acquired by the Museum, it was, as can be seen in the photograph, somewhat darker than at present, and covered in places with a thin layer of calcite, which concealed parts of the decoration. It was also noticed that the third incisor on the broken side of the mandible was loose and slipped in and out easily. (It has since been secured by adhesive.) The decorated horse mandible illustrated by Boyd Dawkins (1880, 158, Fig. A) is undoubtedly the same piece, as can be verified by comparing the position of the blocks of chevron decoration, where these were visible in 1880. It will be noted that Boyd Dawkins's illustration is drawn freehand and is slightly larger than the original, and that the draftsman has removed the loose tooth—though its socket is clearly visible.

The fragment is the symphysis, the front part of the lower jaw (or mandible) of a horse, or, more correctly, as Boyd Dawkins described it, 'the incisors, symphysis, and the diastema, broken away in front of the molar series'. The main teeth-carrying part of the jaw and the articulation with the cheek are missing. There is not really sufficient of the jaw to give a definite idea of size, but Dr. Sutcliffe was able to demonstrate, by comparison with modern horse mandibles, that the Kendrick's Cave specimen appeared to be more robust than such modern material as was readily available. The structure of the symphysis was heavier, i.e. the bone was thicker, and there appeared to be a shorter distance between the cheek teeth (pre-molar) and the incisors than in modern species. A socket for a cheek tooth is in fact present, which allows this observation to be made. Possibly the Kendrick's Cave horse may have been a deeper-jawed animal, resembling Przewalski's horse, but this is purely speculative.

238

When the underside of the mandible fragment was examined after cleaning, it became clear that this was decorated with a number of isolated blocks of carefully incised ornament, placed at regular intervals round the steeply contoured surface. Before cleaning, traces of haematite were visible in the incisors, but these were removed during the cleaning process. A carefully executed rubbing of the decoration (Fig. 5) illustrates the technique of incision, showing where the craftsman allowed his cutting tool to stray beyond the confines of the decorative panels. However, the flattened illustration of this almost cylindrical piece exaggerates apparent irregularities. In the hand the decoration gives a much greater impression of uniformity. Nearly all the incisions appear to be square in cross-section as if a fairly flat cutting edge was used for them. Exceptionally, the narrow block of rather larger single-chevron ornament near the outer margin appears to have been cut with a different implement, perhaps a knife blade, producing a V-sectioned groove. There seems no reason to believe that such decoration could not have been produced by means of flint implements.

In addition to this decoration Boyd Dawkins states that 'the outer surface of the incisors is polished by friction against some soft substance . . . more than it would be naturally in the mouth of a horse'. Ingram's explanation (1885) is that the 'two lower equine jaws[17] . . . were probably hung also from the necks of the cave men as ornaments . . . in the same way as the natives of New Guinea wear lower human jaws as bracelets'. The enamel of the outer surface of the incisors is exceptionally well preserved, but not unnaturally so, and the polish seems likely to be due simply to the animal chewing silicious grass.

The Wild Horse (*Equus Caballus*) is favoured by the open steppe conditions of the Late Glacial and earlier interstadial periods and its extinction in Britain is thought to coincide with the post-glacial expansion of forest in Zone IV.[18] The Kendrick's Cave horse mandible, on this argument, is likely to belong to the Upper Palaeolithic or to the Late Glacial (Epi-palaeolithic) cultures and to date from the Allerød (Zone II) at the latest.[19] Alternatively, the mandible could post-date the reintroduction of the horse into Britain and belong to the Bronze Age or possibly to the late Neolithic.[20] However, though the post-glacial extinction of the horse is well documented for heavily forested regions, it may possibly have persisted in lightly wooded hill-country in the west of Britain. Piggott[21] suggests that, in relatively open country, in Caithness and on the oolitic limestone area of the Severn-Cotswold tombs, horse was a common wild animal in the late Neolithic period. There are also claims, though these are generally disallowed, for the association of horse with a late Creswellian industry of post-glacial date.[22] A Mesolithic or Neolithic date for the Kendrick's Cave mandible, though unlikely, cannot therefore entirely be dismissed on faunal grounds, until further evidence becomes available for the post-glacial extinction of the horse in Britain.

No method of measuring the absolute, or chronometric, age of the mandible by scientific means has so far been carried out, though it is hoped to obtain a thermoluminescent date for the piece, should this method become effective for the dating of bones of Pleistocene age.[23]

A nitrogen analysis of the mandible has been undertaken which provides a comparative dating for the piece (see Appendix I). This analysis shows that the mandible is likely to be considerably older than the Iron Age bone comb from Kendrick's Cave (also analysed) and is comparable in nitrogen content with Pleistocene mammal bone from the Welsh caves, and therefore may be of comparable age. Further analyses of the other Kendrick's Cave pieces, at present being carried out, may be expected to confirm this suggestion.

Comparative study of the decoration

The Palaeolithic date of the horse mandible suggested by the faunal evidence is strongly supported by its style and mode of decoration.

The ornament can be briefly described as four blocks of herringbone, accompanied by a block of single chevrons placed one above the other. The superficial purpose of the ornament, as can be clearly seen from different views illustrated (Pl. LXXXV *a*, *d*), is to fill the available field with a carefully and symmetrically arranged series of ornamental blocks, utilizing the underside of the symphysis, the broadest and most suitable part of the horse mandible for decoration, and making allowances for the natural holes which occur on each side. The two blocks of ornament nearest the teeth (Fig. 5, bottom) are both incomplete as the bone is particularly thin and has broken away to the left and right. The right-hand block of decoration is approximately correct in over-all size and the left-hand block was presumably of equivalent size before the three missing incisors and their sockets broke away from the mandible, as each block has seven rows of herringbone ornament. The two rear blocks of ornament are slightly larger in size, and each contain nine rows of the decorative motif. The design is completed by the block of (ten) parallel single chevrons, for which a different cutting tool seems to have been employed (see above). We have mentioned that the flattened *development* of the design (Fig. 5) is misleading. The photographs show that the underside of the symphysis, though providing a broad surface area for decoration, is steeply contoured, and the appearance of the design on the original is much more symmetrical than it appears in the rubbing. Additionally, the actual carved design on the light-coloured bone emphasizes the intentional negative quality of the incised ornament, which appears to be intended to make the plain areas of bone between the incised lines stand out from the field.

The decoration was incised, presumably with a flint implement. No evidence to the contrary was observed, but the knife or burin, of whatever raw material, must have had a fairly short cutting-edge, as the decorative lines are narrow and close together, much closer than in certain other classes of prehistoric bone engraving. Though the cutting-edge was short and the bone presumably fresh when cut, instances of the tool over-running the desired line of ornament are frequent, and the depth of each individual line is irregular, shallow at one end of the groove and deep at the other. The planning of the ornament in the top right

FIG. 5. Kendrick's Cave, Llandudno. Decorated horse mandible. (Decoration unrolled.) Scale 1:1

panel appears to have gone awry, certain cuts are too far apart or discontinuous, and it looks as if the craftsman was misled here by the change in contour in the centre of the field.

When comparing the mandible with other decorated examples, attention has to be paid to the motifs used, to the formal decorative scheme, described above, the scale of the decoration, the use of incised decoration on bones in general, and the use of animal jawbones, and other pieces of the animal skeleton which are unlikely or impossible to have been tools, as suitable subjects for geometric decoration.

The principal motive used on the Kendrick's Cave mandible is herringbone ornament, of the type described as the disjointed herringbone. As is made clear by Clark in his discussion of Maglemose Art (1938),[24] the motive is quite distinct from single linear chevron ornament (Clark's motive *h*) or single chevrons placed one above the other (Clark's motive *x*). Both of these motives are characteristic of Maglemose art, whereas the disjointed herringbone is thought to be completely absent from the Maglemose culture, and rare even in Western Palaeolithic art. Recent discussion of Maglemose art confirms Clark's judgement.[25] There is only one known piece with ornament similar to herringbone and that is a miniature amber sculptured model animal, the silhouette elk head from Egemarke.[26] On closer examination the decoration on this piece clearly resolves itself into the use of the individual linear chevron (motive *h*), though these are drawn one beneath the other, to produce blocks of ornament at first sight resembling herringbone. Also, the blocks of ornament on the Egemarke head respect the contours of the sculpture and are clearly naturalistic in intention. They were probably an attempt to indicate variation in colour or texture of the animal's pelt, and are not comparable with the abstract decoration on the Kendrick's Cave mandible.

There are two other Maglemose pieces which must be discussed as they have chevron ornament, and were found in Britain. These are the engraved deer antler tine from Romsey, Hants (Clark, no. xxxix) and the ox-bone perforated adze-head from the Thames (Clark, no. vi). These pieces are at present in the British Museum and were published in the *British Museum Quarterly* by Reginald A. Smith in 1934. The Romsey deer tine (*B.M.Q.* viii. 144–5 and Pl. xlvi) is decorated circumferentially in a series of rows of large isolated chevrons, deeply engraved. The Thames adze-head, however, is poorly illustrated in the plate accompanying Mr. Smith's publication. A careful drawing (Fig. 7) shows the beginning of a block of connected chevrons resembling herringbone. This is the nearest parallel to the Kendrick's Cave mandible in Britain, but it is basically unsatisfactory. The Thames perforated adze is very much larger in size and correspondingly coarse in decoration. Liversage has recently discussed the attribution of coarse, deeply cut decoration to the Kongemose culture in Denmark (as opposed to the finely drawn Maglemose decorative styles).[27] Whatever the exact cultural status of the ornament, it seems most likely that this piece (and that from Romsey) both belong to the Mesolithic cultural tradition of Maglemose affinities at present recognized in Britain. Both pieces are found within the presently accepted area of distribution of the Maglemose. The Thames adze-head (Reg. no. 1927, 7–7, 3) is recorded by Smith in manuscript as found at Hammersmith,[28] within the classic area of distribution. It is also a well-known Maglemose type, though it does not closely resemble the elk mattock heads from Star Carr, the only British examples in this class.[29]

The Romsey antler tine, another typical Maglemose product on Clark's analysis, is found within the extension to the Maglemose distribution in Britain proposed by Wainwright in 1956.[30] The area originally recognized as Maglemose comprised the east coast and the low-lying river valleys from Yorkshire to the Thames, where these provided inlets from the east, and as far inland as Thatcham, west of Reading. With the extension of the area it was recognized that riverine penetration probably took place through the Thames valley to the Wiltshire and Somerset lowland, and down into Hampshire, where interfluves and portages from the east are available. But this English distribution is still predominantly a lowland one. The mandible from Kendrick's Cave on the Irish Sea does not fall into the same class in terms of either distribution or design.

British Neolithic portable art, and rock carvings on Megalithic tombs in Britain, Ireland, and the Continent, do not reveal any close parallels for the Kendrick's Cave ornament. Perhaps the nearest examples are the bone points with deeply incised single chevrons from Skara Brae, but their relationship is clearly with the Romsey tine, rather than the Welsh mandible, and Piggott draws attention to their probable Maglemose ancestry.[31] Again, flat stone plaques of one sort or another are common on sites around the Irish Sea, and several of these in the Ronaldsway culture and at Graig Llwyd in north Wales have decoration including zigzags and perhaps (in the case of Graig Llwyd) overlapping chevrons. But it is clear from the other elements in their decoration[32] and from the eccentrically placed and isolated use of the motives (as well as from the use of the carefully shaped stone plaques themselves) that these pieces are in the Irish/Iberian Megalithic art world. There is no trace of herringbone ornament itself on these pieces and though one can find a number of examples in which it is used on the larger scale in Megalithic tomb art,[33] it is always found in combination with other elements and is used in a manner completely foreign to the piece we are studying.

It is the Palaeolithic period which furnishes the best parallels to the Kendrick's Cave mandible, but these parallels are almost entirely from eastern Europe and Russia. The only other British piece with geometric decoration from this period is a small flat bone from the Pin Hole cave, Creswell Crags, incised with a single series of overlapping chevrons in no way resembling herringbone.[34] Simple linear chevron ornament and single chevrons stacked below one another, usually very carelessly drawn, are known from the French Palaeolithic[35] but disjointed herringbone, so characteristic of eastern Palaeolithic art, is almost entirely absent from the Upper Palaeolithic art of western Europe,[36] as it is from the Maglemose culture. In Russia herringbone ornament can be quoted from many of the classic sites. The most striking pieces are those from Mezin, including the phallic figurines or anthropomorphic representations and the ivory bracelets first published by Volkov in 1911–12, and the considerable quantity of further figurines from the same source made available with Rudinsky's illustrations in 1931.[37]

243

The use of herringbone, with the addition of lozenge and Greek key patterns seems to appear on nearly every piece of bone recovered from this site. Similar use of herringbone ornament can be paralleled on other Russian sites such as Kostenki I, Avdeevo, Eliseevichi, and Suponevo.[38] Equally characteristic of eastern Palaeolithic art is the use of blocks of ornament, either free-standing as at Avdeevo in Russia and Dolni Vistonici in Moravia,[39] or in contact as at the Moravian site of Predmost or at Eliseevichi.[40] Decoration in single blocks of rigid ornament is also characteristic of the Russian sites.[41] Further illustrations of related blocks of ornament which include the use of herringbone are found at Mezhirich[42] and at Mezin[43] and it is the latter, probably the richest in portable works of art of all the Russian mammoth sites, which provides the best parallels to the Kendrick's Cave mandible. The scale of decoration, the regularity and closeness between the lines of chevrons, and the relationship of the various blocks of pattern to one another, all seem to resemble the decoration found on the Welsh example.

Animal jawbones and scapulae seem to be in use throughout the eastern art province as subjects for geometric decoration. Knives made from horse mandibles and decorated in incised patterns are well known in central Europe on late Upper Palaeolithic sites such as Pekárna and Petersfels.[44] Scapulae decorated in a similar manner are known from other eastern European sites (Pl. LXXXVI).[45] At Eliseevichi a scapula decorated with chevrons was placed over the burial of a man, with the decorated face downwards towards the burial. At Mezin itself the post-war excavations have revealed both a scapula and a mandible, both of mammoth and not of horse, but both decorated in a similar manner to the examples of block geometric decoration already discussed (Fig. 6). The decoration on the mammoth mandible closely resembles that on the mammoth rib bone from Predmost referred to above, while the decoration on the scapula includes a panel of chevron ornament, no doubt originally more extensive. The unusual thing about these pieces from Mezin is that the designs are executed in red paint, instead of being incised into the bone.[46] However, the decoration itself and the purpose behind the decoration of animal mandibles with geometric ornament does provide a clear cultural connection between the Welsh and the east European sites and the presence of haematite in the incisions on the Kendrick's Cave mandible itself may possibly be another parallel to the Russian painted example.

The nature of the cave occupation

Attention should be drawn to the sparse nature of the cave occupation at the Kendrick's Cave site, as it is represented by the contemporary records of the excavation and the surviving pieces. Finds from the cave range from the extinct

Pleistocene fauna of the cave earth to the Early Iron Age bone comb and the loom weight of comparable date. They are, however, few in number and include a number of human skeletons, presumed by Boyd Dawkins to be Neolithic in date. With these the horse mandibles and the decorated teeth were thought (by Dawkins) to be associated.

The sparseness of the occupation material is partly explained by the smallness and unimportant nature of the cave itself. It is unlikely that a site of this size could ever have been of great importance as a habitation and the finds in their miscellaneous character resemble those from other small caves of north Wales

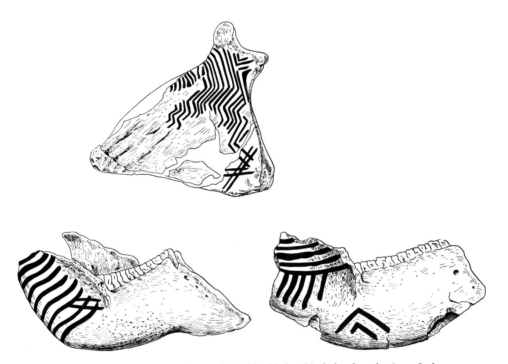

Fig. 6. Mezin. Mammoth bones, jaw and shoulder blade with design in red ochre. Scale *c.* 1:7
(After *Sovietskaya Archeologiya* 4, 1957, 99.)

and elsewhere in Britain. Finds of Iron Age or of Roman date are also a well-known feature of such cave occupations. Palaeolithic cave occupation deposits in Britain fall into two classes. There are a few caves in fortunate areas which contain Upper Palaeolithic occupation debris as rich in flint implements as the French cave sites. Such are the caves near the southern coasts of Great Britain and south of the ice margin in the last glaciation, such as Paviland, Kent's Cavern, and some of the Cheddar caves. Some of the occupation deposits at Cresswell Crags are equally rich but may not be entirely of Pleistocene date. But the

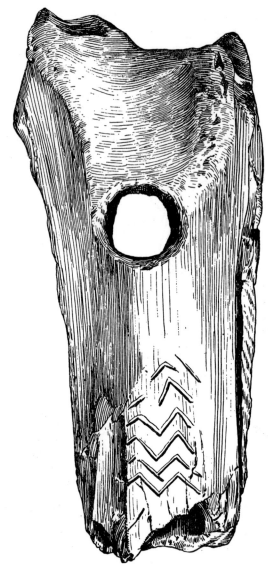

Fɪɢ. 7. River Thames at Hammersmith. Perforated ox-bone implement. Scale 1:1

majority of British Pleistocene cave sites appear to be less fortunately situated in environmental terms. Their occupation debris consists at most of a handful of tools or flakes attributable to the last glaciation. Undoubtedly the Kendrick's Cave occupation deposit belongs to the second category. The Pleistocene occupation debris is so sparse that one might query its very existence and the presence of two groups of artefacts of high quality, the horse mandibles and the decorated teeth, is very surprising in this context. Is it possible that these do not represent *occupation* debris but are the result of deliberate burial, possibly related, as Boyd Dawkins thought, to one or more of the skeletons making up the Kendrick's Cave sepulture? The use of both teeth and mandibles for burials have their parallels in European Palaeolithic archaeology and the fact that almost a string of decorated teeth were found at this site also points in the same direction. At Paviland Cave, in south Wales, was found one famous Upper Palaeolithic burial, accompanied by sophisticated grave goods. One of the Kendrick's Cave burials may have been of equal antiquity. This seems to be the simplest explanation for the appearance of the decorated horse mandible in such a small and isolated site.

G. DE G. SIEVEKING

APPENDIX I

Dr. K. P. Oakley of the British Museum (Natural History) examined the problem of dating the pieces from Kendrick's Cave in the Bloomsbury collection and advised that nitrogen analysis was most suitable for demonstrating the difference in age between the two pieces submitted, the Early Iron Age bone comb and the decorated horse mandible. Samples were taken for analysis by the Anthropology Section, British Museum (Natural History), and the analysis was carried out in December 1958 by Mr. G. J. Johnson of the Department of the Government Chemist. The Kendrick's Cave mandible was cleaned *after* the samples were taken.

The results of the nitrogen analysis, including other samples supplied by Dr. K. P. Oakley for purposes of comparison, are as follows.

	Per cent.
Modern bone	*c.* 4·0
Early Iron Age bone comb from Kendrick's Cave	2·83
Decorated equid mandible from Kendrick's Cave	0·65
Ursus bone (late Pleistocene) Paviland Cave	0·93

The results suggest that the mandible is older than the Iron Age comb from the same cave and comparable in date with Pleistocene material from other caves. This is not a conclusive proof of Pleistocene age as no Neolithic samples have been tested and the Pleistocene mammal, though from a similar environment, is not from the same cave.

APPENDIX II

Report by the Geological Survey and Museum (Petrographical Dept.) on Stone Axe from Kendrick's Cave, Llandudno

B.M. Registered no. 1959, 12–3, 4

The axe is made from a dark-grey fine-grained rock. In thin section (ENQ. 1718) the rock is foliated and contains fibrous hornblende, pleochroic in yellowish-green to blue-green; granules of iron-ore; and feldspar which has been saussuritized. There are some remains of larger feldspar crystals, but for the most part it forms a fine-grained mosaic.

An exact match has not been found for this rock, but it is very similar in type to specimens of sheared epidiorite from Cornwall and it is possible that it comes from that area.

1 It seems likely that Kendrick was something of a builders' merchant and monumental stone mason. Humphreys (1908) says 'as Llandudno developed Kendrick's work increased, and to enlarge his accommodation he began excavating in the back of the cave'.

2 Eskrigge, 1880, 155. It seems likely that Eskrigge was 'the medical gentleman from Bangor'.

3 Information kindly provided by Miss Humphreys, owner of Ardwy Orme in 1957.

4 Kendrick's Cave was visited by the Royal Commission in 1951, and subsequently on behalf of the British Museum by Mr. Peter Wild of Dyserth in 1957, to whom I am greatly indebted for a careful and detailed description of the site, now comprising a garden shed with flower beds laid out round the entrance. It appears that much of the back of the cave is filled with boulders, and that little trace of the breccia or cave earth can be seen. The archaeological relics came from near the entrance, just behind the rear wall of the shed. The floor here is now concrete or rock.

5 Humphreys, 1908.

6 Presumably Glynllivon, 5 miles south of Caernarvon.

7 Houlder, C. H., 'The Excavation of a Neolithic Stone Implement Factory on Mynydd Rhiw', *P.P.S.* xxvii (1961), figs. 12–13.

8 The types are best described in Bulleid, A., and Gray, H. St. G., 1948, *The Meare Lake Village*, i. 64–5.

9 A provisional distribution and illustrations in Bulleid and Gray, 1948, op. cit. 64–88. See also Wheeler, R. E. M., 1943, *Maiden Castle, Dorset*, 298, and Childe, V. G., 1940, *Prehistoric Communities of the British Isles*, 201–3 and note 56; Henshall, A. S., *P.P.S.*, xvi (1950), 146 and 160; and Rahtz, P., *P.P.S.*, xxviii (1962), 323 (a Bronze Age example). For a comb from Kents Cavern see Coughtrey, M., 1873, 'Notes on Materials . . . at Hillswick, Shetland, with Special Reference to Longhandled Combs', *Proc. Soc. Ant. Scot.* ix. 118–43.

10 I am indebted to the Royal Commission for providing the original of their published illustration of these specimens, which have not been available for examination.

11 The nearest Palaeolithic parallels are all more regularly and more deeply incised. See Breuil, H., 1924, 'Voyage paléolithique en Europe Centrale III', *L'Anthrop.* xxxiv. 531, fig. 13. 3–6 (Predmost); Piette, É., 1907, *L'Art pendant l'âge du renne*, pl. LXXIII. 3 and 4, LXXXI. 9 (Brassempouy);

pl. XXIV. 6 (Lourdes); *Collection Piette*, 92, Cat. no. 48599; 70, Cat. no. 51314; 72, Cat. no. 48519D (Gourdan); 165, Cat. no. 47417 (Lortet), all Magdalenian; and Chollot-Legoux, M., 1962, *Arts et Techniques*, fig. 23 (Abri Blanchard) Aurignacian; St-Périer, R., 1951, *La Grotte d'Isturitz*, iii, fig. 28, 9–12 and fig. 29; and Cheynier, A., *La Caverne de Pair-non-Pair*, fig. 47, 1, and numerous other illustrations, Perigordian; and Péquart St-J., Boule, M., and Vallois, H. V., 1937, Teviec *Mémoire 18*, *Institut de Paléontologie humaine*, fig. 38, Tardenoisian. In England the nearest Palaeolithic parallel is from Gough's Cave, Cheddar. See Parry, R. F., 1930, 'Excavations in Cheddar', *Proc. Somerset Arch. and N. H. Soc.* lxxvi. 48, fig. 2. The Kendrick's Cave tallies appear much more carelessly decorated, resembling in general terms finds from such sites as *All Cannings Cross* (Cunnington, M. E., 1923, pls. 12 and 15) and Wookey Hole (Balch, H. E., 1914, pl. XXVI B, no. 4).

12 I am indebted to Mr. C. H. Houlder of the Royal Commission for drawing my attention to this collection and to Mr. F. P. Jowett for making the teeth available for publication.

13 See, for example, the lists of later examples quoted by Bulleid, A., and Gray, H. St. G., 1917, in *The Glastonbury Lake Village*, ii. 482–5, and Greenwell, W., 1877, *British Barrows*, 327.

14 Even within the small number of published examples there is a good deal of variation in decoration patterns, some teeth being merely notched down one edge and down one side of a plane surface, e.g. Gourdan, *Collection Piette*, 58, Cat. no. 48626, and Isturitz, St-Périer, R., 1936, *La Grotte d'Isturitz*, ii, pl. VII, nos. 10, 12, or very faintly incised as St-Périer, R., op. cit. i, pl. VI. 18. The best parallels for the Kendrick's Cave teeth are ox teeth from Laugerie-Basse in the Christy collection (B.M.), and at St-Germain, *Reliquiae Acquitanicae* B, pl. v, nos. 6 and 7; and horse teeth from Mas d'Azil, *Collection Piette*, 275, Cat. no. 47998b, and Brassempouy; Piette, 1907, op. cit., pl. LXXVIII. 2, all Magdalenian, and similar examples are claimed from the Solutrean at Lacave, Vire, A., 1907, *Grotte de Lacave* (Lot), *L'Anthrop.*, xvi. 429; and 'for the Upper Perigordian, St-Périer, op. cit. iii, pl. VII, centre.

In a recent publication Barandiaran Maestu I, 1967, *El Paleomesolítico del Pirano Occidental*, 240–2, the author quotes Spanish examples and divides perforated teeth into a number of different classes according to their manner of decoration.

[15] Sollas, W. J., 1913, 'Paviland Cave. An Aurignacian Station in Wales', *J. Royal Anthrop. Inst.* xliii, pl. XXII.

[16] In addition to the pieces described by Garrod in *The Upper Palaeolithic Age in Britain* there are a number of more recent examples from caves in the Bristol region, including most recently a decorated rib bone from Gough's Cave, Cheddar, published rather eccentrically by Miss Powers (*Proc. Univ. Bristol Spel. Soc.* xii. 2 (1970), 138–42), and the decorated bone from Armstrong's excavations at Pinhole Cave, Creswell Crags, as yet unpublished.

[17] Originally the front parts of *two* lower jaws of horse were found, apparently together. Only one of them was 'ornamented with a herringbone pattern' (Eskrigge, 1880), but Boyd Dawkins (1880) claimed that 'the outer surface of the bone has been scraped by the hand in both'. The second horse mandible is still missing.

[18] Godwin, H., 1956, *History of British Flora*, 18, 38. This phenomenon is known to archaeologists in northern Europe, where horse disappears from prehistoric sites after the Late Glacial period, at least in Denmark and in the north German plain. See faunal lists in Clark, J. G. D., 1938, *The Mesolithic Settlement of Northern Europe*, 223–8.

In parts of Sweden the horse is present throughout the Post-Glacial. Lundholm, 1949, quoted in Zeuner, F. E., 1963, *A History of Domesticated Animals*, fig. 12. 21. True British Upper Palaeolithic sites usually contain a fauna in which horse is abundant, often associated with *R. Tarandus, C. Megaceros,* and *C. Elaphus.* See Garrod, D. A. E., 1925, *The Upper Palaeolithic Age in Britain,* for typical examples.

[19] Clark, J. G. D., 1954, *Excavations at Star Carr,* 192–4.

[20] Jackson, J. W., 1935, 'The Animal Remains from the Stonehenge Excavation', 1920–6, *Ant. J.* xv. 434–6.

[21] Piggott, S., 1952, *Neolithic Communities of the British Isles.* 11. Some of the examples quoted in east and south-east England (i.e. Grimes Graves and Cissbury) may well be post-Neolithic in date.

[22] e.g. Mother Grundy's Parlour, Cresswell Crags upper middle level. See Garrod, D. A. E., 1925, *The Upper Palaeolithic Age in Britain,* 137, and refs. The excavation is an old one and the evidence for the associations is uncertain. Modern excavations at Cresswell Crags, currently awaiting publication, may do much to clarify the situation.

[23] Jasińska, M. and Nicwiadomski, T., 'Thermoluminescence of Biological Materials', in *Nature,* 227 (1970), 1159.

[24] Clark, 1938, op. cit. 177–8.

[25] Liversage, D., 1966, 'Ornamented Mesolithic Artefacts from Denmark', *Acta Archaeologica,* xxxviii. 221–37. Discussion and bibliography of recent literature.

[26] Powell, T. G. E., 1966, *Prehistoric Art,* pl. 63.

[27] Liversage, 1966, op. cit.

[28] In the Departmental Register. For some reason the attribution was omitted from his publication seven years later.

[29] Clark, 1954, op. cit., fig. 69 and pls. XIII–XIV. The usual perforated adzes are made of antler but are similar in design to the Hammersmith example. See Clark, 1938, op. cit. 112, and fig. 40.

[30] Wainwright, G. F., 1960, 'Three Microlithic Industries from S.W. England and their affinities', *Proc. Preh. Soc.* xxvi. 193–201.

[31] Piggott, 1952, op. cit., fig. 54, no. 2.

[32] Piggott, 1952, op. cit., fig. 61, 9, and fig. 46, 4. Piggott describes the Graig Llwyd decoration (290–2) as 'a series of hatched triangles pendant from a double line, probably continued in multiple lozenges'. The related Ronaldsway plaques also have zigzags or lozenges.

[33] e.g. Barclodiad y Gawres, Anglesey; Gavr Innis, Brittany; Gohlitzsch, Germany. Powell, 1966, op. cit., pls. 113, 115, 188. Organ, S. France, Gagnière, S., and Granier, J., 1963, 'Les stèles anthropomorphiques du Musée Calvet d'Avignon', *Gallia Préhistoire,* vi. 31–62. Trets. Sieveking, 1963, in *Vanished Civilisations* (ed. E. Bacon) 271. 7.

[34] Armstrong, A. L., 1956, 'Prehistory: Palaeolithic, Neolithic and Bronze Ages', in *Sheffield and its Region* (British Association), 95.

[35] For example, Breuil, H., and St-Périer, R. de, *Les Poissons . . . dans l'art quaternaire,* figs. 26–7, and Piette, 1907, op. cit., pl. XIV. 1, and Graziosi, P., 1960, *Palaeolithic Art,* pl. 91 e.

[36] Graziosi, P., 1960, op. cit., pl. 103 a. Illustrates an engraved plaque from Parpallo with possible herringbone ornament.

[37] The first publication available in Western Europe was Volkov, T., 1913. Station Paléolithique de Mézine. c.r. *Congrès internat. d'anth. and arch. préhist.* 14. I, 415–34. The major series of illustrations are those published by Rudinsky in 1931 quoted in and made available in the West by Golomshtok, E. A., 1938, 'The Old Stone Age in European Russia', *Trans. American*

K k

Phil. Soc. xxix. 2. 349–53. Similar but slightly different illustrations are available in Abramova, Z. A., 1962. *Palaeolithic Art in the USSR.* Available in translation in *Arctic Anthrop.* iv. no. 2 (1967), 1–180 and also in the recent site publication. Shovkoplyas, I. G., 1965, *Mezinska stoyanka.*

[38] Abramova, 1962, op. cit., pl. XVIII. 14, XXX. 4, and XXXVI. 6. Hančar, F., 1961, 'Die oberpaläolithische Mammutjägerstation Mezin', *Mitt. der Anthrop. Gesell. in Wien.* xci. 64–87, figs. 1–2.

[39] Okladnikov, A. P., 1957, *Paléolithique et néolithique de l' URSS,* fig. 25; and Müller-Karpe, H.,1966, *Handbuch der Vorgeschichte,* i. pl. 231.15.

[40] Maska, K. J., 1886, *Der diluviale Mensch in Mähren,* 101; Breuil, H., 1924, 'Voyage paléolithique en Europe Centrale', *L'Anthrop.* xxxiv.

fig. 16. 10, and fig. 22; and Müller-Karpe, 1966, op. cit., fig. 219A. 2.

[41] Abramova, 1962, op. cit., pls. XVIII–XIX.

[42] Pidoplichko, I. G., 1969, *Late Palaeolithic Mammoth-bone Dwellings in Ukraine,* Fig. 58.

[43] Golomshtock, 1938, op. cit., figs. 59. 2 and fig. 61. 3; Abramova, 1962, op. cit., pls. XXXII. 2. XXXIV. 6, 8.

[44] Müller-Karpe, 1966, op. cit., pl. 220. 11–12 (Pekárna); Breuil, 1924, op. cit. 277, fig. 3 (Kostelik); Peters, E., 1930, *Die Station Petersfels,* pl. X; also at Kesslerloch, Switzerland; Guyan, W., 1941, *Die Steinzeit der Schweiz,* pl. 30.

[45] Abramova, 1962, op. cit., 200.

[46] Abramova, 1962, op. cit., pl. XXXV; Shovkoplyas, 1965, op. cit., pls. LIV–LVI.

BIBLIOGRAPHY

ANON., 1880. Prehistoric inhabitants of Llandudno. *Shrewsbury Chronicle.* 24 September, 1880.

ANON., 1881. Prehistoric Cave at Llandudno. *Archaeologia Cambrensis,* series iv, 12, 335.

ANON., 1885. (Prehistoric discoveries at) Llandudno, copied from Geological Magazine. *Archaeologia Cambrensis,* series v, 2, 234.

BOYD DAWKINS, Professor, 1880. Memorandum on the remains from the cave at Great Orme's head. *Proc. of the Liverpool Geological Society* iv. ii. 156–9.

ESKRIGGE, R. A., 1880. Notes on human skeletons and traces of human workmanship found in a cave at Llandudno. *Proc. of the Liverpool Geological Society,* iv. ii. 153–5.

HUMPHREYS, G. A., 1908. Prehistoric Remains, Kendrick's Cave, Great Orme's head, Llandudno. *Proc. Llandudno and District Field Club,* 1907–8, 49–57.

INGRAM, A. H. W., 1885. On the discovery of human bones and ornaments in a cave in the Great Orme's head. *Geological Magazine,* N.S. Dec. iii, vol. ii. 307.

JACKSON, J. W., 1953. Archaeology and Palaeontology in: *British Caving* (ed. Cullingford, C. H. D.), Bibliography, 209–10.

LOWE, B., 1912. *The Heart of North Wales I,* 13–14.

Royal Commission on Ancient and Historical Monuments in Wales and Monmouthshire, 1956. An Inventory of the Ancient Monuments in *Caernarvonshire, Vol. 1: East,* p. 114. Monument No. 365; fig. 13. 9; and p. l.

UNDERWOOD, 1951. Chairman's Address. *Proc. Llandudno, Colwyn Bay and District Field Club,* xxiv. 11.

WHEELER, R. E. M., 1925. *Prehistoric and Roman Wales,* p. 36.

THE RECONSTRUCTION OF IRON AGE BUCKETS FROM AYLESFORD AND BALDOCK

THERE is much in common between the rich burial discovered at Aylesford, Kent, in 1886 and that found at Baldock, Hertfordshire, in 1967. They were cremation burials of the same culture, and perhaps of the same generation. There is similarity too in the circumstances of their discoveries, for they were found by chance and fully excavated by their finders. In both instances the archaeologist was presented with a collection of fragmentary objects, and many of his questions remain unanswered. But the most striking analogy lies among the grave-goods, for the objects from each burial included bronze bands and wooden staves, handles and curious handle-mounts cast in the form of human heads. Bronze-ornamented wooden buckets of this type are unique to these two burials, and in both the graves the remains were fragmentary, incomplete, and not recorded *in situ*. The various pieces are considered here together, so that details from one site may help to explain material from the other.

THE BALDOCK BURIAL

In December 1967, during shallow excavations for an extension to a road appropriately, but coincidentally, named 'The Tene', in Baldock, Hertfordshire (TL. 248336), a fairly rich La Tène III grave was disturbed. Repeated efforts with a large bulldozer smashed the first obstruction encountered—an iron fire-dog—but in a return run over the same spot a second fire-dog was plucked out virtually undamaged. This piece aroused the interest of the workmen, who set to with picks and shovels and unearthed a number of bronze and iron objects, pottery, bones, and a 'wooden bucket standing inside a bronze dish'. No importance was attached to this discovery, and it was some weeks before information reached the Inspectorate of Ancient Monuments, Ministry of Public Building and Works.[1]

The Inspectorate immediately arranged an excavation and recovered the finds which had been dispersed. The circular grave, 5 ft. 3 in. in diameter and only 2 ft. deep below present ground level, had been thoroughly disturbed before the archaeological excavation started, but it seems likely that the entire grave-group has now been reassembled. It comprises: a bronze cauldron with iron rim and iron handles; two iron fire-dogs; a Dressel type 1 amphora; a pair of bronze dishes; a pair of wooden buckets with bronze fittings; as well as pig bones (possibly the complete skeleton) and some calcined bones. Although in a circular, instead of a rectangular grave, this group may be classed with the 'Welwyn-type burials' of Hertfordshire, Essex, Bedfordshire, and Cambridgeshire.[2]

Only scattered fragments of the buckets were found during the archaeological excavation—the wooden vessel seen by the workmen had, of course, disintegrated. The 'bronze dish' which contained the bucket, according to the workmen's account, is doubtless a series of bands which once decorated it. The many fragments of this sheet bronze, and the handles and handle-mounts, have now been cleaned and studied and it appears that there is not one bucket, but a pair, for which a reconstruction can be suggested.[3]

The remains of the Baldock buckets

A. Three cast bronze heads, each with a hole in the back to receive the end of a swing-handle.

1. The only head found in the grave by the archaeologists—it still has traces of wood and remains of bronze plate and rim-binding attached (Fig. 1 and Pl. LXXXVII).

A human head, with elongated, protruding, and slanting eyes (the left eye more bulbous than the right one) bordered by narrow raised eyelids and surmounted by a continuous brow ridge. The nose is long and pointed, and below a very deep upper lip, just above the chin, the mouth is indicated by a single line, pointing slightly downwards at the edges. The chin is sharply angled, and at each side the bottom of the jaw is marked by two grooves which may be intended to define a torque or possibly a strap for the helmet. Below the chin is a rounded length of neck with a rivet through it. Above the face is a head-dress—a close fitting cap, or helmet, with a broad top-piece raised above the skull and spreading sideways to terminate at each side in a wide drooping horn with deep mouldings at the end. This handle-mount is exactly 2 in. high, and the head-dress is 1·7 in. wide.

At the back the shape of the skull starts below the top-piece but then merges into a long, flat, functional plate. In the centre of this is a hole, 0·25 in. diameter, opening into the hollow of the cast head—this is the socket to take the stub at the end of the handle, H.1. Immediately below the line of the hole, the back-plate separates from the front, leaving a space which is 0·2 in. near the top but widens slightly lower down. The body of the rivet which pinions the neck crosses this space, but from this point the 0·6-in. wide back-plate is broken.

The remains in the space between the face and the back-plate clearly show how this head had been mounted. At the top is a curved bronze binding-strip (G) which at the front covers the top of a sheet of bronze (D), and behind this bronze sheet, capped completely by the binding and filling the entire space between face and back-plate, is some mineralized wood with vertical grain.

2. A similar head, but found before our excavation, and cleaned by the finders (Fig. 1).

Apparently the pair to A.1, although it differs in detail and could not have been cast in the same mould—presumably they were cast by the *cire perdue* technique in which the mould could not be used twice. The most obvious difference is in the moulding at the ends of the horns, which in A.2 is deeper, but also the brow ridge slants (much thicker on the left); the eyes are equal in size, but the right eye is slightly higher than the left; the nose is broader and less pointed; the line of the mouth is carelessly indicated (slanting on the left, but fairly straight on the right); and the jaw is marked by a single line at the side.

There is a hole in the centre of the top-piece, but this may well be due to corrosion, which has also attacked the right-hand horn. The neck is missing, and as the surviving edges are rounded and patinated, this seems to have happened in antiquity. On the left side the face ends at the line defining the jaw, in the centre immediately below the mouth, and on the right side a little of the neck survives below the jaw-line. The front is now 1·75 in. high, and the head-dress 1·65 in. wide.

The back-plate, 0·52 in. wide, survives intact and the full height is 2·3 in. The handle-hole is slightly larger than A.1, 0·28 in., and below it there are two rivet-holes. No other wood or metal remains are attached.

3. Like A.2, this head was found and cleaned before our excavation (Fig. 2).

In all ways it is much cruder than the others. The slanting eyes are narrower and indi-

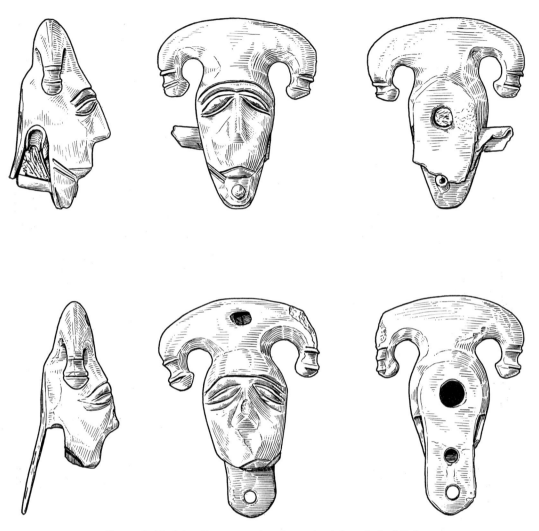

Fig. 1. Baldock handle-mounts: A.1 above; A.2 below. Scale: full size.

cated by fairly straight lines, and only one eyelid, the bottom right, is shown. Like A.2 the brow ridge is thicker on the left side. The cheeks, particularly the left one (emphasized by a corroded hole below the eye where the metal is very thin), are sunken and the nose is flattened and lop-sided—narrow on the left and broad on the right. The outline of the face is straight and fairly flat, and there are no lines to indicate jaw or mouth. Below the chin the large head of a rivet protudes from the neck. The top-piece is lower than A.1 and A.2, and the moulded terminals are very rough. The front is 1·9 in. high and the head-dress 1·7 in. wide.

The back-plate is fairly straight from the top of the head-dress, and unlike the others it is irregular in shape and thicker, with an uneven surface and a more pointed end. The

253

handle-hole has an irregular shape, and here it can be seen that the casting is thicker and heavier than A.1 and A.2. The back-plate is 2·6 in. high, and like A.2 it has two rivet-holes —but the rivets survive, the one through the neck 0·98 in., and the one below 0·65 in. long.

B. Bands of thin sheet bronze, 3·4 in. to 3·5 in. deep, whose edges are each ridged and bordered by a row of stamped S-shapes (Fig. 3).

1. A complete band, one edge well preserved, the other more damaged. There is an overlap of about 0·8 in., and the total length of this piece is 33·6 in. (32·8 in. circumference). The

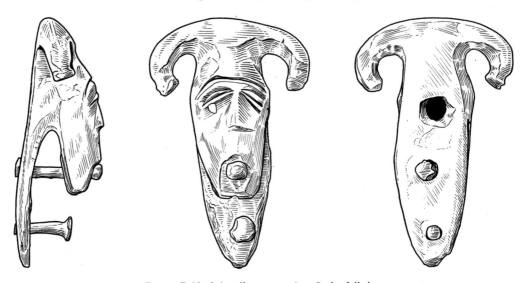

FIG. 2. Baldock handle-mount: A.3. Scale: full size.

overlap has been fastened to the wood below with small pins—there are four holes in a fairly straight vertical line. Two pin-holes are only 0·15 in. apart at the centre of the band and the other two are just within the S-border on either side. Directly opposite the overlap there may have been a similar row of pin-holes—but the two holes surviving (one edge of the band is missing at this point) are larger than those on the overlap.

2. Part of a second band, 10·5 in. long; a pin-hole just within the S-border, near one (broken) end.
3. Another, 15·6 in. long; a central pin-hole survives towards one end.
4. Other small pieces (either B or C).

There must have been at least two bands of this type.

C. Bands of thin sheet bronze, 3·2 in. to 3·3 in. deep, with decoration like B but along one edge only. The other edge is roughly finished and stains show that it had been covered by another band of bronze, so that only a 2·6-in. or 2·7-in. width of band C could have been seen (Fig. 3).

1. A complete band, quite well preserved. There is an overlap of 0·6 in. to 0·7 in., and the total length is 32·7 in. (32 in. circumference). (It is very difficult to get accurate measure-

ments of the circumference because the metal is in places broken, bent, and corroded.) Like B.1 the overlap has been tacked to the wood with three pins (the hole near the undecorated edge is double), and three similar pins have been used to attach the band on the opposite side (Fig. 3).

2. Part of a second band, badly corroded, measures 9·9 in. along the undecorated edge, but only 1·6 in. of the other edge survives.
3. A short length—1·25 in. long decorated edge—whose undecorated edge (only 1·0 in. long) is quite straight (the others are roughly finished with rather wavy edges).
4. Other small pieces (B or C).

There must have been at least two bands of this type.

D. Bands of thin sheet bronze, 1·7 in. deep. One edge is ridged and the other plain. The plain edge has been covered by another bronze band, and stains show that only 1·3 in. of the width of band D was visible. These bands are decorated towards the ends with a simple stamped motif—three discs (each a ring with central boss) arranged in a triangle with two linking ridges on the long sides (Fig. 3).

1. 8·8 in. long, with one original end (at the left, ridge uppermost) with the decorative motif, and broken end. 7·5 in. from the straight end there are holes from which two rivets have been ripped, and this is clearly the position of one of the handle-mounts—the holes on A.2 fit this position exactly. Below these rivet-holes is a pin-hole; there is another at one side and there could have been a third, central, at the straight end of this strip.
2. 6 in. long, with one original end (at the right, ridge uppermost) with decorative motif. A single pin-hole almost central near the straight end. This end could have been overlapped by the straight end of D.1—the two holes are in reasonable positions for a single pin.
3. 3·3 in. long, with one straight end (at the left, ridge uppermost) with decorative motif and single, fairly central, pin-hole.
4. 4·6 in. long, with broken ends—undecorated and no pin-holes.
5. 2·4 in. long, with one straight end (at the left, ridge uppermost), with a single very small pin-hole (0·06 in. by 0·03 in.) at the edge. Apparently no decoration, but it is very corroded.

No complete length of band D survives, but it seems reasonable to suppose that two lengths covered a single circuit, with the decorative motifs facing at opposite sides of the bucket, and the handle-mounts mid-way between the decorated ends. This being so, there are at least three lengths of band D—at least two circuits.

E. Bands of thin sheet bronze, 1·2 in. to 1·5 in. deep, with one edge ridged and the other plain—the visible depth seems to vary between 1·0 in. and 1·35 in. Each band is decorated with a simple repoussé motif, similar to that on band D—a series of discs linked by diagonal ridges, forming a continuous decorative band (Fig. 3).

1. 9·1 in. long. A complete band, with two straight ends. There is one fairly central pin-hole near one end—at the other end the pin has just clipped the edge of the band—and a third pin-hole towards the middle (4·1 in. from one end).
2. 8·8 in. long. A complete band, one pin-hole 0·7 in. away from the end—at the opposite end the pin has just clipped the edge of the band. Another pin-hole near the middle, 4·1 in. from one end.

3. 8·6 in. long, complete band. A double pin-hole at one end, one at the other—none in the middle of the band, but there are corroded holes about the middle.
4. 5·5 in. long, with one original straight end (right, ridge uppermost), with two adjoining pin-holes, and another pin-hole 5·3 in. away from the straight end.
5. 3·75 in. long, one straight edge (left, ridge uppermost) with a single pin-hole.
6. 3·2 in. long, one edge (left, ridge uppermost)—a single pin-hole partly obscured by corrosion.
7. 2·1 in. long, one edge (left, ridge uppermost), but the pin-hole is obscured by corrosion.
8. 2·5 in. long, no original edges.

There must have been at least six bands of this type, and they cannot have been exactly equal in length even allowing for overlaps—the length between pin-holes on the three complete examples is 8·9 in., 8·15 in. and 7·75 in. respectively.

F. Rectangular plaques cut from sheet bronze. Each 3·1 in. to 3·3 in. wide and about 4·5 in. high, with three ridged edges and one edge clearly overlapped by a bronze band. All the plaques are badly corroded, but they seem to have been decorated in the same way: near the plain edge (the top, as illustrated, Fig. 3) are two discs linked by a diagonal ridge—with similar linking ridges leading off the plaque in each direction (this ornament is exactly the same as that on band E); below is a single line of S-motifs (as on bands B and C); below that a fairly square field is covered with a design of similar discs and ridges—a central disc with a double row of stamped dots below surmounts a U-shaped ridge whose terminals curve down again to finish in a disc, with an additional disc on each side below. At the bottom, above the bordering ridge is a second row of S-motifs.

1. 3·3 in. wide and 4·5 in. high—stains show that the visible length would have been 4·15 in. All four edges survive, but the piece is very corroded—as on all these plaques, the band of ornament resembling band E, and the upper row of S-motifs, is in much better condition that the U-shaped design. Two pin-holes survive on each side, and their positions suggest that there would have been others in the bottom corners (corroded).
2. 3·1 in. wide—the top (plain), upper part of the two sides, and much of the design survives—but the bottom edge is corroded. The top pin-holes (one double) are intact, but corrosion has encroached on the two central holes.
3. 3·3 in. wide. Again the top and upper part of the two sides remains, but the piece is badly corroded and there is only one pin-hole of the upper row.
4. 3·2 in. wide. Only the upper part—but it has been bent in antiquity and pinned back again. There is a central pin-hole in the top row, as well as the two side holes (both double); in the second row a double hole on the left-hand side survives.
5. Small corroded fragments include a distinctive top left-hand corner to prove the presence of a fifth plaque.

There must have been at least five plaques of this type.

G. Curved pieces of bronze binding, semicircular in section, with an opening of about 0·2 in. (Fig. 3).
1. 3·9 in. long.
2. 2·6 in. long.
3 2·0 in. long.

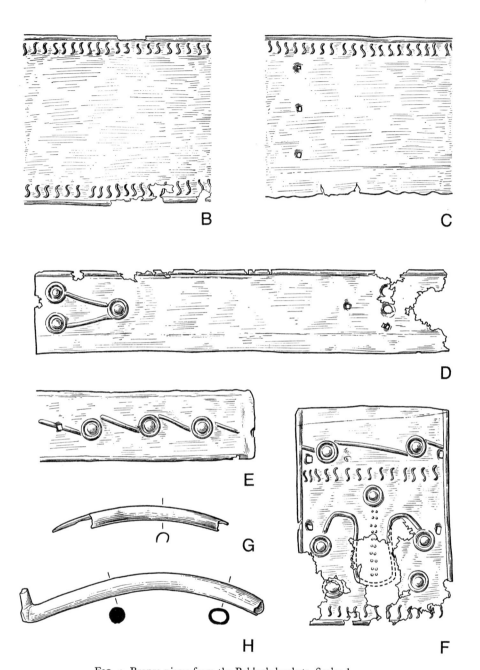

Fig. 3. Bronze pieces from the Baldock buckets. Scale: ½.

4. 2·0 in. long.
5. 1·5 in. long; the ridged edge of this piece has been filed towards one end—possibly to allow a handle-mount to fit over it.
6. 1·1 in. long.

There is less than one circuit of the bucket—these very small pieces give an external diameter of almost 11 in.

H. Pieces from swing-handles, formed from seamed bronze tubing, 0·4 in. diameter, whose joint is on the underside (Fig. 3).
1. 5·4 in. long, with a solid end from which a stub projects at right-angles.
2. 9·7 in. along the circumference—one end has been nipped and is presumably near the solid terminal.
3. 6·6 in. along the circumference.
4. 2·4 in. long—inside one end is a solid rod—presumably approaching the end of the handle.

One terminal and two other pieces nearing ends suggest that these fragments belong to two swing-handles—and this is confirmed by the combined length, which is too great for a single handle. They are presumably the same size—each with a height of just under 6 in., and an outer measurement (excluding projecting stubs) of about 10 in. These measurements are only approximate because the handle is not semicircular—the sides are comparatively straight.

J. The various pieces of sheet bronze had been attached to the wooden bucket with small pins. Curiously not a single pin survives intact, and part of only one shank was found—in the wood. Holes in the bronze show that the pin shanks were square or rectangular in section (some 0·06 in. to 0·08 in. across—the only pin-hole which differs is the very small hole in D.5) and in some instances stains on the upper surface of the bronze preserved the impression of circular heads, 0·3 in. diameter.

K. Several pieces of wood survived—evidently fragments of staves. The longest piece measured 7·5 in. and was 0·45 in. thick, but no other fragment was thicker than 0·35 in. Several pieces measured up to 1·3 in. wide.
   This wood, and that from Aylesford (see below, pp. 269 and 271) has been examined by G. C. Morgan, Ancient Monuments Laboratory, whose report on the material from Baldock states: 'The wood is wet, and thin section shows the structure of yew (*Taxus baccata*).'

Sequence of the bronze fittings

The grave had been so thoroughly disturbed that no information could be gleaned about the relative positions of the various bronze fittings. However, examination of the remains has shown several links between individual pieces, and other evidence which influences a reconstruction:

   (i) The position of the binding-pieces, G, is shown by the survival of a fragment corroded under the head-mount, A.1. Clearly, G was used to bind the rim of the bucket.

(ii) On band D.1 there are holes from which the rivets of a handle-mount have been removed. This shows that band D was at the top of the bucket, with the ridge edge uppermost, and supporting evidence is provided by a small piece of ridged edge *in situ* under the handle-mount A.1. The rivet holes in D.1 also show the position of a handle-mount in relation to the decorative motif on the end of that band—and it falls just short of the half-way mark if one length of D covers half the circumference.

(iii) The link between plaques F and bands E is proved without doubt, not only by the decorative motif—disc and diagonal ridge—which is continuous, but also by the coincidence of pin-holes (particularly, in two instances, double pin-holes), and by discoloration which outlines overlapping metalwork.

(iv) The undecorated edges of bands and plaques bear slight discoloration showing that they had been overlapped by other metal bands, and it seems reasonable to suppose that the overlapping edges were ridged. The bands C, D, and E/F have one ridged edge and one plain edge, and only one band, B, has two ridged edges.

(v) In some instances the mark of an underlying band was preserved on the underside of a ridged edge, and one such stain, on band B.1, clearly showed the outline of a plaque F.

(vi) The absence of stains and pin-holes shows that no band was covered by the body of plaque F.

One of the main factors hindering a reconstruction is the knowledge that not all the bronze fittings have survived. Obviously one handle-mount has been lost, and of the other remains only B.1 and C.1 are fairly complete. Another problem lies in the inadequate excavation of the grave—for although the workmen saw one wooden bucket, this does not preclude the presence of a second.

The handles and handle-mounts come from a bucket with two handles, or from two buckets each with one handle. With the exception of the handle-mounts, the bronze remains cannot be divided into two groups on stylistic grounds, so it is likely that if there were two buckets they were manufactured at the same time and were exactly paired. Two of the handle-mounts are similar (A.1 and A.2), and the third is an inferior copy—but it is just as likely to have been used on the same bucket (? possibly as a replacement) as on a matching pair.

The various pieces of sheet bronze could certainly be fitted on to a single bucket, which would measure at least $18\frac{1}{2}$ in. tall. Such a vessel would have two handle-mounts immediately adjacent on opposite sides of the rim, and the plaques F would be in either interlocking or facing positions—leaving uncovered wood round the middle. This reconstruction produces an ungainly vessel, but it does meet the description of a single wooden bucket found by the workmen. The principal objection lies in the handle-mounts, for it would be difficult, if not impossible, to swing the handles unless they met the mounts at right-angles. When double handles do occur on buckets open ring-mounts are used and these allow much more play than the tight holes in the back of the heads from Baldock. Furthermore, the mounts for double handles are usually cast in one piece, not separately.[4]

It seems more reasonable to suppose that the remains belong to two buckets, although for this one must assume that a considerable length of band D and a lot of rim-binding has been lost. Otherwise the minimum number of pieces deduced from the remains can be fitted exactly into two buckets. The lower edge of D is covered by the decorated edge of C; then B overlaps C above and E/F below. Attached in this way, the bronze pieces have an over-all height of about $11\frac{3}{4}$ in., with vertical walls and a diameter of about $10\frac{1}{2}$ in. (Pl. LXXXVIII).

THE AYLESFORD BURIAL[5]

In 1886 John and Arthur Evans visited a sand and gravel pit at Aylesford, Kent, to search for Palaeolithic implements. Their attention was drawn to a group of Iron Age objects recently discovered, which they subsequently purchased for the British Museum. According to Arthur Evans's account this group comprised: (1) a wooden bucket with bronze fittings, (2) 'a small fragment of another', (3) a bronze jug, (4) a bronze pan with long handle, (5) two bronze brooches, (6) calcined bones, and (7) 'fragments of earthenware vases'.[6] These objects had been found in a circular grave about $3\frac{1}{2}$ ft. deep. The burnt bones and brooches were inside the bucket, and the jug and pan outside, 'while around were the remains of several earthenware urns, some of which had been used as cineraries'.

The collection registered in the British Museum in 1886 consists of the jug, pan, remains of the bucket, bronze fragments from two other vessels, three brooches, and sherds from six pots. The third brooch, not listed by Evans, is the pair to one which he did publish so there can be little doubt that it belongs to the grave-group. The pottery presents more of a problem, because Evans did not publish detailed drawings, contenting himself with a 'diagrammatic sketch' of the grave-group based on the account he had been given by the finders.[7] Only one vessel shown on Evans's sketch resembles a pot in the British Museum 1886 collection.[8] But none of the Aylesford pottery now in the British Museum was excavated under the supervision of an archaeologist, and the records collected by Evans and the Museum Register are at times inadequate and inconsistent.[9] One can place little reliance on the associations of any of the Aylesford pottery found before the excavations directed and recorded by Evans—and the material from those excavations was deposited in the Ashmolean Museum.

However, if the associations of the pottery are confused, there can be no doubt about the bronzes in the grave-group, for these pieces Evans published in detail: the two bronze vessels which had been imported from the Continent;[10] the three brooches, which deserve a more detailed study some time; and the bronzes attached to wood, which can now be considered in the light of the buckets from Baldock.

The remains of the Aylesford bucket

There is no detailed record of these pieces before they were assembled in a reconstruction in the 1880s (Pl. LXXXIX). The bronze bands weret hen restored and pinned to a cylindrical wooden framework; the cast details were attached by an extremely hard mastic; and original wood was fixed to the inside to give some impression of the staves. That reconstruction has required little attention subsequently, and it still stands today. For the purposes of the present paper one head (A.2) was removed in order to study the 'key-hole cover' (B).[11] Any attempt to go beyond this and dismantle the entire reconstruction would be a very long and painstaking job; it would allow a more thorough study, but it might well damage some of the fragile remains and it is doubtful whether there would even then be evidence for a more accurate reconstruction.

A. Two cast bronze heads, each with a hole in the back where the iron handle is corroded in a fixed position (Fig. 4).

1. A human head with broad forehead and low cheeks, tapering to a narrow chin. It has raised almond-shaped eyes, pointed towards the side of the head. The nose is a low narrow ridge broadening at the end and, at the forehead, extending into a sharp continuous brow-ridge. Below the mouth—a wide and neatly cut chip—the rather pointed chin protrudes quite considerably. Indeed, the face has a hollowed profile, for a line linking the eyebrow and chin is not touched by the nose. Nothing survives below the chin. Above the brow-ridge, and following its curve, is a milled band—the milling cut diagonally starting from a V more or less over the nose. This milled band seems to be the border of a cap—or perhaps a narrow fringe of hair; above it a cap fits closely over the skull. Attached to the top of the cap, across its width, is a broad rounded top-piece basically a plaque only 0·1 in. thick. From this plaque two holes have been cut, leaving a central plume springing from a cross-rib and terminating in large circular shapes attached to the ends of the cross-rib. On the front of each circular shape is a domed bronze knob, 0·6 in. diameter, separate from the main plaque, and apparently made of thin sheet bronze. The domes have been repaired in the restoration and their original form of attachment is obscure; presumably each knob had a filling of 'clay', and had been attached to the plaque with adhesive. There are crudely milled bands, defined by engraved lines, bordering the sides of the plume; and the top edge of the plaque—much of it now damaged—is decorated with a central milled band raised between plain borders. The top-piece is 2·32 in. wide, and the head survives to a height of 2·25 in. at the front.

    At the back the top-piece is undecorated, apart from roughly engraved lines outlining the plume, and there is no hint of a rivet, or any other means for attaching the domes on

261

the other side. There is a milled band similar to that defining the cap on the front, and also following a similar curve—raised above the hole for the handle. The milled bands at front and back meet at their lowest point below the ends of the top-piece, at the sides of the head. Below the handle-hole—which is obscured by the iron handle and surrounding corrosion— the back plate is crossed by two ribs bordering a deeper groove, in a position rather high on the neck and slightly below the cutting in the side which allows the head to fit over the rim of the bucket. Below this decorative band the narrow plate extends down and is broken at the line of a rivet-hole. The back survives to a height of 2·45 in.

There is also a separate fragment, in the 1880s reconstruction attached below this head at the front. It is a circular plate, 0·65 in. diameter and 0·1 in. thick, with a stem at one side, 0·35 in. wide and 0·15 in. thick. This stem is very short and has broken at a rivet-hole. The outer, visible, surface of the circular plate does not have the same patina as the stem— it is roughly finished and appears to have been covered. This separate fragment seems likely to have been the lower terminal of one of the head-mounts, either at the front or the back. If it belonged to the front, as displayed on the 1880s reconstruction, it may be that the circular plate was covered by another bronze dome—the same as those on the top-piece. Three bronze domes arranged in this way, in a triangle, would echo the shape of the head.

2. The second head is quite similar to A.1 although taller, and obviously not cast in the same mould. The right eye is larger than the left, and is set lower in the face. The nose is more pronounced, better shaped, and longer. The cutting of the mouth is quite similar, but here the lips are indicated in relief. The chin is as pointed as A.1, but is defined by a fine groove; and in profile the nose projects beyond a line drawn between chin and forehead. Under the chin the upper part of a front plate survives, with a milled band round the top of the neck, and below this the plate is broken at a rivet-hole. There are no major differences in the head-dress, but centrally at both sides of the head a vertical milled band is linked with the similar bands bordering the cap. If the milled band at the front is a fringe of hair, these vertical bands at the sides resemble side-boards; or perhaps they are straps for the head-dress. At the front this piece survives to a height of 2·55 in., and the top-piece is 2·35 in. across. At the back it is broken at the rivet-hole, like A.1, but at the time of writing the details of the decoration here are still obscured by nineteenth-century mastic. The width of the space straddling the rim-binding is 0·3 in.

B. An object consisting of two bronze plates linked by a single rivet. On the 1880s reconstruction this piece is below the head A.2, with one plate outside the bucket and the other inside (Fig. 5, and Pl. xc).

The inner plate (B.1), 1·4 in. long, has been cast in bronze, and in shape it resembles the cover for a key-hole. Its body is curved in section, convex on the outside and concave inside. One end, 0·6 in. wide, is rounded and bordered by a milled band defined by a groove. The other end is narrower and more roughly shaped, with flat sides and rounded corners; and through this end is the head of the rivet. The rivet is now 0·7 in. long, but broken.

The outer plate (B.2), 0·25 in. from the broken end of the rivet, is 1·3 in. long and roughly cut from a sheet of bronze. The rivet passes off-centre through the wider end, an irregular, vaguely circular shape from which springs a stem 0·3 in. wide, expanding to 0·4 in. The other end of this piece seems to have been broken in antiquity—possibly on the line of a rivet-hole.

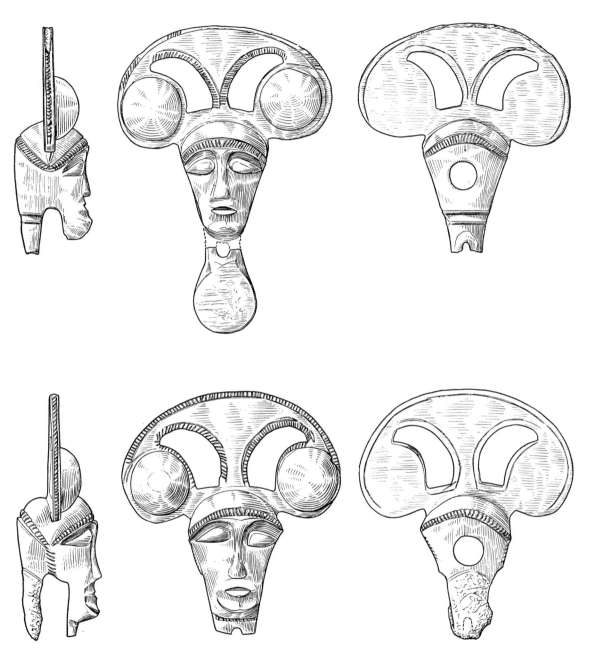

FIG. 4. Aylesford handle-mounts: A.1 above; A.2 below. Scale: full size.

On the 1880s reconstruction the rivet passed through the bucket directly under the head, A.2. The piece B.1 extended upwards and covered the bottom of the head-mount at the back; and at the front B.2 went under the head-mount but outside the rim-binding. Clearly this was a repair and not an original arrangement, but was it done in the nineteenth century or in antiquity? In order to settle this, the piece B and the head A.2 were removed from the bucket.[12]

The piece B.2 was corroded on to the rivet—it had occupied that position since antiquity; and the head of the rivet was in its original position through B.1. On the outside, in bronze band C, there is a crack below the rivet-hole—but there is no corresponding crack in the internal band F, so the piece could not have been inserted here by the nineteenth-century restorers. Furthermore the nineteenth-century mastic was only at the top of B.1, where it had been used to attach the head firmly, and there was none on B.2. If it had been a nineteenth-century repair one would have expected this mastic along the length of both pieces. Lower on B.1, above the rivet, there are traces of original mastic.

So it must have been a repair carried out in antiquity, but a peculiarly ineffective repair. The head A.2 had originally been attached by a single rivet, but both the front and back-plates had broken at this rivet-hole. There may have been an attempt to refix it by the same means, for in the outer band C the hole for this rivet has been enlarged and in the inner band F a second hole has been pierced slightly off the centre of the first. The piece B was successful in hiding the break at the back of the head, and at the front the projecting rivet was no doubt covered by a bronze dome (see above, A.1, separate fragment) which would to some extent mask the clumsiness of the repair. But although it may have been acceptable visually, it can hardly have been effective functionally. The piece B.2 covers the hole for the original rivet through the head A.2—so after the repair the head was not rivetted to the bucket, nor to the piece B; the piece B was rivetted to the bucket and the head was attached to it solely by mastic— although B.2, pressed under the head A.2 and outside the rim-binding, might have helped to secure it.

It is conceivable that the piece B was manufactured specifically for this repair, but its ineffectiveness and clumsiness—particularly about B.2—suggests improvisation. Further- more, B.2 seems to have been broken at its top end, and possibly broken at a rivet-hole. If it did have a previous purpose, B.1 and the rivet might be regarded separately from the cruder B.2, which could have been added for this repair. The milled edge of B.1 is quite in keeping with the milled decoration on the heads, and it is conceivable that this piece was an original fitting, either of this bucket or of an accompanying vessel. The long single rivet suggests that it was attached to wood; and perhaps that it was intended to swing with the rivet as a pivot, but if so it is curious that the piece should be concave underneath. If it was intended as a cover which could be moved aside when need be, like a key-hole cover, then the principle could be matched by an object in the Santon Downham hoard.[13]

C. A bronze band decorated with repoussé ornament (Fig. 5). It is 2·7 in. deep, and has had a bordering ridge round the bottom edge, although this survives only in a short stretch, to the left of head A.1. The top, with a simple straight edge, can be seen in only two places. The joint in this band is below the head A.1, where a straight, but damaged, left-hand end survives. A rivet-hole, just over 0·1 in. diameter, 0·5 in. from this end and 2·2 in. above the bottom of

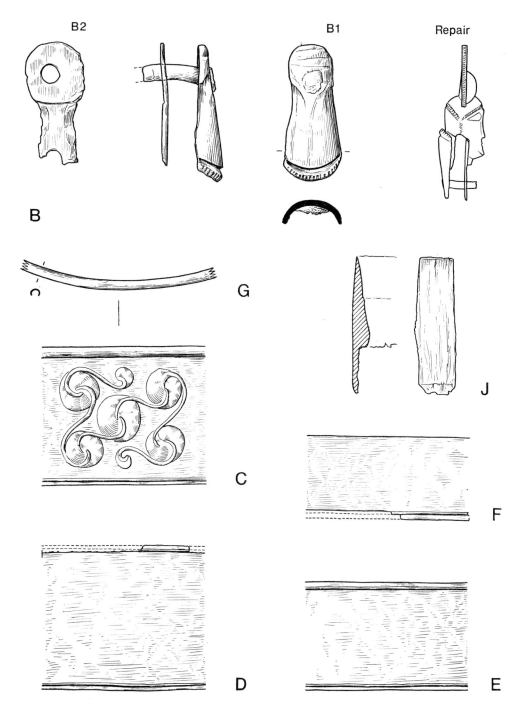

FIG. 5. Pieces from the Aylesford bucket: the bronze piece B (also showing its use as a repair on the handle mount A.2); bronzes C to G; and part of a wooden stave, J. Scales: B, full size; the rest ½.

the band, matches the hole through head A.1, and below it discoloration of the band C suggests that the separate fragment was correctly placed on the nineteenth-century reconstruction. Below this a second rivet-hole, 0·55 in. from the end and 1·1 in. above the bottom of the band, could have held a lower rivet from the back-plate (cf. Baldock), but as there is no single comparable rivet-hole under head A.2 (there are two holes, side by side—see below) it is more likely to have been used only for fastening the band. There is no straight edge at the right-hand end of this band, which is badly corroded.

On the other side of the bucket a rivet-hole in band C matches the position of the hole through the head A.2, and one below it held the rivet through piece B. Below that, 1·2 in. from the bottom of the band—corresponding roughly with the level of the lower hole below head A.1—there are two rivet-holes, 0·85 in. apart between centres, arranged symmetrically on either side of a line directly below A.2.

The band is broken and corroded in several places, but the only complete break, apart from the join under A.1, is through the whirligig motif to the left of head A.2. It seems to have been correctly reassembled at this point, and apart from loss due to corrosion at the extreme right-hand end it seems complete and reconstructed to the correct diameter. The surviving length is about 36 in. and the circumference as restored is 35·5 in. This band was registered (1886. 11–12. 3) as one piece along with the rim-binding, heads, handle, and internal band.

The band is decorated with three different motifs (Fig. 6): (a) A design of interlocking lobes, or commas, linked by S-like stems. From the centre the stems lead diagonally to the top right and bottom left, then vertically, and finally horizontally to end in two single lobes, above and below the central motif. (b) Above and below a central whirligig is an arched line terminating at each side in a bird-like head, with pointed beak and beady eye, wrapped round a ring and dome. (c) Two confronted animals. Perhaps they most resemble horses—certainly in the over-all shape of the body, the mane, and the prancing forelegs—indicated together in profile, as one. The parted lips could be those of a horse, too, but considerably exaggerated. The ears and tails are elaborate appendages, bifurcating to cover the open field. Only the hind legs, shown separated, are anatomically distorted—bending forward, like a human knee, a pantomime horse. The animal on the right, although slightly shorter, is heavier, with a larger head, thicker neck, and a much longer tail. Behind it a space is filled by an isolated trilobate motif.

These motifs are arranged in ten panels, from head A.1 clockwise: a, b, c, a, b, then head A2., b, a, c, b, a. Thus the confronted horses appear only twice, on each side at the mid-point between the human heads—a position similar to that occupied by the triangular arrangement of discs at Baldock—and the other motifs are repeated four times. The details of the motifs are exactly duplicated, so each must have been formed from a single pattern—presumably the design was raised, or sunk, on a wooden block and the metal was then beaten over it.

D. The second band on the 1880s reconstruction is restored as a complete circuit, also 35·5 in. in circumference (Fig. 5). The maximum surviving depth is 2·9 in., but if it had been symmetrical, with ridge and flange at each edge, it would have measured 3 in. There seem to be no straight ends or true overlapping joints, and no rivet- or pin-holes.[14] But the band has been completely broken, and joined by the restorers in five places: one under head A.1; another about 9 in. to the left; another, very obvious and with corroded edges, 2·8 in. to the left;

266

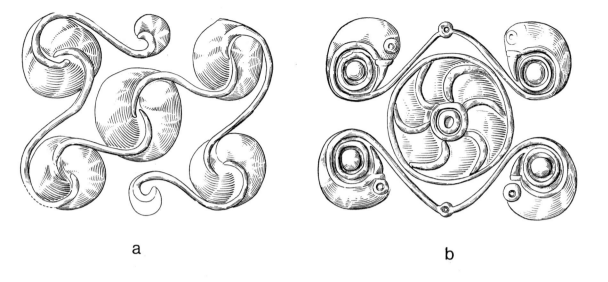

a
b

c

Fig. 6. Repoussé decoration on band C. Scale: full size.

another 8·5 in. to the left—but the corrosion pattern suggests that this has been correctly joined; and two other diagonal breaks in the next 15 in.

This band was registered separately (Reg. no. 1886. 11–12. 4) but both the length, 38 in., and the width, 3·15 in., then recorded are greater than the measurements now taken. Presumably this band would have had two straight ends, overlapped and pinned to the wood; but there is no straight end now, so the full length cannot survive. Furthermore, as the circumference is fully covered by original bronze one must conclude not only that more than one

267

original band has been amalgamated to form a complete circuit, but also, in view of the well-matched joints, that the restorers deliberately tailored the pieces to fit.

E. The third band on the 1880s reconstruction is 2·2 in. deep and ridged at both edges (Fig. 5). It has been restored from three separate pieces, respectively 9 in., 4·5 in., and 10 in. long. But judging from the good state of preservation, with a brownish patina, not green like the rest of the bronze here described, these pieces came originally from the same band. The different patina suggests that the alloy is slightly different from the other bronze bands, but this is no reason for supposing that band E belongs to a different vessel. Among the surviving pieces there are no straight ends and no pin-holes.

These must be the pieces registered (1886. 11–12. 5) as 12 in., 4·5 in., and 10 in. long.

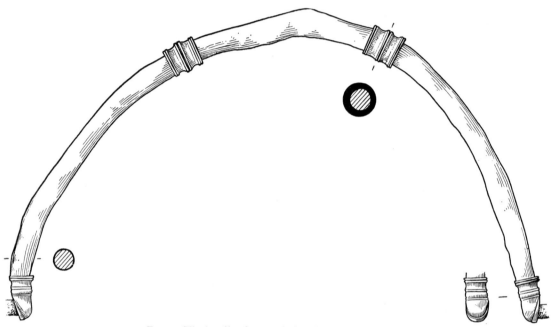

FIG. 7. The handle of the Aylesford bucket. Scale: ½.

F. The internal bronze band, attached to the inside of the rim, is 1·7 in. deep, with a plain straight edge at the top and a ridged edge at the bottom (Fig. 5). There is a single overlap, under head A.1—the same point as the overlap in band C, with a rivet-hole at the same level as the broken rivet-hole in the back plate of A.1 and a second 0·25 in. deeper and 0·5 in. from the end of the band. The band has been broken in one other place, where the two ends seem to match, but a gap of about 0·5 in. has been left in the restoration. This piece was registered in one with the repoussé band, handle, etc.

G. Almost the complete circuit of bronze rim-binding survives, in three separate pieces. It is curved in section, about 0·2 in. wide and 0·15 in. deep (Fig. 5).

H. The handle is formed from an iron rod wrapped in bronze, with the joint in the bronze case on the under side (Fig. 7). At each end there is a cast bronze 'glove' from which the end of the iron handle projects to form a short stub which pivots in the hole in the back of the head-mount. Each 'glove' is ribbed and grooved at one end, and has a deep lip-moulding covering the end from which the iron stub projects. The 'gloves' are respectively 0·9 in. and 0·8 in. long. On the body of the handle, over the top of the bronze casing, are two cast bronze rings, arranged symmetrically 3·8 in. apart. Each ring is 0·7 in. long, 0·45 in. internal diameter—which gives the diameter of the handle before the iron corrosion sprung the bronze case—and is decorated with ribs and grooves.

J. Several pieces of wood survive from the walls, and most of them are about 2·8 in. long and belong to the very top of the bucket (Fig. 5). For display purposes they have been fixed to the inside of the restoration, below the inner band. This wood owes its preservation to being sandwiched between the inner and outer bronze bands at the top, and its surface is perfectly preserved only where the bronze covered it—where the outer band projects below the inner band only the outer surface of wood survives. The wood has been bevelled to a point at the top, and it has a maximum thickness of 0·3 in. The widest piece is 2 in. across—and has a couple of rivet-holes, presumably from A.2, at one edge. The other pieces are narrower, but in no instance can one be certain that the original width of a stave survives.

G. C. Morgan comments: 'The wood is very dry and a thin section showed a very altered structure, making identification difficult. It is however a "soft" wood, showing characteristics of yew (*Taxus baccata*).'

The above pieces, A to J, are included in the 1880s reconstruction of the Aylesford bucket, but the collection includes a number of other pieces, K to O, possibly from the same vessel (1886. 11–12. 7); and others, P to S, certainly from another vessel.

K. A very corroded bronze fragment, 2·1 in. by 1·5 in., with repoussé decoration. The design is the same as (*b*) on band C—apparently taken from the same mould. But at the top (as illustrated on Fig. 8) the ridged edge of the bronze is very much nearer to the design than it is on band C; and at the side there are traces of a second ridged edge. This piece is unique in that it appears to have two finished edges at right angles. It cannot have been part of band C, and it is unlikely to have belonged to another band. It seems more reasonable, on the analogy of Baldock, to suppose that this piece came from a rectangular plaque. The absence of a pin-hole in the corner is curious, but it could have been in the area lost to corrosion—possibly in the flange.

There are two very small and corroded pieces of bronze also decorated with repoussé ornament. They may have belonged to this plaque, or to another, or to band C.

L. Part of a bronze band, 1·4 in. deep and 4·7 in. long, with one original straight end (Fig. 9). Its upper edge is ridged, without a flange beyond; in part this has been flattened, and below the ridge a series of slightly scored lines (? chisel marks) resemble those in some places below the rim-binding on the restored bucket. This suggests that L was an internal band from immediately below a binding—but unlike F its lower edge is roughly cut, not ridged, and one imagines that it would have been covered by another band, below. There are two pin-holes, each 0·1 in. diameter and just below the ridged edge, and each adjoining a smaller pin-hole. Over each hole is the impression of a circular pin-head, about 0·35 in. diameter. Judging from the curvature of this small length, it came from a vessel slightly smaller in diameter than the bucket.

269

M. The straight end of a band, 2·3 in. deep (Fig. 9). One edge is 2·7 in. long and cut along a wavy-line, as Baldock band C, and the other edge, only 0·3 in. long, may have been similar. There may be the edge of a single rivet-hole, 0·2 in. from the straight edge and in the centre of the band—but this area is corroded. This band was clearly overlapped by about 0·4 in. at the straight end.

There is also a small fragment from the same sheet, 2 in. by 1·6 in., with one original edge only 0·5 in. long.

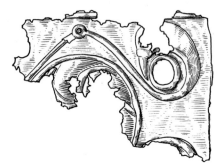

FIG. 8. Bronze sheet K. Scale: full size.

L

 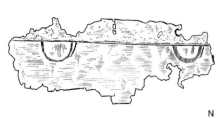

M   N

FIG. 9. Bronze pieces from Aylesford. Scale ½.

N. A fragment from a bronze band, apparently from the inside of a vessel (Fig. 9). The surviving length is 4·4 in. and the width 1·75 in.—but one edge is only 0·35 in. long and is probably a break rather than a true edge, in which case the band would have been wider. The other edge is 1·7 in. long and is cut along a wavy line, as M. A strip 0·5 in. deep, adjoining this edge and defined by an engraved line, is much more corroded than the rest of this piece, and it seems to have been overlapped, or fastened to something. Beyond the corroded band are two semicircular stains, each with the flat side adjacent to the corrosion. One of these stains is quite sharply defined, 0·6 in. diameter; the other is 2·1 in. away and less clear.

270

O. Three small fragments of thin sheet bronze, two with rough edges, but no other features.

The fragments P to S belong to a separate vessel—a stave-built dish or tub—and they were given a different registration number (1886. 11–12. 6) (Fig. 10).

P. Two fragments from the bronze band on the inside of the vessel, each 1·3 in. long. The ridged edge at the top survives, but both pieces are broken near the ridge at the bottom. The surviving depth is 0·7 in., and this neatly fits the impression on the inside of the wood, R.

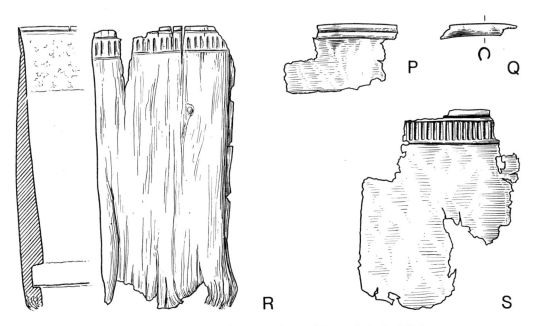

FIG. 10. The wood, R, and bronze, S, from a dish or tub. Scale: full size.

Q. Two short lengths, 1·3 in. and 0·8 in., of rim binding—finer than G and very likely from the same vessel as P, R, and S.

R. Three lengths of wood, 3 in. high and 0.2 in. thick above the base, tapering almost to a point at the rim, as J. The three pieces are respectively 1·4 in., 1·4 in. and 1·3 in. wide, and one of them has two pin-holes one above the other, 0·6 in. from the rim and 1·7 in. below that. Each piece has traces of a groove, cut to insert the base, but only one has the full depth of this groove preserved—0·25 in. The top of the groove is 2·5 in. below the rim. Odd fragments of very thin sheet bronze survive on the outer surface of the wood, and on the inside of two pieces there is a ridge of bronze-corrosion 0·65 in. to 0·7 in. below the rim—possibly indicating the position of a narrow internal band. On the outside of one piece is the very clear impression of the stamped ladder-pattern on the bronze piece S.

G. C. Morgan reports: 'The wood is very dry—in a similar state to that from the bucket (J)—and also shows characteristics of yew (*Taxus baccata*). The absence of resin ducts suggest that it is not a pine, although larch is a possibility.'

271

S. Sheet of very thin bronze, similar to that in small fragments on the wood R. It is 2·1 in. high and 1·6 in. wide (in two pieces) with one edge ridged and decorated with a horizontal band, 0·25 in. deep—a series of stamped ribs arranged in a ladder-pattern. Another piece from the outside of this vessel measures roughly 1·6 in. square, and no decoration survives.

Sequence of the bronze fittings

The upper part of the Aylesford bucket had survived in one piece, with some wood sandwiched between the internal band and the decorated band, and the whole linked by the corroded iron handle. This was registered under a single number, and one can be fairly sure that the pieces are in their correct positions. The only oddity in this upper part, the piece B, has been explained above as a repair in antiquity.

Below this the remains are obviously incomplete: there is a complete circuit of D, but it seems to include pieces from more than one band; there is only two-thirds of a circuit of E; and there are smaller fragments of other bronze bands. It seems that in the reconstruction the more complete remains were assembled into three bands—'there seem to have been three metal bands', recorded Evans,[15] but he was no more definite than that—and the other remains were packed away. It was acknowledged at the start that there were fragments from another vessel.[16]

There is no evidence for spacing the bands at the intervals chosen on the reconstruction, and one wonders if the bucket could have been covered entirely with bronze, as at Baldock. As bands C, D, E, and F are still attached to the reconstruction the reverses cannot be studied for traces of overlapping. One marked difference between the bands on the Aylesford and Baldock buckets is that all those on the Aylesford reconstruction are ridged on both edges—apart from the upper edges of C and F, covered by the rim-binding. On the Baldock bucket there were several wavy edges which were covered by the ridged edges of adjoining bands. This might suggest that the Aylesford reconstruction was correct in leaving spaces between the bands, but for the fact that the Aylesford collection includes fragments (M and N) with wavy edges precisely the same as the covered edges at Baldock. Admittedly the surviving fragments of M and N are very short, but if they are correctly included in the grave-group they must surely have been complete circuits originally.

Apart from the bucket there are remains of two other wooden vessels sheathed in bronze. One of these can be reconstructed—a shallow dish whose wooden profile is still intact (Fig. 10). The other is represented by the internal band L, which duplicates F so cannot belong to the main bucket, whilst it does not match the bronze stain on the inside of the wooden dish, R. The curious band N may belong to this third vessel, as might the band E, now attached to the reconstructed bucket.

There are too many unknown factors—particularly the incomplete remains; the presence in the collection of other vessels with similar wood and bronze; and the features obscured in the nineteenth-century reconstruction—to allow an alternative arrangement of the bronzes to be suggested with any confidence. Perhaps more information will be revealed when the 1880s reconstruction is eventually stripped. Meanwhile, it seems worth suggesting that the Aylesford bucket could have been entirely clothed in bronze, like the buckets from Baldock, possibly with a band M overlapped above and below by ridged edges; and judging from its decoration the piece K must surely belong—on the analogy of Baldock, perhaps one of a series of plaques below the lowest complete bronze band.

COMPARISON

Despite numerous small differences the over-all picture is one of similarity, in technique, in form, and presumably in purpose. The Baldock buckets had no internal band and their handles lacked an iron core, whose corrosion, at Aylesford, combined with the sandwiching effect of internal and external bronze bands to preserve the upper part of that bucket in one piece. But although the Baldock examples were more fragmentary, their examination has produced more clues for the reconstruction, and the sequence of bronzes now suggested (Pl. LXXXVIII) is almost certainly correct. The Aylesford bucket may have been clothed entirely in bronze, too, and a small decorated fragment from a plaque provides a hint that there was a similar arrangement of plaques at the bottom.

Baldock produced nothing to compare with the fine repoussé decoration on the Aylesford bronze, although its simple stamped ornament can be matched on several contemporary pieces.[17] Even so, there is the same symmetry in the top band, with the simple triangular arrangement of discs at a mid-point between the heads, to match the confronted animals at Aylesford. Similarly, the Baldock heads fall short of their Aylesford counterparts. The Aylesford head is a grander conception, a bold symmetrical pattern confidently modelled; whereas Baldock is less powerful, though still impressive, and perhaps more naturalistic, less stylized. But both faces are grim, with remote fixed expressions. Both heads are helmeted—at Baldock with a soft profile, perhaps copying a leather helmet, with drooping, possibly weighted, horns. At Aylesford a close-fitting cap is surmounted by a plume whose curved outline resembles the top of the Baldock helmet, and indeed it may be the Baldock helmet stylized and converted into a simple pattern. It may well be that the helmets should be regarded as an attribute, and both heads may represent the same figure from Celtic mythology.

The Aylesford heads were less securely attached—only a single rivet was used, whereas at Baldock there were two rivets for each head. The broad fitting over the rim-binding would have helped to secure the Aylesford heads, but in time they would have worked loose. This was a defect, and in both pieces front and back plates snapped at the rivet-hole. The one head was repaired by adding a fitting which would have preserved the appearance but served no other function; the other was broken and not repaired. At the time of burial neither head could have been attached to the bucket other than by mastic, and it is unlikely that even the empty bucket could have been held by its handle. The single small piece of plaque suggests that the bottom of the bucket was in poor condition as well. But other instances show that old and repaired objects of no more use to the living were still quite suitable to accompany the dead.

Opinion has been divided as to whether the Aylesford bucket was a native product, or an import from Gaul. For an object so unusual there is a strong argument in favour of manufacture near its ultimate provenance, and this is given overwhelming support by the discovery of the Baldock buckets in another Aylesford culture context. Chronologically, there is nothing to choose between the two. The Baldock buckets are less ambitious pieces from another workshop, but stylistically there is nothing to place them earlier or later than Aylesford. The only dating evidence is provided by continental imports among the grave-goods—the bronze jug and pan at Aylesford and the Dressel type 1 Italian amphora at Baldock; but one need look no further than Welwyn to find all three pieces in the one grave-group.[18]

BUCKETS FROM LE TÈNE III BURIALS IN BRITAIN

Although several buckets have been found in La Tène III burials in Britain, there is nothing to compare closely with those from Aylesford and Baldock.[19] Only one other vessel, from Great Chesterford (Pl. xci), has a swing-handle, and that is the only other piece bound solely in bronze—but with a diameter of 6.3 in. it is considerably smaller than those described above.[20] On the other hand the famous Marlborough bucket, nearly 2 ft. in diameter, is very much larger, and differs in having some iron bands and a fixed iron bar-handle. The Harpenden bucket has fine rams-head handle-mounts, but they support bronze ring-handles, and no bands from that vessel survive; and a possible bucket from Silkstead has decorated sheet bronze, but iron handle-mounts and iron ring-handles.

A different type of bucket, with iron bands and iron ring-handles, has been found in graves at Aylesford ('X'), Swarling (burial 13), Old Warden, and Welwyn Garden City. Finally, there are pieces of iron and bronze, sometimes identified as remains of buckets, from the La Tène III burials at Lexden and Hurstbourne Tarrant.[21] But neither Lexden nor Hurstbourne Tarrant yielded bucket handles, and no reconstruction of a bucket has ever been attempted; furthermore, at both sites the so-called bucket remains were associated with tanged iron bands and dome-headed pins, features which can be matched on an unknown object from Hertford Heath.[22] This feature from three rich La Tène III burials may perhaps be compared with the wooden object decorated with dome-headed studs from Welwyn Garden City;[23] whatever its purpose it is unlikely to have been a bucket, or a container of any kind.

It is worth inquiring how far the term 'bucket-burial' is justified for classifying these sites. They have been defined as 'burials of greater luxury . . . found in

	IN A GRAVE		USED AS CINERARY			HANDLES			METAL BANDS		
	certainly	possibly	yes	no	unknown	swing	ring	other	bronze only	bronze and iron	iron only
AYLESFORD 'Y'	X		X			X			X		
BALDOCK (2)	X			X		X			X		
GT. CHESTERFORD		X			X	X			X		
HARPENDEN		X			X		X		?		
SILKSTEAD		X			X		X			X	
MARLBOROUGH	X		X					X		X	
AYLESFORD 'X'	X			X			X				X
SWARLING 13	X		X				X				X
OLD WARDEN	X		X				?				X
WELWYN GARDEN CITY (2)	X			X			X				X

FIG. 11. Table: Buckets in La Tène III burials in Britain.

wooden buckets', and ten sites have been listed, to which two recent discoveries may be added.[24] Of the twelve examples, nine are certainly from burials, but the remains from two of these (Lexden and Hurstbourne Tarrant) cannot be certainly identified as buckets. Of the others, the burial was not *inside* the buckets at Welwyn Garden City; and as there are two buckets from Baldock it is unlikely that one, or both, was used as a cinerary vessel. This leaves five sites: at Swarling the cremated bones were manifestly inside the bucket; at Old Warden and Marlborough older and less reliable accounts firmly place the bones inside the buckets; but at Aylesford the records are more curious—the one bucket ('X') had several cinerary urns inside, and the other ('Y') contained cremated bones and the fibulae, but there were cinerary urns in the same grave. Modern excavations have shown that the calcined bones in richer Aylesford culture burials were often simply heaped on the floor of the grave.[25] Although there are instances where a cremation has been buried in a bucket, it is perhaps misleading to look on the 'bucket-burial' as a distinctive burial-rite; it may be better to regard the bucket merely as one of the grave-goods.

THE USE OE THE BUCKETS

If these buckets were not specifically cinerary vessels they may have had some other function, to which associated grave-goods may provide a clue. It has been shown that buckets were found with seven La Tène III burials in Britain. At Marlborough there were no other grave-goods; at Aylesford 'X' only native pottery; and at Swarling, burial 13, native pottery and two brooches. Objects imported from the Continent were found with the other four burials—Italian amphorae at Baldock, Old Warden, and, along with an Italian silver cup, Welwyn Garden City; and a bronze jug and pan at Aylesford 'Y'. These imports, as well as the improvised strainer at Welwyn Garden City, are connected with wine, so perhaps the buckets should be viewed in this context too. They may have held water for diluting the wine, or indeed they could have been used as the receptacle in which the wine was mixed. In a classical context the wine service would not be complete without a mixing-bowl. Fox has suggested that bovine handle-mounts on other Iron Age buckets might indicate their use as milk-pails;[26] perhaps our grim and helmeted heads presided over a rather more serious brew.

Here it is worth reverting to the reconstruction of the Aylesford and Baldock buckets, and considering one curious feature. At Baldock the sequence of bronze bands has been established, but there is little known about the wood-work. It has been assumed that the vessel was stave-built, but no complete stave survives, nor any part of the base. Hence the bucket can be reconstructed only where the wood is covered by bronze, and this creates a problem at the bottom where there are three pendant plaques with spaces between (Pl. LXXXVIII). If the bucket was $11\frac{3}{4}$ in. high there was exposed wood between the plaques and no bronze to bind the junction between the staves and the base. The plaques might be merely decorative, comparable in a general way with those on a bucket found in a well at Mount Sorrel, Leicestershire;[27] or perhaps they were non-functional survivals, with an ancestry in the angle-plates on Late Bronze Age metal buckets.[28] But a more convincing explanation is that the bucket was entirely clothed in bronze and the plaques were quite functional, covering three wooden feet. The stave-built bucket would then be only $8\frac{3}{4}$ in. high, with three wooden feet below, and would present a much more balanced appearance with the two deep bands bordered by the two narrow bands (Fig. 12). This explanation might also account for the very poor condition of the surviving plaques, for not only would they be exposed on three sides to attacks of corrosion, but they would

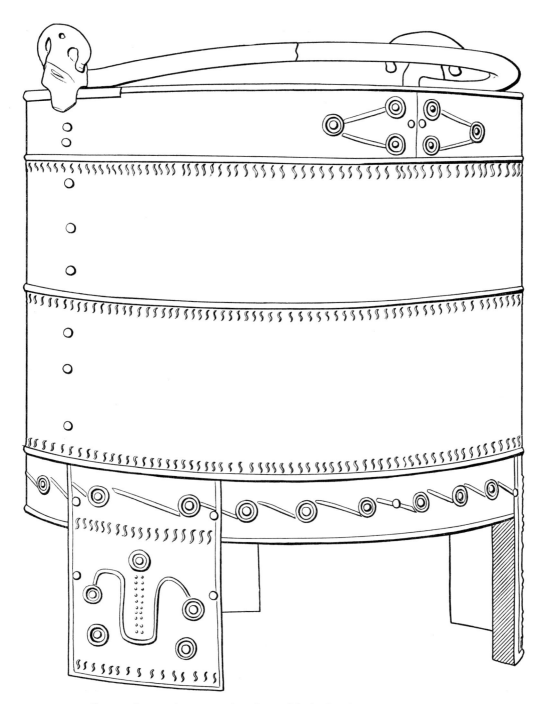

FIG. 12. Suggested reconstruction of one of the buckets from Baldock. Scale: ½.

also be in a vulnerable position when the bucket was in use. The similarity throughout between the Aylesford and Baldock buckets, and particularly the presence in the Aylesford collection of the small fragment, K, apparently from a plaque, suggests that if the Baldock buckets stood on three feet, then so did the one from Aylesford. This case is considerably strengthened by the recent discovery of two similar tripod vessels in an Augustan grave at Goeblingen-Nospelt, Luxemburg.[29]

It remains to link these arguments: that the Aylesford and Baldock buckets (i) might have been used for mixing wine, and (ii) might have been tripod vessels. For occasionally Roman bronze wine-buckets were provided with three feet.[30] The point is well illustrated by another barbarian grave, richly furnished with Roman objects of the Augustan period. This burial, at Hoby, in Denmark, had Roman silver cups, a tray, jug, and pan—and also a large bronze wine-bucket which had human head handle-mounts and stood on three feet.[31] Roman cups, jugs, and pans were imported into Britain and placed with Aylesford culture burials, but no wine-bucket has been found. Perhaps the wooden Aylesford and Baldock buckets stood on three feet in imitation of a contemporary Roman practice—certainly they were used alongside Italian imports by peoples in close contact with the Roman world, shortly after Caesar's expeditions to Britain.

I. M. STEAD

APPENDIX

La Tène III burials in Britain with buckets[32]

AYLESFORD, Kent. Burial 'X'

An iron band and two ring-handles from a large bucket found in a grave at Aylesford were acquired by Henry Lewis, of Camberwell, and were subsequently purchased by the British Museum. According to Lewis several cinerary urns were found inside it; but the grave-group seems to have been muddled.[33]

GREAT CHESTERFORD, Essex

Little is known about the provenance of this vessel. It was donated by one Octavius Green to the Cambridge University Museum of Archaeology and Ethnology, and is labelled 'Great Chesterford 1869'. There are no further details, and it has never been fully published.[34]

It consists of a number of bronze bands, a swing-handle and handle-mounts, and pieces of the original wood (Pl. XCI). These remains have been reconstructed and fitted to a wooden frame, to form a bucket 6·3 in. diameter and 6·3 in. high. The top band in the reconstruction, 1·8 in. deep, has ridged edges and is plain in its lower half, but has simple repoussé decoration in the upper half—a row of domes each ringed by a milled border, and above and below bands of horizontal ribs and punched dots. The reconstruction includes here a short length from a second band, only 1·72 in. deep, but with similar decoration (omitting the top row of ribs and dots). Below this a number of lengths of 0·95 in. deep undecorated band, with ridged edges, have been grouped into two circuits. The handle-mounts are simple lengths of undecorated bronze, each attached by a single rivet to the wooden bucket. These mounts belong *under* the band, which here has traces of another bronze sheet—perhaps a vertical band or a plaque.[35] The swing handle is bronze, without an iron core, wrapped and joined along the top. At either side the handle swings on a single rivet, and above this is a cast feature—an animal head with a stub of a snout and spirally protruding eyes, tapering upwards to end in a small cup inset with a bead of red enamel.

HARPENDEN, Hertfordshire

A collection of objects discovered in 1867 may well have belonged to a grave-group. It consists of a pair of powerfully modelled rams-head handle-mounts, with a large bronze ring-handle suspended from each; a bronze dish with a single handle; and parts of two shale urns.[36] Fox's reconstruction of the handles—with the heads non-functional and the rings mounted in separate brackets (which have not survived)—is not convincing.[37] The rings are well adapted to the position in which they were originally published,[38] and the flanges at the sides of the rams heads have been worn by their movement.

MARLBOROUGH, Wiltshire

This bucket was found about 1807 in an area which produced quantities of Roman material, on the east side of Marlborough. It contained cremated human bones. It was recorded and lifted by the Revd. Charles Francis—a 'drawing was made on the spot . . . while it was entire, and freed from the surrounding earth, so that we had a perfect view of it', but 'it would not bear the smallest jar or shake, and it fell to pieces'. The drawing was published, but the bucket remained in pieces for more than seventy years. Then the surviving fragments were attached to a wooden base, following the original drawing and built to the measurements recorded when it was found.[39]

OLD WARDEN, Bedfordshire

A cremation burial at Quint's Hill, Old Warden, was enclosed by 'two hoops of iron, one on the other's edge', and associated with two amphorae and two shale urns.[40]

SILKSTEAD, OTTERBOURNE, Hampshire

Pieces of iron and bronze found in 1929 in a sand-pit between Silkstead and Otterbourne have been variously published as the remains of a bucket, and a casket.[41] If they all belong to one object—and that cannot be established—it is likely to have been a bucket, but there is no evidence that it was found with a burial.

The remains include five pieces of sheet bronze with simple stamped decoration—a motif comprising two commas enclosing a dot, repeated in lines separated by rows of commas arranged in a scroll.[42] Two of these fragments, with ridged edges on three sides and respectively 2·8 in. and 3·05 in. wide, resemble the plaques on the Baldock bucket—but another similar piece is more than 4 in. wide. Among the iron remains are two pieces which might have been handle-mounts, a ring-handle 3·4 in. diameter, and a short length possibly from a binding strip.

SWARLING, Kent. Burial 13

Three iron hoops from a wooden bucket, one with ring-handles attached, were found in a grave in the Swarling cemetery. It had calcined bones, two brooches, and two pots inside, and there were four other vessels in the grave.[43]

WELWYN GARDEN CITY, Hertfordshire

Iron bands and ring-handles, apparently from two wooden buckets, were found in the rich La Tène III burial at Welwn Garden City in 1965.[44] The calcined bones were heaped on the floor of the grave, some distance away from the buckets.

[1] Through the good offices of Leslie Matthews, Manshead Archaeological Society; John Moss-Eccardt, Curator of Letchworth Museum; and A. C. Eaton, Clerk and Chief Financial Officer to the Baldock U.D.C. The complete excavation report, with full acknowledgements, will be published elsewhere; for a brief note with some illustrations, see *Ant. J.* xlviii, 1968, 306 and pl. lxxvii.

[2] *Arch.* ci, 1967, 44, and distribution map, fig. 1.

[3] Miss Gillian Jones drew all the illustrations for this paper, and contributed ideas for the reconstruction—as did Miss Valerie Rigby, who dealt with the buckets in the field and in the office. Mlle. Jeanette Kocher successfully treated the bronze remains in the Ancient Monuments Laboratory.

[4] e.g. *Later Prehistoric Antiquities of the British Isles*, 1953, pl. xxi, no. 2.

[5] The writer is most grateful to the staff of the new Department, and particularly to Dr. I. H. Longworth, for their help, and patience, in the study and recording of the Aylesford bucket at the British Museum.

[6] *Arch.* lii, 1890, 317.

[7] Op. cit. 318, fig. 1.

[8] *B.M.Q.* xxviii, 1964, 27, no. 4.

[9] The material from the Aylesford cemetery in the British Museum was received in three collections, (1) 1886, 'purchased from Silas Wagon through John Evans, Esq.'; (2) 1887, 'presented by John Hale, Esq.'; (3) 1888, 'purchased from Henry Lewis'. The collection purchased from Silas Wagon includes the bronzes described by Evans as well as sherds from six pots—clearly these sherds were found at Aylesford, but there is no proof that they came from the rich grave—they are not illustrated by Evans and the museum

Register does not describe them as a grave-group. Other graves had already been disturbed at Aylesford, and the Wagon collection may well include stray sherds. The John Hale collection is also unsatisfactory as a grave-group, for its principal item —the remains of a tankard—was found in October 1886, 'buried in the topsoil about 18 ins. deep . . . in close proximity to and apparently within a circle of 5 or 6 coarse earthenware jars . . . some of them containing burnt bones . . .'. This description in the Register seems to be the basis of Evans's account (*Arch.* lii, 1890, 317–18). Evans accepted it as a grave-group (op. cit. 318 and 330), but the description could equally apply to another 'family circle' comprising a group of burials. The Aylesford cemetery seems to have been divided into a number of burial groups (op. cit., 320, and 321–2; this may resemble the grouping noticed in an Aylesford culture cemetery at Verulamium, *Antiquity*, xliii, 1969, 50, and fig. 3). Finally, the Henry Lewis collection includes four pots in the only grave-group specifically listed in the Register —but this association is spoilt because the only pot from this grave illustrated by Evans is not included in the group in the Register (*Arch.* lii, 1890, 319 and 331, no. 16; *B.M.Q.* xxviii, 1964, 25–6).

[10] *Bayerische Vorgeschichtsblätter*, xx, 1954, 43–73.

[11] Miss Mavis Bimson, of the British Museum Laboratory, spent many hours skilfully detaching these pieces, and also took a series of very useful X-ray photographs.

[12] See note 11.

[13] *Proc. Camb. Ant. Soc.* xiii, 1908–9, 154–5, and fig. 8; also *Arch.* ci, 1967, 25; but this Santon Downham piece was attached to metal, not wood.

[14] It cannot be photographed by X-rays because the restoration has a solid wooden shelf just above this band.

[15] *Arch.* lii, 1890, 360.

[16] Ibid. 317.

[17] e.g. Lexden, *Arch.* lxxvi, 1926–7, 249, and pl. lix; Hurstbourne Tarrant, *Arch. Journ.* lxxxvii, 1930, 305, and pl. i, B.

[18] Welwyn B: *Arch.* lxiii, 1911–12, 3 ('second vault'), and *Arch.* ci, 1967, 58.

[19] Among remains of buckets not found with La Tène III burials is a small handle-mount in the form of a Celtic head, with a hole in the back for the end of a swing-handle, found with an inhumation at Brough, east Yorkshire, and dated Romano-British, *Ant. J.* xviii, 1938, 68–74, and pl. xxix. From Thealby, Lincolnshire, there is a pair of ox-head handle-mounts with similar holes in the back, and several others belong to a different type in which the ends of the handle pivoted in a ring above an animal or human head (for the animals, see C. F. C. Hawkes, in W. F. Grimes, ed., *Aspects of Archaeology in Britain and Beyond*, 1951, 172–99; and the human head, S. Piggott, *The Druids*, 1968, 223, and pl. 11).

[20] The sites mentioned in this section are listed in the Appendix and tabulated in Fig. 11.

[21] Lexden: *Arch.* lxxvi, 1926–7, 246 and 249, and pl. lii, fig. 3; pl. liv, fig. 1; and pl. lix. Hurstbourne Tarrant: *Proc. Hants. F.C. & A.S.* x, 1926–30, 122, and *Arch. Journ.* lxxxvii, 1930, 304–8.

[22] *E. Herts. Arch. Soc. Trans.* xiv, part 1, 1959, 5–8, and fig. 3, nos. 8 to 16.

[23] *Arch.* ci, 1967, 27–9, and fig. 4, no. 9.

[24] *Arch. Journ.* lxxxvii, 1930, 304, for a list of seven sites, to which *P.P.S.* xxi, 1965, 257, adds three buckets with iron bands and ring handles (tankards are excluded from the present discussion); the Baldock and Welwyn Garden City graves are the recent discoveries. See Appendix for details.

[25] Snailwell, *Proc. Camb. Ant. Soc.* xlvii, 1953, 26–8; Welwyn Garden City, *Arch.* ci, 1967, 5; Verulamium, *Antiquity*, xliii, 1969, 49.

[26] Sir Cyril Fox, *Pattern and Purpose*, 1958, 73.

[27] W. F. Grimes (ed.), *Aspects of Archaeology in Britain and Beyond*, 1951, 197, and pl. viii A.

[28] *Ant. J.* xxxvii, 1957, 139.

[29] These are stave-built buckets encased in bronze bands. They lack the elaborate handle-mounts, but one of the bands is decorated with repoussé S-motifs like those incorporated in an Aylesford design (Fig. 6 *a*). The grave (Grave B, one of four rich burials) also produced a bronze pan and jug of the same types found at Aylesford. For the buckets see *Hémecht*, 1967, no. 1, 92–3, with drawings, Taf. I, 11 and 12; for photographs see *Publications de la Section Historique de l'Institut G.-D. de Luxembourg*, lxxxiv, 1968, 285 and 286.

[30] The writer is grateful to Professor D. E. Strong for discussion on this point, and for drawing his attention to examples from Pompeii, whose feet were either original or added in antiquity, E. Pernice, *Die hellenistische Kunst in Pompeii*, Band iv, 1925, Abb. 20 and Taf. iv; also for Roman examples, and copies of Roman work, H. J. Eggers, *Der römische Import im freien Germanien*, 1951, types 24, 27–30, and 32–4.

[31] Sir Mortimer Wheeler, *Rome Beyond the Imperial Frontiers*, 1955, 53–6; H. J. Eggers, op. cit., 1951, 88, no. 246—the wine bucket is Eggers type 24.

[32] For facilities to study material in their custody the writer is grateful to Miss M. D. Cra'ster (Cambridge University Museum of Archaeology and Ethnology); Mr. Peter Smith (Luton Museum and Art Gallery); and Messrs. Frank Cottrill and John Dockerill (Winchester City Museum).

[33] *Arch.* lii, 1890, 319; for the confusion about the grave-group see note 9.

[34] C. Fox, *Archaeology of the Cambridge Region*, 1923, 105, devotes a few lines to it.

[35] Possibly something similar to the Mount Sorrel bucket, W. F. Grimes (ed.), op. cit., 1951, 197 and pl. viii A.

[36] J. E. Cussans, *History of Hertfordshire*, iii, Hundred of Dacorum, 1879–81, 350; *Ant. J.* viii, 1928, 520–2; *Ant. J.* xxix, 1949, 196–7; the handle probably belongs to the dish rather than to a chest—one fragment of the dish has a piece of iron attached, and that might well be part of one of the iron rings attaching the handle, cf. Welwyn Garden City, *Arch.* ci, 1967, 26, and fig. 14.

[37] Sir Cyril Fox, *Pattern and Purpose*, 1958, 76–8, and fig. 47.

[38] *Ant. J.* viii, 1928, 520–2, and pls. lxxxii and lxxxiii; E. T. Leeds, *Celtic Ornament*, 1933, 93–4, and fig. 28.

[39] The discovery is recorded by Sir Richard Colt Hoare, *The Ancient History of Wiltshire*, ii, 1821, 35, and pl. vi; further details, from Hoare's notebook, are given in *W.A.M.* xxii, 1885, 234–8; and in a letter from Francis published in a paper

which also describes the reconstruction of the vessel, *W.A.M.* xxiii, 1887, 222–8. For some discrepancies between the original drawing and the reconstruction, omissions from the original drawing, and photographs of the surviving pieces, see *Acta Arch.* xxix, 1958, 1–20, and Sir Cyril Fox, *Pattern and Purpose*, 1958, 69, and pls. 34 to 36.

⁴⁰ Sir Henry Dryden, *Pubs. Camb. Ant. Soc.* i (1840–6), no. 8, 1845, 20. T. Inskip, *Ass. Architect. Soc. Reports and Papers*, i, 1850–1, 169, clarifies Dryden's description of the amphorae and urns, but makes no mention of the iron hoops. The shale urns are at Cambridge (C. Fox, *Archaeology of the Cambridge Region*, 1923, 96–7, pl. xv, 3) and the British Museum (*Later Prehistoric Antiquities of the British Isles*, 1953, 71, pl. xxiii, 3),

but it seems that the bucket remains have not survived.

⁴¹ *Arch. Journ.* lxxxvii, 1930, 304, note 2, followed by *P.P.S.* xxi, 1965, 256–7, treated them as a bucket; but Sir Cyril Fox, *Pattern and Purpose*, 1958, 105, regarded them as part of a casket.

⁴² One piece is illustrated by Sir Cyril Fox, *Pattern and Purpose*, 1958, pl. 77, a.2 (wrongly captioned 'Winchester').

⁴³ J. P. Bushe-Fox, *Excavation of the Late-Celtic Urn-field at Swarling, Kent* (Soc. Ant. Res. Cttee. Report No. V), 1925, 6–7, and pl. ii, fig. 2.

⁴⁴ *Arch.* ci, 1967, 36–8.

PLATES

(a)

(b)

I. THE DEPARTMENT OF PREHISTORIC AND ROMANO-BRITISH ANTIQUITIES

(a) The main offices built on top of offices used by the Department of Printed Books. The Reading Room is on the right

(b) The new Students' Room floor for the Romano-British and Later Prehistoric collections, seen from the north-east. To the left is the shaft of the lift from the Front Hall

(a)

(b)

II. THE CENTRAL PREHISTORIC SALOON

(a) Looking through into the North Wing before 1939

(b) War damage in 1941, looking towards the North Wing

III. THE CENTRAL PREHISTORIC SALOON, 1969

(a) Showing the raised exhibition gallery in the North Wing. The new Roman Britain room is on the right

(b) The rebuilt Saloon, with the staircase well leading to the Front Hall

(a)

(b)

IV. THE ROMAN BRITAIN ROOM

(a) War damage in 1941

(b) Part of the new Room, with the restored Horkstow pavement, previously exhibited in sections

(a)

(b)

V. FACILITIES FOR STUDY

(a) Palaeolithic implements as displayed in 1939 in the long gallery in the North Wing of the Prehistoric Saloon

(b) The new Students' Room for the Romano-British and Later Prehistoric collections

(a)

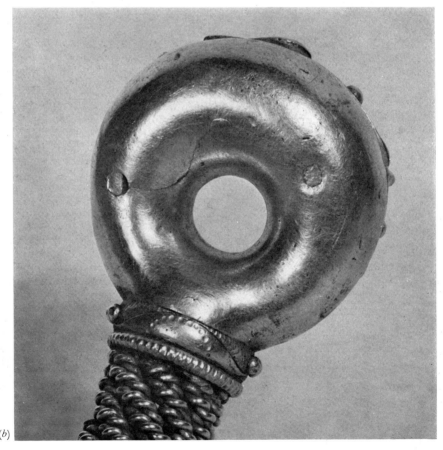

(b)

VI. THE SEDGEFORD TORC
(a) General view. (Scale 3:4)
(b) Plain (repaired) face of terminal. (Scale approx. 3:2)

VII. THE SEDGEFORD TORC: decorated face of the terminal. (Scale approx. 5:2)

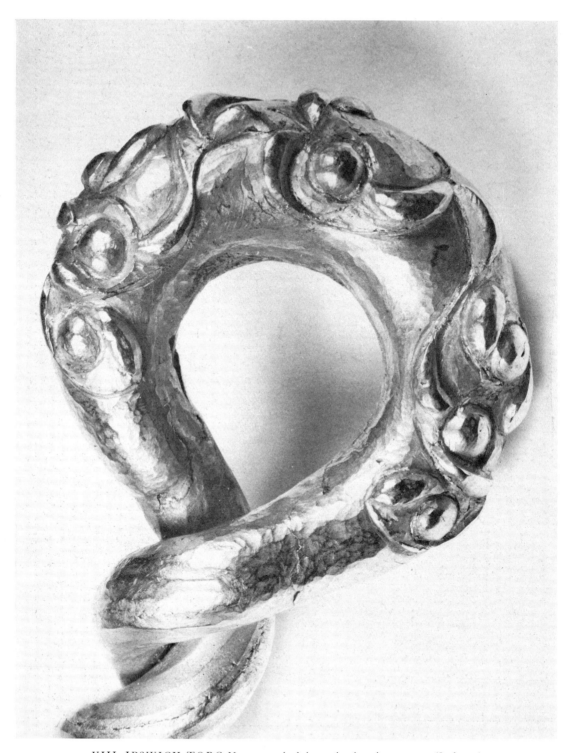

VIII. IPSWICH TORC No. 2: terminal decoration in primary stage. (Scale 5:2)

IX. IPSWICH TORC No. 5: terminal decoration in secondary stage, still unfinished. (Scale 2:1)

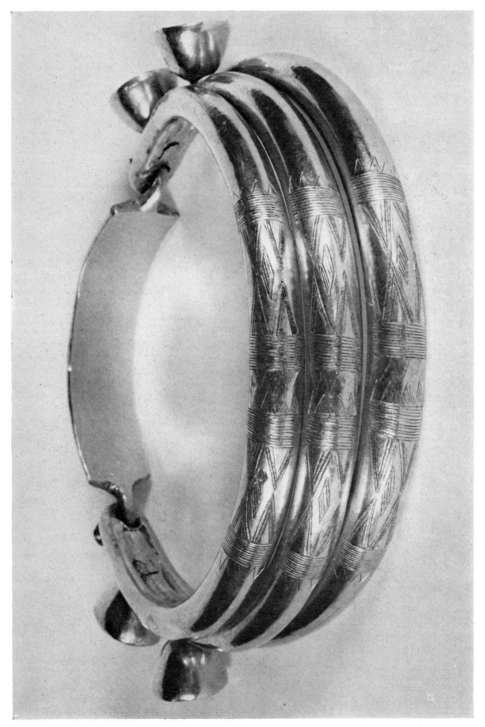

X. THE GOLD COLLAR FROM SINTRA, Portugal

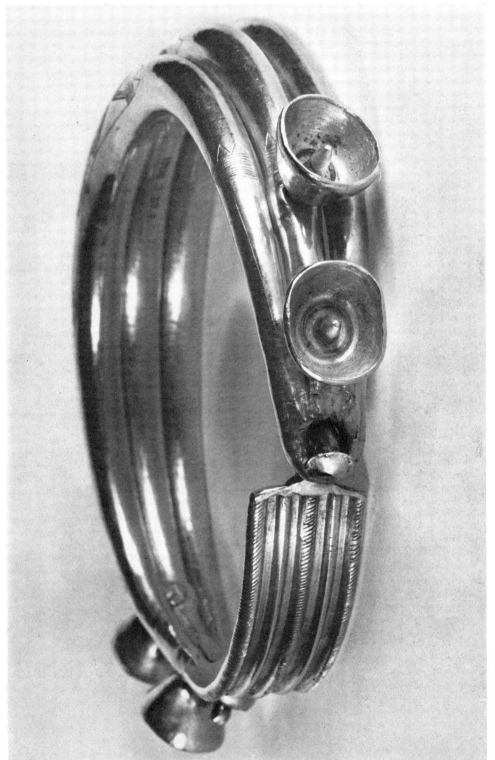

XI. THE SINTRA GOLD COLLAR: showing link and floral cup ornaments

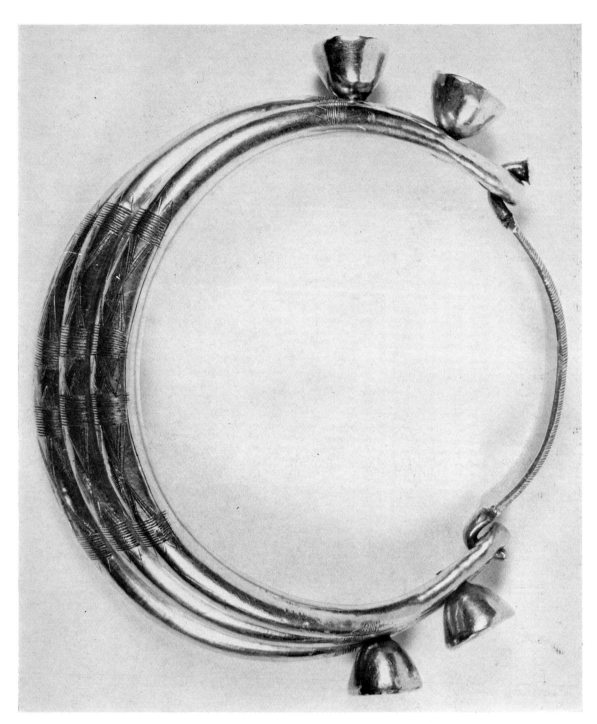

XII. THE SINTRA GOLD COLLAR: showing ornament on body

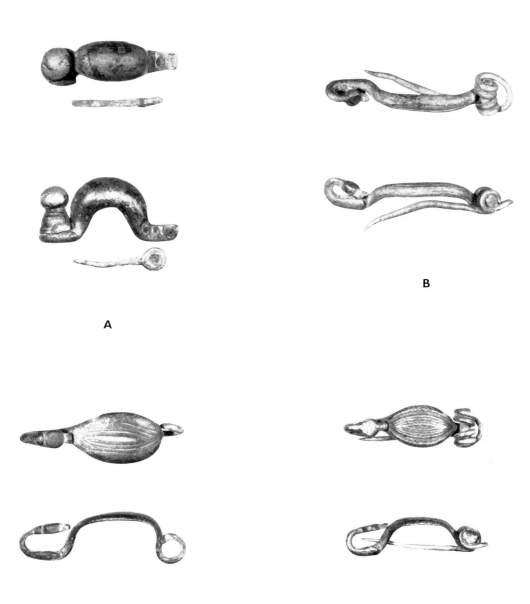

XIII. FIBULAE from Hammersmith (A–C) and 'Thames at London' (D) (British Museum)
Scale 1:1

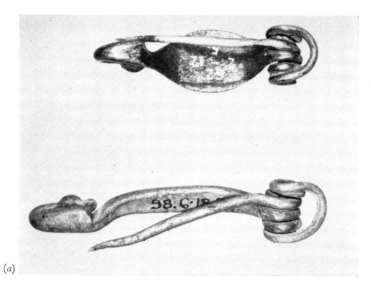

(a)

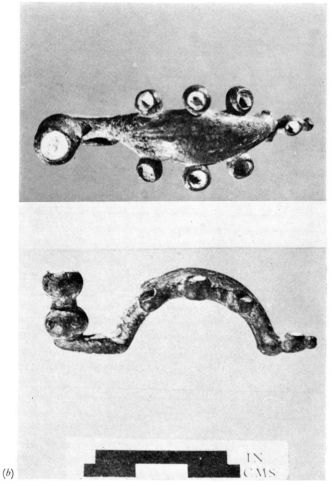

(b)

XIV. (a) UNDERSIDES OF FIBULAE D and B enlarged to show construction of
skeuomorphic springs (see Pl. XIII D and B). Scale 3:2

(b) BRONZE FIBULA with white inlays from Great Chesterford, Essex. (By courtesy
of Cambridge University Museum of Archaeology and Ethnology)

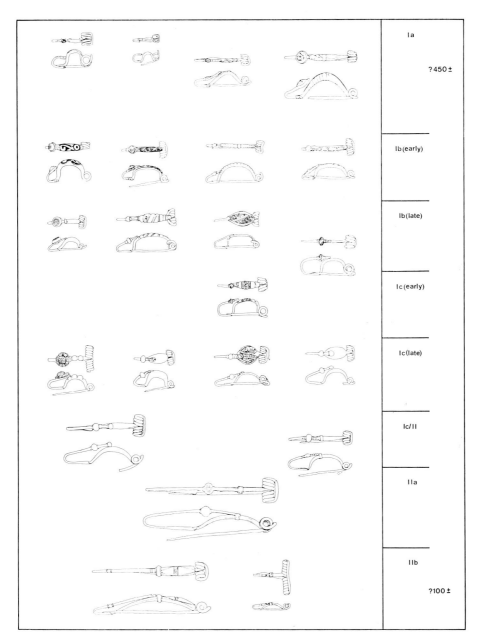

	la
	?450 ±
	lb (early)
	lb (late)
	lc (early)
	lc (late)
	lc/ll
	lla
	llb
	?100 ±

XV. SEQUENCE OF FIBULAE TYPES and phases at Münsingen cemetery (Switzerland)
Dates expressed in years B.C.

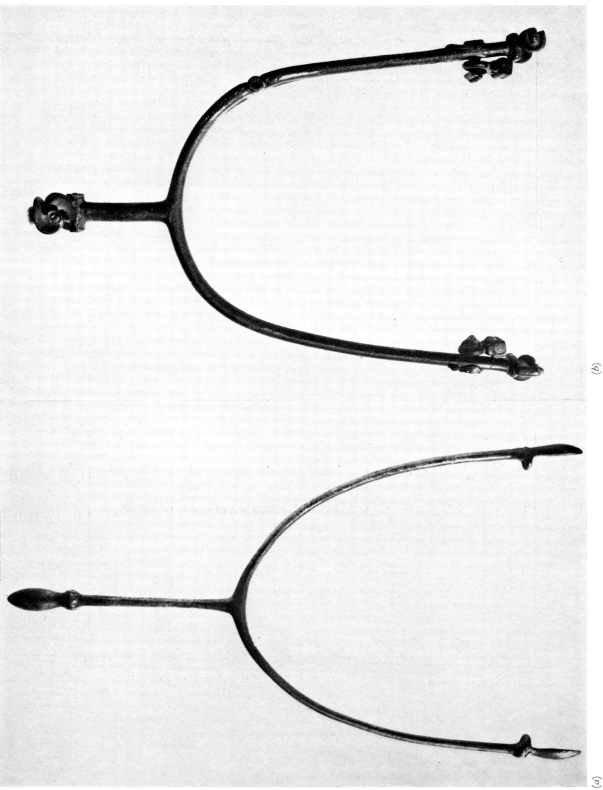

(b)

(a)

XVI. SPUR-SHAPED BRONZES: (a) Catalogue No. 2. (b) Catalogue No. 1. Scale 1:1

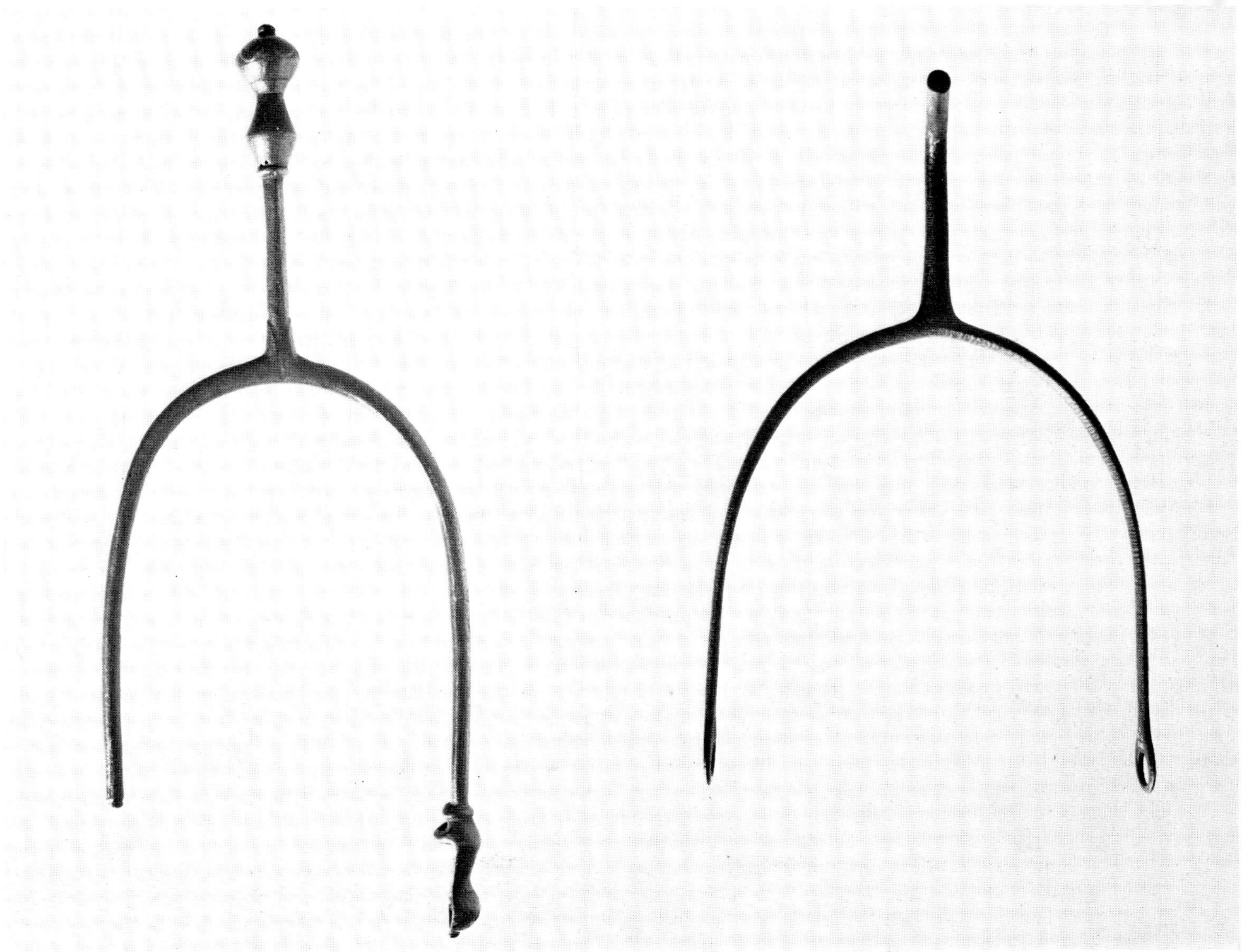

XVII. SPUR-SHAPED BRONZES: (a) Catalogue no. 3; (b) Catalogue no. 4. Scale 1 : 2

(b)

(a)

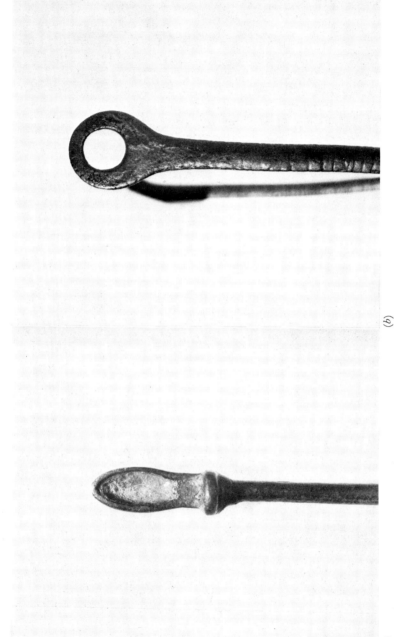

(b)

(a)

XVIII. SPUR-SHAPED BRONZES: (a) Catalogue no. 2 detail. (b) Catalogue no. 4 detail. Scale 1 : 1

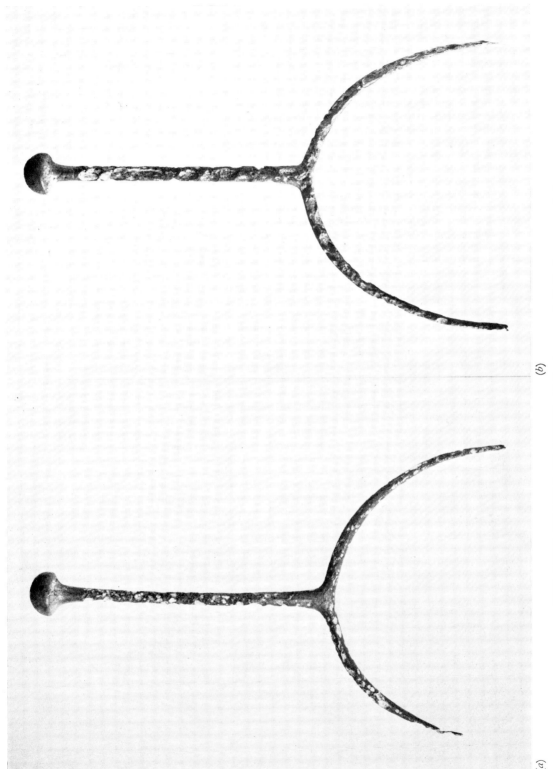

XIX. SPUR-SHAPED BRONZES: (a) Catalogue no. 6. (b) Catalogue no. 5. Scale 1:2

XX. GENERAL VIEW OF THE WITHAM SHIELD

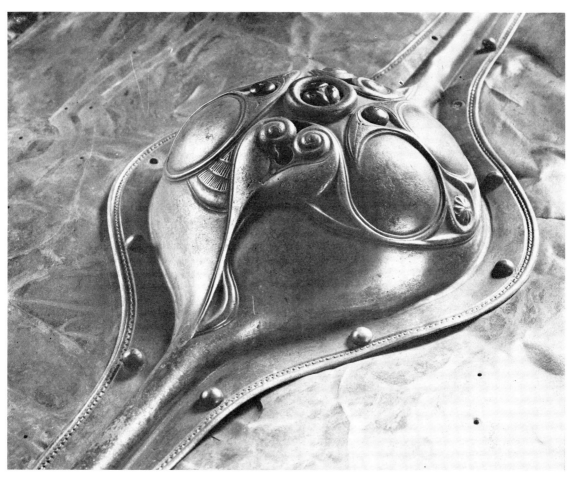

XXI. WITHAM SHIELD: oblique view of central umbo from above (photo. E. Neuffer).

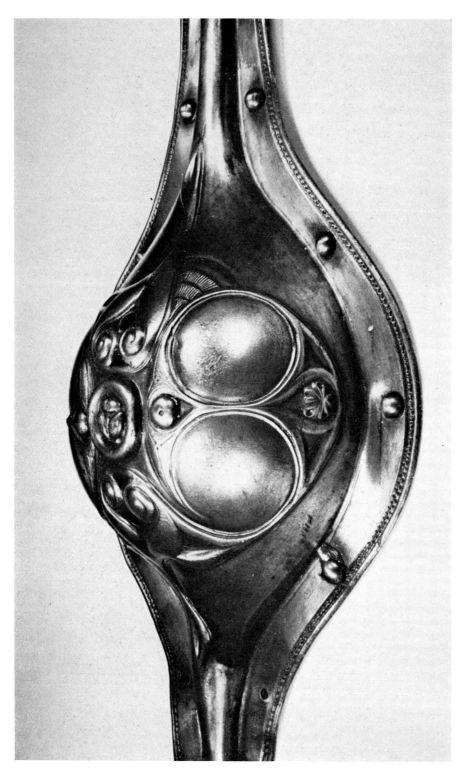

XXII. WITHAM SHIELD electrotype: oblique view of central umbo from one side
(photo. R. E. H. Reid).

XXIII. WITHAM SHIELD electrotype: vertical view of spine and
lower roundel (photo. R. E. H. Reid)

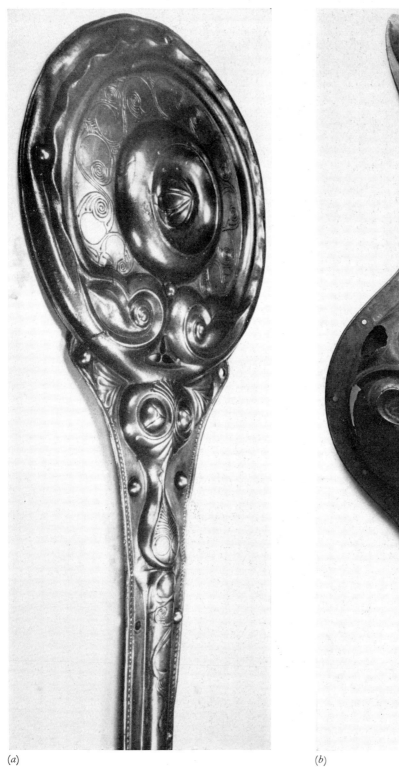

(a)   (b)

XXIV. (a) WITHAM SHIELD electrotype: oblique view of spine and upper roundel, with its central boss restored
(photo. P. D. Shorer)

(b) WANDSWORTH SHIELD-BOSS: spine with central umbo (photo. R. E. H. Reid

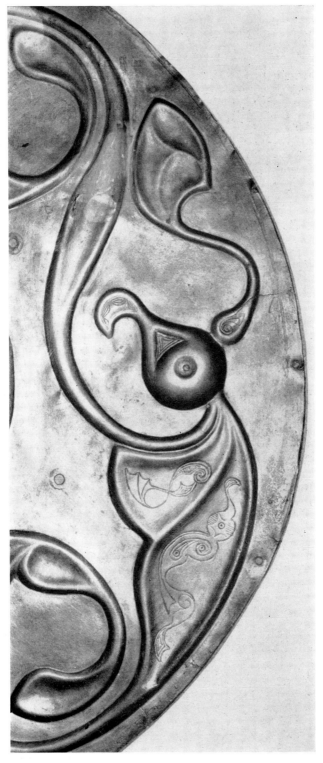

XXV. WANDSWORTH: SECOND SHIELD-BOSS.
Detail from plaque surrounding the hemispherical central boss, showing an embossed bird rising obliquely; note the attempted perspective
(photo. R. E. H. Reid)

(a)

(b)

XXVI. VERULAMIUM. THE RED WALL: (a) General view. (b) Central panel detail

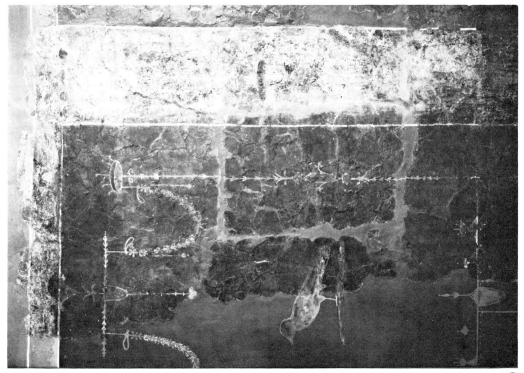

(b)

(a)

XXVII. VERULAMIUM. THE RED WALL: (a) Central panel. (b) Left-hand panel

(b)

(a)

XXVIII. VERULAMIUM. RIGHT-HAND PANEL OF THE RED WALL: (a) Upper portion. (b) Lower portion

(a)

(b)

XXIX. VERULAMIUM. THE RED WALL: (a) *Graffito* of bird. (b) *Graffito* EQVVS

XXX. VERULAMIUM. THE PEOPLED SCROLL FRIEZE

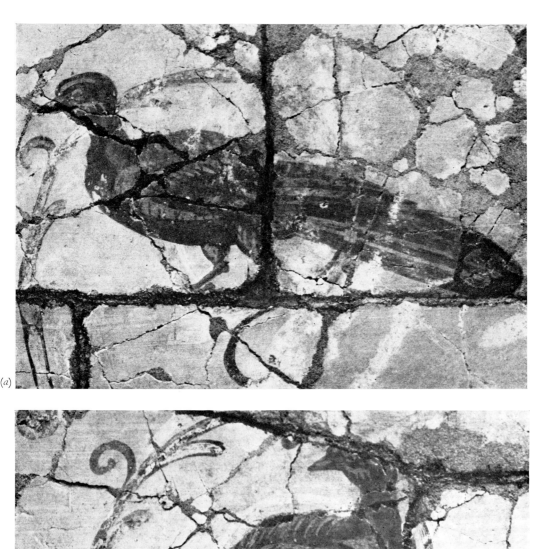

(a)

(b)

XXXI. VERULAMIUM. (a) and (b) Birds in the peopled scroll frieze

(a)

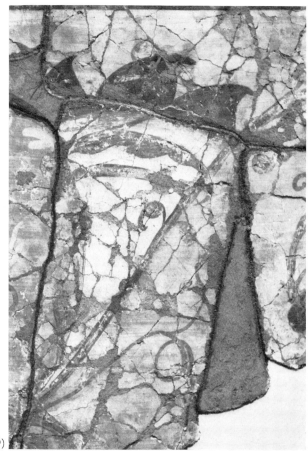

(b)

XXXII. VERULAMIUM. The peopled scroll frieze:
(a) Feline mask. (b) Funnel-shaped motif

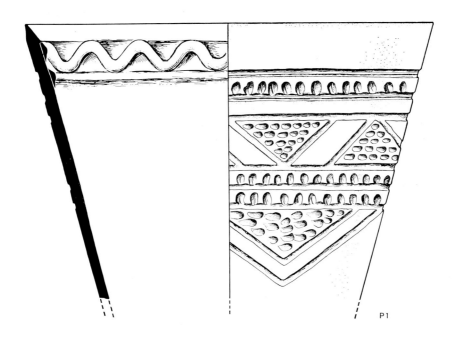

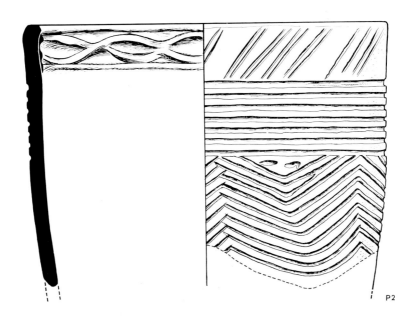

XXXIII. GROOVED WARE FROM LION POINT, CLACTON: P1–P2

Scale 1:3

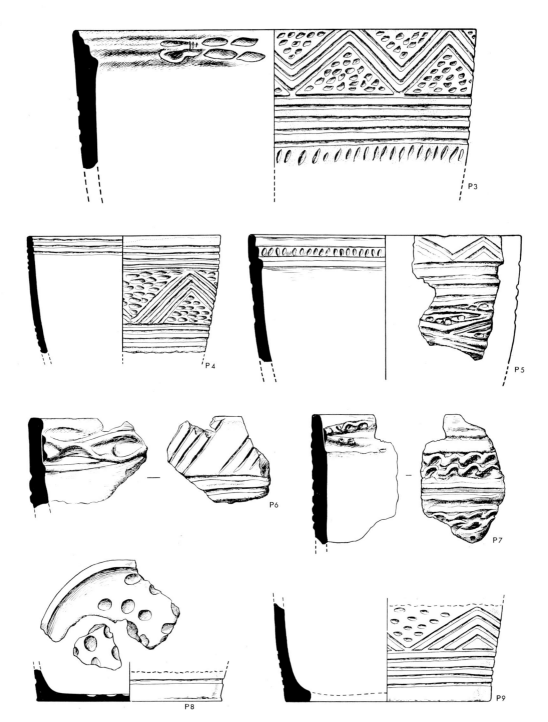

XXXIV. GROOVED WARE FROM LION POINT, CLACTON: P3-P9

Scale 1:3

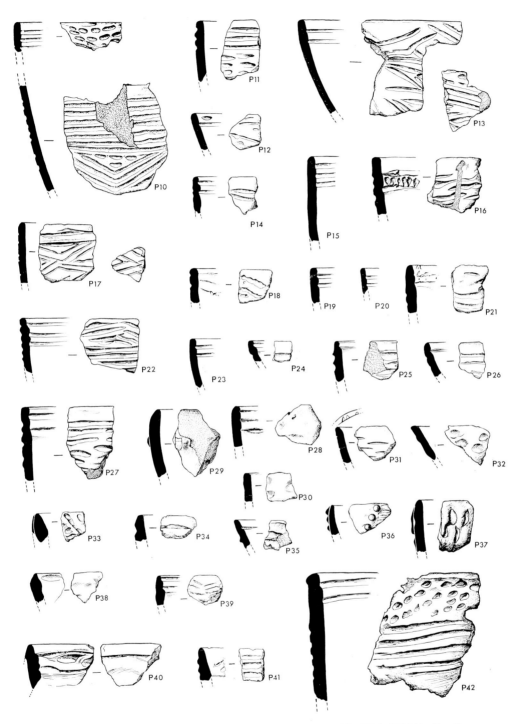

XXXV. GROOVED WARE FROM LION POINT, CLACTON: P10–P42

Scale 1:3

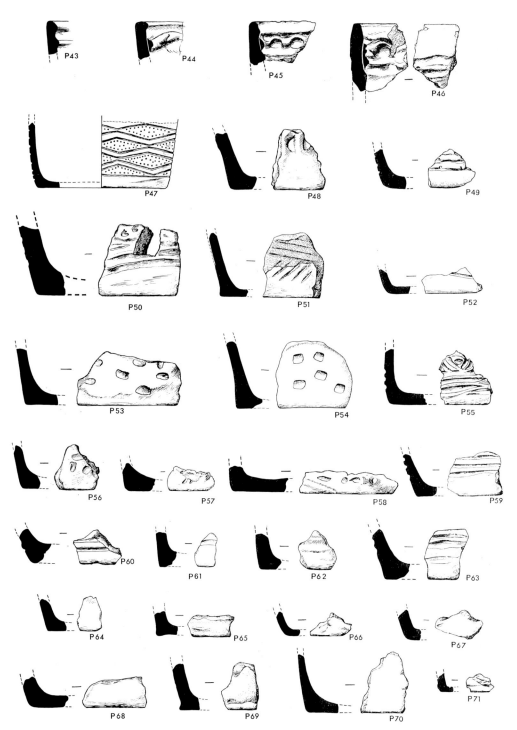

XXXVI. GROOVED WARE FROM LION POINT, CLACTON: P43–P71

Scale 1:3

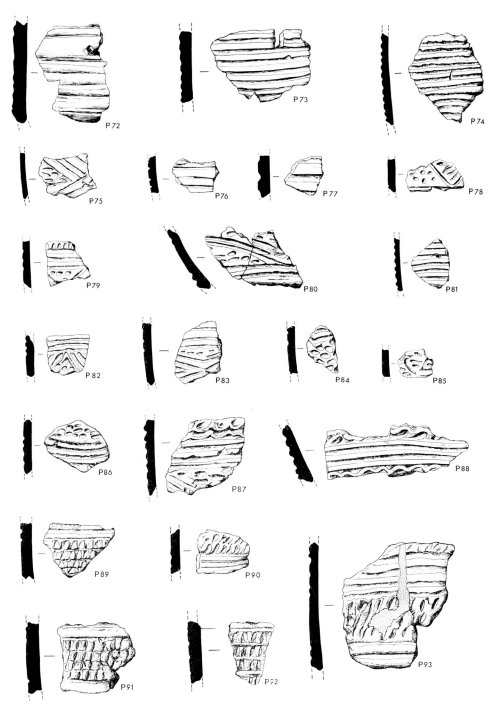

XXXVII. GROOVED WARE FROM LION POINT, CLACTON: P72–P93

Scale 1:3

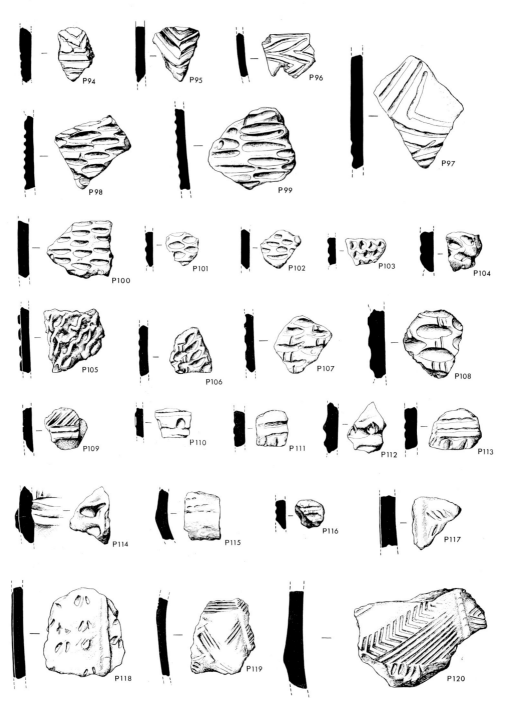

XXXVIII. GROOVED WARE FROM LION POINT, CLACTON: P94–P120

Scale 1:3

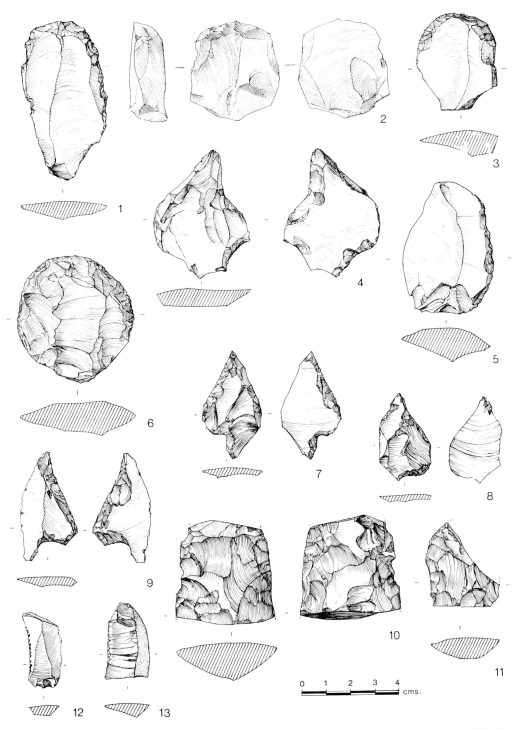

0   1   2   3   4
cms.

XXXIX. FLINTS FROM GROOVED WARE SITE AT LION POINT, CLACTON

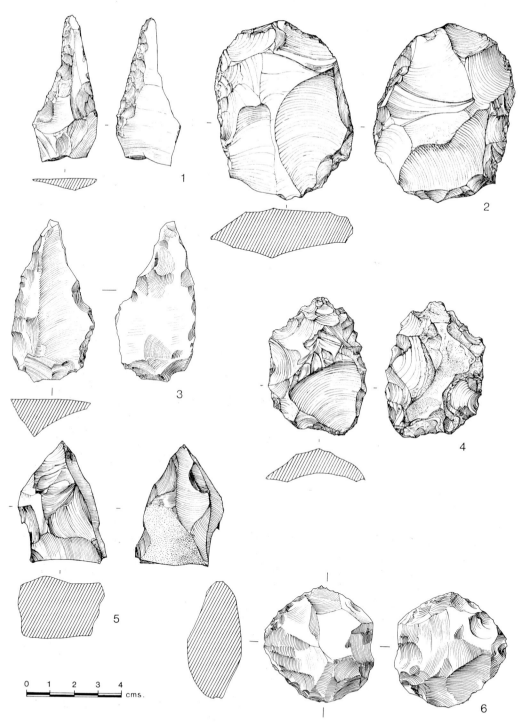

XL. FLINTS FROM GROOVED WARE SITE AT LION POINT, CLACTON

XLI. THE PIERCEBRIDGE PLOUGH GROUP: viewed from the right

XLII. THE PIERCEBRIDGE PLOUGH GROUP: *viewed from the left*

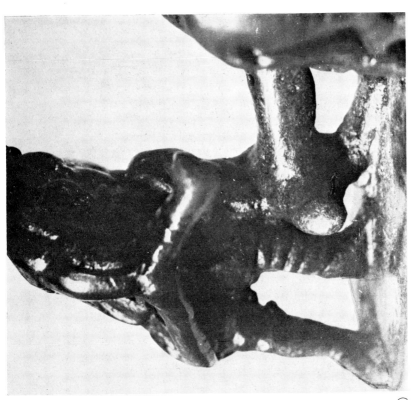

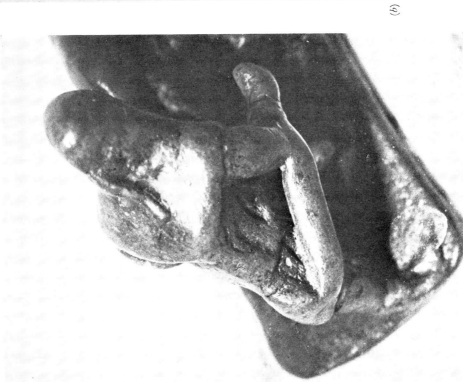

XLIII. THE PIERCEBRIDGE PLOUGHMAN

(a) View showing the casting-strip that was left in position. (b) View showing the rear end of the plough

(b)

(a)

XLIV. (a) THE PLOUGHMAN HOLDING THE REMAINS OF AN OX-GOAD
(b) THE TWO BEASTS FROM THE FRONT

XLV. THE PLOUGHMAN FROM THE FRONT

XLVI. THE PLOUGH GROUP: *oblique view from above*

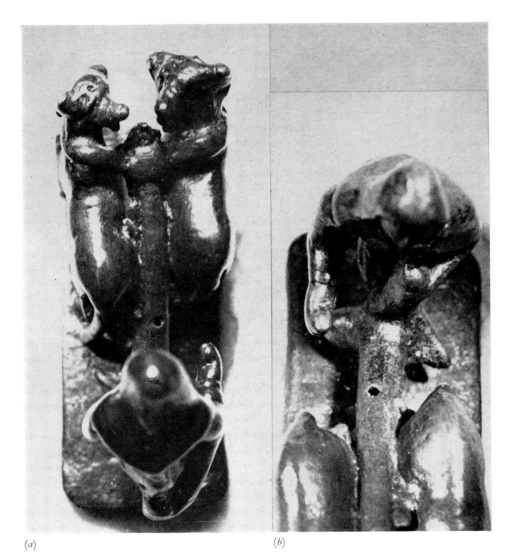

XLVII. THE PLOUGH GROUP VIEWED FROM ABOVE:

(a) Looking forward

(b) Looking back

XLVIII. ENGRAVED BONE FRAGMENT from the Gorge d'Enfer. Aurignacian (British Museum). First face

XLIX. ENGRAVED BONE FRAGMENT from the Gorge d'Enfer. Aurignacian (British Museum). Second face

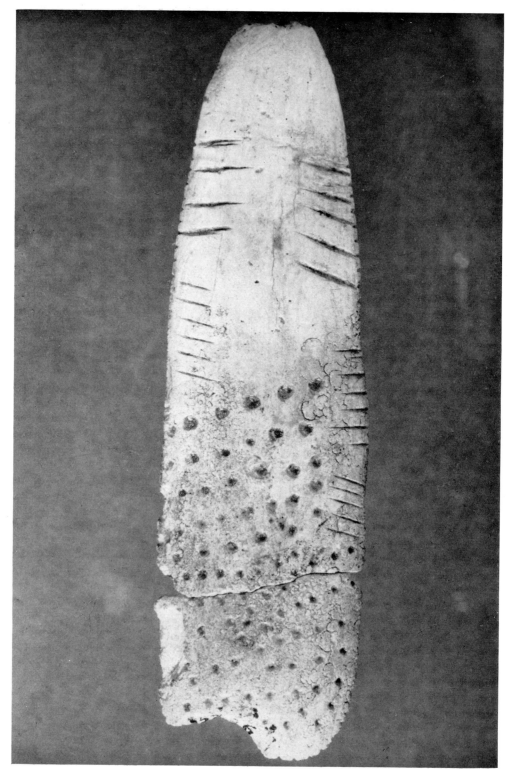

L. ENGRAVED AND OCHRED BONE FRAGMENT from the Gorge d'Enfer. Aurignacian (St-Germain Museum)

LI. DETAIL OF ENGRAVED AND OCHRED FRAGMENT from the Gorge d'Enfer

LII. ENGRAVED BONE FRAGMENT, supposedly Aurignacian. Site unknown (Les Eyzies Museum). First face

LIII. ENGRAVED BONE FRAGMENT, supposedly Aurignacian. Site unknown (Les Eyzies Museum). Second face

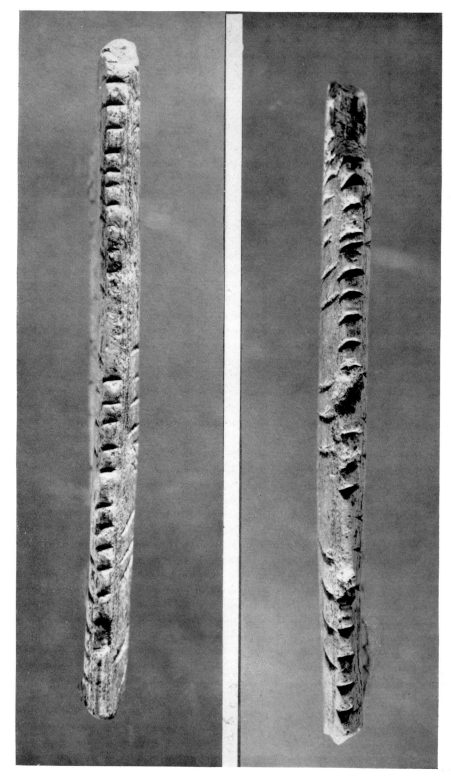

LIV. ENGRAVED BONE FRAGMENT from Les Eyzies Museum. Two edges

LV. ENGRAVED BONE FRAGMENT from Trou des Forges, Bruniquel (de Lastic collection, British Museum). Late Magdalenian. Showing engraved insect (ant) and a block of marks

LVI. ENGRAVED FRAGMENT from Trou des Forges, Bruniquel. Detail showing intentional marks additional to the main series

LVII ENGRAVED FRAGMENT from Trou des Forges, Bruniquel. Detail showing intentional marks additional to the main series

LVIII. ENGRAVED FRAGMENT from Trou des Forges, Bruniquel. Detail showing the two 'primary marks' formed by two strokes at an angle. The long line crossing over at the left is cut by a different point.

(a)

(b)

LIX. (a) WRAXALL, SOMERSET. Bronze collar. List no. 1. City Museum, Bristol. Scale: ½
(b) LLANDYSSUL, CARDIGANSHIRE. Half of bronze collar. List no. 2. City Museum, Bristol. Scale: ¾

(a)

(b)

LX. PORTLAND ISLAND, DORSET. List no. 3. Details of (a) terminals and (b) rear hinge of collar. British Museum. Scale: $\frac{4}{5}$

(a)

(b)

LXI. UNPROVENANCED ?DORSET. List no. 4. Details of (a) terminals and (b) rear hinge of collar. British Museum. Scale: $\frac{4}{5}$

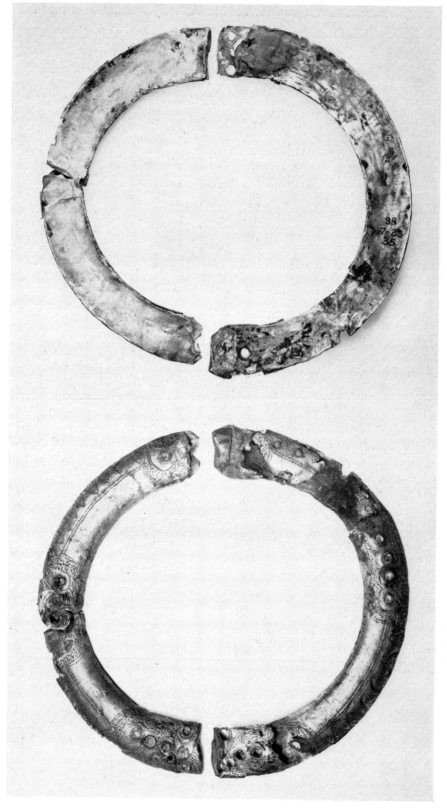

LXII. TRENOWETH, CORNWALL. List no. 7. Separate front and back plates of collar. British Museum. Scale: $\frac{1}{2}$

LXIII. DORCHESTER, DORSET. List no. 5. Detail of decoration on bronze collar.
Dorset County Museum, Dorchester.

LXIV. PART OF THE MILDENHALL TREASURE

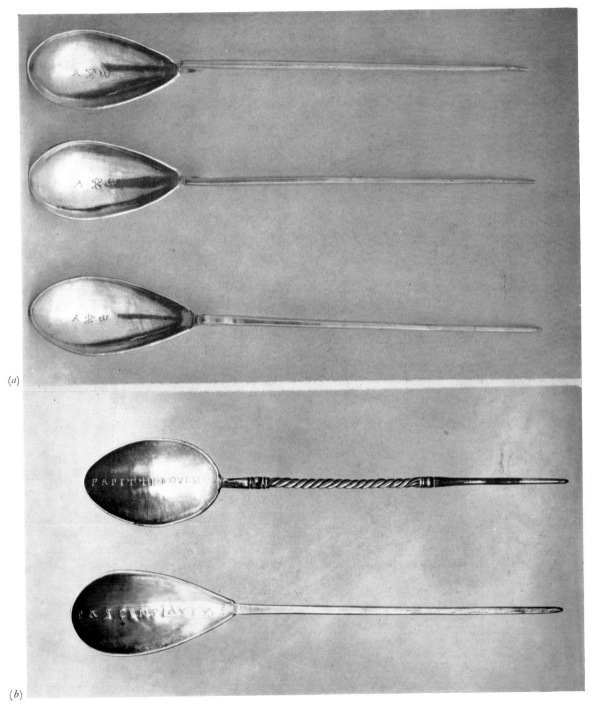

LXV. THE MILDENHALL TREASURE: (*a*) Spoons inscribed with alpha and omega and with the Chi-Rho.
(*b*) Spoons inscribed PAPITTEDO VIVAS and PASCENTIA VIVAS

(a)

(b)

LXVI. (a) LEAD TANK from Icklingham, Suffolk, with applied inscription, alpha and omega, and Chi-Rho.
(b) FRAGMENT OF LEAD TANK from Walesby, Lincolnshire, with applied Chi-Rho and figured frieze.
(Photograph by courtesy of Lincoln City Libraries, Museum and Art Gallery)

LXVII. LEAD TANK FROM WALESBY: detail of figured frieze. (Photograph by courtesy of Lincoln City Libraries, Museum and Art Gallery)

LXVIII. LULLINGSTONE VILLA. Reconstruction of part of the Christian wall-plaster, as exhibited in the British Museum in 1969. The wall on the left was shortened for the purposes of the exhibition, and the blank panels will probably prove to have been figured

(a)

(b)

LXIX. LULLINGSTONE VILLA. THE CHRISTIAN WALL-PLASTER:
(a) Detail of the Chi-Rho, incorporating all the surviving fragments
(b) Detail of the figured frieze: the central figure incorporates all its surviving fragments

LXX. HINTON ST. MARY MOSAIC

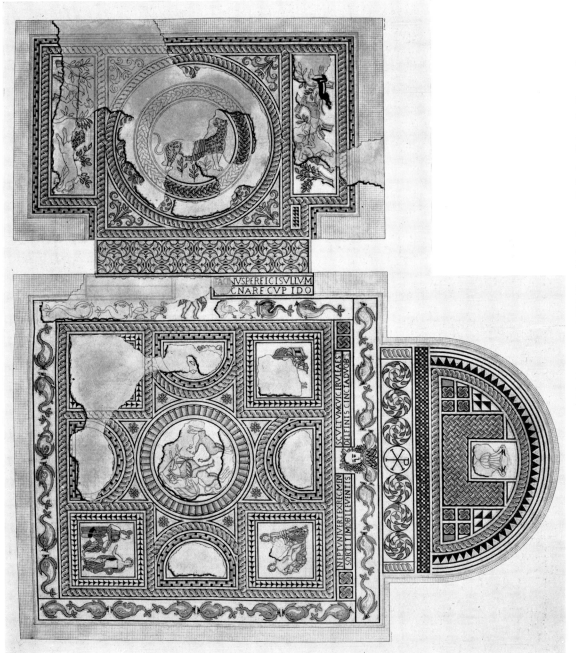

LXXI. FRAMPTON MOSAIC, with Neptune and Chi-Rho. (After Lysons, *Reliquiae Britannico-Romanae*)

LXXII. WITHINGTON MOSAIC, with Orpheus and the beasts and with hunting
scenes. (After Lysons, *Reliquiae Britannico-Romanae*)

(a)

(b)　　　　　　　　　　　　　　　　　　(c)

LXXIII. (a) SCRAPER MS 1, showing two of the 3–4 rows of hinged flake scars removed from the scraper edge by use. The newly formed edge of the scraper shows some further damage by small scalar flakelets which precede (further) damage by hinged flaking. No abrasion. Optical magnification 8×; photographic enlargement to *c.* 30×

(b) SCRAPER MS 26, showing hinged flaking, particularly in the centre of the scraper front, followed by abrasion; the blade edge is also rounded by abrasion. Optical magnification 2·5×; photographic enlargement to *c.* 4×

(c) SCRAPER MS 34, showing very intensely abraded scraper edge with parallel grooves perpendicular to the edge. The grooves have a rounded cross-section and result from the inclusion of 'dirt' of the fine sand grade between the scraper and worked surface. Optical magnification 10×; photographic enlargement to *c.* 40×

(a)

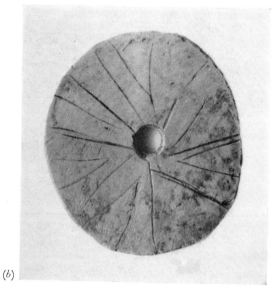

(b)

LXXIV. DECORATED BONE DISCS. Scale 1:1
(a) Bruniquel (British Museum)
(b) Křížova Jeskyně (Brno Museum)

LXXV. DECORATED DISCS OF BONE AND STONE from Brno II burial (Brno Museum). Scale 1:1

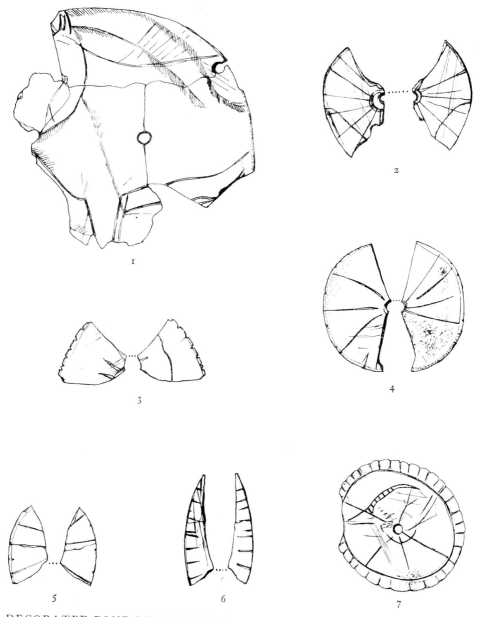

LXXVI. DECORATED BONE DISCS. (1) La Tuilière (B.M.). (2–6) Bruniquel (B.M.). (7) Bruniquel. Scale 1:1

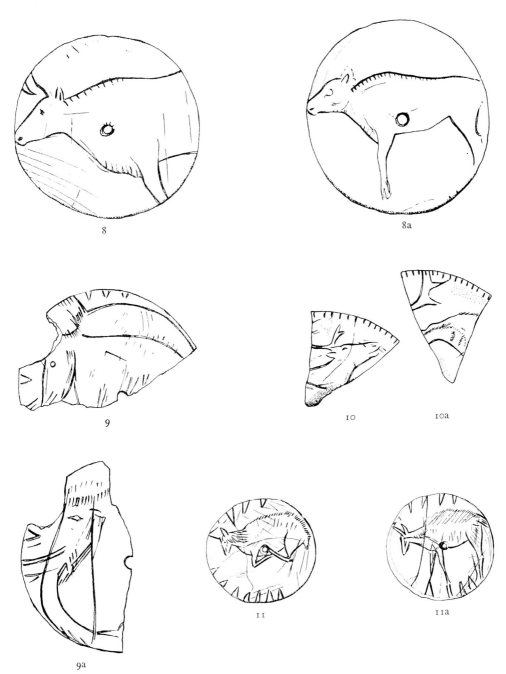

LXXVII. DECORATED BONE DISCS. (8) Mas d'Azil. (9) Raymonden. (10) Mas d'Azil
(11) Laugerie-Basse. Scale 1 : 1

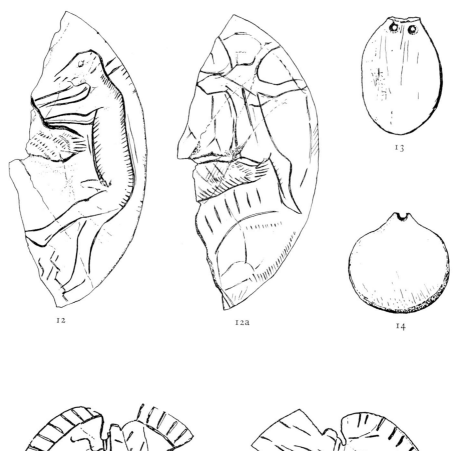

12   12a   13

14

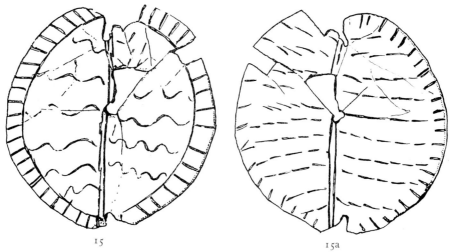

15   15a

LXXVIII. DECORATED PIECES. (12) Bone disc from Mas d'Azil. (13) Cro-Magnon ivory pendant. (14) Isturitz bone pendant. (15) Bone disc from Mas d'Azil. Scale 1 : 1

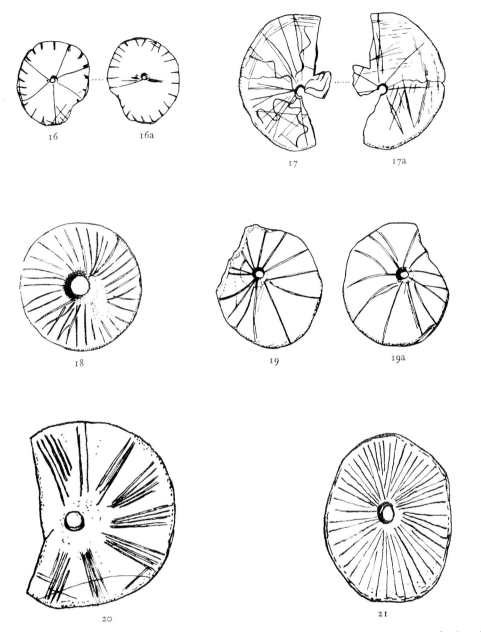

LXXIX. DECORATED DISCS. (16–17) Le Portel (bone). (18) Isturitz (bone). (19) Lourdes (stone). (20–1) Laugerie-Basse (bone). Scale 1 : 1

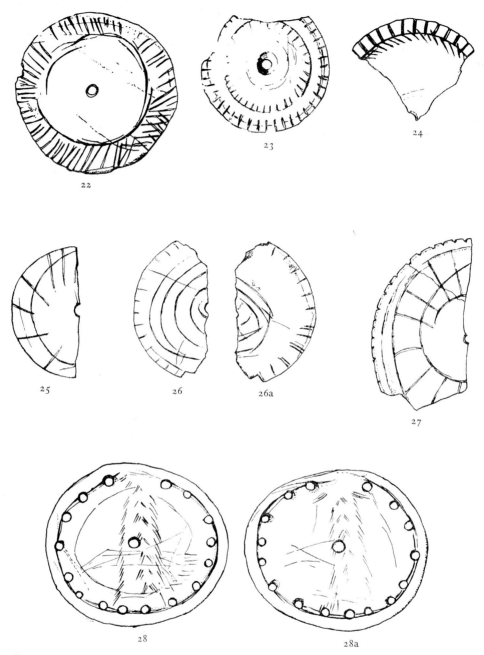

LXXX. DECORATED BONE DISCS. (22, 26–8) Mas d'Azil. (23–5) Isturitz. Scale 1:1

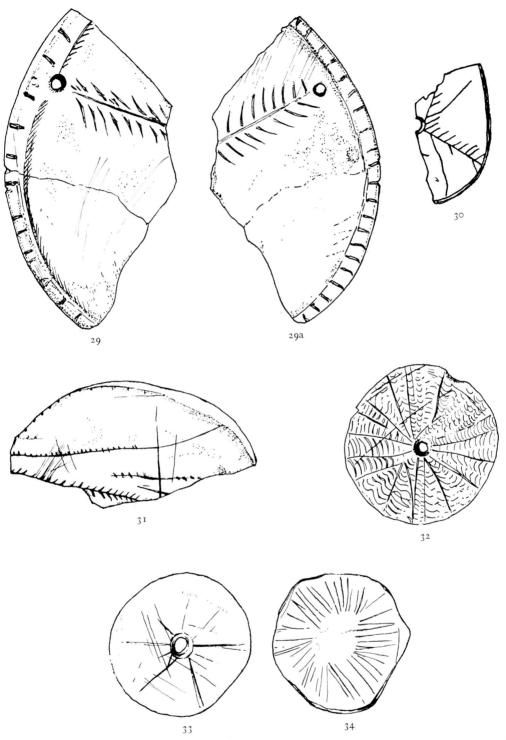

LXXXI. DECORATED DISCS. (29) Bone, from Mas d'Azil. (30) Bone, from Kesslerloch. (31) Bone, from Gourdan. (32) Ivory, from Petersfels. (33–4) Lignite, from Petersfels. Scale 1 : 1

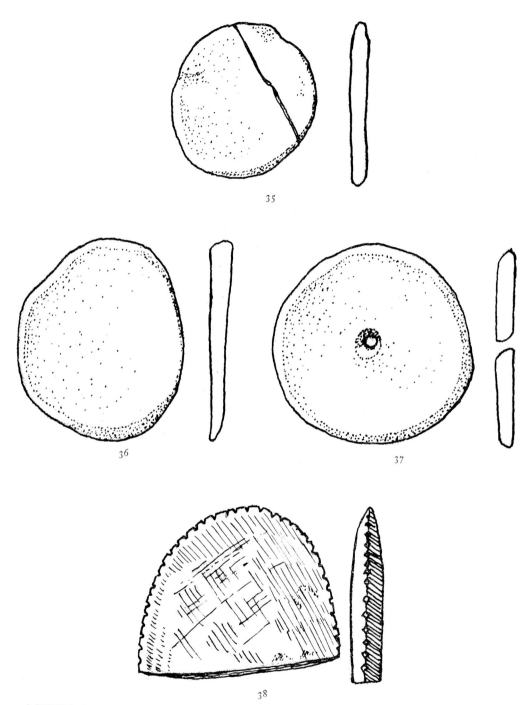

LXXXII. DISCS AND FRAGMENT OF STONE. (35-7) Stone discs from Molodova V.
(38) Decorated stone fragment from Molodova V. Scale 1:1

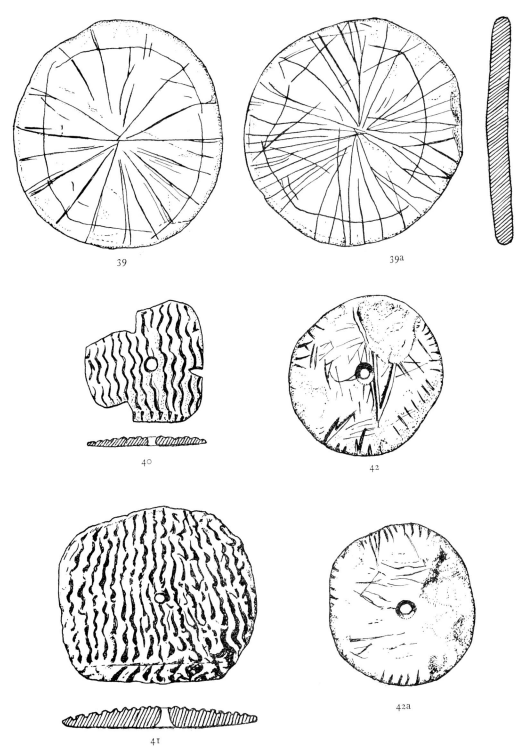

LXXXIII. DECORATED DISCS AND ALLIED PIECES. (39) Stone, from Afontova Gora III.
(40–1) Mammoth Ivory, from Mal'ta. (42) Stone, from Afontova Gora II. Scale 1 : 1

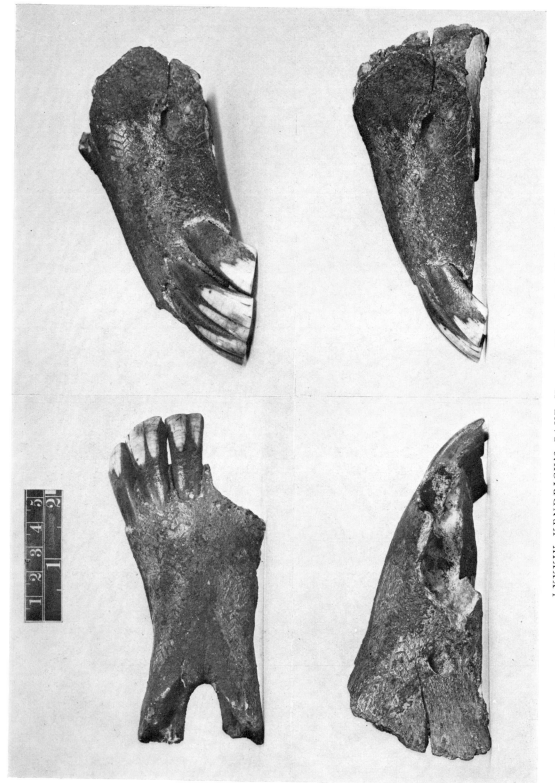

LXXXIV. KENDRICK'S CAVE. Horse mandible symphysis. Before cleaning

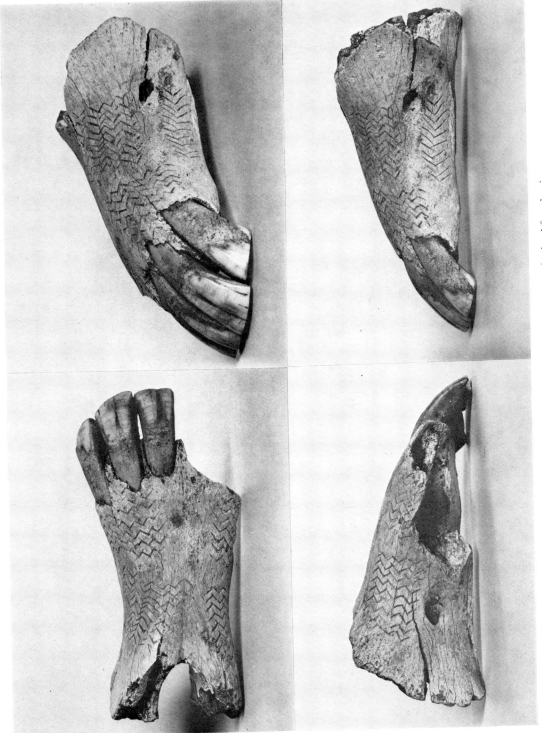

LXXXV. KENDRICK'S CAVE. Horse mandible symphysis. After cleaning

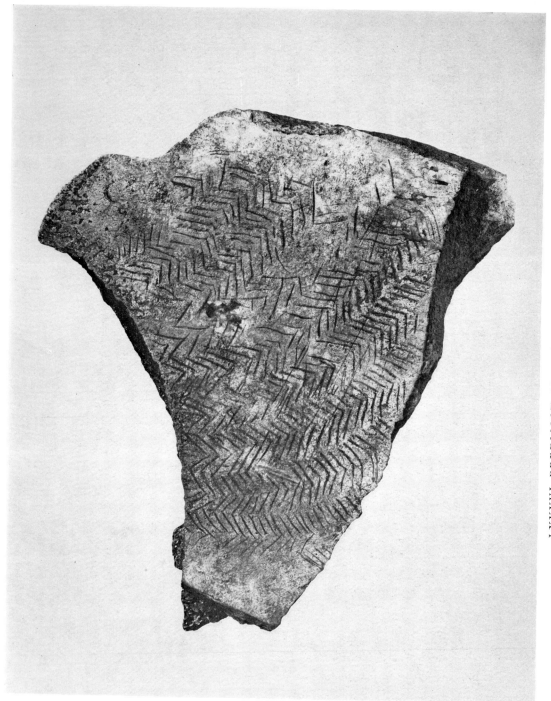

LXXXVI. PREDMOST. Mammoth scapula fragment (Brno Museum)

LXXXVII. BALDOCK. The handle-mount. (Photograph: A. L. Pacitto)

LXXXVIII. RECONSTRUCTION OF THE BALDOCK BUCKET, showing the sequence of bronze remains on a temporary cardboard frame (the pin-heads are not original). (Photograph: A. L. Pacitto)

LXXXIX. 1880s RECONSTRUCTION OF THE AYLESFORD BUCKET. (Photograph: A. L. Pacitto)

XC. AYLESFORD: the handle-mount A.2, and the repair B. (Photograph: A. L. Pacitto)

XCI. GREAT CHESTERFORD, ESSEX, BUCKET. (Photograph: Museum of Archaeology
and Ethnology, Cambridge)